The Russian Revolutions

The Russian Revolutions

Max Weber

Translated and Edited by
Gordon C. Wells and Peter Baehr

Original German edition edited by
Wolfgang J. Mommsen
in collaboration with
Dittmar Dahlmann and Gangolf Hübinger

Polity Press

This English translation copyright © Polity Press 1995.
Introduction copyright © Gordon C. Wells and Peter Baehr.
All other chapters published in the original German in
Max Weber Gesamtausgabe copyright © J. C. B. Mohr
(Paul Siebeck) Tübingen, 1984, 1989.

First published in 1995 by Polity Press
in association with Blackwell Publishers Ltd.

First published in paperback 1997.

Editorial office:
Polity Press
65 Bridge Street
Cambridge CB2 1UR, UK

Marketing and production:
Blackwell Publishers Ltd
108 Cowley Road
Oxford OX4 1JF, UK

All rights reserved. Except for the quotation of short
passages for the purposes of criticism and review, no part of
this publication may be reproduced, stored in a retrieval
system, or transmitted, in any form or by any means,
electronic, mechanical, photocopying, recording or
otherwise, without the prior permission of the publisher.

Except in the United States of America, this book is sold
subject to the condition that it shall not, by way of trade or
otherwise, be lent, re-sold, hired out, or otherwise circulated
without the publisher's prior consent in any form of binding
or cover other than that in which it is published and without
a similar condition including this condition being imposed on
the subsequent purchaser.

ISBN 0–7456–0943–0
ISBN 0–7456–1752–2 (pbk)

A CIP catalogue record for this book is available from the
British Library.

Typeset in 10/12 pt Times
by Acorn Bookwork, Salisbury, Wiltshire
Printed in Great Britain by Hartnolls Ltd, Bodmin, Cornwall

This book is printed on acid-free paper.

Contents

Abbreviations	vii
Dates	viii
Editors' Introduction	1
The Essays of 1905–1906	3
The Essays of 1917	12
The Place of the Russian Essays in Weber's Oeuvre	15
The Political Significance of the Essays Today	24
Note on the Translation	28
Acknowledgements	31
Notes	32
1 Bourgeois Democracy in Russia	41
The Zemstvo Movement in Russia	41
The Constitutional Draft of the 'Union of Liberation'	45
The Nationalities and Language Question	54
Church and State	63
The Socialist Parties	65
The Intelligentsia and the Bourgeois Parties	70
The Agrarian Question	74
The Progress of the Revolution	101
Notes	113
2 Russia's Transition to Pseudo-constitutionalism	148
The General Policy of the Interim Ministry	148
Analysis of the General Political Legislation of the Interim Ministry	158

Completing the Bureaucratization of the Autocracy	174
The 'Constitution'	181
Analysis of the Electoral Law of the Duma	184
The Social and Political Background to the Election	191
Analysis of the Duma Elections	213
After the Elections	215
Notes	233

3 Russia's Transition to Pseudo-democracy — 241
Notes — 256

4 The Russian Revolution and the Peace — 261
Notes — 265

Political Parties and Associations in Russia, 1905–1906	267
References	270
Glossary	275
Index	282

Abbreviations

BD	Weber, 'Bourgeois Democracy in Russia'
M–D	W. J. Mommsen and D. Dahlmann (German Editors of BD and PC)
M–H	W. J. Mommsen and G. Hübinger (German Editors of P and PD)
MWG	*Max Weber Gesamtausgabe*: see 'Note on the Translation', p. 28
P	Weber, 'The Russian Revolution and the Peace'
PC	Weber, 'Russia's Transition to Pseudo-constitutionalism'
PD	Weber, 'Russia's Transition to Pseudo-democracy'
PSR	Socialist Revolutionary Party: see BD n. 6
RSDRP	Russian Social Democratic Workers' Party: see BD n. 99
SRD	Council of Workers' Deputies: see p. 148

Dates

In BD and PC (published in 1906) dates are given in the Julian calendar, in use in Russia at the time, which was 13 days behind the Gregorian calendar, used in the West. In many instances both dates are given (the Julian calendar first).

In the case of two essays published in 1917 (PD and P), dates are given first according to the Gregorian calendar, with the earlier date following.

Editors' Introduction

In the autumn of 1905, Max Weber embarked on a project which, even by his own exacting standards, was demanding and audacious. Intrigued by the revolution unfolding in Russia, and dismayed by the mostly patronizing and hostile coverage it was receiving in the established German press, Weber set out to write his own 'chronicles' documenting the crisis. The result was the articles in part translated here as 'Bourgeois Democracy in Russia' (hereafter, BD) and 'Russia's Transition to Pseudo-constitutionalism' (hereafter, PC). In them Weber examines, among other things, the prospects for liberalism in Russia and the constitutional facade erected by the forces of autocracy to frustrate both civil freedom and parliamentary reform.

These two essays are remarkable in many respects, not least of which is that they were written at all: in a mere three months, Weber learned enough Russian to enable him to dissect the bewildering array of party programmes and constitutional proposals that flourished in this vertiginous period.[1] The sheer amount of detail in these studies, it must be acknowledged, is not always calculated to keep the reader dangling in suspense. Weber wrote mainly to inform his audience, rather than keep it entertained, and the price of his meticulousness is a prose style which is at times laboured and dense. In compensation, Weber's essays also contain some particularly stirring passages. The most striking of them is the long peroration in 'Bourgeois Democracy' on the struggle for individual freedom in an ecologically shrinking, bureaucratically dominated world. Impressive, too, are Weber's shrewd cameos of some of the key figures of the drama, and – against the *realpolitiker* of his day – his passionate depictions of the 'uncompromising idealism, the relentless energy, the ups and downs of tempestuous hope and agonizing disappointment experienced by those in the thick of the fight' (PC: 231).

Weber's two 1905–6 treatises on Russia contain a multitude of themes, some of which we shall address in the following sections. They also harbour a distinctive *mood*: it is the plight of idealistic liberalism that captures Weber's sympathy and enlists his support. However, while Weber was a liberal, albeit one of idiosyncratic persuasion,[2] he was also a convinced German nationalist; and this helps to explain the very different atmosphere which pervades the other two essays on Russia, penned in 1917, which we have also included in this volume. In 1905–6, the forces of liberalism were fighting for their life in Russia, and Weber's own liberal convictions reached out to theirs, moved by the heroic pathos of their efforts. A concern with civil justice, the rule of law, and freedom took precedence over the possible geopolitical impact that any major change in Russia would have for his own native land. By 1917, however, the political geography of Europe had been drastically transformed. Now it was Germany itself that was fighting for survival – and Russia was one of its adversaries. Accordingly, in 'Russia's Transition to Pseudo-democracy' (hereafter, PD) and 'The Russian Revolution and the Peace' (hereafter, P) the aperture through which Weber viewed that country is largely patriotic and (quite literally) defensive in resolution: in 1917 it is the interests and *security* of the German nation-state that are foremost in his mind.

To be sure, this broad distinction between the 1905–6 and the 1917 essays should not be pushed too far.[3] From at least 1905 onwards, Weber was keenly aware of the geopolitical importance of Russian domestic upheavals for German interests. During the same period, he remained consistently sympathetic to a principled liberalism in Russia – even if by 1917 he was convinced of its malaise. On Weber's account, liberalism in Russia had been gradually forsaken by the Russian Constitutional Democrats (Kadets) who, as a result of defeat and disappointment at home, had in large part become imperialists and opportunists. Despite this qualification, however, it is highly misleading to say of the 1905–6 essays that '[w]hat agitated Weber most was the question of the probable influence of the events in Russia upon German development' (Marianne Weber 1988 [1926]: 328). This judgement collapses the later essays into the earlier ones, and is likely to have been the result of Marianne Weber's own perspective, writing in the decade after the First World War, as distinct from her husband's during 1905–6.

In the remainder of this Introduction we offer first (next two sections) a sketch of the sociopolitical context and content of Weber's essays. We concentrate on the studies of 1905–6 since these are far more substantial than their largely polemical 1917 counterparts. In the following section we seek to locate the writings on Russia in Weber's work more generally. We then enquire into their present political significance.

The Essays of 1905–1906

'Contemporary history' is the most swiftly antiquated of all narrative forms. Current reportage may strike us momentarily with great force, only to be revealed as erroneous or oversimplified just a week later. It was doubtless for this reason that Weber approached his own writings on Russia with such ambivalence. On the one hand, he seems to claim very little for them; the essays of 1905–6 are described as mere 'chronicles', 'a poorly structured collection of notes', rather than an authentic history. On the other, his examination of Russian conditions is far more than a simple narrative account; Weber seeks to uncover what is 'significant' about the 'general situation' (BD: 113 n. 2), its tendencies and dynamics, in a manner that has drawn comparison with Marx's analysis of Bonapartism (Scaff and Arnold 1985). In any event, once he had commenced his analytical sojourn in 1905, Weber moved at a relentless pace, determined to keep abreast of developments, and to report on them with as much rigour as his energies could summon and the available documents allowed.

By the time Weber devoted his full attention to Russia, the revolution of 1905 was approaching its dénouement. In 1904, as the war with Japan became ever more disastrous, the autocracy of Tsar Nicholas II attempted to reach some accommodation with the liberal reform movement as a means of stabilizing the regime, but no coherent policy developed. The core of the liberal movement was the *zemstvos*, the provincial and district organs of local self-government that had been established in Russia in 1864 (Szamuely 1974: 226). Increasingly, they were pressing for civil liberties and a working parliament. From the autocracy's standpoint, they were asking for too much and their demands – trenchantly enunciated in the 'Eleven Theses' of the First Zemstvo Congress of November 1904[4] – were effectively ignored. Pressure built up. On 'Bloody Sunday' (9/22 January 1905[5]) scores of demonstrators petitioning for basic civil rights and improved working conditions outside the Tsar's Winter Palace were massacred by government troops, precipitating a rash of strikes and mutinies which continued intermittently through the winter, spring and summer. Towards the end of February, and again in August, Tsar Nicholas offered concessions, in the latter case the so-called Bulygin Duma (named after A. G. Bulygin, the Minister of the Interior). The proposed Duma (parliament) would allow limited popular representation based on a curial voting system, and would give consultative and advisory powers to a lower chamber of deputies (Doctorow 1975: 124f). This concession, however, did nothing to quell rural and urban upheaval; the projected Bulygin Duma was stillborn.

In October, an explosive compound of terrorism, agrarian rebellion, mutiny within the armed forces, nationalist insurrection in the Ukraine, the Baltic, Poland and Finland, and a general strike finally persuaded the autocracy to yield further ground. Faced with what Lenin described in retrospect as 'a bourgeois-democratic revolution in its social content, but a proletarian revolution in its methods of struggle' (Lenin, 1967 [1925]: 790), the Tsar promulgated the Manifesto of 17/30 October. In essence it promised: 'effective' civil liberties of thought, speech, assembly and association, underwritten by a habeas corpus provision; increased popular representation; and the 'immutable principle' that all laws would require the express approval of the Imperial Duma. Through the Manifesto, the Tsar and premier-designate Count Sergei Witte sought to split the opposition forces, dividing reformist liberals, for instance, from Marxist and other radicals. In this the provisions of the Manifesto, and later clarifications, were partly successful (Doctorow 1975: 135). By the time of the next major challenge to autocratic power – the general strike of December and the armed uprising in Moscow that accompanied it – the government was better organized. The insurrection was speedily and violently suppressed, and in March of the new year elections for the Duma at last took place.

It is into this maelstrom that the reader descends in 'Bourgeois Democracy in Russia'. The article, of book-length proportions in the German original, takes us up to December 1905. Its point of entry is a scrutiny of the constitutional draft of the liberal-leaning Union of Liberation, published earlier that year in Paris under the title *Loi fondamentale de l'Empire Russe*, and composed by the legal experts F. F. Kokoshkin and S. Kotliarevskii. The 'preceding exposition' to which Weber alludes in his first sentence refers to a review of that draft by Sergei I. Zhivago; Weber had commissioned it for the *Archiv für Sozialwissenschaft und Sozialpolitik*, the premier German social science journal of its day, edited by Werner Sombart, Edgar Jaffé – and Weber himself. To Zhivago's review Weber appends not the 'few remarks' he promises, but instead a massive investigation into the 'bearers of the liberal and democratic movement' (BD: 41), the forces arrayed against them, and the outlook for a political system in Russia approaching Western constitutional forms.

Weber had little doubt that, eventually, the Russian autocracy would fall. Though it would probably require a major European war to deliver the final blow (BD: 142 n. 200), the regime had so alienated its subjects that, domestically, 'a *permanent* compromise' with it was 'practically impossible' (BD: 74).[6] Even so, a liberal democratic system would not automatically replace the regime. On the contrary, an improvement of the position of the peasants was more likely to encourage 'communist radicalism' (BD: 90) than liberal individualism. Moreover, an examination of some of the socialist programmes and personalities (notably Lenin and Plekhanov,[7] but especially the 'Socialist Revolutionary' Peshekhonov, whom Weber described as a modern Jacobin) led Weber to discern 'a worrying foretaste of the *centralist-bureaucratic* path which Russia could all too easily take, under the influence of radical theoreticians' (BD: 89). Who, then, composed the liberal-democratic forces? And what were their chances of political success in the near future?

In regard to the first question, Weber quite sharply distinguished between the Russian bourgeoisie as a social class and as a status-group. The former, with their various capitalist fractions – big industry and manufacture, finance capital – were either cool in their attitude towards liberal constitutionalism, or (and more usually) expressly hostile towards it, even 'reactionary' in political temperament (BD: 74). By contrast, the latter grouping – bourgeois in virtue of a certain 'general attitude to life and standard of education' (BD: 45) – formed the bulwark of the liberal movement. Comprising the honorary, landed members (the so-called Second Element) of the zemstvos, members of the Union of Liberation, and the Constitutional Democrat Party (founded in October 1905) which grew out of both, this grouping of 'notables' sought to modernize Russian political life in the direction of the *Rechtsstaat*, that is, a state grounded in the rule of law.[8] Alongside, and in some tension with it, was the 'Third Element': 'the quasi-proletarian intelligentsia of the salaried zemstvo officials' (BD: 45) – schoolteachers, agronomists, statisticians, journalists, doctors, nurses – whose outlook was more leftist and populist in character, and whose way of life was closer to subordinate classes, than their patrician zemstvo counterparts (BD: 45, 71; PD: 242; cf. Perrie 1972: 125).[9]

Weber admired both zemstvo groupings for different reasons. More important, he saw in the institution as a whole the clearest refutation of facile claims that Russia was a society unprepared for self-government. The administrative achievements of the zemstvos in the spheres of education, health, road-building, tax assessment, among others, were impressive, particularly so since these accomplishments were realized in the teeth of resentful opposition from the central bureaucracy. Comparing the zemstvo favourably with local government in the United States, Weber envisaged the former as an institution which in embryo prefigured an expanded system of self-rule throughout the Russian empire. All the more regrettable, then, that the constitutional document of the Union of Liberation failed adequately to build on that potential. True, this found some compensation in the more federalist programme of the Constitutional Democrats (BD: 49). But even that programme was to run aground on the complexities of the nationalities problem, a vortex which threatened to turn all plans for federation into demands for fully-fledged national autonomy – a prospect which only very few liberals at the time could accept with calm nerves.

According to Weber, the zemstvos were doubly consequential for Russian liberalism. On the one hand, they furnished an arena in which the liberals could legally agitate for change. On the other, the existence of a permanent Zemstvo Board, charged with the job of preparing congress agendas and facilities, provided a durable, continuous apparatus for the canvassing of liberal ideas. Nonetheless, Weber's treatment of the division within the zemstvo intelligentsia, of the limitations of the liberal constitutional programmes, and of the problems that dogged the nationalities question establishes fairly early on in 'Bourgeois Democracy' a gloomy surmise: the chances of liberal democratic success in the revolution were slim. This was only partly because of the restricted constituency and orientation of the liberals themselves. Historical conditions of some magnitude were also unfavourable to the constitutional movement, a point to which we will return. Moreover, the ability of the liberals to forge an alliance with groups close to the state, or with social classes opposed to it, was confounded by various kinds of intransigence and incompatibility.

Predictably, the central bureaucracy old guard loathed the liberals. And little could be expected from the Church. In general, its institutional interests and doctrinal orientation made it a pillar of autocracy and thus, with important exceptions, highly resistant to change. Nor were firm bases of liberal support evident in the wider society. The socialist parties were, of course, radical foes of the Tsar. Influenced by a distinctively Russian 'pragmatic rationalism' which declared that the formation of a socialist society was not dependent on a prior bourgeois stage of development, they scorned the 'naturalist rationalism' of economistic and evolutionary versions of Marxism. But these parties too – Weber's animus is especially directed towards the Bolshevik faction of Russian Social Democracy – suffered from their own injurious liabilities. Their 'pragmatic rationalism' freed them from mechanistic historicism only to encourage instead a putschist mentality and practice. Their attitude to the liberal movement was cynical and opportunistic. And their own ranks were riven with sectarian animosities. In consequence, '(a)ny agreement between oppositional elements is . . . rendered impossible' (BD: 69).

None of this was calculated, Weber declared, to offer the urban 'masses' mature and responsible leadership, or incline them towards a principled alliance with liberalism. Nor could the liberals, or any other grouping for that matter, count on the volatile petty bourgeoisie. Their proclivity for antisemitism and collaboration with the police all too often threw them into the arms of the most reactionary and bloodthirsty strata. Finally, the peasantry offered the least hope of all for the short-term prospects of the liberal movement. In by far the longest section of 'Bourgeois Democracy', which draws on his extensive knowledge of agrarian political economy, Weber observes that the 'communist' traditions of the Russian peasant community had made it highly resistant to liberal individualism. The peasants' economic interests in agrarian reform – for instance, in the abolition of redemption payments, the provision of more land to deal with the rising rural population and 'land hunger' – were not to be confused with either a desire for a capitalist economic system centred on the individual entrepreneur and 'economic selection', or for a parliamentary government. For in the first case, peasant traditions stressed collective rights to the use of land. Economic-technical efficiency was ancillary to this value, and private ownership antithetical to it. Second, though the peasants responded with furious or muted indignation to the local gentry, nobility and civil servants who mistreated them with impunity, their estimation for the Tsar was something quite different. Peasant hardship was typically attributed not to their 'Lord', but rather to the corrupt behaviour of those officials who claimed to serve him. What was required to correct this parlous state of affairs was not so much a representative parliamentary system, interposing yet one more body between peasants and Tsar, as direct access to the ear of the Tsar himself (BD: 98–9). For this reason and others – notably, the massive costs involved in financing agrarian reform (BD: 100–1) – the liberals faced an intimidating set of challenges. Still, they were challenges the liberals must try to meet. Weber concludes:

> The further development of capitalism will put an end to 'populist' romanticism. No doubt its place will be largely taken by Marxism. But the work to be done on the formidable and fundamental agrarian problem cannot possibly be undertaken with the intellectual tools of Marxism . . . Clearly this work can only be done by the organs of self-government and for this reason alone it seems vital that liberalism continues to see its vocation as fighting against both bureaucratic and Jacobin *centralism* and working at the permeation of the masses with the old individualistic basic

idea of the 'inalienable rights of man', which have become as 'boring' to us Western Europeans as black bread is for the person who has enough to eat. (BD: 107–8)

Whereas 'Bourgeois Democracy' had tended to focus on the personalities, programmes, conflicts, and dilemmas of the anti-autocratic movements, 'Pseudo-constitutionalism', the second essay we translate below, deals mainly with the tsarist political system, particularly during the 'interim ministry'. This was the ministry which spanned the appointment of Witte as Premier in October 1905 through to his resignation on the 14/27 April (and, in a sense, actually beyond that to the convocation of the First Imperial Duma on 27 April/10 May 1906). The essay was probably begun in the middle of March 1906 (Mommsen and Dahlmann 1989c: 282–3); it covers mainly the period from January to July 1906 (PC: 224), when the Duma was dissolved by the Tsar. The backdrop to Weber's comments is the crumbling of the revolutionary movement in December. The main topics addressed are the retrenchment of autocratic power, the mechanisms through which this was effected, and the background to the startling electoral success of the Kadets.

'Pseudo-constitutionalism' commences with a description of the means employed by the autocracy to regain the political initiative. The first mechanism was a policy of brute repression directed both by the Minister of the Interior I. N. Durnovo, as well as by various governors in the provinces which became 'de facto . . . regional satrapies' (PC: 154). For this policy to work, the forces of coercion – notably the police, army and cossacks – had to be mollified and bribed back into support for the regime, and this was duly attempted, with some success. However, if the aim of naked force was to restore order, rather than wreak revenge on those who had possessed the temerity to challenge autocratic rule, the policy was largely a failure. Police violence – 'the purely "random" and senseless brutality of power' (PC: 191) – only served to increase the general lawlessness.

In tandem with this strategy, a second one was adopted. The government attempted 'to create institutions which would give the outward impression abroad that the Manifesto of 1/ October was being carried out, though without seriously jeopardizing the power of the bureaucracy' (PC: 158). The reference to the impression created 'abroad' is an allusion to foreign financial interests which, with some equivocation, were demanding social order *and* a Western-style constitution as a condition for their loans. 'Russia is a debtor state' (PC: 151), Weber reminded his readers, and even the insufferable arrogance of the Tsar was no match for 'the impersonal but ineluctable power of the money market' (PC: 152). The Russian state's dependence on foreign finance capital, and the consequences of this for domestic policy, is a theme that weaves its way throughout the whole essay (and also PD, and P). In particular, Weber shows how such pressure encouraged not genuine reforms in Russia so much as a pseudo-constitutional charade. It is this subterfuge that he then proceeds to expose by revealing, with surgical precision, the broken promises of the October Manifesto, a travesty which came to be enshrined in the 'Fundamental Laws' of 27 April/10 May 1906.

Consider first the promise to establish fundamental civil liberties. While some freedom of conscience was achieved in the realm of religious affairs, 'freedoms' of the press, association, assembly, movement and of the person turned out to be illusory. Administrative arbitrariness was the rule, not the rule of law. It could hardly have been otherwise in the circumstances. Habeas corpus and the entrenched protection of other rights 'assumes the existence of bodies with *constitutionally* guaranteed independence, which can exercise effective control of the administration' (PC: 171). Nothing approaching such autonomy could be permitted by a Tsar for whom 'there were only police interests' (PC: 152). Consider, too, the pledges to extend the franchise, and to establish the 'actual participation of the Duma "in the supervision of the legality of the actions" of the state authorities' (PC: 158). In regard to the former, Weber describes how the franchise was indeed extended, albeit using indirect methods of voting of byzantine complexity. Massively expensive and cumbersome to boot, the electoral process aimed to confound the opposition rather than facilitate its expression. In addition, the autocracy relied on prohibition of meetings and intimidation of voters to secure the favoured result. All this, however, was to prove counterproductive – 'It should come as no surprise that in the eyes of both the urban masses and the peasants, whatever the bureaucracy banned must necessarily be something excellent' (PC: 188).

And, what, finally, of the October Manifesto's commitment to give the Duma real power in the supervision of the state's activities? Again, this turned out to be a mirage. The tsarist system ceded as little real power as possible to the Duma. 'The entire relationship between government and people's representation presupposes that it is axiomatic that the representative body of the people was and always will be the natural enemy of the state power' (PC: 181; emphasis omitted). Accordingly, the remit of Duma authority was countermanded by the existence of an appointed Imperial Council with near equivalent prerogatives (PC: 181). And, crucially, the powers of the Duma to approve state expenditures and to raise revenue – budgetary control is 'the vital nerve of any constitutionalism' (PC: 182) – were negated by a plethora of countervailing rules and stipulations, so that 'every movement of parliament runs up against legal barbed wire' (PC: 184). The result was a rigged system, a 'farce' (PC: 183), not genuine constitutionalism, and it was a dissimulation, Weber predicted, which would eventually prove deadly to the credibility of tsarism itself.

> The machinery grinds on as if nothing has happened. And yet things have been done which cannot be undone. The insincerity by which liberties are officially granted, and at the moment when one is about to avail oneself of them, are taken away again with the other hand, *must* become the source of constantly repeated conflicts and fierce hatred, and be far more provocative than the old blatantly crushing system of repression. (PC: 173)

This remark also highlights a contention that links 'Bourgeois Democracy' to 'Pseudo-constitutionalism', namely, that the very machinery of power employed by the 'trickster' autocracy to retain control would, in the longer term, be its undoing.

For the meantime, however, the ploys of force and evasion were being supplemented by an internal reorganization of the administration (PC: 174–80). The effect of this reorganization was to bifurcate the regime, making the Tsar ever more dependent on the central bureaucracy and the Prime Minister. In particular, the relationship of the Council of Ministers to the Tsar was radically changed by a decree promulgated in October 1905. From being a largely advisory body, consisting of departmental heads and other sundry appointees under the Tsar's patronage and control, it became an organ subject to the Prime Minister, whose powers were accordingly enhanced. Previously, the Tsar had normally presided over the Council; now this was to be the exception: instead the Prime Minister managed it and tightly controlled its agenda. Previously, Council ministers had been able to report directly to the Tsar; now they were expected to go through the channel – and filter – of the Prime Minister's office. Previously, various departments had competed against one another for the favour of the Tsar, and by their very rivalry had tended to constrain the efficient functioning of the overall mechanism. Now, this system had been rationalized, and its fearsome coordination lent the Prime Minister even more power. In short, a 'cabinet' system was imposed on a monarchical one – to the detriment of the latter. Ironically, the Tsar's own desire for a pseudo-, rather than a substantive, constitutional system helped curtail his prerogatives. Had he implemented a real constitutional system, with a working parliament, the bureaucracy would have had many reasons to unite with him against the new order. As a result of recent changes, conversely, the central bureaucracy's own autonomy was enhanced at the Tsar's expense.

Yet despite every ruse, every internal transformation, every act of brutality, the election produced an assembly largely opposed to the autocratic system. Against all odds, when the first Imperial Duma met on 27 April/10 May, the Kadets were the single largest group with 179 – just over 37 per cent – of the deputies. In a long section on the background to the election, Weber traces the various forces and processes that converged to produce a Kadet victory. He describes the remarkable regrouping of the workers' movement, and the peculiarities, quandaries and conflicts between and within the parties agitating for change, stabilization or reaction. The peasant and agrarian question is at the forefront of discussion (we return to it below); and the tactics of tsarist repression are once again rehearsed. The Kadets' triumph was nonetheless highly unstable, Weber argued. Essentially, their electoral success was due more to the incompetent tactics of the regime and the intransigence of the far left than to widespread support for a liberal democratic programme *per se*. For by failing to provide guarantees for a real constitution, the regime had alienated much of the bourgeois vote, which deserted rightist organizations like the Trade and Industry Party, and the Party of Legal Order, and voted Kadet instead. More generally, the regime's cynicism and brutality encouraged a protest vote from many strata prepared to override class interests temporarily to punish the autocracy, and which found in the Kadets the best instrument for this chastisement. Finally, the official boycott of the election staged by the Social Democratic leadership prompted many of the party's rank and file to look elsewhere to express their feelings – and vote Kadet. But all this – including peasant support for elements of the Kadet agrarian programme – made for a highly volatile constituency. The fate of the Kadets rested on a loose coalition of voters which could disintegrate as quickly as it had come together. Concessions from the regime were likely to detach sections of the bourgeois vote. The agrarian programme might be insufficiently radical for the peasants. And where Social Democracy abandoned its official boycott, and put up candidates of its own, experience showed that the workers would tend to vote socialist rather than liberal.

Weber concludes the essay by examining the state of the various parties following the election result, the government's financial capitulation to a consortium of European banks, and the confrontation between Duma groupings and the autocracy. The latter responded to the opposition by stalling-tactics, provocation, and finally by dissolution of the assembly on 7/20 July 1906. The first Imperial Duma had lasted less than two and a half months.

The Essays of 1917

When the tide of the revolutionary movement receded in 1906, Weber turned his attention to other projects. His interest in the affairs of Russia remained lively, however. He continued to subscribe to a number of Russian newspapers, remained in touch with Russian scholars (Mommsen and Dahlmann 1989a: 22–3), and offered observations on the Russian scene in various public settings. Thus, in a discussion held in November 1908 on parliamentary monarchies and in a clarification of March 1909, Weber argued that a parliamentary and democratic system would make Russia a far more formidable force than it currently was under tsarism (Weber 1989: 685–92). And again, in December 1912, delivering a speech to commemorate the fiftieth anniversary of the Heidelberg Russian Reading Room, Weber addressed recent conflicts between Russian and German students and spoke about the cultural relationship of the two countries. (We only have newspaper, and other people's, very sketchy accounts of the 1912 intervention. Nothing survives of the original speech.) Weber also planned to write an essay on the ethics of Tolstoy, but the project never materialized.

When Weber did start to write again specifically on Russian themes (in the form of political journalism), Germany was in the final stages of a war with the Anglo-Franco-Russian 'Triple Entente'. Weber's view of the causes of the war, and of the methods and policy that Germany should employ in prosecuting it, are too complex to be described here in any detail (see, instead, Mommsen 1984 [1974, 1959]: 137–282). Suffice it to say that he envisaged the conflict as a consequence of German foreign policy mismanagement and, more fundamentally, of Entente determination to stop Germany from becoming a 'great' European power. But that, according to Weber, was exactly what Germany should strive to be: first, to redeem the potential of German unification in 1871; and second, to provide a counterweight to the division of the globe between Anglo-Saxon and Russian hegemony. Even so, Weber did not consider Germany's 'Western' and 'Eastern' opponents to be equally menacing. It was Russia that was the greater threat on account of its rising population, its expansionist tendencies, and its geopolitical interest in the Balkans. Moreover, the mantle of Russian chauvinism was being assumed by the Kadets as well as by the autocracy. It was imperative, therefore, that Germany consider its post-war future and do nothing in the short term that would lastingly estrange it from potential Western allies (Weber 1984b [1916]: 161–94; cf. Pipes 1954–5: 388–9; Mommsen 1984 [1959]: 140, esp. n. 13).

'Russia's Transition to Pseudo-democracy' and 'The Russian Revolution and the Peace' were prompted by a series of events that began with the February 1917 'revolution' in Russia, the abdication of the Tsar, and the formation on 1/14 March of a 'Provisional Government' under the direction of Prince G. E. Lvov (Prime Minister), Paul Miliukov, the leader of the Kadets (Foreign Minister), and Alexander Kerensky, leader of the Socialist Revolutionaries (Minister of Justice). Alongside it emerged an alternative, shadow government centred on the Petrograd Workers' and Soldiers' Council (Soviet). The Menshevik N. S. Chkheidze was its chairman; and Kerensky, the conduit between the Provisional Government and the Petrograd Soviet, was its deputy chairman. In March 1917, the Petrograd Soviet called for an immediate cessation of the war 'without annexations or indemnities', a declaration which Weber welcomed even if he doubted its ability to deliver the peace. The failure of German Social Democracy to understand this – it had taken up the Soviet's call – would make Germany weaker, he believed. In the event, the split over war aims between the Provisional Government (still formally loyal to France and Britain) and the Petrograd Soviet made the status quo untenable. Miliukov resigned, and on 6/19 May the so-called first coalition government was formed, which included socialist members. This 'republic of literati' (Weber 1978b [1917]: 1406), in which Kerensky became Minister of War, was short-lived. It was followed by the second coalition government formed on 25 July/7 August. In it, Kerensky reached his zenith as Prime Minister, surviving a botched counter-revolutionary coup by General L. G. Kornilov in September, only to be finally ousted by the Bolsheviks in October/November 1917.

Against this backdrop, Weber wrote the 1917 essays which we will summarize together. Despite his earlier prognosis that only a European war would topple the autocracy, Weber, like most observers, was taken by surprise by the February revolution and the abdication of the Tsar. Both events had seemed unlikely for at least three reasons. First, since 1906, P. A. Stolypin's agrarian reforms had gradually cleaved the peasantry into two antagonistic groupings – private owners with a vested interest in the persistence of the regime, and the mass of poor, land-hungry peasants. More divided than ever, the peasants had appeared a less potent force than they had been in 1905–6. Second, though the radical industrial proletariat had 'greatly increased' during the previous decade, it still remained relatively small – and, this is the third reason, unable to form a durable alliance with elements of the bourgeoisie. All experience demonstrated, Weber claimed, that without such an alliance revolutions were doomed to fail. The reason was simple: only the bourgeoisie was able to secure the credit-worthiness necessary to finance 'the organization of a permanent administration' (PD: 243). The question was, then, 'how bourgeois circles would react to another revolution' (PD: 243). In this particular case not only was 'heavy industry' violently opposed to it; that was to be expected. Also, after years of frustration at home, 'the bourgeois intelligentsia and the zemstvo circles' (PD: 243) had abandoned the revolutionary movement, and turned their eyes instead towards foreign adventurism.

So why did the revolution occur? Weber assigns much of the responsibility to Nicholas II. Throughout all four of the essays on Russia, Weber's remarks on the Tsar and his regime are typically scathing. In 'Bourgeois Democracy', he incessantly condemns the tsarist system for its viciousness, shallowness and insincerity. In 'Pseudo-constitutionalism', elaborating on these accusations, he even argues that the appalling ruthlessness of the regime tended to impede the development of political skills and orientations which would be required to remove it. For the struggle with the tsarist system 'had inevitably to consume so much strength in mere "tactics", and place so much emphasis on "technical party considerations", that scarcely any room was left for "great leaders" ' (PC: 231). And Weber adds: 'One cannot accomplish "great" deeds against vermin' (PC: 231). The venom in these words is also evident in 'Pseudo-democracy', where Weber claims that the Tsar's wish to maintain the 'vain romanticism and self-pity' (PD: 246) of the semblance of power, rather than its substance, turned out to be catastrophic. Had he been receptive to a constitutional monarchy, Nicholas II might well have succeeded in co-opting bourgeois strata. He might also have been able to maintain the loyalty of disaffected officers, and stave off an alliance between middle-class and proletarian intellectuals (PD: 247–8). Instead, the Tsar had encouraged a momentary unification of disaffected forces – and had lost his throne as a result.

That a revolution had come, however, did not mean that either peace or democracy would follow immediately in its wake. The system of dual power – the Provisional Government on the one side, the Petrograd Soviet on the other – produced an erratic 'diplomatic seesaw' (P: 261). Consider first the Provisional Government in which Miliukov continued to make bellicose statements; he showed no interest at all in a 'democratic and federalist Russia' (P: 261). Supporting the Government were the reactionary elements of the Duma, particularly the big landowners. Indeed, neither the Provisional Government nor the dominant class in the Duma had any immediate incentive to achieve peace or democracy. On the contrary, the war discharged the invaluable function of pinning down the revolutionary peasants in the trenches under military discipline. Moreover, the Provisional Government and its allies required money to stay in power – and such funds would be provided by domestic and foreign banks only on the understanding that 'the radical and revolutionary peasants are suppressed, and the war continues' (P: 265; also PD: 256). The engine of war was thus being driven no longer by the conflict with Germany, or because of fear of a Japanese attack on Russia's Asian colonies. The war was continuing because of domestic political considerations: primarily, trepidation about the consequences of peasant participation in elections for a constituent assembly, and peasant demand for land (PD: 250–1). The peasants themselves had much to gain from a speedy resolution of the conflict, 'the expropriation in entirety of non-peasant land' that was likely to follow, 'and the cancellation of Russia's foreign debts' (PD: 249; emphasis omitted), the interest on which they would otherwise be compelled to pay. But the peasants were not in control. Nor was the socialist Kerensky, who uncomfortably straddled for a time both the Provisional Government and the Petrograd Soviet. Any political alternative to the current situation that he might envisage would require financial backing, a prospect rendered implausible by the banks' implacable demand for order and profit. So Kerensky – the 'gravedigger of Russia's young freedom' (Weber 1978b [1917]: 1465 n. 17; cf. P: 265) – was compelled to play a game that was both duplicitous and futile (PD: 252–3).

And what about the other side of this political equation, the Petrograd Soviet? Weber concluded that its chairman, Chkheidze, was a typical Russian intellectual, with the propensity to turn nationalist and imperialist once he became actively embroiled in state affairs. 'There is *only one* reliable *test* of a genuine democratic and non-imperialist attitude,' Weber insisted. 'Does the politician in question restrict himself to cleaning up in his own backyard, i.e. to creating a democracy within his own country *or not*? If he does not, he is an imperialist, whether or not he intends to be' (P: 263). By calling upon the Germans to depose the Kaiser, Weber argued tortuously, Chkheidze exposed himself as a socialist-imperialist, and 'whether Russian imperialism takes a despotic, a liberal or a socialist form is neither here nor there' (P: 263).

What existed in Russia in April/May 1917, then, was a pseudo-democracy by means of which real democracy and federalism were being forestalled. For that reason, Weber warned his compatriots, hopes for an immediate end to hostilities were likely to be disappointed.

The Place of the Russian Essays in Weber's Oeuvre

How are we to position the essays on Russia, particularly the very substantial pieces of 1905–6, in Weber's work more generally? At least two strategies suggest themselves. The first might seek to locate the 1905–6 essays within a particular Weberian 'period' or 'phase'. The problem arising from such an approach, however, is the obvious one of what period or phase to choose.[10] Weberian scholarship offers little consensus on how to map Weber's work or how to 'weigh' the impact on it of neo-Kantianism, *Nationalökonomie*, cultural philosophy, history and sociology. But of one thing we can be certain. In the years contiguous to the Russian writings, Weber published two works which have since become emblematic of a specifically Weberian approach to 'social science': in 1904, ' "Objectivity" in Social Science and Social Policy', the essay in which Weber set out the editorial 'line' of the *Archiv für Sozialwissenschaft und Sozialpolitik*; and in 1905 'The Protestant Ethic and the "Spirit" of Capitalism'. What bearing, if any, do these essays have on the 1905–6 writings on Russia?

Various answers are possible. But if we consider these writings as a 'cluster', rather than as a discrete series of publications, Weber's critical engagement with historical materialism is especially salient. ' "Objectivity" in Social Science', as is well known, records Weber's attempt to delineate the presuppositions (purpose, character) of the cultural sciences, and the type of concept-formation appropriate to them. Yet in doing this, Weber could not just be programmatic; he had also to defend his theory against its rivals (cf. Wolin 1981). Chief among these was Marxism, and Weber offers both a critique of historical materialism *and* an attempt to 'trump' it. His formula is to reject 'most emphatically' the 'so-called "materialist conception of history" as a *Weltanschauung*', while simultaneously insisting that the 'advancement of the economic *interpretation* of history is one of the most important aims of our journal' (Weber 1949a [1904]: 68). As we shall show towards the end of this section, it is precisely this formula that Weber seeks to vindicate in the Russian studies of 1905–6.

It is also credible to see the latter (among other things) as an empirical counterpoint to the famous methodological statement that concludes the 'Protestant Ethic'. There Weber insisted that it was no part of his aim 'to substitute for a one-sided materialistic an equally one-sided spiritualistic causal interpretation of culture and of history' (Weber 1930 [1905]: 183). His epistemology required no such alternative.[11] As Merleau-Ponty (1973 [1955]: 18–19) once observed of it:

> The ambiguity of historical facts, their *Vielseitigkeit*, the plurality of their aspects . . . allows us to read in a religious fact the first draft of an economic system or read, in an economic system, positions taken with regard to the absolute. Religion, law, and economy make up a single

history because any fact in any one of the three orders arises, in a sense, from the other two.

In the Russian treatises, Weber redeems the qualification registered in the closing lines of the 'Protestant Ethic' by examining those conditions – economic, organizational, and religious too – which were decidedly unfavourable to the establishing of the 'spirit' of capitalism and a liberal-democratic system. This he attempts alongside a critique of Marxism that excoriates the limitations of its 'intellectual tools', and the political strategy for modernization it advances.

We mentioned above that there are at least two ways in which one might seek to locate the writings on Russia in the Weberian oeuvre. The aforementioned reference to the conditions underlying bourgeois democracy conveniently brings us to the second. In this case, rather than designating a particular period or phase in which to situate the Russian studies, we might be more concerned to identify their relationship to the broader span of Weber's life-interests and substantive preoccupations. In particular, we find cogent David Beetham's (1985 [1974]: 183–4, 203–10) emphasis on the thematic bridge that connects the Russian essays to Weber's earlier (and later) writings on the German predicament. (Again, there are clear echoes here of Weber's ongoing debate with historical materialism.) In both countries, as Beetham points out, Weber was concerned to identify the historical conditions which both facilitated and hindered the rise of a vibrant parliamentary and democratic system. The facilitating conditions – largely absent in the cases of Russia and Germany themselves – are touched on towards the end of 'Bourgeois Democracy'. They included 'overseas expansion', the 'peculiarity of the economic and social structure of the "early capitalist" era in Western Europe', the rise of science and its domination of social life, and 'certain ideal values, which, emerging from the concrete historical peculiarity of a certain religious thought world, have, together with numerous particular political constellations and in collaboration with those (aforementioned) material conditions, gone to make up the particular "ethical" character and the cultural values of modern man' (BD: 109).

Conversely, among the chief impediments to liberal democracy were, first, the relatively late industrialization experienced by both Russia and Germany. During capitalism's nascent phase, Weber explains, material interest and individualistic ethos had tended to coincide in a pincer attack on late feudal society. In Russia and Germany, in contrast, this developmental stage had been missed and, consequently, individualism now found itself swimming ' "against the tide" of material constellations' (BD: 109). Re-emphasizing this point, Weber added that, in Russia, all 'those intermediate stages are missing, which in the West placed the powerful *economic* interests of propertied strata in the service of the bourgeois freedom movement' (PC: 232). A second obstacle to the establishment of liberal democracy common to both Germany and Russia was the subordinate political position of the 'bourgeoisie' itself. Heavy industry, big manufacture, finance capital, wealthy commercial interests, far from achieving political power, had largely capitulated to the authoritarian state. Again, developmental conditions were the critical factor. The emergence of a restive working class *before* the consolidation of middle-class power and confidence had conspired to throw the bourgeoisie into a fearful and dependent alliance with traditional ruling strata. Finally, the existence of religious traditions such as Lutheranism and Russian Orthodoxy, highly statist and politically conformist in character, were also unfavourable to the advancement of liberal individualism. In Russia, even what appeared to be radical religious movements, like the 'Christian Fighting Brotherhood', were in fact institutionally quite weak and vulnerable to co-option by the established order. 'A *purely* religious, biblical and *ascetic* movement, on the other hand, could be a serious danger for the Orthodox Church and thus for the authoritarian regime in a moment of outward weakness, but the age of fully developed capitalism offers little basis for this' (BD: 128 n. 84).[12]

For all these related reasons, then, the opportunities available to democratic liberals in Russia, as in Germany, were more circumscribed than had been the case in Britain or America during an earlier epoch. The parallels between Germany and Russia should not, however, be exaggerated. For, to begin with, Weber recognized that Russia had potentialities that Germany evidently lacked. Russia, like the United States, comprised a 'virtually limitless geographical arena' (BD: 110). Its economic and political modernization was relatively recent and uneven. And devoid of the complacency and ennui of nations no longer excited by the concept of 'human rights', it might eventually prove capable of producing something unique.[13]

But there were also liabilities. Weber was aware that Russian economic conditions were marked by a far larger gap between advanced capitalism (*Hochkapitalismus*) and paternalistic social relations than in the Germany of his day. Indeed, Russia was a 'country whose most "national" institutions scarcely a century ago showed strong similarities to the monarchy of Diocletian' (BD: 46). In particular, the Russian countryside bore the indelible impress of archaic peasant 'communism', the obshchina system.[14] The obshchina (village or peasant community) was to a large degree a 'compulsory association' (BD: 77) equipped with the ability to control a person's movement, and with the right to use a person's labour power. As a result, Weber claimed, the Russian peasant had not been truly emancipated, and remained ' "in bondage to his commune" ' (BD: 77). Furthermore, while the economic situation of the Russian peasantry was often desperate – 'the worst conditions of economic slavery can exist within' it (Weber 1989: 211 n. 62) – the peasants themselves were divided on the merits of the obshchina. Some may have found it an unwelcome restraint on, for instance, economic acquisition. But the

> overwhelming majority of peasants, in the regions where it exists, is undoubtedly favourably disposed to its basic principle: right to land according to need, and in favour also of its fundamental institutional function, the redistribution of land where there has been a shift in the 'correct' proportion between size of family and land share. (PC: 210; emphasis omitted)

This was yet another reason why reform along individualistic, capitalist lines met so many problems, and why discussion in Kadet agrarian debates regarding *which* land to expropriate, and on the basis of which norms, was so controversial and complicated (PC: 196–200; cf. Fleischhauer 1979: 179–80). Moreover, favouring one group (e.g. the land-hungry) was likely to provoke the hostility of another (e.g. the Kulaks); 'as so often "value stands against value" ' (PC: 211).

The German agrarian configuration was very different, a point Weber sought to clarify in his 1918 lecture on 'Socialism'. While there might be an affinity of sorts between Marxist doctrine and the aspirations of 'land-hungry' Russian peasants 'used to agrarian communism', the German farmer 'is an individualist nowadays and clings to his inheritance and his soil. He will hardly let himself be driven from it. He will sooner ally himself with the landed proprietor than with the radical socialist worker, if he believes himself threatened' (Weber 1971 [1918]: 216, 218).

Equally, Russian autocratic power and domestic coercion was far more severe than that exercised by its western neighbour. It is true that Weber often used his Russian essays as an occasion to attack, directly or through allusion, Bismarck's legacy and the 'personal rule' of Wilhelm II (e.g. BD: 107, 121 n. 47, PD: 246). Nonetheless, he was clear where such comparisons ended. Even the most basic political and civil liberties were still to be achieved in Russia, as was a functioning parliament. The German Reichstag may have stood condemned, as Weber later expressed it, as the bearer of 'negative politics', unable to pursue responsible and decisive leadership because of the constitution imposed by Bismarck, and the ideological posturing such arrangements encouraged (Weber 1978b [1918]: 1407–16). But at least Germany in 1905 *had* an established parliament, and with it political parties which to a considerable degree could openly and legally mobilize for social and political reform. Since 1867 Germany (with the exception of Prussia) had secured universal manhood suffrage, the secret ballot, and equal weighting of votes. And by 1912 the Social Democrats were the single largest party in the Reichstag. The First Imperial Duma, in contrast, had to wait till May 1906 to be convened, and was based on a graded franchise. When, against all odds, it still managed to produce a combative parliament, the Tsar promptly dismissed it. The cavalier mismanagement of Germany under the German Kaiser was, for Weber, a travesty of political life and a national disgrace.[15] But it was not a 'mechanism maintained merely by daily executions', a phrase he used in 1909 to describe the Romanov autocracy (Weber 1989: 691).[16] Such distinctions only served to sharpen Weber's appreciation of the sheer range of authoritarian systems. Beside Bismarck's Caesarism (cf. Baehr 1988), and the Kaiserism of Wilhelm II, lay another kind of 'personal regime': that of Nicholas II and the 'Caesaropapist' order he manipulated.[17]

We stated above that Weber's Russian articles reveal tangible continuities with earlier concerns. But if that was all they provided, these essays would be less interesting than they are. For in addition they also furnish some of the discursive conditions of ideas and arguments which tend to be associated with Weber's later sociology. In practice, Weber's political and academic writings were rarely sharply separated (cf. Giddens 1972). More usual was his habit of textual reconstitution, in which observations first registered in a political context were later reshaped and expanded into more clinical, abstract formulae, becoming instances of Weber's 'ideal-types'. For instance, when Weber, in *Economy and Society* (1910–1914 version), outlines the ruler's dependence on bureaucracy, the German Kaiser and the Russian Tsar are employed as illustrations. In the latter case, Weber draws directly (though with changed emphasis) on remarks he had made in 'Pseudo-constitutionalism' (1978a: 993–4, PC: 174–9). A similar practice of textual reformulation is evident in the sociology of law, where Weber discusses natural law ideologies of the small peasantry (1978a: 871–2; PC: 198). Or one might consider those passages on intellectuals and secular salvation ideologies (1978a: 500–17) in which the 'Russian revolutionary intelligentsia' (1978a: 516) are accorded an important place – as they are in all four of the essays translated below. (See also the allusion, in the 1918–20 version of *Economy and Society*, to disputes between Lenin and Plekhanov, and compare with 'Bourgeois Democracy': Weber, 1978a: 112; BD: 67, 131 n. 103; cf. PC: 194, 217)

Weber's articles on Russia also enable us to trace the development and refinement of his political ideas. As a man of strong political sensibility,

Weber was always curious about the character of those attracted to politics, about what political actors hoped to gain from their involvement, how much uncertainty they could bear, and the manner in which particular institutional arrangements 'selected' definite personality traits. His studies of Russia contain some relevant material on this subject. Of particular note are those sections where Weber sketches the sectarianism of Russian Social Democracy:

> Like the thorough-going Jesuit, the devout Marxist is imbued by his dogma with a blithe superiority and the self-assurance of the somnambulist. Disdaining to strive for lasting political success, and confident of being above reproach, he accepts with equanimity and a mocking laugh the collapse of all hopes – his own included – of overcoming the mortal foe he shares with other groups; is always exclusively concerned with the preservation of the pure faith and – if possible – the increase of his own sect by a few souls; and seeks the 'unmasking' of 'those who are also catholics' here, of 'traitors to the people' there, in neighbouring groups. (BD: 69; cf. 132–3 n. 114)

This acidic depiction of the apostles of the 'unconditional ethical imperative' (BD: 52) will at once be familiar to students of Weber; it prefigures the more extended treatment, in 'Politics as a Vocation' (Weber 1948b [1919]: 120–8), of the follower of the 'ethic of conviction'. The contrasting political type – the follower of the 'ethic of responsibility' – also makes an appearance in one of the essays on Russia: to wit, in 'Pseudo-democracy' where Weber mentions 'strict *objectivity*, the steady sense of *proportion*, the restrained *self-control*, and the capacity for *unobtrusive* action which it calls for' as the key qualities necessary for the capable politician (PD: 245; compare with Weber 1948b [1919]: 115–17).

Yet besides the actual substance of these essays, two other characteristics are also worth mentioning: first, Weber's enduring sense of the paradoxical; second, his more general approach to social relations and human conduct. It is a commonplace to note that Weber's work is permeated by various kinds of conceptual opposition: for instance, bureaucracy and charisma, the politics of conviction and responsibility, formal and substantive rationality. But it should be just as plain that Weber formulated these polarities not because he himself thought the social world was indeed binary in structure – that was the psychology of the sectarian fanatic or utopian visionary he frequently criticized – but precisely for the opposite reason. The formulation of stark, coordinating oppositions allows us to plot the actual course of history as it steers unsteadily between these extremes (cf. Scaff 1989: 181–5). Weber recognized that our reasoning capacity, and our expository frameworks, will inevitably tend to impose some sort of regularity on the social world around us. Even so, history itself is fluid, unstable, evasive of our categorical schemata, and only rarely synchronistic. An appreciation of this attitude helps explain the extensive treatment Weber offers in 'Bourgeois Democracy' of the Populist and the Socialist Revolutionary party programmes. It is the 'hybrid interstitial thought worlds, created by the victorious march of capitalism' that fascinates him, that conceptual space 'between the bourgeois and the modern proletarian thought world on the one hand and romantic-revolutionary utopianism on the other' (Weber 1989: 209 n. 61). And from a broadly similar perspective, he observes that the bearer of 'bourgeois democracy' in Russia is not actually the economic bourgeoisie itself; that the Russian 'autocracy is not capable of solving any of the great social problems without thereby fatally wounding itself' (BD: 111); that immediate universal suffrage would not democratize and liberalize the zemstvos, but would lead to the 'complete bureaucratization of the zemstvo administration' (BD: 51); that 'any attempt at systematic and general land distribution . . . would require a government which was at the same time inspired by strictly democratic ideals and was prepared to repress any opposition to its orders with iron authority and power' (PC: 200; emphasis omitted).

Second, the writings on Russia should help to erode further what remains of Weber's reputation as a writer biased towards 'idealist' explanations of social life. That this reputation persists is indubitable; and it is not just in textbook expositions that one continues to find it.[18] Thus after acknowledging her indebtedness to Weber's analysis of 'the state/ society relationship' in *Economy and Society*, chs 9–13, Theda Skocpol (1979: 304 n. 4) enters the following two caveats:

> Weber tended to theorize about major forms of political structures in terms of the dominant kinds of ideas – tradition, charisma, rational-legal norms – through which the authority of rulers or their staffs was legitimated, whereas the focus here [i.e. in Skocpol's own comparative study of revolutions in France, Russia and China] is much more on the material-resource base and organizational form of state power. Second, insofar as Weber was willing to theorize about societal sociopolitical structures as wholes, he tended to use categories that referred to political forms alone, in isolation from socioeconomic structures.

This, at best, represents a very partial and particular reading of *Economy and Society* (for a contrary view see Collins 1986: 2–3, 145–209). It also quite evidently ignores the entire corpus of Weber's political writings on revolutionary Russia. Yet throughout the 1905–6 pieces in particular,

Weber's precise and deliberate objective is to establish the *limits* of idealinterests and doctrinal principles when faced with social classes and state agencies determined to oppose them. The forces of liberalism failed, Weber shows, because they lacked potent bearers (institutions, social strata) to carry forward, and resources to sustain, the liberal idea. With regard to the individual actor, Weber's approach is also revealing. Typically, he portrays the individual in the 1905–6 studies as a quintessentially social being, existing at the intersection of historical legacies, ideological commitments, personal ambitions. 'External', institutional conditions are presented as the essential locus in which the person must face up to inner 'demands' and challenges (cf. Schluchter 1979 [1971]: 71). As a result, he is able to assess figures as ideologically remote as Plehve and Plekhanov, not by some rationalistic or moralistic calculus, but in the context of the organizational and doctrinal dilemmas they found themselves compelled to confront or, with varying degrees of ingenuity, to evade.

Furthermore, the emphasis on liberalism in the treatises of 1905–6 should not disguise Weber's very real respect for 'the indefatigable energy' of those currents 'of Russian radicalism' (PC: 230) which were decidedly anti-liberal in persuasion, and for the idealism and 'class solidarity' of the workers' movement (PC: 193). Weber's grasp of the harsh realities of social power meant that he was happy to draw on a Marxian lexicon where he found it appropriate – as he often did; thus his references in 'Pseudo-constitutionalism' to 'the reserve army of the unemployed', 'class solidarity', 'class interests', 'class offences . . . dealt with by class-based courts' and so on (respectively, PC: 192, 193, 172, 172; emphasis omitted). On the power of the money-markets to influence Russian domestic policy, Weber is equally unsentimental:

> Their influence is the most significant. In the previous revolution one could follow step by step how the government of Count Witte did whatever the foreign banks and stock exchanges regarded as being advantageous for the *credit-worthiness* of the regime, whether this meant making concessions or applying repression. The bourgeois leaders of the present regime, if they wish to have credit, have no choice other than to behave likewise. (PD: 248)

Nonetheless, Weber's distance from Marxism is in other respects immense. In his philosophy of history, Weber expanded the range of factors capable of assuming causal force and simultaneously released them from a logical hierarchy of determination. Politically, his chief enemy was not the market or the state *per se* so much as their modern manifestation: bureaucratic paternalism, a social order in which maximum regulation, instrumental reason and impersonality had triumphed at the expense of individual responsibility. Socialism, in his judgement, was poised to intensify this system rather than abolish it. And by dint of character, too, Weber occupies a different thought world from the Marxists he criticized. His discomfited sense of 'irrationality' – of a world inevitably characterized by 'undeserved suffering, unpunished injustice, and hopeless stupidity' (Weber 1948b [1919]: 122) – deprived him of chiliastic hopes, promoting instead an ironic distance towards any 'final' appropriation of truth, virtue or progress.

At the time of their original publication in Germany, the 1905–6 interventions passed largely unnoticed (Mommsen and Dahlmann 1989a: 44–7). Their fate in Russia before the First World War, on the other hand, was kinder: 'Bourgeois Democracy', translated into Russian in 1906, was generally well received in liberal circles, though Lenin dismissed its description of the 'foolish', 'putschist' December uprising as a 'piece of professorial wisdom of the cowardly bourgeoisie' (Lenin 1967 [1925]: 800). The concept of 'pseudo-constitutionalism' also attracted attention, and was taken up by 'historians and teachers of constitutional law' such as 'Borodin, Reysner, Kovalevskii, Kotliarevskii and Miliukov' (Mommsen and Dahlmann 1989a: 48–9). More recently, a growing body of literature has emerged which explicitly or incidentally is testing Weber's hypotheses and examining his research on, for instance, the Duma elections of 1906.[19] It is not within the competence of the editors of this volume to judge the empirical and historical accuracy of Weber's treatises on Russia. We leave that estimation to scholars of the field (but see especially Ascher 1988, 1992) and we hope that the *MWG* edition, and our partial translation of it, will facilitate such an appraisal.

The Political Significance of the Essays Today

The scholarly reception of a complex author's work is never a smooth and linear process. Inevitably, the work is read selectively, and Weber's fate in this regard has been proverbial. The single most influential volume for the Anglo-Saxon reception of Weber as a wide-ranging sociological thinker is undoubtedly the anthology *From Max Weber*.[20] Edited by Hans H. Gerth and C. Wright Mills, it has sold over 200,000 copies since its original publication in 1948 (Roth, 1992: 454). But aside from a long quote from 'Bourgeois Democracy' in the editors' Introduction (71–2), it contains nothing of substance on Russia. Nor does the next most important work in the career of Weber's reception as a sociologist: A. M.

Editors' Introduction 25

Henderson's and Talcott Parsons's *The Theory of Social and Economic Organization* (Weber 1947), a translation of the first part of Weber's *Economy and Society*, the full version of which had to wait till 1968 to be published in English (Weber 1978a; the English-language edition also contains an important political essay as an Appendix: Weber 1978b). To be sure, this does include many more references to Russian conditions, even if the longest of them by far (on 'Tsarist patrimonialism', 1978a: 1064–8) is under four pages long.

Yet if all three of these works contain relatively little on Russia specifically, they do enshrine something else of major significance: to wit, the analysis of bureaucracy, and the classification of the three types of legitimate domination or authority (traditional, rational-legal, and charismatic) which, *par excellence*, typify Weber the sociologist. And it is these seminal discussions[21] to which scholars have typically gravitated when they have sought to apply Weberian ideas to the Russian/Soviet cases (see, for instance, Rigby 1980; Fehér et al. 1983: 138–86; Breuer 1992);[22] or when, more generally, they have argued for the relevance of Weber's geopolitical or 'neo-Machiavellian'[23] approach to the study of social life. Particularly instructive in the circumstances is an unjustly overlooked discussion by Randall Collins in his *Weberian Sociological Theory* (1986). Comprising chapter 8 of that book, and entitled 'The future decline of the Russian Empire', it ventured the forecast that 'Particular combinations of events may . . . bring about precipitous losses of territorial power within the next thirty years' (1986: 187).[24]

However, if it is possible to argue for the continued utility of the categories of *Economy and Society*, what about that of the essays translated in the present volume? Here we must be more cautious, mindful of the tasks for which they were intended. The Russian studies of 1905–6 lack the conceptual apparatus of *Economy and Society*, and were penned for a different purpose. It makes little sense to expect from them what they were never supposed to accomplish. It is true that some scholars have discerned striking parallels between modern conditions in Russia and those of 1905. For instance, Alan Kimball and Gary Ulmen (1991), comparing the 'Russian Empire in 1905' and 'the Soviet Empire in 1991', enumerate the following resemblances:

> costly defeat in an unpopular imperialist war with a small and supposedly weaker Asian foe (Japan then, Afghanistan now), growing unrest among reform-minded bureaucrats and intellectuals . . . widespread popular unrest among the poor, separatist pressures from nations subordinated to the central imperial authority, startling projects for extensive change directed by the political leadership and the splintering of both official and

public activists into factions. The attempt to solve the 1905 crisis was no less state-directed than in 1991, and in both cases a solution was sought in the introduction of capitalism. Then, as now, the revolution planned and executed from above caught the imagination of the people below, who called for democracy. Then, the prospects for democracy could not be realized without either restricting or removing the Tsar. Now, they could not be divorced from the removal of the Communist Party. (1991: 189; cf. 195)

Since those lines were written, the Soviet Union has completely unravelled, and its aftermath offers us paradox, as much as analogy, to reflect on. Indeed, the extent of the paradoxes might even have surprised Max Weber. The Russian parliament building stands charred and pockmarked, a ghostly monument to 'democratic renewal'. Nationalist fervour and economic hardship coagulate in support for a party laughably called 'Liberal Democratic'. Under present Russian conditions, events move at a dizzying pace. Personalities and programmes come and go, so that to 'the outsider, all those individual fates, so dramatic in themselves, become interwoven to form an impenetrable tangle' (PC: 231). Political judgement could not be faced with a more formidable challenge. It would be unrealistic as well as unhistorical to expect too much illumination from Weber's political essays. It would also, of course, be un-Weberian. What interested Weber as a political writer and as a historian was less ' "analogies" and "parallels" ' and more the 'individuality' of each formation. Identifying the differences allows us then to 'determine the causes which led to these differences' (Weber 1976 [1909]: 385). In any case, a dispassionate examination of Weber's writings on the Russia of his day would show that prescience was not their only characteristic; they also contained verdicts that were to prove questionable or mistaken. In April 1917, Weber expected a quick reversion to the conservative-monarchist status quo ante (1984a: 236-7). And his later description of the Bolshevik government as a 'military dictatorship, not, it is true, of generals, but of corporals' (1971 [1918]: 216) had more polemical charge to it than analytical insight.

Yet if these writings provide no simple 'lesson' to be applied to current conditions, nor offer the theoretical scope and sophistication that *Economy and Society* can be claimed to possess, they do offer a historical resonance of sorts. This goes beyond the important catalytic role played by the incumbent leaderships of 1917 and 1989. In the first case, as Weber contended, Nicholas refused to countenance radical change until it was too late; in the second, Mikhail Gorbachev encouraged change without realizing its full implications, and before the consequences of 'reform' span out of his control. The historical resonance also goes beyond the nature of the nationalities question sketched by Weber, and his analysis of the haemorrhage of legitimacy that accompanies a regime's terminal decline. There is something more important still to be drawn from Weber's analysis.

In 1905–6, Weber argued that the introduction of advanced capitalism alone could not be expected to bring liberal democracy to Russia. He recognized that the destruction of tsarism was one thing; the consolidation of constitutional democracy quite another. For it was:

> absolutely ridiculous to attribute to the high capitalism which is today being imported into Russia and already exists in America – this 'inevitable' economic development – any elective affinity with 'democracy' let alone 'liberty' (in *any* sense of the word). The question should be: how can these things exist at all for any length of time under the domination of capitalism? In fact they are only possible where they are backed up by the determined *will* of a nation not to be ruled like a flock of sheep. (BD: 109)

How do things stand today? The destruction of an authoritarian order, and the implanting of capitalism in its stead, does not guarantee a stable constitutional democratic system today in Russia, any more than it did in the time of the Tsar. Indeed, the financial conditions in which Russia is supposed to make its great transformation are especially daunting. In the West, the current anathema attached to public management, controlled exchange rates, and the welfare state palpably attests to the victory of deregulation economics. Among its corollaries are social fragmentation and the pauperization of a growing underclass. These are the same forces and consequences that are now being imported pell-mell into Russia. It is true that they are also being resisted in both purposive and inchoate ways. But the decisions of electorates committed to pluralist democracy – and they are clearly heterogeneous decisions – face formidable obstacles, not only within Russia, but also from outside of it. If the policies of government become inconsistent with those of global financial markets, and the latter's judgements on 'credit-worthiness and sustainability' (Hutton 1994: 21), the national currency comes under attack and the government is pressured back into line. Whatever this is, it is not 'democracy' and it would be fraudulent to pretend otherwise. Marxism may be largely discredited in Russia, but a genuinely pluralistic and representative system has still to be firmly established there. And this will require cultural and political conditions, not just economic ones.[25]

Once again, then, the road ahead for Russia is stony and uncertain. Once again, too, political actors will continue to require the 'steadfastness of heart which can brave even the crumbling of all hopes' (Weber 1948b [1919]: 128). Few expected the Soviet Union to collapse in the way that it did, and as suddenly as it did. And we can only hypothesize today what course the latest Russian revolution will take. Even so, the sentiments Weber expressed of that first great revolution in 1905 retain an enduring pertinence for modern times:

> 'Millennia had to pass before you came into being, and more millennia wait silently to see what you will do with your life.' These impassioned words of Carlyle, originally addressed to individuals, can, without exaggeration, be applied not only to the United States, but also to Russia, to some extent now, and probably more fully after another generation. And this is why, despite all differences of national character and – let us be honest about it – probably those of national interests too, we cannot do other than to look with profound inner emotion and concern at the struggle for freedom in Russia and those who engage in it – of whatever 'orientation' and 'class'. (BD: 111; cf. Weber 1948a [1906]: 385)

Note on the Translation

The translations that follow are based on the texts published in two of the volumes of the *Max Weber Gesamtausgabe* (*MWG*), the annotated compilation of Weber's complete works, edited by Horst Baier, M. Rainer Lepsius, Wolfgang J. Mommsen, Wolfgang Schluchter, and the late Johannes Winckelmann. When completed, the *MWG* (1984–) is expected to amount to over thirty volumes.

'Bourgeois Democracy in Russia' (= 'Zur Lage der bürgerlichen Demokratie in Rußland') and 'Russia's Transition to Pseudo-constitutionalism' (= 'Rußlands Übergang zum Scheinkonstitutionalismus') are to be found in Max Weber, *Zur Russischen Revolution von 1905. Schriften und Reden 1905–1912*, *MWG* I/10 (Tübingen, J. C. B. Mohr [Paul Siebeck], 1989), pp. 86–279, 293–679, edited by Wolfgang J. Mommsen in collaboration with Dittmar Dahlmann. Both articles appeared originally in 1906 as supplements to the *Archiv für Sozialwissenschaft und Sozialpolitik*, respectively, vol. 22 (1) and vol. 23 (1), edited by Weber, Werner Sombart and Edgar Jaffé.[26]

Weber had written both studies with the objective that they should be highly topical, and the delays in publication which resulted from typesetting difficulties, problems in deciphering his handwriting, the author's constant revisions to keep up with events, and some disagreements between Jaffé and Weber regarding journal stylistics, caused the latter to be particularly bitter and irascible. 'It is a good thing that I am the only one who can hear him cursing and swearing at people', wrote Marianne Weber to her mother-in-law, Helene Weber, on 13 July 1906 (Weber 1989: 285).

'Bourgeois Democracy' was finally published on 6 February 1906 (final corrections had been sent to the printers on 29 January); 'Pseudo-constitutionalism' bears the date 25 August 1906; Weber had submitted the final proofs on 6 August. It is a measure of Weber's commitment to these topical supplements that he paid the production costs out of his own funds. Both appeared in a print run of 2,000 copies, 1,200 of which went free to subscribers of the *Archiv*, the remaining 800 were put on sale. (The previous two paragraphs draw on Mommsen and Dahlmann 1989b, 1989c.)

'Russia's Transition to Pseudo-democracy' (= 'Rußlands Übergang zur Scheindemokratie'), and 'The Russian Revolution and the Peace' (= 'Die russische Revolution und der Friede') are to be found in Max Weber, *Zur Politik im Weltkrieg. Schriften und Reden 1914–1918*, *MWG* I/15 (Tübingen: J. C. B. Mohr [Paul Siebeck], 1984), pp. 238–60, 291–7), edited by Wolfgang J. Mommsen in collaboration with Gangolf Hübinger. The former was originally published in Friedrich Naumann's weekly *Die Hilfe*, 23 (17) (26 April 1917); the latter, in the *Berliner Tageblatt*, 241 (12 May 1917), evening edition.

None of the original manuscripts have been preserved.

We are particularly indebted to the German editors of the *MWG*; the scholarship in the two volumes we have employed, but especially in *MWG* I/10, is extraordinary. Readers puzzled by the expression 'German thoroughness' are invited to peruse the *MWG* texts, where, in copious footnotes, Weber's sources and statistical computations have been checked by the German editors, and corrected where necessary; where poetic or other allusions have been assiduously traced wherever possible; and where historical events have been explained and contextualized. Where we have drawn on these notes we have marked them [M–H] and [M–D] as appropriate; Weber's own notes by [Weber]; and our own notes as English editors and translators by [Tr.], or simply enclosed in square brackets. The glossary and the list of parties and organizations, to be found at the end of this volume, are taken almost entirely from the *MWG* I/10.

The 1917 essays ('Russia's Transition to Pseudo-democracy' and 'The Russian Revolution and the Peace') are presented here in their entirety. In contrast, the 1905–6 essays ('Bourgeois Democracy in Russia' and 'Russia's Transition to Pseudo-constitutionalism') are offered in a truncated version; just over half of the original has been omitted. In particular, we were compelled to prune drastically Weber's own voluminous footnotes comprising his sources, various statistical calculations, qualifications, and other miscellaneous addenda. Deciding on what to delete, and how to translate, are never simple tasks, but we have attempted in the main text to strike a balance, respectively, between fidelity to Weber's own substantive emphases and interest to the modern reader, and between Weberianese and English readability. Naturally, there are dangers in attempting such balances, as readers acquainted with the historicist–presentist controversy (see, for instance, Jones 1983) or with *Begriffsgeschichte* (notably, Koselleck 1985 [1979]), will be eager to remind us. But there are dangers, too, in seeking to insist on purity (even assuming that publishing houses would accept such purism!) – of which some unintelligibility is the most obvious.

All translations of a work are simultaneously interpretations of it, but there is at least one reason to believe that Weber's political writings pose fewer hermeneutic difficulties than their philosophical-methodological counterparts. Translating the latter accurately, Gisela Hinkle (1986) has persuasively argued, requires a thorough appreciation of the neo-Kantian idioms – logic, theory of cognition, etc. – to which Weber subscribed, and which translators from Anglo-Saxon traditions have tended to underestimate or downplay. Reasons adduced for this state of affairs have included everything from carelessness to unconscious or deliberate domestication by a translator keen to conjoin a certain text to a particular scientific project (for more on the reception process, see Baehr and O'Brien 1994: ch. 4). With Weber's political writings, on the other hand, we have a rather different situation. Politically, Weber wrote as a liberal Anglophile (Roth 1992: 452), addressing a German audience to convince them of the virtues of some British–American political and ethical traditions. The vocabulary and conceptual apparatus he employed are thus more familiar and accessible to an English-reader than his methodological writings are. This is not of course to say that any translation of Weber is straightforward. Nor is it to say that any translation is definitive. It can never be, and not only because a translation is something different from the original, and 'improvements' on it 'improve the translation, not the original' (Greenberg 1993: 32). A translation also involves a constant stream of semantic choices between roughly equivalent alternatives.

Deletions in the main text of less than a sentence are represented thus: . . . Deletions in the main text of a sentence or more are represented thus: [. . .]. Where we have deemed it helpful for the reader, we have provided our own interpolation summarizing what has been omitted. Generally, we have avoided doing so for omissions from the German footnotes.

Editors' Introduction 31

The spelling of Russian words is complicated by the fact that Weber, naturally, gives German forms of the words in question. In putting these words into English, we have endeavoured to ascertain the original Russian spellings and then to apply a consistent scheme of transliteration. In the case of most letters the equivalent choice of English letter is straightforward. But in a few cases there is more than one possible choice. The cases in question are principally: (1) the Russian letter 'e', which may be rendered by the English letter 'e' (the solution we have adopted) or by letters chosen to indicate the pronunciation ('ye' or 'yo', as the case may be), e.g. we have written 'Solovev' rather than 'Solovyov'. (2) The Russian letter И may be rendered by either 'i' or 'y'. Our preferred option is 'i'. Where the customary English spelling of a well-known Russian name differs from the scheme, we have retained the customary spelling (e.g. 'Gorky', instead of 'Gorkii').

Acknowledgements

We wish to record our gratitude to colleagues at Coventry University and the Memorial University of Newfoundland for their help and encouragement throughout this project. At Coventry, we would like warmly to thank: the former Dean of the School of International Studies and Law, Michael Smith, for providing some relief from teaching duties, Roy Benwell, for assistance with word-processing, and Ann Benwell and other members of the German subject area, past and present, for their support and their readiness to discuss some of the knotty problems posed by Weber's language. Thanks also to colleagues in Russian and History, especially Patrick Corness for advice on transliteration of Russian words, and Alexander Chubarov for sharing so generously with us his knowledge of the language and history of Russia.

At Memorial, we have benefited greatly from the advice of Kim Ducey, Mark Knighton, Hedda Schuurman, Ron Schwartz, Peter Sinclair, Victor Zaslavsky, but especially Bill McGrath and Volker Meja. We are grateful also to Memorial for financially backing the project through the good offices of the former Dean of Arts, Michael Staveley. A trip from Newfoundland to Coventry was thus made possible, and the editors were able to work together in person. Peter Baehr would also like to record his great debt to former teachers at the Department of Sociology, University of Leicester, particularly Clive Ashworth, Chris Dandeker and Terry Johnson. During a period in the 1970s, notable for its chronic academic polarization, Leicester offered a refreshingly open and ecumenical forum for sociological discussion; in that setting, the work of Weber figured prominently. We have also been fortunate in having in Andrew Winnard at Polity Press an able, responsive and efficient editor. We should also like to thank Kate Pool and Gordon Fielden of the Translators' Association of the Society of Authors for their helpful advice and assistance in the early stages of this project. Responsibility for the end result of our work is, of course, entirely our own.

Finally, a very special note of thanks is due to our respective families who have given us such tremendous support during the course of this project, and who have made many sacrifices so that we could devote our energy to it.

The editors of this English-language version of Weber's writings on Russia dedicate their work to Anita, Penny and Sally Wells, and to Hedda Schuurman.

Notes

1 Heidelberg, Weber's home and base-camp, boasted one of the most thriving Russian 'colonies' in Germany, consisting of a lively and highly politicized Russian émigré and academic community. Centred around the university, clubs and the Heidelberg Reading Room, Russian intellectuals vigorously debated the cultural and political events of the day. Weber was thus able to engage in discussion with Russian scholars and radicals, and afforded access to Russian newspapers (often printed outside Russia), periodicals and other documents. It appears that Bogdan Kistiakovskii, a Russian scholar, and a former pupil of Wilhelm Windelband and Georg Simmel, was particularly important in directing Weber's attention to the liberal constitutional movement unfolding in Russia in 1905. He also helped Weber to acquire relevant sources for his investigations. Kistiakovskii was a member of the 'Union of Liberation', an association seeking to modernize Russian political life in a liberal democratic direction. It was the Union of Liberation's constitutional draft, published in Paris, first in Russian in March, then in a French version in August 1905 as 'Loi fondamentale de l'Empire Russe', that Weber examines in 'Bourgeois Democracy' and that provides the springboard for the analysis of Russian conditions.

   For a discussion of the Russian colony, and Weber's contacts with it, see Mommsen and Dahlmann 1989a: 5–8, from which our own note is drawn.

2 The nature of Weber's liberalism continues to be the subject of spirited debate. Among helpful recent appraisals are Bellamy 1992: ch. 4; Beetham 1989; Hennis 1988: ch. 5; Warren 1988.

3 Weber wrote to a Russian paper in March 1909, after having been quoted out of context, 'I cling to the view that the renewal of Russia *will come* and that it is consequently in Germany's interests for this renewal to come *as quickly as possible*, so that we can solve the problems which divide us by

Editors' Introduction 33

immediate contact between nation and nation. So, not only with regard to the lofty cultural tasks which are common to all of us, but in consideration of the immediate tasks facing German interests, all my sympathies have been for a long time on the side of the Russian freedom movement' (Weber 1989: 692).

4 A translation of the 'Eleven Theses' of this Congress can be found in the Appendix to Harcave 1964: 279–81.
5 The Russian (Julian) calendar of this period was thirteen days behind the Gregorian calendar used today. Both datings are provided in this Introduction.
6 Unless otherwise indicated, all emphases in the text are Weber's.
7 Historically, the term 'Jacobin' is generally associated with the so-called Jacobin Republic of Year II (June 1793–July 1794), the populist dictatorship established during the French Revolution which forged a temporary alliance of urban labour and the little-propertied on the one hand (the 'Sansculottes'), with a section of the radical middle class on the other. Its leaders included Saint-Just, Marat, Danton and, most notoriously, Robespierre. It is best known for the 'Terror' – responsible for the executions of at least 17,000 people – and the Committee of Public Safety which directed it. A brief assessment can be found in Hobsbawm 1973 [1962]: 89–94.

For the argument that Lenin too was strongly influenced by Jacobin thinking, especially via the ideas of Pyotr Tkachev, see Szamuely 1974: 287–319. Lenin's own definition of Jacobinism appears in Lenin 1964 [1917]: 'Proletarian historians see Jacobinism as one of the highest *peaks* in the emancipation struggle of an oppressed class. The Jacobins gave France the best models of a democratic revolution and of resistance to a coalition of monarchs against a republic', etc.

8 For the programmes of the Union of Liberation and of the Kadets see, respectively, Harcave 1964: 273–9, 292–300.
9 In *Economy and Society* (1978a [1910–14]: 516), Weber returns to this split between 'patrician, academic and aristocratic intellectuals' (i.e. the Second Element) and 'Plebeian intellectualism . . . represented by the proletaroid minor officialdom, which was highly sophisticated in its sociological thinking and broad cultural interests; it was composed especially of the *zemstvo* officials (the so-called "third element")'.
10 For discussions of the putative phases of Weber's work, see Antoni 1962 [1959, 1940]: ch. 4; Mommsen 1974: ch. 1; Scaff 1984.

Consider also, in more detail, the division offered by one of Britain's foremost Weber scholars, Keith Tribe. According to Tribe, it is useful to distinguish between three phases in Weber's intellectual trajectory. The first period, spanning roughly 1892–7, 'is one of "public" politics played out in the new institutions of post-Bismarckian politics: the *Verein für Sozialpolitik*, the *Evangelisch-soziale Kongress*, the *Alldeutscher Verband* – institutions which held conferences, addressed themselves to a "public opinion" and circulated literature and newspapers' (Tribe 1989 [1983]: 86). During these years, Weber's thought turned on the agrarian labour question in Prussia and its implications for German politics. Then, following a hiatus of some years as Weber first suffered, then strained to recover, from mental breakdown, a different set of preoccupations dominates his bibliographic record. From 1903 to the outbreak of the First World War, 'it is evident that his focus has become more strictly academic: opposing certain aspects of University appointment policy, taking up the editorship of a social science journal, assisting in the founding of a Sociological Association' (Tribe 1989: 87). Finally, between the outbreak of war and his death in 1920, Weber's writings oscillate 'between writings on religion and reflections on the consequences of the war for German politics' (Tribe 1989: 87).

This is a useful classification, and Tribe is the first to recognize that none of these phases are hermetically sealed. Still, it is also just as well to notice what such a typology obscures. The more we read Weber, the more aware we become of a mind which disregards all categorical borders established by his interpreters. Weber's 1905–6 writings on Russia illustrate the point well enough. Falling under Tribe's phase II, Weber's 'domain of engagement' is actually political rather than 'academic'. On this he was unequivocal. Both 'Bourgeois Democracy' and 'Pseudo-constitutionalism' were envisaged as 'social-political' reports, designed to deal with questions of pressing topicality; as such, they lacked the personal and temporal 'distance' he thought a more judicious academic perspective demanded. Not only did Weber, with quirky understatement, call his own efforts on Russia 'journalistic' (Weber 1989: 282); he even issued the following instruction to his publisher Paul Siebeck: 'please do not send the supplement ['Bourgeois Democracy in Russia'] *on any account* to academic periodicals. That would give the impression that it was a piece of work claiming *academic* qualities. That is just what it is *not*, but rather a *collection of material* and *popular* information' (postcard to Siebeck, dated 26 January, 1906, and cited in Weber 1989: 74 n. 20; emphasis in original). To this it will be objected that any periodization is a matter of emphasis, and that two treatises alone do not undermine Tribe's main point. They do not, but nor are these essays mere deviations of a 'phase': at almost a quarter of a million words, they amount to the most bulky of Weber's political writings.

11 Weber parodies 'spiritualistic' explanations of cultural history in his article 'Stammler's "Refutation" of the Materialist Conception of History' = *Critique of Stammler* (1977 [1907]: 62–70). Through a fictional dialogue between a 'historical spiritualist' and an 'empiricist', Weber draws out the reductionist reasoning of the former, and taxes its 'scholastic mystification'. However, this dialogue turns out to be simply a literary device for criticizing the isomorphic logic of the 'materialist conception of history' which, according to Weber, recapitulates in all essentials the absurdity of 'historical spiritualism'.

Weber's bad-tempered attack on the work of Rudolf Stammler – jurist, epistemologist, and author of *The Historical Materialist Conception of*

Economy and Law: A Sociophilosophical Investigation (2nd edn, 1906) – appears to have been among the first major compositions he attempted since halting his analysis of (what he would later refer to as) 'the catastrophe of the Russian revolution' (Weber 1987a [1910–14]: 516). For some biographical details on the mental depression ('the Evil One') that followed the 1905–6 writings on Russia, and which may help to explain the bilious tone of the Stammler piece, see Marianne Weber 1988 [1926]: 361–6.

12 The *Heidelberger Tageblatt*, covering a discussion organized by the Nationalsoziale Verein on 5 June 1905 in Heidelberg, reported that 'Weber does not believe in the possibility of success for liberal strivings [in Russia] *as long as* the *religious* convictions of the people lead them to see in the existing regime the unchangeable order instituted by *God*. And there was little chance of any change in this regard for the foreseeable future (Weber 1989: 700).

13 In this passage Weber also writes, incongruously, of the 'absence of the "historical" dimension' in Russia, and its opportunity to construct a free culture 'from scratch' (BD: 110–11). This is probably best taken metaphorically to refer to a Russia whose future was still very much open. If so, it is poorly phrased, but that still does not warrant Richard Pipes' astonishing extrapolation from it. Comparing Weber's 'philosophical' orientation with that of Leibniz, Pipes takes both to task for a failure to consider the specificity of Russian development. 'Behind both attitudes lie the same static concept of history, the same deductive method, the same disregard for local traditions and stress on universal values, and the same tendency to judge progress in terms of rational criteria' (Pipes 1955: 399). Can this be the Weber for whom *everything* was historically conditioned; for whom the aim of social science as a 'science of concrete reality' is 'the understanding of the characteristic uniqueness of the reality in which we move' (Weber 1949a [1904]: 72; cf. 68, 94); for whom local traditions are either the vectors for or the obstacles to liberal constitutionalism; for whom 'universal values' like 'human rights' are not ontological attributes, but the creations of civilization; and for whom progress itself, when not used in a purely technical sense, is an inherently evaluative and contestable notion (Weber 1949b [1917]: 27–37)? Weber's philosophy of science, and of social life more generally, is certainly ambiguous in formulation and bristles with thematic tensions (Oakes 1982). But from a year or so before he started his writings on Russia, to the end of the First World War and beyond, Weber made great efforts to criticize the very attitudes that Pipes imputes to him.

14 The obshchina emerged during the 16th century and quickly became a fundamental administrative unit of the Russian state. Peasants referred to it as the *mir* – meaning the world, earth, universe. More specifically, this village community 'was a compulsory fiscal group, created . . . to ensure the orderly payment of *tiaglo* [lit. 'burden' = state tax] by its members. It was based upon the principle of the joint performance by its members of their tax-paying duty, on the collective responsibility, and indeed under the collective guarantee of the community as a whole. To cope with its task the *obshchina*

gradually gained wide-ranging powers: it distributed the tax obligation among its members, enforced payment, prevented members from escaping (which would have meant a corresponding increase in the tax burden of the remaining peasants); later it became responsible for supplying recruits, administering punishments, exiling lazy or criminal members to Siberia, etc. Its most important function became the management of the village's economy, the provision of the wherewithal to pay tax by assigning each member a plot of land . . . roughly commensurate with the size of his family. The community periodically reapportioned the land among its members' (Szamuely 1974: 47).

15 For details, see Röhl and Sombart 1982.
16 Vatro Murvar is right to say that Weber was not a Russophobe, but he underestimates the viciousness of the latter's attacks on the tsarist system. See Murvar 1984: 238. Murvar's depiction of the late-tsarist and Soviet political regimes as 'patrimonial' is convincingly rebutted by Stefan Breuer 1992: 272–5. One might add that Weber's discussion of 'tsarist patrimonialism' (in 1978a: 1064–8) on which Murvar puts so much store, is almost exclusively concerned with the period of Peter the Great to Catherine II (who died in 1796). In contrast, neither Alexander III nor Nicholas II are so much as mentioned in this passage.
17 For a contrast of the German and Russian states, see also Perry Anderson 1974: 354. Anderson's grasp of Weber's work – widely cited in *Lineages* – is normally excellent; mysteriously, however, there is no reference at all to Weber's 1905–6 writings on Russia.
18 The best of such expositions have always sought to avoid this caricature. See e.g. the sensible and illuminating account in Parkin 1982: 40–70.
19 For a sample of this literature, see the long documentary n. 176 in Mommsen and Dahlmann 1989a: 51. Richard Pipes (1955), more than anyone, was responsible for introducing Weber's writings on Russia to an academic audience of historians and social scientists, both in Germany and elsewhere.
20 Weber's most *famous* text is certainly *The Protestant Ethic and the Spirit of Capitalism* (1930 [1905]). Though later associated with Weber the 'sociologist', it first attracted attention in the English-speaking world as a work of economic history. Moreover, even when it entered the Weber sociological canon, it could never offer the 'general' sociology which the Gerth and Mills reader, and the versions of *Economy and Society*, provided. There is also wide agreement that the single most important person in elevating Weber into a *sociological* colossus – in Germany as well as outside it – was an American, Talcott Parsons.
21 And, to a lesser extent, ch. 9 part II of *Economy and Society* on 'Political Communities'. (Most of this chapter was translated in Gerth and Mills as 'Structures of Power' and 'Class Status and Party'.)
22 And now post-Soviet cases. See the searing critique of Lech Walesa by Adam Michnik (1990: 47f). Michnik describes Walesa as a charismatic figure, brilliant and necessary in a time of crisis, disastrous once a democracy has

been established. Weber's name is not cited by Michnik but the influence of the German writer is pervasive and unmistakable in this article.
23 The expression 'neo-Machiavellian' was revived recently by Clive Ashworth and Christopher Dandeker (1987: 3–8). Broadly, it denotes the emphasis placed on 'inter-societal relations' (i.e. war, diplomacy and geopolitics more generally) by such writers as Pareto, Mosca, Michels, and especially Max Weber. Ashworth and Dandeker might also have mentioned Otto Hintze. See his 'Military organization and the organization of the state' (1975 [1906]). His comments on Machiavelli ('one of the great theorists on the threshold of the new epoch . . . who linked the art of war and statecraft') appear on pp. 195–6. Also of general relevance is Mann 1986.
24 Since Collins's prediction was based on the self-conscious application and development of Weberian theory – particularly as formulated in *Economy and Society* – it is worth pausing to explore his comments a little more closely.

The geopolitical theory Collins offers embraces three cumulative and interacting principles: first, size and resource advantage ('military power is a function of the size of the economy and of the population, not of the average economic level per individual'); second, positional advantage ('States with militarily capable neighbours in fewer directions ["marchland states"] have an advantage over states with powerful neighbours in more directions ["interior states"] . . . marchland advantage sets in motion cumulative size and resource advantage'); third, interior state fragmentation ('Interior territories, facing enemies on several fronts, tend to fragment into an increasing number of smaller states over long periods of time . . . the power of such states fluctuates rather than cumulates' (Collins 1986: 187–8). To these three principles, Collins adds further theses on the problematic implications of great-power stalemate, and of imperial overextension. With that theoretical grid constructed, the case of 'the Russian Empire' (i.e. the Soviet Union as dominated by Russia) is then considered. According to Collins, that empire's demise was highly likely because of critical structural weaknesses. In particular, Russia had lost its 'marchland advantage' and become an 'interior' state. In addition, faced with the stalemate imposed by the Cold War, it was presiding over the 'reemergence of a polycentric world', a situation aggravated by Russia's overextended commitments in both economic and political domains.

This is a rough sketch of a more precise and nuanced argument, but it will suffice here. It has been presented because Collins's analysis appears to offer an impressive demonstration of the fecundity of Weberian-style thinking. It also offers testimony to Collins's own exceptional gifts as an applied sociological theorist. Some of the statements in the chapter we have been summarizing are uncanny: 'in the long-term future Russia will fragment into successively smaller states' (1986: 196); 'the success (of) any one satellite in pulling free sharply would increase the chance that a number of adjacent states would also achieve independence' (p. 202); 'it is highly likely that, once a first round of serious crises caused the loss of Eastern Europe . . . there would be set in motion cumulative processes of internal weakening, culminating in the eventual loss of the next tier of ethnically distinct conquest: the Baltic states, the Ukraine, the Caucasus, and the central-Asian Moslem territories' (p. 203); the 'importance of the autonomous-ethnic-state structure ... is that it both maintains ethnic identities and provides an organizational framework that would allow genuinely separate states to emerge whenever the central government were seriously weakened' (p. 204).

Finally, let us note that his analysis is also consistent with (indeed anticipates and systematizes) many of the other candidates that have more recently been proposed to explain the disintegration of the Soviet Union and its satellite regimes in Central-Eastern Europe. They include: the long-term consequences of a command economy, systematically inefficient and wasteful; a nuclear arms race and more general militarization of the society which, in the Brezhnev era, was devouring 'between 25 and 30 per cent of GDP' (Hirst 1991: 227), and diverting valuable resources from the civilian sector; the erosion of confidence among political elites no longer convinced of their right to rule (Ash 1990: 19); the decomposition of Soviet-Marxist ideology as a socially cohesive force, and the courage of those willing to challenge the system openly (yet see Gellner 1992–3: 191). Another cause of dissolution was Soviet nationality policy. Techniques of ethnic segmentation and integration, preferment and coercion, actually helped to build nations, rather than level them, promoting a centrifugality the results of which are now unfolding before our eyes (Zaslavsky, 1992: esp. 105–6; cf. Suny 1992).

Collins's argument (itself an elaboration of Collins 1981, 1978) was published two years before Paul Kennedy's acclaimed but less accurate *The Rise and Fall of the Great Powers* (1988), and three years before the fall of the Berlin Wall.

25 The radical political and economic transformation needed in Russia will also require leadership, and here again there is a resonance – or perhaps an antiresonance – with Weber's writings. The locus of the relevant discussion is Weber's analysis of the problems faced by his own society after its defeat in war, and the collapse of the old order. Claiming that, under such crisis conditions, shifting parliamentary and interest-group allegiance dramatically impeded political leadership and major social transformation, Weber advocated the formation of a 'plebiscitarian' presidential system: that is, the President of the German Reich should be elected by the people directly and *en masse*, rather than by parliamentary deputies, as in the French Third Republic. A 'plebiscitarian' president offered the prospect, Weber editorialized, of affirming the unity of the infant Republic in the face of centrifugal forces; of piloting through economic measures to facilitate Germany's postwar financial and manufacturing recovery; and of offering strong, personal leadership. In short, a president elected by the people would furnish a concentrated source of legitimacy which (unlike a parliament divided between competing interests and parties) might just be able to mobilize sufficient public support to modernize the society. Unabashedly, and drawing on

Roman Republican usage, Weber described the president as a 'democratic dictator' without whom 'the reconstruction of our economy, on whatever foundation, is impossible' (Weber 1986 [1919]: 129; cf. Baehr 1989). The danger of such an approach for civil and political freedoms is obvious, and Weber tended to minimize it; at this juncture in his thinking, the tension between libertarian and 'democratic' commitments was fraught to the point of incoherence. However, it was just such a strategy that the first plebiscitarian president of Russia, Boris Yeltsin, was presumably banking on when, in conflict with parliament, he chose in October 1993 to dissolve the assembly and, through a referendum and new elections, appeal to the people for support. The contradictory result in December 1993 was both to enhance the powers available to the presidential office as a result of a referendum, and to produce a parliament that drifted sharply to the right, and which was largely opposed to the presidential reforms the enhanced powers were supposed to serve. But all this, of course, is 'contemporary history' and will be obsolete long before this book is published.

26 Part of the concluding section to 'Bourgeois Democracy' has previously been translated by Eric Matthews as 'The Prospects for Liberal Democracy in Tsarist Russia', in Runciman 1978: 269–84. Admirable for its combination of fluency and accuracy, Matthews's translation is hard to surpass.

1
Bourgeois Democracy in Russia

The Zemstvo Movement in Russia

May I be permitted to add to the preceding exposition,[1] which has kindly been placed at our disposal, a few remarks concerning the political tendency from which the draft originated.[2] It remains to be seen what practical significance this draft might acquire in the coming political debates; it suffices for our purposes that it is a symptom of a particular political way of thinking of outstandingly able and idealistic Russian patriots, for whom personally we have a great liking, whatever may be the ultimate success of their work, given the tremendous difficulties of their position. The fact that in general they are by no means friends of German culture – on Russian soil often bitter enemies – and that politically too they are predominantly hostile to Germany does not affect the respect we have for them. The draft was drawn up by members of the 'Union of Liberation' (Soiuz Osvobozhdeniia) and was one of the drafts discussed at the Congresses of the Members of the Zemstvos and Dumas.[3]

Now a few words about each of these organizations, bearers of the liberal and democratic movement.

The 'Union of Liberation' was founded in the summer of 1903[4] (its official constitution, framed in Petersburg, had to wait until January 1904[5]) on what was supposed to be a communal holiday trip in the Black Forest presided over by Petrunkevich,[6] the landowner disciplined along with the Tver Zemstvo by Plehve.[7] The persons involved, ranging from Zemstvo Constitutionalists to 'Socialist Revolutionaries', came from very different camps. Only official Social Democracy had excluded itself. About one-third were zemstvo members. The remainder came from various groups of the 'intelligentsia'.

The principal organ of the movement, supported by the Union, was Peter Struve's fortnightly *Osvobozhdenie*, appearing from 1902 at first in Stuttgart, then, after harassment from the German Police,[8] who were, regrettably, acting as henchmen for the Russian government, in Paris; its subscribers have been estimated at about 4,000 abroad during the period of censorship, and about double that (?) in Russia.[9] The cost, especially that of smuggling it into Russia, must have been very significant. Its influence in favour of – in the broadest sense of the word – 'bourgeois democracy', especially for driving 'populist' romanticism out of the heads of the social reformers, must be seen as very great. Peter Struve himself, who is well known to readers of this journal, with his profound and expert knowledge of capitalism, originally strongly influenced by Marx, found his true life's work in the struggle against these romantic illusions.[10] The Union did not have the capital for the foundation of its own daily newspaper; it did, on the other hand, support morally, and doubtless also through subsidies, existing press enterprises.[11] The disparate nature of its elements and its necessarily 'conspiratorial' organization undoubtedly led to a dissipation of energy,[12] which, however, would probably have been even greater without Struve to hold it together.

Alongside the Union of Liberation there was, in its final form since autumn 1904, the Organization of the Zemstvos and Dumas. Both kinds of bodies are today, as is known, representations of the property-owning classes of the country or the cities chosen by means of periodical (three-yearly) elections, according to 'estate' and 'census' [see Glossary]; the zemstvos are organized at two levels, that of the district (*uezd*) and of the province [*guberniia*], and staffed entirely by honorary officials – with the exception of the permanent *uprava* [see Glossary] – the bureau elected by the zemstvo assembly, which has a chairman and between two and five paid members. Although they were, of course, officially banned, the 'Pan-Russian Congresses' of the provincial zemstvos and the dumas of the larger cities began to be organized from the autumn of 1904; they came to represent the Constitutional-Democratic Movement, whose members were increasingly prominent in them.[13]

The First Zemstvo Congress took place – with the participation of only 20 provinces – in November 1904 in Petersburg, because the vacillating government, under Sviatopolk-Mirskii, had at first only agreed to allow it to meet there, where it could be monitored, and not in Moscow. At the last moment the government banned it after all, but without success, since in this case as in the following congresses in Moscow the participants assembled despite the ban, refusing to disperse, and had the police compile a report on their meetings.

It is a measure of how unsure of itself the liberal movement felt, and how enormously the congresses have since developed, that before the first congress they did not dare to hope for more than 14 votes for a constitutional resolution. In fact the '11 points', including the demand for a people's representative body, were passed with only the vote of Count Stenbok-Fermor (Kherson) against ... The resolution was not sent directly to the Tsar, but to the Minister (Sviatopolk-Mirskii), and in fact, since the congress itself was illegal, it was sent by the provincial zemstvos, to whom it had been forwarded by the congress for consultation.[14] The corresponding resolution of the provincial zemstvo of Chernigov was then, as we know, described as 'impudent' by the Tsar.

A further zemstvo congress took place in February 1905, and another one in April (to which two-thirds of the provinces sent delegates).

Both parties – the Constitutional Democrats and the Slavophiles – had called special congresses of their groups for May; under the impact of the battle of Tsushima they united in a 'Coalition Congress' (24 and 25 May), which sent the deputation to Peterhof (6 June).

The July Congress, whose participants were personally described by the Tsar as windbags, was at the same time the last of the congresses to be treated by the police as in some sense 'illegal'.[15] The subsequent zemstvo congress in September, meeting to consult on the Bulygin Duma Project, went unmolested, as did, after the issuing of the October Manifesto, the congress of 6–13 November, which made 'confidence' in Count Witte conditional on certain general 'conditions', and about which the German press has reported in detail.[16] The first congresses were pure zemstvo assemblies. The representatives of the cities had from time to time held separate congresses; only in the July Congress was their representation a general one – with the exception of a few reactionary dumas. The Constitutional-Democratic group of zemstvo members regularly held their meetings before the congress – only in July 1905 did they hold it afterwards.

The association of the liberal movement with the zemstvo organization had two great advantages: firstly, it ensured a basis in legality, which would guarantee that the government – after the experience of the Moscow Zemstvo mentioned below – at least at the present moment, would not dare to suppress it entirely.

Secondly, there was, in the shape of the legally required Zemstvo Board (the 'uprava'), which made the preparations for the congress, a permanent apparatus available at all times, to serve as a bureau and prepare and introduce the resolutions of the assemblies. This board existed outside of the usual annual (late autumn) assemblies of the individual zemstvos. This was all the more important as the legally appointed chairmen of the official provincial and district zemstvo assemblies, the Marshals of the Nobility, elected *by* the nobility, were in general reactionary in character.

The leadership of the Pan-Russian Congresses was taken by the Moscow Uprava, which as early as 1902/3 had arranged the debates, which were then still non-political, amongst the zemstvos. Plehve had involuntarily ensured that it was outstandingly well suited to the task of leading the political movement by dismissing the 'moderately liberal' Slavophile Shipov on the grounds of zemstvo opposition to arbitrary rule.[17] Shipov's temporary popularity rested on this dismissal. In his place the radical Golovin was elected, and since Plehve had only shortly before dissolved the Tver Zemstvo on account of similar opposition by its leading members (Petrunkevich, de Roberti and others), he did not then dare to intervene. With Shipov as leader of the uprava, however, the great radical zemstvo congresses in Moscow, according to participants, would not have been possible in the form that they took under Golovin.

As regards the social composition of this zemstvo liberalism, the enfranchised members of the zemstvos and dumas are, it is true, elected partly according to property ownership, partly according to electoral classes determined by estate, and must meet the criteria of the wealth census. The Social Democrats in Berlin learnt how to achieve artificially the house-owner qualification by the assignment of, for example, one-hundredth of a share in a house. In the same way, through fictitious transfer of wealth, a passive franchise [the right to stand for election] has been created for members of the Russian 'intelligentsia', when for instance there was a need for the active involvement of an expert for particular administrative reforms in a city administration. Thus we find in the zemstvo congresses, alongside the liberal landowners, the flower of the Russian academic intelligentsia and political writers,[18] or at least those of liberal persuasion. The nature of the composition of the congresses reminds one, insofar as such comparisons are possible, more than anything of the 1848 Pre-Parliament and the Frankfurt – not the Berlin – National Assembly.[19]

Aside from the 34 provinces in which zemstvos are organized, *ad hoc* electoral bodies have been created by the existing agricultural and other associations for the purposes of congress representation and other associations – how, it is not possible for me to establish in detail. At any rate, at the last zemstvo congresses even the non-organized areas were represented, together with Siberia and Transcaucasus, and at the November Congress even the Poles were there. There has never been true comprehensiveness, as hitherto many zemstvos and dumas have either refused to participate (as in Kiev) or had only individual representatives (as in Petersburg). (A number of the uezd zemstvos are, indeed, quite reactionary.)

The honorary elected zemstvo members (*deiateli*, or officially *glasnyie*) represent mainly the 'bourgeois' intelligentsia, if one takes the word not in the sense of an economic class but in the sense of a general attitude to life and standard of education. The true 'bourgeoisie', in particular the big industrialists, are, on the other hand, relatively lacking in influence in the zemstvos.

Thus as early as 11 March 1905 the representatives of the central *raion* [district] under the leadership of Morozov (Moscow), those of the Petersburg capitalists under the leadership of Nobel, and those of the South Russian miners under Avdakov, protested to Minister Bulygin, who had given them an audience, disputing the competence of the zemstvo and duma representatives to represent 'public opinion'.

From the economic point of view, the zemstvo liberals were in general 'non-interested parties', representing a political and social idealism of a kind which at the moment is not easy to organize as a force in public life here in Germany, as the fate of the National Social Association (*Nationalsozialer Verein*) has shown.[20] In the official Russian expression they form the 'Second Element' in the zemstvos, in contrast to the quasi-proletarian ['*proletaroid*'] intelligentsia of the salaried zemstvo officials, who – hence the former term – were on occasion called by Plehve sourly and threateningly the 'Third Element',[21] and who, as we shall see later, are organized with other strata of similar social stamp primarily, if not exclusively, in the 'Union of Unions'.[22]

This Third Element forms a very numerous bureaucracy (allegedly 50,000 persons strong) which, together with the 'uprava', carries the regular workload of the zemstvos.[23] There is a tendency to laugh at the inclination towards the 'systematic' which inspires the radical ideologues of this stratum, and the foreigner who groans at the ocean of zemstvo statistics will at times sense a lack of ability to distinguish between the important and the unimportant. At the same time the evident idealism and willingness to make sacrifices shown by these men, the only category of civil servants who really live 'among and with the people', is one of the most ethically pleasing and estimable things that today's Russia has to offer.

The Constitutional Draft of the 'Union of Liberation'

Out of the 'Union of Liberation' and the Zemstvo Constitutionalists there grew the Constitutional Democratic Party. The July Congress of the Zemstvos accepted the proposal to nominate 40 members for negotiations with the delegates of the Union of Liberation and the Union of Unions; the Union of Liberation did the same, and in the period from 12 to 18 October 1905 (Old Calendar) the party was constituted in Moscow. As the city was at that time cut off from the outside world by the strikes, I have no further reports on the procedure. What is certain is that the Union of Unions did not join the party, which, in the eyes of its members, was too moderate.

The Union of Liberation was dissolved, it is true, but not before the Petersburg group had rejected an application from Prof. Miliukov and Struve to join the Constitutional Democratic Party, fiercely attacking Struve as a 'genteel foreigner'. This group continued to exist for the time being as a rump and was then transformed, in December, into a social-political club, to which Struve, according to press reports, responded by founding a society modelled on the Fabians.

Those elements which had hitherto been united in the Union of Liberation now fell apart, and the quasi-proletarian intelligentsia, represented in the Union of Unions, went its own way, as did the 'bourgeois' intelligentsia, which was in essence a zemstvo party.

The April congress of the zemstvos now took the draft of some 'Osvobozhdenians', which is here being reviewed,[24] as a basis for consultation, and at the same time a committee was commissioned by the bureau to amend it. The result is now available in Russian under the same title. Where it deviates from the original is mainly in the deletion of the reference to the 'Supreme Court' and the elimination of the Finnish question (the Polish question is not mentioned either). The thus altered draft was accepted in principle by the July Congress with seven votes against, subject to discussion in the local self-governing corporations.[25] No further constitutional draft has been put forward by the liberals; one which is said to have been written by the 'Party of Legal Order' (to be mentioned below), is at the moment unavailable to me.[26]

It may at first be objected that the draft discussed here is thoroughly 'unhistorical', a reasonable objection, one might think, in the case of a modern piece of international law such as this. But what is truly 'historical' in the Russia of today? With the exception of the Church and the peasant commune, to which we shall turn later, there is nothing whatever, except for the absolute power of the Tsar, which dates back to the age of the Tartars, and today, after the breakup of all those 'organic' structures which shaped the Russia of the seventeenth and eighteenth centuries, lingers on in quite unhistorical 'freedom'. A country whose most 'national' institutions scarcely a century ago showed strong similarities to the monarchy of Diocletian is indeed unable to undertake any 'historically' orientated and yet still viable 'reform'. The most vital institution in Russian public life, one which is most firmly rooted in public awareness and has been most thoroughly tested for its efficiency, is the zemstvo; this is at the same time the one which is most foreign to the old Muscovite idea of a collective obligation to perform duties allotted according to estate-based principles. The zemstvo is a modern body of self-government, no more than 40 years old and already remodelled once – from one which represented purely land ownership as such (including the peasants) to a body structured essentially on estate principles.[27]

It is of course not possible for me to judge its performance. Merely to go by the state of the bridges and roads, as West European travellers are accustomed to do, is no more an appropriate measure there than in America and for the same economic reasons. Belief in the importance of the 'systematic' and of theories in general is, as everyone knows, incomparably greater in Russia than in America, with whose local administration the zemstvos can best be compared; the conviction of the fundamental importance of popular education is equally great in the local government of the two countries; and the idealism of the majority of zemstvos shown by their willingness to make financial sacrifices in the service of such 'ideal' purposes is worthy of the highest respect and is in every way equal to the behaviour of our East Prussian Representatives of the Estates in 1847.[28] Even in its present atrophied form and in view of the amazing variety of its area of activities, from the founding of primary schools, statistics, medicine, veterinary services, road-building, tax distribution and agricultural instruction to the important area of meal provision at times of famine – all this demonstrates an achievement, given the difficulty of the situation, which ought to give the lie to the view, which is still widely held, that the Russians are unready for free self-government. This much is evident even from the material available abroad. To the zemstvo the state power appears, understandably, in spite of all its superiority in bureaucratic 'technique',[29] as a parasite existing only for the preservation of the existing political distribution of power, almost devoid of relevant interests other than those of finance and therefore filled with the deepest mistrust towards its rival.

The zemstvo has thus had to fight for its successes against constant obstruction from the state police, on whose coercive force it was dependent for the execution of its resolutions; and it achieved these successes in spite of the fact that the envy of the government more and more noticeably and finally quite systematically frustrated its work, prohibiting it from increasing taxation, required especially for educational purposes,[30] and, for example, in the last war, suppressing the zemstvo charitable organization in favour of the hopelessly corrupt state 'Red

Cross', and attempting to nationalize the meals service. Having thus forced the zemstvo increasingly into the role of a mere passive association whose purpose was to shoulder burdens imposed by the government and for the government's benefit, and preventing the extension of the zemstvo constitution to the Ukrainian and Belorussian provinces,[31] Plehve finally in his last period made a serious attempt completely to destroy the zemstvos and replace them with the state bureaucracy.

After all this it is striking that there is no attempt in the draft to establish the constitutionally determined competence and authority of local government. Thus the central political question of the last 25 years is completely ignored, namely whether the zemstvos should remain local interest bodies or should become 'delegatees' [*Delegatare*][32] or, finally, passive '*Zweckverbände*'[33] – all of which would still be possible under a 'democratic' government.

It is all the more striking that the draft makes no attempt to place self-government on a secure footing, since in 1884 the Ukrainian [Little Russian] writer Dragomanov made an attempt to solve this problem in a most ingenious way in a draft of his own.[34] This included: constitutionally guaranteed tasks for the representatives of village, town, *volost*, district and province (*oblast*) with expressly established compulsory powers and possibly their own authority over the military, subject to the *legally* binding veto of the governor [*Statthalter*] in the case of *constitutional* problems; the right of all electoral bodies to give their deputies in the self-governing body the imperative mandate; and the right of the 19 oblast representatives to do the same for their deputies in the upper house of the two-part Imperial Duma, the 'Federal Assembly', and to recall them at any time; the right of the self-governing bodies legally to challenge the constitutionality of the Imperial laws etc. The 'Federal Assembly' (Soiuznaia Duma) of this draft was thus a body partly modelled on the United States Senate, partly on the Swiss Bundesrat and partly on the German Bundesrat.

The draft we are considering here, on the other hand, speaks only of the two houses of the Duma, each of which rests on the 'four-part' franchise, i.e. 'universal, equal, direct and secret'. The Lower House is to be directly elected, the Upper House indirectly by the zemstvos, which here are conceived as communal bodies without any authority to act against the central power. The draft restricts itself to *electoral* law of this kind in the case of the zemstvos too. We shall see later that this caution had to do with the involvement of the *nationalities* problem in the question of decentralization. Nevertheless, the fact that the draft deals with the zemstvo at all is the closest one can expect it to come to 'historicism' in the circumstances.

Bourgeois Democracy in Russia   49

The party programme of the Constitutional Democrats, on the other hand, has reverted to the ideas of Dragomanov – perhaps without actually knowing them – to the extent that in principle all areas of state administration are assigned to the self-governing body, 'with the exception of those areas which, under present circumstances, must be concentrated in the hands of the central power' (point 22) and (point 23) to the extent that the activity of the local representative of the central power is limited to the veto in cases of illegality, on which, however, the *courts* must rule – one of the most important principles to be adopted by the party.

The unconditional execution of the principle of the four-part franchise, i.e. universal, equal, direct, and secret, distinguishes the Constitutional Democratic Party, which advocates this, from other constitutional groups to the right, which support census or indirect franchise, and from Shipov's antibureaucratic Slavophile group with their idea that a consultative popular assembly controlling the finances should emerge from the existing zemstvos.

The demand for that franchise, the most controversial point of the draft, is for the Democrats firstly the logical result of the lack of other 'historical' foundations on which to build, since the government has worked for 25 years now to discredit the zemstvos. On top of this of course there is that circumstance which today everywhere makes it impossible for the representatives of fundamental reforms to defend a graded franchise fully and with inner honesty: the effect of capitalism with its class-forming power. For the economic clash of interests and the class character of the proletariat is a stab in the back for the specifically bourgeois reformers: that is the fate of their work here as everywhere.

Only as long as the predominance of craft work gave the mass of workers, at least in theory, the opportunity to become 'autonomous' could anyone honestly regard a census electoral system as also representing those who are not yet autonomous. In Russia not only is (for historical reasons) the development of the urban 'middle class' in the West European sense very weak in itself, but also capitalism has long since begun to make its mark there too, and any attempt to advocate the census system would be considered by the reforming agitator to be a case of 'officers without soldiers'. It would, understandably, never occur to the workers in the cities to agree to it.

In the countryside, moreover, the census franchise in the areas of the obshchina (village commune) could scarcely be carried out without the most arbitrary effects. In the village commune *equal* voting rights for heads of households is 'historical'. Of course, an autocratic government could, if it acted *promptly*, have enforced any scheme of franchise, for instance one of an educational qualification or a plural franchise. However, a party of reform could draw scarcely any other consequences from the situation than that reached in the draft. If it were to do otherwise – and this is the final compelling reason – at the first sign of opposition from the Duma, the autocracy would have it in its power to play the workers off against it, as for years the previous regime used to do, with at least apparent success, in order to intimidate the property-owning classes who were suspected of liberalism.[35] And the moment the Democratic Party accepted the census franchise, i.e. the evident exclusion of the mass of peasants from the election, reactionary forces would be able to align these behind it without exception, for it is precisely against the enfranchised owners of private property, the landowners and especially the *kulaks* ('fists' i.e. newly rich peasants and petty rural capitalists) and the rest of the 'village bourgeoisie' that the hatred of the rural masses is directed. In the eyes of the peasants, the Tsar is never responsible for their misery. Where once it was the civil servants, in future it would be the great mass of the peasants who would be excluded, since they would be placed *behind* all urban proletarians in the census. Already the representatives of the reactionary nobility have been busy spreading the news that the goal of the liberals is to allow no peasants into the Duma.[36] And this demagogic policy of the government was particularly prominent in the Bulygin Duma Project.

According to the attached electoral order, the Assembly proposed in the Manifesto of 6/19 August [Bulygin Duma Project], whose task is to consider the laws and control the state budget, is to be chosen by electors in 26 cities and in provincial electoral assemblies. In order to restrict the candidature of the 'intelligentsia' as much as possible, candidates are to be selected from the ranks of the electors themselves.

The election of these electors in the provinces is distributed amongst three classes: (1) the largest private landowners; (2) the towns; (3) the peasants. There are variations in the different provinces. But whereas the first two classes have a census franchise of a rather plutocratic type[37] – the workers are always completely excluded – the peasant electors are elected from the volost assemblies, which in their turn rest on the equality of all landowners in the village.

In other words, the only people for whom there is no census limit are to be the usually illiterate peasants. And moreover the peasant electors selected in this way are, in contrast to the other classes, to have the right to nominate one deputy from their own members before the election of the other Duma deputies. After this they, together with the others, elect the remainder. In other words the representatives of the peasants have an estate-like privileged franchise for at least 51 deputies (the number of the

European Russian provinces) and of the remainder with census [qualifying] land ownership they usually make up more than two-thirds of the electors.

The Manifesto of 17/30 October[38] states the 'firm principle' that from now on no law should come into force without the consent of the Duma, adding that, in general, as far as this was possible in the short time available, the franchise should be given to the classes which had hitherto been deprived of it and the 'further development' of the 'principle' of the general franchise should be left to the 'newly created legislative order'. As Peter Struve has quite correctly said in his introduction to the draft under discussion, it is now 'too late' for any other liberal franchise programme in Russia today. It was the idea of 'human rights' and the demand for a 'four-part franchise' that united the radical bourgeois with the quasi-proletarian (and even part of the Socialist Revolutionary) intelligentsia in the Union of Liberation. Commitment to the achievement of these aims was all that prevented a division amongst the intelligentsia in the struggle.

If one wanted – and were able – to disregard this situation, *then* of course even the most convinced Democrat or Social Democrat would be very doubtful about the wisdom of choosing this particular franchise as the first one to be introduced in this country, especially at the *present* moment.[39]

For the Russian Democrats hold very varied opinions amongst themselves on the decisive point: the probable effect of this franchise. The greatest misgivings are felt against handing over the *zemstvos* to completely untrained illiterates, however strongly the necessity of a much stronger representation of the peasants (who are at present restricted to a minority representation without influence) is stressed.

In fact, complete bureaucratization of the zemstvo administration would be the immediate result, and, despite every acknowledgement of the outstanding achievements of the zemstvo officials, the 'Third Element' (*tretii element*), this could only be the precursor of a centralization on the French model. The 'economic independence' of the honorary members of the zemstvo was what guaranteed the autonomy of the zemstvo 'from above' and, under our economic order, could guarantee its independence against any centralizing parliamentary party government, as long as the peasants remain shackled to the agrarian communism of their communes.

Opinions differ concerning the probable effect of universal, equal franchise for the *Duma*. I know Russian Democrats who take the view '*fiat justitia, pereat mundus*'.[40] Even if the masses reject all cultural advance or destroy it, we can only ask what is just, and we have done our duty if we give them the franchise and thus pass to them the responsibility for their actions. 'Even the most extreme ochlocracy', they add, 'cannot go as far as the "black hundreds", hired by civil servants whose power is threatened. However that may be, it is better to suffer generations of cultural darkness than to do a political wrong. And perhaps sometime in the future the educational impact of the franchise will do its part.'[41]

Implicit in such views is perhaps also something of Solovev's belief in the ethical and religious peculiarity of the political task of Russianness,[42] as an advocate of this view pointed out to me. Absolute rejection of the 'success ethic' here means, in the political sphere, that only the unconditional ethical imperative is valid as the guiding star of positive action; there is only the possibility of struggle for justice *or* holy renunciation. Once that which is recognized as positive 'duty' is done, then, because *all* values other than ethical ones have been excluded, that biblical injunction comes into force again which has become ingrained not only in the soul of Tolstoy but in that of the Russian people as a whole: 'Resist not evil'.[43]

This abrupt alternation between tempestuous activity and resignation is the consequence of a refusal to acknowledge the status of the ethically indifferent as a 'value', or even its very existence, an attitude which fits the panmoralism of Solovev's 'sanctity' just as it does a purely ethically orientated democracy. Besides these extreme ideologues there are other people (and they are undoubtedly in the majority) who take a more optimistic view of the future of democracy than those foreigners who are inclined to infer a certain degree of integrity of constitutional intentions on the part of the present regime from the fact that the regime does *not* hand over the arithmetically equal franchise at the present moment to the politically uneducated mass of the people. The Russians cite certain *economic* reasons why the masses, armed with the franchise, would simply *have to* follow political and cultural ideals of liberty. These reasons will be examined later,[44] as in the view of some Democratic leaders they are especially important.

Aside from the general reference to the 'educational' function of the franchise, which, however, if it is claimed for *equal* franchise, does require certain 'developmental' conditions to be fulfilled, the only purely political argument is actually, even in the 'evidence' contained in the draft, that relating to the experience of Bulgaria's introduction of the universal franchise, which seems to the authors to have been favourable.[45] In this, apart from other considerations, there has been an underestimation of the difference between a small state and one which is – even in the opinion of people like Struve – a great nation compelled towards 'world politics', and even more between the traditional position of the nationally and religiously consecrated Tsar and a petty princeling who has for the time being been hired and imported.[46]

Moreover it should be expressly emphasized that the draft is very far removed from having a 'radical' character in constitutional law. The authors rightly reject, it is true, the fashionable talk of the 'outdated' nature of parliamentarism.[47] But their draft is careful to be protective towards the position of the Tsar.[48] It allows for no elected officials apart from the 'Justices of the Peace'. Neither does it advocate parliamentary sovereignty on the British model. Nor rule by the parliamentary majority as in France. This consideration of the position of the monarch distinguishes the supporters of the Constitutional Democratic groups from radical groups to their left; the latter, even if they are not republicans, place the emphasis on the calling of a 'constituent assembly' as an expression of the principle of popular sovereignty, and specifically wish to establish a parliamentary determination of the course of policy.

For the constitutional supporters it is clear that the determining factors have been not only compelling considerations of *realpolitik*, but also the idea that only the monarch effectively represents the unity of the Empire, once wide-ranging autonomy is accorded to the individual nationalities.

In its consideration of the position of the Tsar the draft could thus not carry through the complete separation of the executive from the legislative as in America. Therefore it attempted, as Zhivago has stressed in his review, to create something in certain respects new in the shape of the 'Supreme Tribunal', outside the structure of legal institutions. The functions of this were to include the following:

1 The quashing of unconstitutional government actions and court judgements, including those which rested on formally correct but substantively unconstitutional laws, on appeal by private interested parties, by one of the two chambers, or one of the constitutionally supreme Imperial authorities. In this function the authors regard it, curiously, as a copy of the American Supreme Court – a mistake which can only surprise us given the great familiarity of the Russians with the well-known book by James Bryce.[49]
2 Electoral examination, which should take place before the Tribunal.
3 The latter – strengthened by the judges of the Court of Appeal – should be the court for political prosecution of ministers brought by one of the chambers.

This political prosecution is intended to stand independently alongside prosecution before the regular courts – which is permissible against all officials – and may only carry dismissal and removal from office for five years for reasons of unsuitability for office. According to the draft, it can be based on (1) deliberate infringement of the constitution and (2) 'serious infringement of state interests' by abuse, exceeding one's powers, and negligence.

This procedure was quite obviously supposed to transfer the parliamentary 'vote of no confidence' into the form of a court case which can be measured by 'objective' standards. However, the factual content of 'interests of state' cannot be 'objectively' established, i.e. without regard for those ideals and interests, which is to say those 'value judgements', which characterize different political and social groupings. The strictly formal task of guarding the constitution and passing legally based judgements on the question of what 'is allowed', and the task of uttering political sentiments regarding what 'ought to be allowed' would thus be placed in the same hands: in itself a most dubious idea. [. . .]

The second draft[50] omitted this institution [the 'Supreme Tribunal'], and the constituent congress of the Constitutional Democratic Party contented itself, in contrast to the Manifesto of 17 October,[51] with establishing ministerial responsibility and demanding the right of the Duma to discuss not only the legality but also the advisability of ministers' actions.[52]

The Nationalities and Language Question

Instead of attempting to criticize, from the point of view of constitutional law, a draft of problematical significance, I should prefer at this point to indicate something else which strikes the foreign reader about it from the political angle. For what it does *not* contain is frequently more interesting than what it does contain.

The reviewer [of the draft constitution, Zhivago] has already called attention to the silence of the draft on the *nationalities problem,* in particular the *Polish question.*[53]

It is all the more striking since this was the problem on which again and again the unity of the pro-liberty parties of Russia foundered. This disunity worked strongly to the advantage of the government, and one of the lasting political achievements of the Russian zemstvo movement is that to a very considerable degree it assisted *bourgeois* liberalism in surmounting these obstacles to unity.

At the time the draft was drawn up this unity had not yet been achieved, and views were divided. The draft thus contains merely the right of the zemstvos to join together into associations for particular purposes connected with local administration (art. 70), on the grounds that this was the best way to provide the ten provinces of Congress Poland with the means to achieve for themselves that degree of national autonomy which could be granted them.

The programme of the Union of Liberation, published in the *Osvobozhdenie* of P. Struve, however, contained quite different concessions. Here 'autonomy' of a 'sharply defined historical character' was promised to all parts of the Empire, in particular to the people of Poland, Lithuania, the Ukraine and Transcaucasus. Furthermore those peoples who do not live in clearly defined areas, but mingle together with the Russians, should have the right – as was neatly formulated – to 'cultural self-determination'. In particular the right to instruction in the native language for primary schools and its use in all local offices was recognized absolutely. The draft contains nothing of all that.

Given that attempts to solve internal nationality problems on a democratic basis will need to be put into practice in the foreseeable future in many places, the work achieved in this area by the Russian liberation movement must first be *noted* in more detail, with the proviso that in future a more thorough scholarly study, taking account of social strata, should be produced.

It is firstly of interest to note on what grounds P. Struve justifies his opposing viewpoint with regard to the *Poles* in his foreword to the draft:[54] recognition of the Constitution of 1815 for Congress Poland[55] was the very least with which Polish liberals would be satisfied. The creation of such complete political autonomy for Poland meant no danger for Russia and in particular no real detachment of Poland from it. Poland was – as Rosa Luxemburg's well-known publication[56] put it – economically bound to Russia as the market for its industry, and Russia therefore had the means, in the revival of its customs boundary which had disappeared in 1851, to execute everything it wished to demand of Poland politically, especially since Poland, as Iasnopolskii has shown, was a region of subsidy for the Russian financial administration.[57] The political autonomy of Poland was, however, also the means of – as we should have said 50 years ago – making 'moral conquests' amongst the Slavs. [. . .] Today's party circumstances and the development of political views in Poland would be a separate topic. The politically most significant fact seems to be the emergence and strengthening of the Progressive Democratic Party, whose programmes show an affinity with Russian liberalism and which stands for national autonomy on the basis of belonging to the Russian empire. As late as the spring of 1905, however, the Polish resolutions spoke of autonomy for Congress Poland, just as did Struve, as being the 'minimum'.

This 'minimum' has, however, had to be considerably scaled down by the Poles in their negotiations with Russian Democracy. After the July Congress of the Zemstvos and the Cities the committee of this congress started to confer with the representatives of the Poles to discuss their participation in further zemstvo congresses. After the publication by the Russians of the report of the congress, the Poles, that is, delegates of the Progressive Democratic Party, demanded, chiefly, that there should be an appendix to the aforementioned second draft[58] of the July Congress stating that the areas of authority of the Empire should be constitutionally separated from those of the autonomous areas, on the principle that Imperial laws have no validity within these areas. Added to this should be constitutional autonomy for schools of every nationality, and equality of national languages in all areas of mixed language. Politically, Poland should (in the view of the Polish representatives) after the introduction of its own constitution, and of the autonomous parliament, remain united with the Empire through the person of the Tsar 'and King'[59] and the participation of deputies in the central Duma, and Poland should be under an Imperial governor and a state secretary who is subject to the Polish provincial Parliament [*Landtag*]. The following should be Imperial affairs: coinage, army, customs, excise, railways, post, telegraph and telephone, though in Poland they should be under national Polish administration; income and expenditure of the common areas of administration mentioned below should be divided up according to population figures. The Poles described the acceptance of these terms in principle as a condition of their participation in the zemstvo congresses.

The Bureau of the Congress then debated these demands and similar claims of other nationalities and laid down the result in a very clear and objective memorandum for the preparation of the resolutions of the following congress. An unnamed member had included proposals which went beyond Dragomanov's ideas: splitting up the Empire into 'provinces' on an economic, geographical and national basis; national proportional election in the individual provinces; a supreme court to rule on the governor's veto against unconstitutional resolutions of the parliaments and on disputes between the provinces; imperative mandate and the ability to recall representatives of the provinces in the Upper House of the central Duma; alteration of the constitution only with the consent of two-thirds of the provinces and the majority of the Duma on the basis of a resolution of a constituent assembly to be called forthwith; all other cases in which the Upper House criticized a resolution of the Duma for infringing the rights of the provinces should be treated similarly. A precise delineation of authority was not attempted.

The Congress Bureau took the view, by contrast, that while the question of decentralization and autonomy did indeed overlap with the nationalities problem, the establishment of provinces [*Länder*] was completely consistent with national aspirations, and that the questions should thus be treated separately. For example, Siberia's demand for autonomy was not for national reasons, and in Austria the struggle of the nationalities took place partly in spite of, and in part because of, its *Länder* constitution.

Only the *language* problem was of a purely national character. The upholding of the Russian language as 'state language' was absolutely essential in the *army* and the central offices, whereas in the central parliament the use of Russian was in the interest of the individual nationalities themselves, though not essential; in the courts and administrative departments the internal official language must basically be left to the discretion of these authorities: which meant that the authorities with control of the central administration should operate in Russian, whilst the others should amongst themselves use the local languages; in dealing with the public they should use the local language of the latter, and where the different parties had different languages they should employ interpreters. The local officials must be able to speak the languages in question. (A detailed study of the Austrian language problem would show the authors that they have not yet fully understood important aspects of the practical difficulties, in particular, the limitation of freedom of movement for officials consequent upon the requirement of multilingual ability.[60])

The situation in the *schools* was crucial. The principle was to be: the Russian language was at all times the *object* of instruction, while in private schools of every level the language of instruction was a matter for the head teacher. Everyone in the Empire should, in principle, have the opportunity to be instructed in his native language (as language of instruction, not only as the object) and this at public expense. Thus (1) national language of instruction, everywhere, including for minorities, in the elementary school; (2) subsidies for parallel classes of national minorities both in schools and in the higher educational institutions.

With regard to the question of *decentralization*, the memorandum does not conceal the difference of opinion which exists in leading zemstvo circles. The draft states that views in favour of general decentralization of the *administration* or general 'political' decentralization (of legislation too), which could not in any case be absolutely clearly distinguished, were represented, as were a 'middling' opinion which wished to admit general political autonomy for certain individual parts of the Empire, primarily of course for Poland, alongside general administrative autonomy. The

Bureau adopts this mediating viewpoint,[61] and supports it with clear and detailed argument.

'Administrative decentralization' means that not only (1) the group of tasks of the local administration from now on must extend to everything that cannot 'in the nature of things' be administered from the centre, such as customs, post, telegraph, excise, railways, but also that (2) the representatives of the central power – that is, the provincial governors – should have supervisory and veto rights in the case of illegality, but no active administrative authority over the self-governing bodies – that is, the zemstvos and their upravas. [. . .]

The Bureau does not conceal the fact that [a limited degree of] local independence does not meet the demands of the specifically *political* national demands of certain territories. Transforming the whole of Russia into a federal state, however, was at the moment out of the question, not only on account of the 'novelty' of the whole problem for public opinion, but also because while one could easily undertake a purely mechanical 'division' 'on paper', one would not, without much greater experience, be able to link up historical or 'natural' borders between the individual territories which corresponded to the needs of the people. Only for a few countries of the Empire – e.g. for Poland – did matters appear sufficiently simple in this regard.

A general explanation of the 'federal' principle could, what is more, easily arouse chauvinist feelings, and the following principles were therefore proposed: granting of autonomy to the individual areas must only occur after a proper Imperial constitution had been set up, not before, for all the forces of the Empire must work together to achieve this; it should therefore take the form of a legislative act of the Empire, which must occur wherever the population of an area demanded autonomy for itself and, perhaps in the form of a mass petition, applied for it. One could then either establish the substantial and regional limits of autonomy in each individual case by special law, or, as some in the Bureau proposed, once and for all create a legal scheme, a 'normal statute' of autonomy, on the basis of which – probably by analogy with American examples[62] – an area could constitute itself at any time it saw fit and demand recognition of its authority.

The majority in the Bureau regarded the first course as the correct one, as the extent of autonomy was not necessarily everywhere the same. The general principle must only be the execution of democratic constitutional principles, validity of bourgeois 'basic rights', and the participation of the autonomous area in the Imperial Duma. Nothing further could at the moment be contained within the programme. Execution of autonomy should be carried out on this basis immediately in the case of the

'Tsardom of Poland', given the historical importance and urgency of the 'Polish question'. Other areas should be considered on an individual basis.

The Congress of the Zemstvos and Cities in Moscow in September 1905 accordingly accepted a special resolution regarding Polish autonomy, alongside general resolutions for the cultural autonomy of the particular nationalities.

[*There follows the Constitutional-Democratic Programme for Poland and Finland, granting them limited autonomy.*]

According to reports, of the (allegedly) approximately 300 district zemstvos, which, at the request of the September congress of the zemstvos, debated the matter in the following weeks, only about two dozen protested against the position taken by the congress.

Much more vigorous was the dissent in the press against the resolutions of this congress and the Constitutional Democratic Programme. They were accused of intending to divide Russia, and the 'Party of Legal Order'[63] (to be mentioned later[64]) emerged more clearly at that time as an opponent of the liberals, expressing doubts about parliamentarism, which it regarded as a danger to Imperial unity.

The liberals (such as Kusmin-Karavaev) in several articles in *Russ*, by contrast, emphasized that 'autonomy' should only be granted to Congress Poland; the other territories should receive only local self-administration for certain 'individual objects', which is to say, the overall authority of the Empire should be guaranteed.

On the other hand, Polish nationalists stepped up their claims. In November 1905, *Goniec*, the organ of the Polish National Democrats, demanded a Polish army of its own, whereas up to then only the garrisoning of Polish recruits in Poland had been demanded. Similarly the use of the Polish language was demanded right up to the level of the Polish central offices. Over against this, *Russ* (which then often functioned as the organ of the Petersburg Democrats) stated very firmly that military service, finance and the state language were common Imperial affairs. And in a polemical attack on the Petersburg lecturer Dr Pilenko, who, in *Novoe Vremia*, had pointed the finger at Hungary as an awful warning, the liberals stressed that there could be no question of granting the Poles the right of citizenship, their own railways, or postal and customs officers, let alone *honveds*.[65]

The government of Witte, on receiving Polish and other delegates, handed over the entire question to the future Duma, in the full knowledge that the views of the proponents of democracy differed, and that any strengthening of Russian nationalist elements would be to the government's political advantage. The fear of the awakening of Russian chauvinism, on the other hand, encouraged Russian and Polish Democrats to reach an agreement. Such an agreement was in fact reached by the zemstvo congress of 6–13/19–23 November, to which by far the majority of provinces, districts and cities sent deputies, and which was attended by 23 Polish representatives, thanks largely to the very considerable readiness of the Poles to compromise.

The resolution introduced by the Bureau of the Congress demanded for Poland: (1) immediate ending of the state of war (this has – in part – now happened[66]) and introduction of the local language in elementary schools, local courts and peace courts – which on Rodichev's suggestion was modified to read: 'to the extent to which this is technically possible'; (2) that the first People's Assembly introduce an autonomous order in the Tsardom of Poland 'on condition that the unity of the Empire be maintained'. The second demand was accepted (apart from one abstention) unanimously. The Poles replied with a proclamation signed by (it is claimed) 30,000 members of the different parties, led by Henryk Sienkievicz, protesting against the imputation of an intention to separate from Russia. [. . .] In their speeches Prince Peter Dolgorukov and Maxim Kovalevskii supported the idea of a democratically based Slav Federation. The former recalled the great period of the first Slavophiles, and the latter expressed the view that if Austria and Turkey should disintegrate, then 'we need friends on our Western border'.

The ideas concerning the nationalities question which underlie the programme of the Union of Liberation (and in part this agreement as well) are of different origins. The extremely nationalistic and ritualistic change of direction of the Slavophile movement was most pointedly expressed by Katkov and Leontev. In the view of the latter, Russia should turn away from the corrupted western Slavs and towards the following idea: in the interests of autocracy, the East should be faced up to for the purpose of subjection of the Asiatics, accustomed as they are to authority. Even after this change of direction, at least V. S. Solovev's irenic, religious nature has not ceased to support the idea of the free, peaceful Slavic union, or, as ultimate goal, of world union.

Whereas amongst the socialists, especially from the orthodox Marxist sector, the existence of the nationalities problem was not infrequently denied until recently, as early as the beginning of the 1880s Dragomanov attempted to reconcile the unity of pan-Russian culture with the ideal of cultural autonomy for the individual peoples on a democratic basis. [. . .] His great strength clearly lay in the way in which he combined economic and national ideals and in his acute sense of what was possible in the ethnographic circumstances and economic conditions of Russia.

[Weber then expands on Dragomanov's realism and moderation.]

Out of Dragomanov's aforementioned programme for the dismemberment of Russia into provinces with guaranteed autonomy, the zemstvo congresses have basically accepted that *Poland*, towards which country their whole programme was geared, should have autonomy, and its own parliament, and have thus gone beyond what he regarded as necessary.

For the Ukraine and other national areas on the other hand they accept, *for the moment*, on grounds previously explained,[67] only his two basic demands 'in natural law', viz. 'cultural autonomy' and democratic self-government, and even these not in the clearly structured manner and with the guarantees that he had demanded or as they were contained in the programme of the Union of Liberation, which placed all nationalities living there on the same footing as the Poles.

Admittedly the position of the Ukrainians themselves does not seem to be uniform. The radical demands, which were previously (about 1890) made by the (now defunct) *Pravda* and most recently again in the Vienna *Ruthenian Revue* (vol. 3 (13)), especially the return to personal union as set out in the Treaty of 1654,[68] combined with violent attacks on the Russian Liberals, go beyond those of the upper strata of the Ukrainian intelligentsia.

The latter not only do not call into question Imperial unity, i.e. hegemony of Russia, but many of them, including notably supporters of Dragomanov's ideas, do not necessarily claim the measure of decentralization that 'Ukrainian Democracy' demands (see below),[69] and they seem to be content with national 'cultural autonomy' – i.e. national language of instruction in the lower-level schools (where the state language is only to be the object of instruction), admission of the national language on conditions of parity in the local administrative offices and its academic study at the university, and a high degree of local self-government. The cities of the Ukraine (Kiev, Poltava), the seats of the intelligentsia, *are* de facto successfully *Russianized*.

All the same, the representatives of the Ukraine within the Democratic groups have made considerably more far-reaching demands and have occasionally been able to achieve them. At the end of March and beginning of April 1905 the congress of the Union of Liberation did, it is true, reject recognition of the genuine Dragomanov idea – the division of Russia into provinces – as a general principle, but demanded autonomy, not only for Poland, Lithuania and Transcaucasus, but also, even if only after a long debate, for the Ukraine.[70]

During the preparation of the negotiations on the nationalities question, the Bureau of the July Congress has available to it two programmes from the Ukraine, of which the more substantial and interesting contained the proposal of the Ukrainian Democratic Party, which bases its constitutional structure on the principles of the Dragomanov constitutional draft, though in a less consistent form. Actually it goes further in the matter of the degree of decentralization: it envisages a separate parliament ('Narodnaia Rada'), responsible for all matters other than foreign policy (e.g. war, trade treaties) and the budget of the central administration. The central body is to consist of a Chamber of Deputies and a Federal Council of representatives of the autonomous areas. However, the autonomy of the approximately 30 million Ukrainians is too much for even the most ardent democrat to stomach.

The Congress of the Zemstvos and Cities of November 1905 resolved merely to approve linguistic freedom and the use of the local language in the lower-level schools 'as far as possible' for the Latvians, Lithuanians, Estonians and Ukrainians. This will not satisfy the local leaders of the Ukrainians, especially those in the rural areas. But in these questions the *realpolitiker* amongst the Democrats are on the side of the Poles, just as God, according to Frederick the Great, 'is on the side of the big battalions'.[71]

Struve for instance (in 1901) anchored his nationalism, which was founded on the strict individualism of 'human rights', essentially on Fichte's concept of culture. But it is typical of his total political philosophy that when faced with the practical problems of the present, he expressly rejects equal treatment for Ukrainians, Latvians and (naturally) the Transcaucasians with the Poles, in contrast to the programme of the Union of Liberation. His particular view of the Polish question fits in for him with a wider 'world political' programme: Entente with the liberal powers, especially England; Russia to confront Asia Minor; etc. The result is, then, that the solution of the nationalities question is left to the Duma, and the difficulties here – if indeed it proves viable at all – will not be minor ones.

Nevertheless, it must be stated that an agreement in principle is perfectly possible, and that this is likely to be made easier than ever before with regard to the Poles by Germany's unsuccessful policy towards Poland,[72] with regard to the Ukrainians by the government's successful Russification policy, and with regard to the non-German Baltic peoples by the historically conditioned reliance of their radical parties on the example of Russian radicalism.[73]

Like the nationalities and language question, the *school question*, which belongs with it, has also been passed over in silence. The programme of the Union of Liberation contains, in this respect, far-reaching demands: re-establishment of university autonomy (since conceded), autonomy for all local associations in the school system, and absolutely free provision of all public education – which Struve at the time had opposed as unworkable and wrong. The draft is silent on the subject, although (or perhaps because) at the moment the most violent struggle, one which has been fomented by the government for two decades, is raging between zemstvo schools, private ABC Schools,[74] and Church schools.

Church and State

This silence [on the schools question] is probably also connected with the fact that the draft does not have a word to say about relations to the *Church* either, but contents itself with promising, within the bounds of public order, absolute tolerance and freedom of worship.

By contrast, the programme of the Union of Liberation demands 'Liberation of the Church from the state and of the state from the Church', i.e. the undoing of the work which Ivan the Terrible and political monasticism of the sixteenth century had begun and Peter the Great had completed.[75] The relationship between State and Church seems to the authors of the draft too complex a matter to be dealt with in 'a few paragraphs'. But when the draft calls for the Emperor to swear the constitutional oath before the Holy Synod,[76] it directly recognizes this Caesaropapist institution.[77] The Constitutional Democratic programme contents itself with demanding liberation of the Orthodox Church (and every other church) *from the state* (point 2), without stating more precisely what consequences should follow. How will the Church behave towards the constitutional movement and within a future constitutional state?

The many thousands of newly founded Church schools show, much more clearly than the Church's home mission, which was revived principally in the struggle against the 'Stunda',[78] that the new situation will find the Orthodox Church (which, it is said, is due to meet again for the first time for a Council in the summer) 'taking up arms' – however much it may have been worn down by the regime of the Chief Procurator.[79] The only question is how intensively and in which direction it will work.

It is no secret that both within and outside the circles of the bishops and even in the ranks of the high state bureaucracy, the idea of a revival of the chair of the Patriarch,[80] vacant for 200 years, is not dead. Bishop Isidor, suffragan of the Eparchie Nizhnii Novgorod, has given public expression to this idea, firmly rejecting the antagonism of the *Moskauer Zeitung*.

Admittedly, the setting up of the chair of the Patriarch does sometimes meet with opposition from the politically liberal sections of the 'white' clergy,[81] through demands for an elected (instead of, as now, appointed) synod, elected bishops and admission of a lay secretary to the synod in an advisory capacity, instead of a Patriarch who is inclined to put pressure on those below and to be subservient to those above him. But despite its national character, the very history and organizational form of the Orthodox Church, especially in view of the total situation into which it would have to find its way, make it quite unlikely that, however it be reshaped, it could ever raise itself up to be the representative of rights of liberty against the power of the police state in the manner of the Roman Church. It would be satisfied with a greater degree of self-government and emancipation from the bureaucracy. The idea of the 'Third Rome' is Caesaropapist, and has been so from the beginning.[82]

On the other hand, it could become quite a respectable instrument of power in the hands of the Tsar. For it is quite improbable that the Russian Church would comply with a *parliamentary* Caesaropapism in the manner of the Greek, much less the Romanian, Church, since this would contradict its interests and traditions. Of course, in view of the profound personal contempt in which the clergy are held,[83] and the undeniable conflict between the 'white clergy' and the 'black clergy' (the monks), it is hard (especially for the foreigner) to assess the potential strength of the Church; this conflict is after all one of the reasons for the power of the State, since it is the only possible protector of the priests against pressure from the celibates. Even less can the outsider assess the significance for the Tsardom (and they could be either a help or a hindrance) of the Christian Social and Christian Democratic movements, which have emerged here and there amongst the clergy and the younger members of a number of seminaries.[84]

However, to judge by the experience of other countries,[85] it seems unlikely that a modern, liberal Russia will be able to judge these opportunities correctly and will not underestimate the religious foundation of autocracy – especially as, in the words of Miliukov at the end of the second volume of his *Ocherki*, history has not taught the educated Russian to be, like the Frenchman, an enemy, nor, like the Englishman, to be a supporter, of his Church, but rather to be 'absolutely indifferent' to it.[86]

The particularly consistent theory of Nikolai K. Leontev, according to which autocracy, being a divine right, could not even be abrogated by the Tsar himself, and any oath opposing it would be a sin, not binding on the oath taker, let alone his successors[87] – analogous to the views of Charles I of England,[88] – may now, after the resignation of Pobedonostsev,[89] have become a blunt instrument. Whether its role in the struggle for autocracy is over remains to be seen. The most truly successful field of operations for the demagogy of modern absolutist Churches is in the confessional and in the cure of souls, in pilgrimages and processions, and in economic cooperatives and associations.[90]

A number of characteristics of the Orthodox Church undoubtedly make this Church's struggle with Liberalism more difficult. These are: the type of confession, which is quite summary in character, lacking in all casuistry and also in all true searching of the conscience, recalling rather the Old Lutheran practice, and connected with the absence of celibacy; the lack of a unified authoritarian power of jurisdiction of a religiously sanctified character in the manner of the papacy; above all the absence of a monasticism which is capable of being active in the 'world'; and finally the lack of a system of holy orders able to rationalize asceticism.

However that may be, the Tsar could not do better in the interests of supporting his authority than to liberate the Church from the domination of the civil servants and restore it to the Patriarchate, especially if a period of liberal rule should really be in the offing.

The Raskol – orthodox in dogma, but since the simultaneously papist and hellenistic 'Renaissance' of the Patriarch Nikon in the seventeenth century in schism from the Church – has placed itself firmly on the basis of the Manifesto of 17/30 October, though in practice only the Edict of Toleration has been of any assistance to it.[91]

When *Moskovskiia Vedomosti* published an anonymous call by a so-called League of Old Believers to support the Tsar and to fight against Liberalism, there followed immediately in the liberal *Russkiia Vedomosti* a proclamation by Old Believers denying the existence of this League. As this proclamation speaks of the 'recollections of the Rogozh Cemetery', it must come from the ritualistic, i.e. religiously conservative, schismatics.[92]

Of the non-hierarchical sects the specifically Protestant will of course be most pleased with the creation of guaranteed rights. The 'pneumatic' sects,[93] on the other hand, are in part strictly apolitical or antipolitical, and in part they have flourished, hitherto at least, only as Churches 'under the cross'.[94] When persecution fell below a certain minimum level, their idealism was often dissipated with remarkable speed. In the central Russian peasant areas the essentially 'Protestant' sects, which can be regarded as supporting individualistic ideals, have been able to gain relatively few supporters. Whether the hopes which the liberals of the Ukraine and southern Russia place in the rapid growth of the Stundists will be fulfilled, remains to be seen.

The Socialist Parties

The political 'individualism' of West European 'human rights' of the kind subscribed to by men like Struve was, to the extent that it was conditioned by 'ideal' factors, inspired partly by religious convictions which rejected unconditionally all subjection to human authorities as atheistic worship of the creature[95] – convictions such as the present-day form of 'enlightenment' does not allow to appear at all – and partly by an optimistic belief in the natural harmony of interests of free individuals, a belief which has now been finally destroyed by capitalism.

These stages of development cannot, if only for 'ideal' reasons, be repeated in the Russia of today. Specifically bourgeois individualism has already been superseded even within the classes of 'education and property' and will certainly not be embraced by the 'petty bourgeoisie'. And as regards the 'masses', when one considers that universal franchise would, and according to the stated purpose of the liberals, should, place power in their hands, the question must be asked as to how they would find the impulse for participation in a movement which goes beyond purely material demands, such as the movement that politicians of bourgeois-democratic stamp have called into being in the shape of the 'Union of Liberation'. That is, how would the masses respond to (1) guaranteed rights of freedom for the individual, (2) the constitutional state [*Rechtsstaat*] on the basis of the 'four-part' franchise, (3) social reform on the West European model, (4) agrarian reform?

Socialist agitation now flourishes in the big cities. It is well known that even prior to those events which allowed Russian Social Democracy to operate openly in Russia itself, the movement had already split into the two groups led respectively by Plekhanov, Axelrod, Martov and Starover [the pseudonym of A. N. Potresov] on the one hand, and by 'Lenin' (Ulianov) on the other.[96]

The former remained in possession of the previously common party organ, the Geneva *Iskra*, and was officially represented at the Pan-Russian Workers' Party Conference, first held in 1905.[97] At the time of the schism this group rejected armed revolt at that particular point in time, and rejected equally firmly the idea of participation in a revolutionary government, placing rather the development of the trade unions at the centre of their activity.

The other group, which had been represented since 1903 by Lenin's journal *Vpered*, refused to recognize *Iskra* as the party organ any longer.[98] Since it formed the majority within the whole party, it functioned as a continuation of the common organization in the Third Congress of the Russian Social Democratic Workers' Party and founded *Proletarii* as its organ.[99] This group emphasized the demand for the eight-hour day rather than the formation of trade unions, preached revolt and participation in a revolutionary government, should one be formed, rejected all legal forms of agitation, and demanded, unlike the supporters

Bourgeois Democracy in Russia 67

of the *Iskra* group, immediate 'confiscation' of all non-peasant land for the peasants. The latter is in strict antithesis to the official programme of Social Democracy, which demanded the transference of the *obrezki* to the peasants, i.e. allocation of the land taken from them at the liberation (about one-fifth),[100] always scorned the Socialist Revolutionary demand for confiscation of all land as 'utopian', and, for example, demonstratively distanced itself, in the spring of 1905, from the Pan-Russian Engineers Congress when this demand was so much as discussed.[101] The Lenin party, in contrast to the Plekhanov group,[102] regarded it as useful to maintain 'occasional alliances' with the Socialist Revolutionaries 'while maintaining its autonomy'.

Both groups declare it to be the duty of the party to support the liberals in their struggle against autocracy, but at the same time to discredit all liberal groups, including the Union of Liberation and the Union of Unions, in the eyes of the workers. The second congress, before the separation, had, by contrast, approved a resolution of Starover which declared a convergence with the bourgeois democrats to be possible and in certain circumstances useful. This resolution was expressly rescinded by the Lenin group, and even the Plekhanov group scarcely pays any further attention to it.

The causes of the split are evidently not ones of principle, but are in part personal, in part tactical in nature, while some of the reasons lie in the intellectual peculiarity of Russian socialism.[103] At the moment it has a very natural source in the conflict between the leaders of orthodoxy, who hitherto have lived mainly abroad and been influenced by the traditions of West European Social Democratic Parties, and the 'putschism' which, with the arrival of press freedom, has now seized the huge numbers of organizations which have arisen within Russia itself. Thus even Bebel's attempts at mediation failed: Lenin refused to accept the advice of foreigners who were not aware of the situation in Russia.[104]

This putsch mood itself, however, is undoubtedly not only the result of the passionate hope, born of the situation of the moment, that the great day has come to overthrow autocracy once and for all and to realize at least the 'minimum programme' of socialism. Revolutionism and opposition to the 'laws of development' has been in the blood of the specifically Russian kind of socialism from the time of its fathers, Herzen and Lavrov, who were influenced in this by some of Hegel's ideas. Herzen rejected as 'nonsense' the idea that socialism could only arise via capitalism,[105] and Lavrov, like the older representatives of the 'Narodnichestvo' [see Glossary], stressed the 'creative' nature of the human mind – the spirit 'come to itself'.[106]

This pragmatic rationalism has never been completely supplanted by the naturalistic rationalism of any 'developmental theory'. Of course, its most telling argument was to be found in the actual existence of communism in the Russian village commune, whose living presence marks not only the views of the workers who mostly even now belong in law to their home commune, but influences views on the decisive agrarian questions deep into the ranks of the liberals, as we shall shortly see.

Putschism is therefore not only the result of the current situation. But of course the latter has had a powerful effect in strengthening this trend. The 'economism' of foreigners schooled in 'historical development' does not mean much to today's organized workers in their present seemingly hopeless power situation. The Lenin tendency rejected it in principle in a resolution of its own, which stated that the view that 'organization was a [gradual] process' was likely to 'weaken the revolutionary consciousness of the proletariat'. However, the 'economistic' tendency of local organizations should be no hindrance to the latter belonging to the party, provided they observe discipline.

To a large extent both groups work together – in Petersburg there is a 'Federal Council',[107] especially as the Plekhanov group had to make the most of extensive concession to the idea of the early 'dictatorship' of the proletariat when their leaders transferred to Petersburg; and the group can, in view of what we are experiencing in German Social Democracy,[108] do this with a clear conscience. Both now possess a Petersburg daily newspaper, the Plekhanov group the *Nachalo*, and the Lenin group the *Novaia Zhizn*. Both papers were at first published without hindrance, in spite of their legends: 'Organ of the Social Democratic Workers' Party' and 'Workers of the World, Unite!'[109] The editors of both papers were, however, prosecuted, because their programmes demanded a republic, something their leading articles continue to advocate. The Lenin group was joined by the 'epistemological' tendencies, which had been rejected or ignored by orthodoxy – such as 'empiriocritics' like Bogdanov and others.

The editorial team of *Nachalo* comprised almost all the well-known leaders, Plekhanov, Axelrod, Martov, 'Starover', Totomiants, Rappoport, 'Parvus' (Helphand), Vera Zasulich, and so on; as regards foreigners: V. Adler, Bebel, Kautsky, Mehring, Rosa Luxemburg, Klara Zetkin: thus this paper is recognized internationally too as 'orthodox'. (I have not had sight of *Novaia Zhizn*, and both papers have now been suppressed.)[110]

The question as to how strong politically the socialist organizations are today, and what their present electoral significance would be, is not easily answered, even in Russia. Suffice it to say that their zeal in campaigning and in detailed work is undoubtedly far greater than that of the liberals, that they are not inferior to them in the number of their centres of organization in the cities, and are probably more united.

But this alone is not decisive. Far more important is the fact that, with the open emergence of what is, despite some deviation from the party line, still essentially 'correct' socialism, a further extremely effective 'element of decomposition' has, as a result of the *sect-like* character of Social Democracy with its close ties to strictly precise *dogmas*, entered into the anti-authoritarian movement, which was until a few months ago still largely united in the Union of Liberation.

Like the thoroughgoing Jesuit, the devout Marxist is imbued by his dogma with a blithe superiority and the self-assurance of the somnambulist. Disdaining to strive for lasting political success, and confident of being above reproach, he accepts with equanimity and a mocking laugh the collapse of all hopes – his own included – of overcoming the mortal foe he shares with other groups; is always exclusively concerned with the preservation of the pure faith and – if possible – the increase of his own sect by a few souls; and seeks the 'unmasking' of 'those who are also catholics' here, of 'traitors to the people' there, in neighbouring groups. This is exactly like the attitude of the Social Democratic press [in Germany] towards the 'bloc'[111] (the expression has been adopted in Russia). Any agreement between oppositional elements is thus rendered impossible, even though the programmes of the Socialist Revolutionaries – to be mentioned below[112] – did not, on account of the greater vagueness of their dogmatic foundation, exclude such an agreement, and many Socialist Revolutionaries, as we have seen,[113] belonged to the Union of Liberation, together with radical princes etc.[114]

The workers' organization which is at present most prominent among those of a socialist character (though not created by the party) is the Council of Workers' Deputies (Soviet Rabochikh Deputatov) in Petersburg.[115] It came into being after the slaughter of 9/22 January, when the government sought to approach the workers by means of a senator (Shidlovskii) and to this end called for the election of deputies.[116] Since their political conditions were not accepted, the workers refused to enter into negotiations, though they continued to provide representatives – at first for local purposes.

In accordance with the regulations accepted at the end of November 1905, the Council of Workers' Deputies now consists of deputies of each factory with at least 400 workers, and is thus a representation of the specifically workers' elite of big industry on a local basis, not on the basis of specific industries. It did, however, determine in its session of 28 November to ally itself with the Union of Trade Associations [*Fachvereine*] in such a way that delegates of the latter could be admitted to the sessions. The question as to whether they would have voting rights remained doubtful when the vote was taken, and was apparently left unanswered. On the other hand it was resolved to give both seats and votes in the Council of Workers' Deputies to the radical Peasant League – to be discussed later.[117]

With regard to its general attitude, it was at first undecided over the question of *another* political general strike (end of November). The point was made in the session of 28 November that it would be too expensive. The Council of Workers' Deputies, in *Izvestiia*, warned repeatedly against pointless revolts and provocation. Apart from the fact that the most economically and politically developed, and therefore most calculating, stratum of industrial worker is represented, there are signs here of the original attitude of the Plekhanov tendency, which was very much involved in the formation of the organization.

Since then, all this has changed. The arrest of its president, the lawyer Khrustalev-Nosar,[118] – hitherto not a prominent political personality – for inflammatory propaganda, gave rise to a sharply worded resolution in favour of immediate armed revolt. At the same time the radical Union of Unions (Soiuz Soiuzov) approached the Council of Workers' Deputies (and at the same time all other isolated associations within Russia) by means of a public announcement, with the proposal for the formation of a 'General Union' (Obshchii Soiuz), which should comprise the Council of Workers' Deputies, the Peasant League, the trade associations, especially of the railway workers and the post and telegraph officers, and all organizations belonging to the Union of Unions.

The Intelligentsia and the Bourgeois Parties

The heart of the Union of Unions,[119] which seems to have been constituted at the beginning of May, was represented by the free associations of *liberal* professions, which were formed in huge numbers in the course of the first months of the year 1905, especially since the manifesto of 18 February,[120] with the purpose of pursuing primarily political and democratic aims. It included the 'Pan-Russian' Union of lawyers, doctors, engineers, journalists, booksellers, primary school teachers, middle school teachers, agriculturalists, statisticians, pharmacists, veterinary surgeons, and also state civil servants. Count Tolstoy, for example, Secretary of the Imperial Council, was reprimanded for membership.[121] There were also insurance employees, clerks, and actors, as well as representatives of women's and of Jewish rights organizations.

At first, 14 organizations joined together in the Union of Unions, but the number is obviously in flux and cannot be accurately estimated from outside the country. (There was even an appeal by *police* officers from

Bourgeois Democracy in Russia 71

Moscow, for example, calling for 'the comrades' to organize, in view of the 'great strength' of this union.)

The general purpose and character of these associations is evidently not uniform. Some actually did pursue professional interests (if not exclusively), but others, and indeed the majority, pursued chiefly general political interests. In the course of last year, no teachers' conference or the like could take place without passing a constitutional resolution.

Then, however, the Union, to coincide with its definitely joining the 'proletarian' camp, announced its intention to subject its member unions to an examination at the Congress planned for mid-December, to determine whether they were purely professional or 'professional-social', or 'professional-political'.[122] For in spite of its radical character the proletarians had gained the impression that it was still too 'bourgeois' – the Engineers' Union had, for instance, rejected the idea of a republic as impracticable – and doubtless the Union aimed to rectify this impression.

Those members of the 'intelligentsia' who were not members of the zemstvos, and who originally belonged to the Union of Unions, had from the beginning a predominantly quasi-proletarian character. The 'Third Element' held predominantly 'populist' and Socialist Revolutionary, or modern socialist views, and tended to act accordingly. For example, the Union boycotted the Bulygin Duma, unlike the Union of Liberation, and, more significantly, it did not join the Constitutional Democratic Party. Exactly how these events, which were so important for the political situation of the Russian 'intelligentsia', unfolded, remains a mystery for the foreign observer, just as it is at the moment quite impossible for him to piece together from the mutually contradictory press reports the course of the inner development of the Union of Unions.

Fundamental to the situation is the quite understandable and deep-seated antagonism of the Third Element, whose members play such an important part within the Union and who feel they provide the intellectual basis on which the achievements of the zemstvos rest, towards the honorary members from the landowning classes, who have the decisive voice.

The political turn-around achieved by Witte in October came so quickly (in addition to the fact that it appeared to be due to the effect of the strike) that it made the structural weakness of the old regime seem considerably greater than it was. The great mass of professional associations, which were formed on the basis of a sudden freedom,[123] were chiefly inspired by the jubilant hope of witnessing the final liberation from the terrible pressure of autocracy. It is not possible to assess the political significance of the involvement of sections of the 'landowning class' in this movement.

After the dissolution of the Union of Liberation[124] there was an increase in the influence on the radical intelligentsia within the Union exercised by the putschist elements of Social Democracy, which regarded the alliance of some of the Socialist Revolutionaries with the bourgeoisie with profound dislike and opposed it with increasing vigour. Moreover, the 'radical' character of the Union was from the very beginning connected, as it was in the case of other liberal groupings, with the fact that up to the October Manifesto many 'moderate' elements in the liberal professions distanced themselves from any form of organization because it was, strictly speaking, illegal.

The union of the radical intelligentsia with the politically organized workers and the Peasant League proposed by the Union of Unions was to be essentially on the basis of the demand for a 'constituent' Imperial Duma, i.e. the principle of popular sovereignty. The resolution of 20 November, requested by the Poles, offered an extremely 'simple' solution: both an Imperial Duma and one constituent Duma each for Poland, Finland and all regions which wished to have one, should convene, though 'the unity of the Empire was to be preserved'. The question of whether the first Duma should be a 'constituent' one had been discussed by the zemstvo constitutionalists. The Constitutional Democratic programme retained this proposal.[125]

When the telegram from Count Witte requesting the sending of party representatives arrived, the Moscow uprava decided to refrain from making individual demands, since 'the only demand could be the calling of the constituent assembly'.

In the November Congress the resolution of the Bureau, supported by Miliukov, in agreement with the original programme of the Union of Liberation, likewise demanded a constituent assembly, which 'with the permission of the Sovereign' was to 'draw up' a constitution. However, this 'republican-sounding' term was removed because of, amongst other reasons, a speech by Maxim Kovalevskii, who declared that he would be happy to live in a republic, as in Paris, but, as things stood in Russia, declared himself to be a monarchist.

However, the Social Democrats, as well as the radical elements of the Union of Liberation, the Socialist Revolutionaries and the Union of Unions (ever since its founding), insisted on the term 'constituent' as a cardinal point. The rift between 'bourgeois' and 'proletarian' intelligentsia, which of course does not rest simply on this trivial point, grew wider after the failure of the former to obtain 'guarantees' from Witte.

The more anarchy spread, and police and military intervention by the government increased, and, in particular, the longer the announcement of the electoral law and the proclamation of the elections were delayed, the

Bourgeois Democracy in Russia 73

greater became the flood of republican radicalism, especially after the extremely cool and non-committal answer of the Council of Ministers to the Bureau of the Zemstvo Representatives.

The Union of Unions, in the aforementioned public announcement regarding the founding of the 'General Union',[126] expressed the conviction that armed revolt was the only means of achieving liberation. It published at the same time the draft of a constituent assembly which should comprise the entire legislative, executive and *judicial* power in itself, in 968 (!) constituencies of the Empire, elected by all citizens, of both sexes, aged over 21. This would amount to the dictatorship of the '*Mass*' and the creation of a monstrous central revolutionary tribunal.

Shortly afterwards a 'manifesto' of the Council of Workers' Deputies was published, which called on everyone to withdraw all deposits from savings banks, reject all paper money and present all bank notes for cashing, as state bankruptcy was just around the corner.[127]

The government responded to these and similar publications by arresting the board of the Union of Unions and all editors of newspapers which had printed the manifestos. The initial reaction to this was a general strike, with further action likely to follow. But of course the high degree to which democracy is discredited after the failure of such efforts, not only affects those who set up the hopeless trial of strength, but has an effect on the prospects of the constitutional movement as a whole, on whose non-participation the masses place the blame for failure.

Within the urban proletariat, which is being worked on from another direction by the Christian Social[128] and Socialist Revolutionary supporters of extreme radicalism, and within the group of 'liberal professions', then, the chances for bourgeois democracy, even under a democratic franchise, are extremely problematical, as even the Democrats would probably concede, although their programme contains all the demands of radical West European social reformers.[129]

As far as the narrow stratum of the genuine 'bourgeoisie' is concerned, the manufacturers have, up to a point, moved quite close to the liberals and even the Democrats. This is understandable when one considers that though they used to be the bearers of nationalism, as described to us by Schulze-Gävernitz, nevertheless it is quite natural that in the circumstances of recent years they should incline this way, since Plehve's government has tried to win over the workers and play them off against the 'intelligentsia',[130] by for example building the eleven huts which were at the heart of the Gapon Movement.[131] However in the constitutional Democratic Party *none* of their names are to be found. They were, as we have seen,[132] sceptical of the zemstvo movement, and the programme of the antiprotectionist Union of Liberation held no attractions for them at all. From the social point of view the mass of their representatives even at the beginning of 1905 acted in an essentially reactionary way and hoped for repression. (This was not universal: there were a number of petitions by manufacturers calling for the right of combination.) Politically, very many of them seem to belong to the Party of Legal Order,[133] which will be mentioned later,[134] or the Union of 17 October,[135] which is close to it. At least, after their experiences, they are not necessarily at the disposal of the government and the reactionaries against the liberals. When, at a meeting of the Association of Traders and Industrialists in Petersburg, a representative of the Party of Legal Order, Philin, invited people to join with the government in the struggle against the Council of Workers' Deputies, other speakers sharply rejected this: 'society' must carry on the struggle alone. If the association now sought protection from the government, the day would come when others would seek protection *against the association* from the very same place and with the same degree of success.

Finally, the petty bourgeoisie, whose attitude, as ever, is most difficult to predict, will probably after all be prevented from joining with the liberals on account of its antisemitism. That is the conclusion suggested by their strong participation in the movement of the 'Black Gangs'. Admittedly, it should not be forgotten that in the big cities and in a few other 'suspicious' places[136] the current organization of police espionage creates such a degree of deeply hated dependency on corrupt, arbitrary and servile officials that for the next few years protest will again override all other considerations. For example, every house must have a porter (*dvornik*),[137] charged with keeping a check on the occupants. The house owners are responsible for employing the porter and must meet the costs. Moreover, it is compulsory to carry a passport at all times, there is 'administrative' – i.e. extra-legal – deportation and no assurance that the house may not be searched at any time. (In fact, such searches are usually carried out at night.)

A *permanent* compromise with a system which requires such methods is practically impossible.

The Agrarian Question

The crucial question which will determine the future not only of the Constitutional Democratic movement but, more importantly, of its fundamental programme, and beyond that the chances of a liberal 'development' in the Western European sense, concerns the *peasants*. This remains true even if the census franchise should give the liberals a majority, for then, if the peasants are reactionary, a reactionary government would be able to use them any time it chose as a rod with which to beat a recalcitrant Duma.

Bourgeois Democracy in Russia

In fact the programme of Bourgeois Democracy is essentially aimed at the peasants. It is precisely the peasants that Peter Struve would like to make a 'personality', by accustoming them not only to the law, in the objective sense, but also to rights in the subjective sense, by which he means 'human rights' of English individualism.[138]

It is constantly stressed with the greatest force that agrarian reform stands at the centre of all questions, that political reforms will and must essentially benefit it and that agrarian reform for its part will benefit political reform.

This does not, of course, mean that the peasants themselves will be democratic. Both Peter Struve and likewise the authors of the draft[139] rely in this respect essentially on the economic interests of the peasants, whose demands in this respect *cannot* be satisfied by a reactionary government.

The questions are, then: what are the demands of the peasants themselves, and what are the demands of the democratic agrarian reformers in the interests of the peasants?

The February Zemstvo Congress had already concerned itself with the agrarian question and in so doing had adopted the slogan of 'supplementation' (*dopolnenie*) of the peasant allotment of land (*nadel*), a characteristic slogan of liberal agrarian reform. Everything else was reserved for a special council.

The March 1905[140] programme of the Union of Liberation then made the following substantial agrarian demands.

1 Abolition of the redemption payments of the peasants (since conceded by the government, to be reduced by half in 1906, and completely waived in 1907).
2 The provision of land for the landless peasants and those with insufficient share of land through division of domain, Crown and treasury lands and, in the absence of these, through *expropriation* of private landowners.
3 Formation of a state land fund for the purpose of planned internal colonization.
4 Reform of the lease law so that the tenant would be guaranteed improvements to his land. Provision of arbitration courts 'for regulation of rent in the interest of workers' and for the resolution of disputes between them and the landlord.
5 Extension of labour law to the farm workers 'in accordance with basic agricultural conditions'.

In addition there were in the programme the following evidently 'physiocratically' inspired points: gradual abolition of indirect taxation and development of direct taxes on the basis of progressive income tax, abolition of protectionist favouring of individual entrepreneurs with simultaneous 'powerful protection of the development of the productive forces of the people': a gradual reduction of duty would, it is said, 'benefit agriculture and stimulate industry'. In a criticism of the draft's budgetary stance, Peter Struve rejected the complete abolition of indirect taxes as an 'editorial error'. And yet this very point seems to be popular with those landowners who would perhaps support a liberal leadership. For example, an apparently authentic petition of 56 'literate' and 84 illiterate 'bourgeois' landowners of the district of Kherson demanded the abolition of the taxes on tea, sugar, machines and matches; so have other similar indubitably peasant petitions, which can be found everywhere in newspapers and periodicals.

It is obvious that a progressive income tax would today in Russia be financially no substitute for duties and consumer taxes – this much at least should be said. Quite apart from economic conditions, moral conditions are lacking for such a truly effective tax, which, as is well known, is impossible even in the United States for the same reasons. Also, it remains completely obscure with what funds the huge reforms here demanded would be carried out. But let us return to those reforms themselves.

German readers must have noticed that the characteristic institution of the Russian agrarian social order [*Agrarverfassung*], the obshchina (mir, or village commune) has not been mentioned. Now, the current peasant question is not by any means confined to areas with village communes,[141] that is, in the centre and the eastern Black Earth regions and areas to the north and north-east of these. In fact, the peasant question relates to the whole Empire from the Baltic to the steppes and is as burning a question in some parts of the Ukraine as for instance in the Moscow area.

The agrarian problems of the hegemonic Russian race itself, however, are all linked directly or indirectly to the commune, and it affects the areas of great peasant density just as much as the principle areas of chronic mass poverty. The influence of the village commune 'ideal' is universal: the whole of the social and political party life of Russia is most intimately connected with the question of its fate, which has been passionately debated for years; it occupies the imagination of the masses just as much as of the socially concerned politicians of all shades, determining their feelings far beyond its actual direct significance.

This provides a clue as to why the programme of the liberals is silent about the village commune. There is no doubt that this silence is a concession to, on the one hand, Slavophiles who have become liberal and to 'Populists', and on the other hand to the socialists, Socialist Revolutionaries and land reformers, all of whom, for opposing reasons, could not agree to an express attack on the commune. In addition, specifically economic liberals, especially such individualists who, like Struve, have been through a strict Marxist school, oppose the linkage of agrarian reform proposals to the commune as 'utopian'.

Moreover, this silence can be explained, of course, by the fact that the legislative treatment of this problem, in whichever direction it may lie, would take a decade and that for practical politicians there are much more urgent agrarian tasks. Nevertheless any kind of comprehensive agrarian policy must immediately come up against the village commune.

[*Weber gives an account of the agrarian programme adopted by the Zemstvo Congress of 24 and 25 February 1905. This looked at ways of increasing the peasants' share of land, including expropriation of private land, and the creation of a land fund, or reserve, for distribution to peasants with little or no land of their own.*]

Leaving aside many economic considerations, it can be stated with all due caution that the question of the future development of the obshchina must be addressed with some urgency if agrarian reform is to solve the problem of what legal fate awaits the land to be newly distributed to the peasants. Distribution of the land as purely individual property is of course regarded even by economically liberal members of the Congress – such as Prince Volkonskii – as impracticable. Firm opposition to the idea of assigning the land to the communes was expressed by Koliubakin, who pointed to conditions in the Novogorod region, where internal colonization, mostly in the form of leasehold settlement, took place by means of immigration by strangers, who would be excluded by the local obshchina associations. Reforming the obshchina would, however, lead to just such a monopoly of the new land by the local peasants, and discriminate against migrants.

In fact it seems clear, at least as viewed from abroad, that liberal political reform must lead to quite profound changes in the obshchina from the legal angle alone. Today it is still at one and the same time both a cooperative and a compulsory association, *Realgemeinde*[142] and political community; the individual is, in principle, as much bound to it as it is – normally – to him. In principle, he has the right to his share of land, and it, in principle, has the right to his labour. He may return to it at any time, and it can oblige him to do so at any time by not renewing his passport, the issuing of which is tied to its approval as well as that of the state authorities. So, even after the abolition of joint liability for taxes (1904),[143] the individual (whose bondage to the estate owner ceased on the abolition of serfdom) remains, at least in principle, 'in bondage to his commune'.

According to the programme of the Union of Liberation, absolute freedom of movement and freedom to settle anywhere should apply to everyone, including the peasant, and the passport system should be abolished.[144] If this were put into practice and, furthermore, universal franchise were unconditionally introduced, in the communes too – and this ought to happen, if they are not to remain on the lowest stage as a community which is at the same time both legally bound and privileged – then the divorce between *Realgemeinde* and political community would be the immediate consequence and it would become impossible, for administrative reasons, to maintain the 'right to land' in the home community even in a formal sense.

Something which is de facto coming into being must – it seems – now occur de jure: the obshchina must become, immediately in law, and in the not too distant future in fact also, an economic special community within the villages. Should the new peasant land now be assigned to such a community? As I have remarked, I cannot tell from the fragmentary reports which are available to me whether anything was said on the subject at that Congress [of Constitutional Democrats] and if so what, nor whether the question was raised as to how to halt the renewed overpopulation in the villages, which is markedly encouraged by the distribution according to the number of 'mouths to feed', i.e. according to the size of families.

The outside observer would, for example, think of the setting of a minimum size of share below which no redistribution could occur, and so on, although it would be impossible to judge whether anything of that kind had any chance of being put into practice. Though it is certain that agrarian politicians like Manuilov, Herzenstein, Chuprov, Kaufmann and others have their opinions about this, it is clearly shown at every opportunity that within the radical parties, right into the ranks of bourgeois democracy, a chaos of conflicting opinions reigns on all questions concerning the commune.

In order to clarify this to ourselves, we must cast a glance at the groups of agrarian reformers to the 'left' of the liberals, especially the different branches of the 'Socialist Revolutionary' tendency.

In its present organization and with its present programme, the party is of fairly recent origin. After the fine work of von Schulze-Gävernitz and Simkhovich,[145] it can be assumed that the reader knows how, on the basis of the commune and local peasant industries (*kustar*), the Narodnichestvo formed the theory that in Russia the right to land enshrined in the obshchina could entirely prevent the separation of the commercial producer from production by the kustar, and indeed prevent the rise of a proletariat detached from the soil; Russia might thus be spared from capitalism and the 'individualism' of the West.

Authoritarian orthodoxy and the imperialistic Slavophile movement saw in this the guarantee of the permanence of the inner unity of Russia under the sceptre of the Tsar: the humble muzhik[146] seemed to them the victorious future type of Russian humanity, subservient both to the Church and to the Tsar. By contrast, radical anarchosocialism saw in him the man who would bypass the painful intermediate steps of Western development and – if the slogan 'peasant take the land, worker take the factory', were carried through – would soon bring about the free society of the future. To the irenic Slavophile, finally, he was the still undeveloped bearer of the ethical qualities of Russianness, especially of holy self-denial.

Alongside the Narodnichestvo of the 'Russian school of sociology', who essentially represented decentralization against bureaucracy, stood peaceful revolutionary groupings, such as the *chernyi peredel* (the 'black redistribution', which accepted the peasants' conviction that the bureaucracy had thwarted the full allocation of the land which the Tsar had promised), other groupings which did not necessarily reject violence, and finally the '*narodnaia volia*', which employed terror to disrupt the ruling classes as a prelude to their violent expropriation.[147] Their history belongs elsewhere.

The 1880s and 1890s proved to be hard times for all groupings directly or indirectly based on those ideas – with the exception of the extreme nationalists. The political pressure became more intense than ever when Russia was invaded by capitalism with all its economic and intellectual side-effects. None of the different groupings could avoid taking a position on this fact, and at the same time, alongside Marx, the influence of Henry George made itself felt particularly strongly in Russia, where not all the land was yet in ownership.[148]

Out of the chaos of opinions which thus arose there crystallized, from the beginning of the new century, the present (still rather vague) Populist and Socialist Revolutionary party programmes. Essentially, the Populists have emphasized the social aspects of liberation from oppression (which capitalism had intensified), and the Socialist Revolutionaries have stressed the political aspects, whilst both have had to take account of the fact that neither kustar nor obshchina had delivered what they seemed to have promised.[149]

The radical parties, even in the 1890s, divided up the work amongst themselves so that the Social Democrats worked on the urban proletariat, and the Populists (Narodniki) worked on the peasants, both from a *social* political angle, though from quite opposing theoretical and practical points of view. Alongside these, on the one hand, was the activity of the terrorists (narodnaia volia); their aims were purely political and were directed at the autocracy and all arbitrary 'crimes' of the civil servants; and on the other hand there was the essentially urban revolutionary 'intelligentsia', with divergent theories but with the same sphere of work as the Social Democrats.

Aside from all these, the Socialist Revolutionary Party[150] – reorganized around the turn of the century – attempted a synthesis of the various spheres of influence and methods: agitation, putsch or systematic terror, depending on the circumstances. Furthermore, their area of work sought to encompass not only the peasants and the workers but also – they laid considerable stress on this point – 'educated society'.

The ultimate aim (of the party) was 'the full realization of the socialist society'. The necessary condition of its achievement in Russia, however, as was continually stressed in constant polemics against the Social Democratic *Saria* and *Iskra*, was a *political*, democratic revolution and an anticapitalist agrarian reform to follow it on the basis of 'right to a full return on one's labour'.

Contrary to what the orthodox Social Democrats believed, this revolution must not (in the view of the Socialist Revolutionaries) be a bourgeois revolution, since in that case, as a result of the further development of agrarian capitalism, the 'purchasing power of the land would be weakened' – a particularly *modern* type of 'populist' argument – and thus a modern 'political superstructure' would be rendered impossible. Furthermore, in the case of a purely bourgeois revolution the peasants would fall back into the arms of the Tsar.

To do as the Social Democrats do, and regard the peasants as cannon fodder for the purely bourgeois revolution, which inevitably had to come first, was therefore not acceptable. The Russian peasant, unlike his Western European cousin, was not anticollectivist: in the struggle against the landowners and the kulaks [see Glossary], in the settlement of new land (Siberia) and in redistribution, he acted anti-individualistically, and this tendency would be reinforced as cultivation expanded.

When Social Democrats objected that the idea of the 'equal' or 'just' division, in fact the very idea of 'division', was petty bourgeois and fissiparous in character, that it contradicted technical and economic 'progress' and was thus reactionary, the reply was to point to the 'Socialist Revolutionary' character of this idea, its opposition to property as such, and the necessity of considering it if only for reasons of *realpolitik*.

The danger lay, however, firstly in the ambiguity of the term 'socialization' of the land, which to the peasants meant simply village communism, and secondly in the hope they placed in the Tsar, which could easily be strengthened by any agrarian reforms carried out by the government. The government of Alexander III, with its bureaucratic destruction of the autonomy of the mir, and the increasing lack of land for peasants fettered to their village, had actually helped promote the revolution. The zemstvo, the influence of the millions of peasants travelling about as workers or small producers and traders, seeing the world and observing social distinctions, and also the sects, had begun to make a different person out of the peasant to what he was 30 years previously, when the 'intellectual' who went among the people was just the 'man with white hands'.

It was thus important to form 'brotherhoods' of convinced comrades in the villages, who would call attention to themselves at all resolutions of the commune, who would organize a boycott of landowners and kulaks, and organize the struggle for reduction of rent and the raising of wages for agricultural work on the estates, and who would spread the idea that the land belonged to no one but 'society' and should only be entrusted to those who worked it with their hands; a man had the right to the product of his own hands and this was already (incompletely) realized in today's mir. However, one should only use these economic factors as arguments for political liberty since political liberty was the only means of achieving real improvement; and one must join together with democratically minded 'intelligentsia' of all strata. It must be made clear to the peasant that in practice he was *already* a 'Socialist Revolutionary'; one must base oneself on that and not on the false and (to him) incomprehensible 'developmental theory' of the Social Democrats, with their doctrine that private property was an inevitable 'transitional phase'.

This line of thought finds expression in the programme of the Socialist Revolutionary Party (Partiia Sotsialistov-Revoliutsionerov) which was presented in draft form in *Revoliutsionnaia Rossiia*, no. 46, of 5 May 1904.

The programme recognizes capitalist development as a fact, with the reservation that the effect of capitalism may be different according to both population strata and country, so that whereas it is relatively positive in 'industrial countries of classical capitalism', in 'agrarian countries and those least favoured in international competition', especially Russia, it is exclusively negative, even when measured by purely technical production standards (here the Social Democrats differ).

Accordingly, the struggle to shake off the yoke of the exploiting and leisured classes in Russia and to transform the people into a single great union of workers – the precondition of the 'comprehensive harmonious development of the human personality' – must here be specially adapted to particular historical conditions and must take the existing situation as its starting-point.

The progressive Socialist Revolutionary minority must above all strive for the fall of autocracy, in order then, should the minority not yet have been transformed into a majority, to demand the following as a minimum programme: eight-hour day for workers, minimum wage, compulsory insurance, and participation of the workers in factory administration. In the agrarian question, however, it should develop 'the traditions and way of life of the Russian peasantry' in the struggle against the rural bourgeoisie, the landowners and kulaks. All land privately owned by individual persons should be confiscated – or, should this not be feasible immediately, expropriated by the communes – and handed over to the village communities and the territorial associations which would be formed, to enable them to dispose of it on the principle of *equality* of rights of use (this was what the socialists chiefly objected to). This was known as the socialization of the land.

Transitional measures would be: taxing the yield which exceeds the 'normal yield' of the farms, compensation for improvements when land is transferred, special taxation of income in favour of the communes. With regard to the question of 'socialization', the draft declares that the 'nationalization' of 'parts of the national economy' under the bourgeois regime is only to be striven for to the extent that the democratic character of the regime in question, and the arrangements made, offer guarantees against this 'state socialism' becoming in fact a 'government capitalism' serving to increase the power of the ruling classes.

It is easy to see here that the standpoint of the Narodnichestvo, i.e. village communism, appropriates ideas from Henry George, Marx and others, and that faith in the 'creative' ability of the 'people' finds expression in the 'progressive minority', and proclaims the leading role of the 'intelligentsia', in spite of concessions to 'developmental' thinking. The present essentially *political* democratic aim of the movement – overthrow of autocracy as precondition of everything else – makes possible a far-reaching understanding with the leaders of 'bourgeois' democracy, who, in the form of the Union of Liberation, and even in the zemstvos, have adopted physiocratic aims which go a long way to satisfy the 'land hunger' of the peasants.

As we have seen, some of the Socialist Revolutionaries belonged to the Union of Liberation. However, when the programme of the liberal [Constitutional Democrat] Agrarian Congress (28 and 29 April 1905) appeared, the Socialist Revolutionaries of *Revoliutsionnaia Rossiia* rejected this as totally inadequate, since in the meantime the chances of revolution seemed to have improved. Their party demanded 'all the land' and 'without new redemption payments'; and there could be no question of having to convert ground rents, devalued by the revolutionaries, into government stocks, on which the people would then have to pay interest.[151]

The incompleteness of these reform proposals seemed no less suspect to the Narodniki (who stood outside the party), whose former leader Mikhailovskii had died just at the outbreak of the war in the East. The mighty political movement, which at the same time transformed the

Socialist Revolutionaries from a group conspiring from abroad into a domestic party, forced it as well as the other groups to lay a renewed programmatic statement before the public, and I should like here to analyse two programmes in rather more detail. One is of the Narodnichestvo, and the other a Socialist Revolutionary programme; they oppose each other in typical fashion precisely in regard to the point which interests us, the village commune, and should not be without interest for those German readers who are unfamiliar with these problems of Russian agrarian politics.

[*Weber now distinguishes the programme of the Young Populists from the Old Populists; the latter was primarily unpolitical and theoretical; the former attempted to establish a position distinct from both economic liberalism and Marxism, at least with regard to agrarian politics. Weber examines the Young Populist programme in some detail. He bases his exposition of the ideas of the Young Populists on an open letter from G. Novotorzhskii to A. V. Peshekhonov. The former proposes, among other things, that the state should have the right to move the surplus population of the poorer villages and resettle them in the richer ones. He regards the commune as a good basis for future developments.*]

The economically characteristic feature of this programme is, aside from the belief in the possibility of preventing the rise of leasing and wage labour by means of prohibitions, commitment to the viewpoint that the village should remain both compulsory association and cooperative at one and the same time, indeed should in a sense become both, and that the individual should thus remain bound to the commune, in part passively, through the necessity of negotiating with it about his departure, in part actively, through permanent claim to a share of land.

At this point the criticism by the Socialist Revolutionary land reformers begins – they are a split from the radical Narodnichestvo which has greatly modernized itself under the influence of Henry George and Marx and whose organ today is the previously mentioned monthly *Russkoe Bogatstvo*.[152]

For them, today's village is a product of division along estate lines [*Ständescheidung*], a 'peasants' ghetto', which hinders the free and 'natural' movement of the population between the individual regions and between town and country, and hinders their decisions as to where to settle and when to move, which should be based on 'market' conditions, determined by natural or economic factors.

To distribute land to the village means not only to replace a privileged minority (of private landowners) by a privileged majority (the mir), but, together with the continuation of the ban on land sale, it completely undermines the basic principle of land reform: 'free access to the land'. At the same time the 'ghetto' character of the village is strengthened still further by the state's right to carry out 'compulsory resettlement' into the commune. That is something that not even today's Russian police state dare do, as Peshekhonov rightly remarks in his reply to the previously mentioned 'open letter' of Novotorzhskii.[153] [. . .]

But further – and here the criticism strikes at the weakest point of the ideas of the 'populists' – the condition for this right (of the state) to practise compulsory resettlement is based on an economically faulty foundation: the concept of the 'adequate' area for cultivation by the commune with its own resources is economically ambiguous. The labour necessary for cultivation of the land does not depend only on size and quality of the land, but above all on (1) what is produced and (2) the technical means by which it is produced.

The granting of permission to pay leaving bonuses simply encourages the creation of incentives for the commune to opt out of a transition to a more rational economic system or to more intensive culture.

If the state does not wish to favour the accumulation of income at the expense of agricultural progress, then, in order to permit 'emigration' or 'immigration', it must control and regiment the entire peasant economy.

Equally, for the same reason, it is quite impossible to prohibit wage labour – unless, by means of endless casuistry, the quite indispensable help of neighbours for wages or payment in kind is not so defined. Also . . . the one who is formally the employer is not necessarily the exploiter (an example given by Peshekhonov does, however, refer to the hiring of *material* means of production which is therefore a capital loan). That is all in principle correct, and Peshekhonov could have supported his argument with far more theoretical considerations: thus the idea that the agricultural product is on the one hand the result of natural soil quality, and on the other the working product of the farmers and nothing more, is invalidated every time means of production are introduced into the agricultural production process which are not produced by the peasant himself, e.g. improved tools, modern buildings, or artificial fertilizer.

Not only the yield, but even the nutrients in the soil are no longer produced by the farmer with the aid of the gifts of nature within the natural soil, but far away in machine and tool factories, potash mines, Thomas blast furnaces, fitters' workshops and the like.

A continually growing proportion of the 'socially necessary labour' required for the achievement of the yield – all Narodniki tend to employ different shades of Marxist terminology – is transported away from the land to those centres of mining and industry.

And not only departures due to leaving bonuses, but just as much resettlement of new people in a village, coupled with the obligation to remain, is bound to restrict 'technical progress' in the customary sense of the word. For the latter brings not only a relative but, compared with small farms, an absolute *reduction*, not an increase, in the number of hands employed on the land, for the same area – a displacement of these 'hands' by 'capital'.

It cannot here be investigated what the technical and economic limits on these developments in agriculture would be, as these would depend on the crop and on the social order. What is certain is that, if the goal is to be 'technical progress', the growing of *grain* for the foreign market would require a tremendous reduction in the agricultural population of today, which is employed on small farms in which the soil is tilled by hand.

The same principle applies to the farm run on private capitalist lines, at least in areas where the country has remained truly 'rural', i.e. in the absence of numerous strong local markets or industry to create favourable economic conditions for small farmers and leaseholders under the conditions of *private land ownership*. Conversely, it would not apply where the peasant, by increasing the natural character of his farm, i.e. by restricting those needs which must be met by purchasing, withdraws from involvement in the machinery of the market, and thus also from 'technical progress'.

The programme of the Young Populists rests on the narrow 'subsistence principle' [*Nahrungsstandpunkt*]; it does not ask: how can I achieve a maximum of produce from a given area with a minimum of labour (the watchword of agrarian capitalism), but: how can I, within the given area, provide a living for a maximum number of people by the utilization of their labour in the village?

This principle can *only* operate consistently when coupled with a determined rejection of 'technical progress', since it would have to fight against the increasing importance of the 'production of means of production' and of the supersession of manual labour by tools. Otherwise the obshchina is simply one item in the maelstrom of the capitalist socialization process, in which there is no room for the 'subsistence principle'.

The weakness of the Young Populists lies, however, in the fact that they would like to be 'modern' in the 'technical' sense. They speak, for example, of the 'increasing purchasing power' that their programme would give the peasants, and thus give up the original Old Narodnichestvo idea, which Mikhailovskii formulated thus: that the approach towards the 'wholeness' of individuals should be the goal, and therefore whereas there should be 'maximum division of labour between organic groups', there should be the *least* possible division of labour among individuals: the glorification of the kustar (home industry) and of the peasant's own production was founded on this, indeed Vorontsov saw in the high lease payments of the peasants – thus in their exploitation – the defensive rampart against capitalist development in agriculture.

What such 'romantic' orientations have in common is simply that they try to fight against capitalism without a theoretical understanding of its essential nature. It therefore enters their camp from behind whilst they are outside jousting with windmills. For their information on the essence of capitalism they have mostly only read Marx and not understood him properly, since they constantly leaf through him looking for 'the moral'.

In their knowledge of the capitalist machinery the land reformers, especially with regard to the tracing and analysis of the process of income accumulation which is after all their special interest, are far ahead of these reactionaries.

They are quite familiar with the significance of market production in the development of the forms of land ownership and the processes of the development of differential incomes. One such is Peshekhonov, whose article in *Russkoe Bogatstvo* we have just analysed. Let us now consider the programme of the land reformers.

It was presented in journalistic form recently in the Petersburg *Syn Otechestva*, an organ which formerly gave a platform to the ideas of the Union of Liberation, and which has been, since 15 November, the party organ of the 'Socialist Revolutionary' Populists under the editorship of G. J. Schreider, N. Kudrin, V. A. Mäkotin, A. V. Peshekhonov, and V. M. Chernov.

In its programme it picks up the ideas of Chernyshevskii, as well as Lavrov, and finally Mikhailovskii, and expressly advocates 'socialism' in the sense of 'socializing all means of production and all the economic activity of man'. It designates the rejection of developmental theory as a feature which distinguishes it from Marxism:

> Our party does not have the tendency to bend before reality and to make fetishes out of facts. The idea that new principles of social order cannot be called into being until the existing social order has completed its development is foreign to us. The 'framework' of this order has nothing sacred about it.

As we see, this is the same pragmatic, rationalist idea which underlies the socialism of Lavrov and the 'sociology' of Mikhailovskii, which attributes the 'unplanned nature' of social development in Western Europe to the idea that science and 'knowledge of social matters' did not exist in the past. The next tasks of the party should be: the achievement of political liberty on the basis of absolute domination by the 'will of the people', 'in whatever form it may express itself' – a connection to the old narodnaia volia.

The objective is a democratic federal state with proportional elections and referendum; the basic social demand is that land ownership is to be 'socialized' and placed in the hands of 'territorial associations', and that 'all working people' should have the right to land use. The question of a general socialization ('nationalization' or 'municipalization') of all means of production is, they say, at the moment not being considered, but the party would approve any take-over of economic activity by the community whenever and wherever possible, especially in the form of local businesses. Its immediate demands are for the eight-hour day, prohibition of child and female night work, and compulsory insurance.

It is scarcely likely that this group will gain ground among the peasants, in view of its highly 'intellectual' character. Nevertheless let us now return once again, for a closer illustration of Socialist Revolutionary ideas, to the agrarian thinking of Peshekhonov, who, as joint editor of the journal, seems best fitted to interpret their views.

The utilization of land by 'all workers' assumes, he argues, if it is not to be bondage, free 'access to the land' – for those, we should add, who *own* the *capital* to utilize it – and this free access in turn requires the breaking open of the 'peasants' ghetto', the granting of full economic freedom of movement. A 'free obshchina' can only – remarks Peshekhonov *contra* Novotorzhskii – be a 'voluntary' one, that is, a cooperative with no coercive character. Western Europe has attempted to achieve the same end by making land available for sale. But this (he continues) could lead to a system of income from land and – when competition from cheaper land emerged – could lead to agrarian crisis, against which Russia, as an exporting country, could not simply apply the remedy of customs duties but would instead be forced to accept the (evidently unthinkable) idea of cash subsidies. Approval of income from land and thus of private ownership of land is, however, absolutely out of the question: a natural process might create ownership of land, says Peshekhonov in characteristic vein – but deliberately to help to bring about the proletarianization which would be sure to follow would be morally unacceptable.

'But what should be done, then?' one asks oneself in the face of this comment, which reveals a high degree of resigned acceptance of the 'natural process' of capitalism's development. The reply is that the surplus yield [*Differenzialrente*], which arises through differences in the natural soil quality and the market situation, 'is due to society' and must therefore be transferred to society from the owners who have benefited. This transfer cannot, of course, be achieved by means of a fixed basic tax, but, since every new railway, every local industrial development or shift in the market yields further income, only through an 'elastic basic contribution'. (This, by the way, is not intended to be the 'Single Tax',[154] which Peshekhonov expressly rejects.) This contribution may be lowered in cases of emergency, and – we may add – in new cases of surplus yield – increased, in the form of a value added tax on the farmers who have benefited. To carry this process through is thus the essential purpose of 'socialization' of the land, and the purpose of abolition of private property is to bring about 'free access to the land'.[155]

If the democratic state of the future is here envisaged as an entity untouched by 'partisan hatreds and affections'[156] and operating according to 'objective' principles, the reformers cannot really be blamed, as even quite outstanding German economists [*Nationalökonomen*], and especially those who are most anxious to be seen as *realpolitiker*, sometimes hold similar views with regard to the present-day Prussian state.

The question now is: how should the state set about acquiring the land and collecting the tax? Certainly not simply by decree. Peshekhonov is quite clear about the astonishment that would greet his reforms if the impoverished peasants of the Black Earth, on the one hand, and the progressive peasants close to the cities, docks and railways, on the other, were informed, in effect, that his reforms would mean new taxes, and, what is more, on their land.

Instead, he believes one should proceed 'organically': the state should proceed to land acquisition in three cases: (1) in order to promote natural population distribution it should grant the peasant help in resettlement and receive in return his share of land (nadel) from his previous commune; it should (2) buy the share of every peasant who leaves a village commune; and finally (3) every instance of transition to a 'capitalist' economy should be followed by immediate expropriation. Of course, in all these cases, depending on the sums of money involved, this could equally well hasten the breakup of the village communes, as well as acting as a brake on the development of a technically 'progressive' economy.

It is not yet certain what the characteristics of a 'capitalist' economy should be, in view of the very broad definition that is commonly applied to it in Russia: whether it should include not only the landowners and kulaks, who cultivate purchased or leased land, but also all owners of individual farms or indeed all farmers who employ waged labour. Peshekhonov does not wish the village communes to be compulsory associations [*Zwangsverbände*]; only public regional corporations [*Gebietskörperschaften*] should have this function. A (socialist) 'national economy' i.e. control by public associations [*Herrschaftsverbände*] is more likely to be achieved by 'municipalization' than by a system of profes-

Bourgeois Democracy in Russia   89

sional associations, with their concomitant private economic conflicts of interest; these public associations should be as large as possible, since the larger they are, the better suited they are to developing the 'spirit of society'. Just as today the local zemstvos are less democratic than the provincial zemstvos, so large associations are in general more progressive than small communes. Only in large associations is the intelligentsia active, and democracy only flourishes where the intelligentsia is to be found.

Where it is a question of 'ideals', one must *centralize*, and only where the interests of the mass, which recognizes no ideals, are directly concerned, should the local associations have control. With this Jacobin idea, well-known from the history of the French 'Convention',[157] which is at the opposite pole from the original ideals of all categories of 'Populism' and of the federalist Socialist Revolutionaries,[158] as well as from socialists like Dragomanov, Peshekhonov makes a pragmatic defence of the all-powerful state: a worrying foretaste of the *centralist-bureaucratic* path which Russia could all too easily take, under the influence of radical theoreticians.

Today's obshchina should, then, according to Peshekhonov, be divested of its character as landowner – and yet the state should negotiate (either solely or at least principally) with 'cooperatives' of farmers about its proposed distribution of land. Again, this is difficult to reconcile with what has been said about the reprehensible nature of trade associations.

Here once again, then, is the link with the village commune, from which, however, every trace of coercion is to be eliminated. The obshchina, where it exists, cannot in fact, either technically or psychologically, be easily dispensed with.

The Young Populists are clearly quite correct in their view that the mass of the *peasants themselves* will not support an agrarian programme which is 'individualistic' in the West European sense. This also explains why the Democrats are reluctant to tackle the issue. First of all there is no doubt that in the question of the preservation of the village commune – however much the resolutions on redistribution are the product of an extremely bitter class struggle – by no means *only* economic class interest, but also firmly rooted concepts of 'natural law', are at work.

There can be no question that resolutions in favour of land redistribution are not normally passed solely by the votes of those who hope for an improvement of their situation from it or who have been intimidated by beatings or boycotts. On the other hand, admittedly, it is also certain that land redistribution, perhaps the most important agrarian democratic element of this social constitution, is frequently little more than a paper exercise, as far as its effect on social policy is concerned. The well-off peasants lease, sell, bequeath their land (naturally only within the commune), trusting that no redistribution will be agreed – or fellow members of the commune may be in debt to these wealthy peasants, and any redistribution in practice merely strengthens their control. And since it is only land that is redistributed, not livestock or economic capital, it is compatible with the most ruthless exploitation of the weak.

Increased land values and increased differentiation bring with them radicalism among the masses, angered by the discrepancy between the law and the facts. This communist radicalism seems bound to increase, *especially* if the situation of the peasants is improved, that is, if their burdens are lightened and the amount of land at the disposal of the commune is increased. For in regions where the obligations placed upon the land holdings exceed the yield – and these are not uncommon – land ownership is regarded as an imposition which every member of the village cooperative tries to evade. Conversely, redistribution is always sought after by the masses in those cases where the yield exceeds the obligations. The regions of best land are therefore the regions where the mass of the people have the most compelling interest in redistribution, and where the wealthy peasants have the most powerful contrary interest. Every alleviation of taxes and burdens, such as the current remission of redemption payments, must then – *if* the commune is to remain – serve to *increase* these focal points of communism and social struggle.

It is a well-known fact that in many cases the German peasants in southern Russia only introduced a strict commune system when the government increased land ownership, and it is not difficult to understand why. Any expansion of nadel[159] is almost certain to give a considerable boost to faith in communism. The hopes of the Socialist Revolutionaries in this regard seem well founded. Yet for honest agrarian reformers there is *today* no alternative to this programme of nadel extension.

The Constitutional Democratic Party has determined to stick, in its agrarian programme (points 36–40), to the relevant demands of the Union of Liberation and of the Liberal Agrarian Congress, while making some far-reaching concessions to the objections of the Socialist Revolutionaries. Amongst these concessions are:

1 the demand that compensation of landowners to be expropriated must *not be based on the market value*, but on a 'fair price' (point 36);
2 the express demand of legal guarantee of renewal of lease, possibly of the right of the leaseholder to compensation for improvements made, and, especially, the creation of *courts of law* (on the Irish model)[160] for the reduction of 'disproportionately high' rents (point 39);

Bourgeois Democracy in Russia 91

3 the creation of an agricultural inspectorate to control the handling of the legislation for protection of workers, which is to be extended to agriculture.

The principles according to which expropriated land is to be assigned to the peasants (either personal or community assignment for property or utilization) should be established 'according to the particular nature of land ownership and utilization of land in the various areas of Russia'.

We have already seen[161] that the regulation of agrarian conditions was to be a matter for the democratic self-governing bodies – a clear approach to the Socialist Revolutionary idea of 'territorial associations' as upholders of the 'right to land'.

This strongly radical agrarian programme does not lag very far behind what the *Revoliutsionnaia Rossiia* regarded as achievable a few years ago – but, under the impact of the unexpected successes of the revolution, it no longer satisfies either the politically radicalized Populists, nor the land-reforming Socialist Revolutionaries, nor the Leninist Social Democrats – nor, understandably, the broad lower strata of the peasants themselves, to the extent that they have been 'awakened', as it still leaves private ownership of the land unscathed.

When the peasants and the radical social reformers demand that the landowners' land be confiscated as 'unjust goods' and given to them, it is hardly surprising that they are unimpressed by the occasionally heard practical objection that they could not, without more implements, cultivate this land. If their own land, as is usually the case, does not suffice, the peasants have only the choice of either being leaseholders (often subleaseholders) of or labourers for the estate owner, or of working (very often with their own implements) in the extensive regions in which grain is produced for export. Where these conditions exist, it is these people who even today work the estate land with their own tools. Four-fifths of the grain coming on to the market is said to be the product of 'peasant' labour (although in the Black Earth region the extent of private property is usually given as five-twelfths of the total area and one-third of the cultivated land). Confiscation of farmland can thus only appear to the peasant as expropriation of a monopolistic class of *rentiers*.[162]

The government has done its part, both centuries ago and in recent times, to increase still further the communist character of the peasant movement, which (character) has its origins in the agrarian social order [*Agrarverfassung*], and, for reasons which have already been mentioned,[163] seems bound to intensify anyway.

The idea that land ownership is subject to the sovereign will of the state power (which overrides any private right, however properly acquired)[164] has its origins in the old Muscovite state, like the village commune, although some maintain that the latter owes its origin entirely to the Moscow tax legislation and *glebae adscriptio*.[165] It is also a fact – even if some liberal civil servants have proceeded differently in practice – that the eradication of 'acquired' rights and transfer to the commune was part of the government programme of Count Kiselev[166] under Nicholas I, and that this programme has been implemented and remains in force in our century.

The policy of the last decade has, however, been to replace 'historical' peasant communism with the principle of '*state* provision of all peasants with land';[167] until then, peasant communism had been, as the peasants wished, 'village communism', that is, it had lawfully claimed the land of the home village as the property of the villagers and of these only,[168] and in addition had looked to the estate land as having been really promised to the peasants by the 'Tsar Liberator'.[169]

Ever since the law of 1893,[170] the government has increasingly divested the mir of its actively cooperative character and attempted to transform it into a passive object of the activity of its officials, under authoritarian control and leadership. Land redistribution takes place increasingly under the control of, and that means, normally, on the instructions of, the authorities, even if the redistribution resolution itself is the outcome of an internal class struggle in the village. And above all, by the law of 1893 the government has treated the peasants' private property with contempt, property which has, according to existing laws and promises made, been validly *acquired* by means of the redemption payments. It has done this by arbitrarily restricting the utilization of this property to the commune. If, now that the state has thus weakened their sense of property and claimed the right and ability to exercise control, the peasants hand over to the state the duty to bear the responsibility to provide for them and to provide land, from wherever it might come – this is no more than a natural consequence of state policy.

All things considered, then, the execution of the reform programme of the Bourgeois Democrats would be most likely to lead to a massive increase of the agrarian communist and social revolutionary 'spirit' amongst the peasants, a spirit which is today already so strong that at least the mass of the peasants could not be won over[171] to an individualistic programme such as the one advocated by Struve.[172]

The peculiarity of the situation of Russia seems to be that an increase in 'capitalist' development, together with the simultaneously rising value of the land and its products, *can* bring with it *beside* the further development of the industrial proletariat and thus of 'modern' socialism, also an increase in 'archaic' *agrarian* communism.

In the sphere of the 'intellectual movement' too there is still doubt about the 'possibilities' inherent in current developments.

The aura of the Narodnichestvo, which is still discernible throughout the 'intelligentsia' of every shade of opinion, and of all classes and political programmes, will fade, but the question remains as to what will replace it. Such a purely factual conception of things as that represented by social reforming liberalism will not, without a hard struggle, succeed in capturing the 'broad' character of the Russian spirit. For in the case of the Socialist Revolutionary intelligentsia this romantic radicalism has another side to it: the leap to the authoritarian and reactionary camp is an extremely easy one for it. This is due to its closeness to 'state socialism', a proximity which, though disputed, is none the less a fact. Thus the relatively common phenomenon of the rapid metamorphosis of extremely radical students into highly 'authoritarian' civil servants, of which chiefly foreign, but also conscientious Russian observers often tell, does not – assuming the accuracy of the fact – arise from innate characteristics or contemptible materialism, as is sometimes asserted. The opposite process, the sudden transition from firm support for the pragmatic bureaucratic rationalism represented by Plehve and Pobedonostsev into the extreme Socialist Revolutionary camp, has also occurred in recent years a number of times.

Underlying these extremes is a pragmatic rationalism which thirsts for the 'deed' in the service of the absolute social and ethical norm, and, on the sounding board of agrarian communist ideas, wavers between the 'creative' deed from 'above' and that from 'below', and thus falls prey to a romanticism which may be either reactionary or revolutionary.

We come now to the views expressed by the peasants themselves.

To the extent that the demands of the peasants are spontaneously expressed, as in the numerous resolutions of their assemblies and again in addresses, such as the impromptu speech at the spring conference of an agricultural cooperative in the Kharkov province, the subject is always, apart from the reduction of taxes and dues and the constantly recurring demand for compulsory schooling, two simple things.

1 To do away with the interference of the minor [*subaltern*], and even more, the noble country civil servants, especially the *Zemskie Nachalniki* (the land captains created by the government as police controllers).[173] 'We beg you, lord, save us from our civil servants, these overseers,[174] gendarmes and land captains. They cost you and us dear, lord, and they do not even keep order for us but prevent us from living and working, and they offend us . . . Ask them sternly, lord, who is to blame that the people are kept in ignorance, why there are no good schools here, why we

have to read books and newspapers which suit them,[175] why we are all so downtrodden. It is all their fault, lord. Let us elect our own officials, lord; we have sensible people with good ideas, who know our needs. They will not cost us or you much money and they will be more use.'[176] To this they always add the desire to meet freely to discuss their own affairs again as they once could.[177]

2   The second general demand is for *more land*: 'The land your grandfather gave remains the same, but the people have multiplied without number. Those who received land shares have already five or six grandchildren, and these also have growing children, and they are without land.' With elemental force this common denominator, to which all the popular movements without exception reduce the agrarian question, found expression in the constituting congress of the Pan-Russian Peasant League of 31 July and 1 August (Old Calendar) 1905 in Moscow – or, to be more exact, in a large barn off the main road near Moscow![178]

This was really a parade of leaders of the Socialist Revolutionary Party and a trumpeting of their agitational successes. Its deliberations do provide symptomatic interest, in that they provide an indication of the state of the movement.

In May the organizations led by the Socialist Revolutionaries had spread over only 40 volosts in 7 provinces. At the congress 28 provinces were represented by about 100 deputies. The north-west and west had hardly any representatives at all, the extreme north, south and south-east scarcely any, but on the other hand there was a fair representation of the centre and the Black Earth region including eastern Ukraine. To judge by the deputies, the organization for which Moscow was responsible was particularly far advanced in parts of the Ukraine and of the province of Kursk (Black Earth). For Vladimir, Tula (both are industrial areas), Kazan (east), Vologda (north), its weakness was expressly stated and was explained by the lack of unity of interest amongst the peasantry; in Orel it had been able, in spite of its weakness, to achieve a reduction of rent by half.

This kind of organization of the peasants for the purpose of achieving purely practical economic aims within the given social order – mostly, admittedly, identical with the *political* order – has since, to judge by the numerous reports in the press, made extraordinarily significant progress. However, it appears that this progress has been greatest in those areas of the south and Ukraine which are not strictly commune areas, and is less apparent in the centre and in Belorussia,[179] where perhaps the purely destructive character of the *kramola* [see Glossary] is predominant.

Everywhere the incentive was provided by the rescript of 18 February 1905, which was made known to the peasants both by the newspapers and by the eager activity of the proletarian intelligentsia.[180] What especially gave rise to determined resistance was the fact, noted almost everywhere, that the officials had tried to conceal it. People had appealed to the rescript to support their opposition to police prohibitions on assembly. They had begun to read newspapers or to have them read to them (especially *Syn Otechestva*), they had drawn up *prigovors* (resolutions) in the *skhod* (village assembly), and written proclamations and petitions to the Tsar. Everywhere the authorities tried to frustrate the movement, as did often – but by no means always – the priests, and regularly the landowners and kulaks.

It was therefore proposed in the congress to have a maximum census qualification (50 desiatins [see Glossary]) and to admit no non-peasant, not even the 'intelligentsia'; yet, after a turbulent debate, a decision on this was left to the local organizations. The suspicion of all authority, which led to the demand that committees of the League should be given 'executive only' mandates, and the strictly democratic climate of the congress,[181] and finally the fact that it wished to be regarded only as the representative of people who 'live by the labour of their hands', in strict contrast to the landowners and their representatives in the zemstvos – all this did not prevent the *urgent warning* being sounded by various deputies, despite their own radical convictions, against personal attacks on the Tsar. Similarly there emerged, alongside hatred and contempt for the priests and the monasteries, fear of their influence and, at least here and there, also sympathy for the monasteries as organizations of altruism and communism. In the land question, which was at the centre of the debate, there was a difference of opinion in only two points:

(1) In whose favour was the land to be formally expropriated? With one vote against, the decision was in favour of the 'generality', though the question was to be further discussed in the village assemblies.

A representative of the Chernigov province had spoken out decidedly against any theory of 'nationalization', another from Vladimir had come forward to speak in favour of the peasant commune as a future bearer of property – both were, however, for expropriation in the same degree as the rest.

The only one to come out against expropriation in principle was the representative of *Social Democracy*, who, like other 'intelligentsia', had only a consultative vote; this view was quite in harmony with the earlier theories of the Plekhanov group, but was contrary to current Social Democratic practice.[182] Abolition of private ownership, not only of factories and industrial means of production, but also of farm land, was said to be impossible at present, because the capitalist development of agriculture was not yet sufficiently advanced. The land was only a 'gift of nature' – the other speakers usually said 'gift of God' – in the same sense as are wood, cotton, or wool, which all have to be first turned into consumer goods by means of labour and tools, that is, by 'capital'. The peasants today needed capital, but capital could at this time only be formed on the basis of private ownership.[183] Only a political revolution was possible in Russia at the moment, not an economic one.[184]

However, this assembly would hear nothing of theories derived from 'developmental history'.[185]

(2) The assembly sought only general principles for a just decision on the second question: whether the land, i.e. all agriculturally utilizable land, should be expropriated with or without compensation. As an example of 'unconstrained ethical thinking', the discussion was quite interesting.

There was unanimous agreement that the Tsar, the Grand Dukes, the Church and – after a few initial objections on account of their 'communist' character – the monasteries, should give up their land for nothing, since it was essentially public property and was in many cases not really used. The principle of remuneration for all private property was asserted by individual representatives from the north (Vologda), the Black Sea region and the Ukraine, i.e. those areas where because of the absence of the commune system the sense of property is relatively the most developed. The great majority, and in particular the representatives of the Black Earth region, as well as those from the north-east (Viatka), where the land even today often has no commercial value, were of a different opinion, and sought only to consider those peasants who had bought land; their interests were energetically defended. There was first an attempt to distinguish between inherited and purchased land, whereby the inherited land was regarded as less sacred. For the original acquisition of land which initiates all inheritance rights was always an act of force, or at least an act of acquisition without payment – listeners were reminded of Catherine II's gifts of land to her lovers – just as unlawful as the appropriating of air and light would be. Thus the mere fact of inheriting could not confer legal title – a view which completely corresponds to the situation in commune areas, where it is not the family but the village which confers ownership on an individual. By contrast, purchase by an individual was not illegal: even the spontaneous 'prigovers' of the peasants, as was admitted by an opponent of compensation, had permitted compensation for land which had been purchased. Of course, though, a time limit in the past must be established, was the rejoinder. After a certain time, be it 20 or 30 years, the purchased land had reimbursed the owner for the purchase price or the capital outlay, or could have done, and must therefore be allowed to be taken away without compensation – a kind of reversal of usucapion.[186] This is thoroughly in accord with the consideration customarily shown by the commune when redistributing land (where its technique is sufficiently refined) towards owners who have carried out improvements.

However: land bought by the larger owners, including the kulaks, it was objected, was not morally justified acquisition at all: one does not earn sufficient money 'with calloused hands' to buy land – and the representative of the Socialist Revolutionaries reminded his listeners of the saying that was used against the kulaks: 'You do not get to live in stone houses from honest toil.' Anyhow, the majority finally agreed that one never acquires much land from one's wages – and this alone was merited income – and that a maximum area of land should be determined, above which nothing should be paid in compensation. Figures of either 50 or 100 desiatins were suggested. Given the differing quality of the soil, a deputy finally proposed making the minimum living wage of a 'civilized person' the basis and thus establishing a yield of 600 roubles, equivalent to a capital value of 10,000 roubles, as the maximum level of compensation. The representative of the Socialist Revolutionaries regarded it as lacking in humanity to expose the landowners (who have no experience of work) to privation and hunger, and therefore proposed a pension for life. But there could be no question of compensation for land ownership as such. That was greeted with loud applause. The delegates finally agreed on a vague formula: that the land should be expropriated partly with and partly without compensation. The rather rambling appeal of the League calls for a struggle for justice, freedom and land in union with the workers and the intelligentsia, singles out the police as the chief enemy, speaks of the need not to allow other classes 'to shut the door of the Duma in their faces', and declares as its goal: 'the land to those who work it with their hands'.

No one can say to what extent this Socialist Revolutionary programme is today the conscious possession of the peasants. Certainly, it is true to say that as far as they 'think' politically, it would be impossible to win them over to an antiliberal union with the nobility: this is a peculiarity of the situation in Russia, in contrast to Germany.[187] On the other hand they are certainly not 'liberal'.

It remains uncertain how strongly the economically more advanced peasants, e.g. those in the south and south-east, or the stratum of 'village bourgeoisie' will influence opinion in favour of 'bourgeois' democracy in the election, and it remains unclear what role the priests, who are essentially peasants too,[188] will play.[189]

The difficulties of any anti-authoritarian agitation which does not content itself with incitement to violence but aims to work for political parties must of course be tremendous, since Witte has not removed press censorship in the countryside and a great many of the nobility, the civil servants, and, more importantly, many of the Orthodox clergy have begun to organize the peasants in a conservative direction from Moscow.

Press reports to the effect that in many provinces, such as Vladimir, peasant organizations have joined the Constitutional Democratic Party, merely reserving the right to their own 'interpretation' of the liberal agrarian programme, cause one to question what this really means, since one can read at the same time that the Constitutional Democratic Congress was attended not only by the nobility and the clergy, but also by the state civil service, including the Zemskie Nachalniki, a class of civil servants which represents, as we have seen, the main enemy of the peasants. However, the radical zemstvo officialdom, the 'Third Element', which generally adopts the same standpoint as the Union of Unions, that is, in part that of the Socialist Revolutionaries and in part that of the Social Democrats, is in the closest touch with the peasants, indeed at the peasants' congress the inclination was expressly stated of merging with them.[190]

[*Weber gives a brief account of the Second Pan-Russian Peasants Congress, about which he could obtain only scanty information.*]

What will the peasants now do in the election? The resistance of the peasants to the influence of civil servants and conservative clerics is clearly of varying strength. It is apparently at its strongest, understandably, not in the genuinely poverty-stricken districts but for instance in the south, in the cossack villages, and in the Chernigov and Kursk provinces.

In these and moreover in many districts of the industrial zone the peasants have not infrequently drawn up the most severe resolutions, in spite of the presence of either the state police, or the marshals of the nobility. They have covered petitions with thousands of signatures for the removal of bureaucratic supervision and for the permission to hold elections for people's representatives, who – and this is crucial and *quite unlike modern parliamentarism* – should deal *directly with the Tsar*, instead of the paid officialdom interposing between them.

In other words, they wish for the disappearance of the bureaucracy of autocracy, but – here the Slavophiles are quite right – they cherish no wish for its replacement by a bureaucracy led by parliament.

The energy of this antibureaucratic trend is, at the moment, not inconsiderable. There are quite a few cases in which the peasants have rejected 'loyal' resolutions prepared by the civil servants for the skhod, and others where they have accepted them in the presence of the civil servants, and later withdrawn them, or have sent back publications of reactionary associations which had been sent to them. However, it is unlikely that this mood could be powerful enough to determine the outcome of the elections, in the face of the oppressive authority of the civil servants.

The electoral law, even in the version of 11 December,[191] seeks to nullify free electoral agitation by permitting assemblies of voters and electors to hold 'preparatory' discussions on the person of the candidates without the police being present, but only allows those entitled to vote and the electors to take part in these discussions (admission is checked by the police!). An exception to this principle, amazingly, is made for the *civil servant* (marshal of the nobility or his representative) who is *the president in charge of the election, even when he is not himself a voter or elector.*

The principle of election 'from amongst their own members', or 'from the number of those entitled to participate', is maintained,[192] although the practical application of this principle at elections in the United States[193] is known to depress the level of the legislatures greatly – undoubtedly one of the purposes of this regulation. In the cities all this has a largely formal significance. However, what the supervision of the electoral assemblies in the country means, particularly amongst the peasants themselves, is something which everyone, *especially* the peasants themselves, whose *principal demand* is the removal of supervision by the civil servants, must answer for themselves. The government, which is obviously *only* focusing on the *short term*, has thus handed over *permanently* to the radicals the most convenient (and most legitimate) propaganda argument. It will, most probably, 'gain' conservative peasant representatives – but every peasant will know that they do not represent *him*. The number of reasons for him to hate the bureaucracy is increased by one.

Yet no one can say how the peasant vote at the Duma elections will turn out. Foreigners generally tend to expect an extreme reactionary composition of the Duma, whereas Russians rather expect in spite of everything an extreme revolutionary one, as far as the peasants are concerned. Either could be right, and, what is more important, the end result could be the same in either case. In the European revolutions of modern times the peasants have in general veered from the most extreme radicalism imaginable to apathy or virtually to political reaction, once their immediate economic demands have been met. There is in fact no doubt that, *if* a complete or partial act of force by the autocracy should stop the peasants' mouths with land or if they were to take the land for themselves in a state of anarchy and were allowed, in one way or another, to keep it, for the vast majority of them that would be the end of the matter and their interest in the form of government would thereby be ended.[194]

The opinion of the representatives of Bourgeois Democracy – especially that of Struve – is, by contrast, that the desire of the peasants for land cannot be fulfilled by a reactionary government, since the realization of that desire would mean economic dispossession not only of the nobility, but also of the Grand Dukes and finally of the Tsar himself. Their view is that the interests of the peasants are irreconcilable with the interest of self-preservation of these powers. And yet in spite of the formidable extent of the estates of the Imperial house, this is still greatly exceeded by that in private ownership, and the hatred of the peasants is directed particularly against the latter.

The question then arises as to which and how many of the peasants' demands the Democrats would be able to satisfy.

Struve spoke out against a simple confiscation of land with the greatest vigour. Nevertheless, the Constitutional Democratic programme states that those expropriated should *not* be reimbursed at the market value of the land, which, from the 'bourgeois' standpoint, amounts to 'confiscation'. [. . .] All the same, it appears that some of the nobility, this very diverse stratum, which extends, according to one of Nicholas I's Education Ministers, 'from the steps of the throne to the ranks of the peasantry', is, under current conditions, not disinclined to hand over its land. 'One prefers to live in liberty in a country house without land than, as now, possessing land but in a fortress,' said Prince Dolgorukov at the Liberal Moscow Agrarian Congress. In contrast, the Congress of Agricultural Entrepreneurs, which was held behind closed doors in Moscow in December 1905, called for unconditional repression.

Whichever way one looks at it, for a non-repressive government land costs a tremendous amount of *money*. Land suitable for colonization is there to be won, especially in the south-east, and in the north-east of the vast empire too – if huge capital sums are made available for irrigation and (in Siberia) for clearing forests. The abolition of redemption payments, tax reductions for the peasants, *civil list* expenditure to compensate the Imperial family for the loss of their land, the loss of rent from the domains, provision of melioration capital, all this means a huge reduction in state income and tremendous extra requirements. In short, it means the problem of raising unprecedented amounts of money.

Bourgeois Democracy in Russia 101

And finally, since the increase of land ownership alone simply cannot solve the agrarian problem (indeed this strategy, if pursued as the *only* solution, may threaten 'technical progress'); and since one would have to expect major disappointment amongst the peasants even after having satisfied all their demands; and since the peasants at their present state of development can scarcely be considered as 'bearers' or 'pillars' but essentially as 'objects' of agrarian policy – in view of all these factors, the party that aims to carry through the reform *by legal means* has an unenviable task.

On the other hand the government has so far only agreed to the waiving of redemption payments, the extension (by means of 30 million roubles of new capital) of the activity of the Peasant Land Bank [see Glossary] to include the transfer of land from the estate-owners to the peasants, and finally, in rather vague words, it has agreed to put in hand agrarian reform to 'reconcile' the interests of the estate-owners with those of the peasants.[195] In spite of all the 'committees' of the past years, it remains most questionable whether the government has the least idea about how to do these things.

The vitally important question remains, as to how the government on the one hand, and the peasants on the other, will come to terms with the legal *right* of *every* peasant, once redemption payments have been ended, *to be allocated his share of private property.*

The Progress of the Revolution

Sacrifices will be necessary for Russian Liberal Democrats seeking social reform.

They have no choice, both according to their conception of duty and according to considerations which are determined by the demogogic behaviour of the old regime, than unconditionally to demand universal equal franchise. And yet their own ideas could, probably, only achieve political influence under an electoral process similar to the zemstvo franchise. They are duty bound to help to defend a type of agrarian reform which, in all probability, must powerfully strengthen (as both economic practice and attitude of the masses) not economically and technically 'progressive' voluntarist socialism, but the essentially archaic communism of the peasants – that is, not economic selection of the most efficient in the 'business' sense, but 'ethical' equalization of opportunity – and thus retard the development of Western European individualistic culture, a development which most believe inevitable.

The type of 'complacent' German who cannot bear not to be 'on the side of the victors', puffed up by the elevating consciousness of his quality as a *realpolitiker*,[196] can only look with pity on such a movement.

It is true that the liberals' instruments of power are flimsy, a fact to which the extreme Socialist Revolutionaries, too, constantly point with scorn. In fact nobody knows where things would stand today without the intimidation of the autocracy brought about by the death of Plehve and of Grand Duke Sergei.

The only comparable instrument of power possessed by the liberals lies in the fact that the *officer corps* could not for ever remain willing to act as executioners of families from which they themselves to a large degree have come.

Indeed the tactic recommended by the liberals has often been effective, namely, not, as some of the Socialist Revolutionaries constantly did, to goad the troops into fighting by means of bombs and armed resistance, but to place themselves unarmed in their path. Admittedly, all this would have its limitations faced with a determined military leadership, and the present uprising in Moscow[197] will be *very* beneficial to the discipline of the army.

In addition to this there is now another, specifically 'bourgeois' instrument of power, but it is not in the hands of the Russian liberals. Without the warning from foreign financiers – not in so many words but by implication[198] – the Manifesto of 17 October would perhaps never have been issued or at least it would soon have been revoked. Fear of the rage of the masses and of the mutiny of the troops, and the weakening of the authoritarian regime by defeat in the east, would have been ineffective had not the autocracy been at the mercy of the cool, hard hand of the banks and stock exchanges.

The position of politicians like Witte and Timiriazev rests upon this fact. And when the Social Democratic *Nachalo* termed Count Witte an 'agent of the stock market', this crude description was not entirely without justification. After all, in the area of constitutional questions and domestic administration Witte scarcely has any particular convictions.

At any rate his various declarations on these subjects clearly contradict each other, and he has also acquired the habit of denying as 'misunderstandings' statements which people beyond suspicion have reported him as making, even in the case of negotiations with party delegates, i.e. not confidential conversations. His interests centre quite definitely on matters of economic policy.

For example, and whatever else one may think of him, he has had the 'courage' (from his point of view) to defend peasant private ownership. Accordingly, he is viewed with an equal amount of odium by both the reactionary bureaucracy and the revolutionary democrats. Equally, he now bears the increased hatred of the Slavophiles and even the personal dislike of the Tsar, which is only exacerbated by his 'indispensability'.[199] Without any doubt his thinking is 'capitalist' in orientation – as is also that of liberals of Struve's stripe.

In contrast to Plehve's attempts to govern with the aid of the masses, under authoritarian leadership, against the 'bourgeoisie', Witte would no doubt be very pleased to have an understanding with the property-owning classes against the masses. He, and perhaps only he, is able to preserve Russia's credit and its currency at the present time, and it is certain that he possesses the will to do this. He undoubtedly knows very well that, in order to do this, it is an essential requirement that Russia be transformed into a state governed by the rule of law, backed by certain constitutional guarantees. If he were able, he would probably take the appropriate domestic political action, in order not to jeopardize his life's ambition to make Russia financially powerful. In addition, there is the idea that a 'genuinely' liberal regime would strengthen the political alliance with France.

These motives in favour of a liberal policy carry, of course, only limited weight with Witte, let alone with the Tsar and his entourage. The question is only: what degree of stress will they withstand, before the temptation to resort to a military dictatorship as a preliminary to some kind of fake constitutionalism becomes too strong to resist? Such an outcome is of course well within the bounds of possibility in the near future. If even a tenth of the officer corps and the troops remain at the disposal of the government – and the fraction would be likely to be closer to nine-tenths[200] – then any number of rebels would be powerless against them. The stock market welcomed the first blood in the streets of Moscow with a boom – and everything that has happened since has shown how powerfully this has strengthened the forces of reaction and changed Witte's mind.

The economic distress that must follow the dreadful devastation of industry, will, after having shattered political illusions, inevitably paralyse the proletariat's fighting spirit. And the foreign observer is bound to anticipate the emergence of a government which, in effect, preserves the power position of the centralist *civil service* – this is what counts. For the social forces which maintained the previous regime are undoubtedly now better organized than appearances suggest.

The resurgence of these social forces was boosted by the sectarian and small-minded attitude of the 'professional socialists', who (despite the organized murdering gangs of police officers whose very existence was under threat) urged their supporters to attack the bourgeois democratic parties 'competing' with them and thus gave vent to their need to hurl insults, a need which, as we in Germany well know, is politically impotent and above all destructive of all political education, however 'humanly' understandable it may be.[201]

Their only triumph is likely to be either that the forces of reaction completely gain the upper hand, or that broad strata of the property owners go over to the 'moderate' camp, thus securing the right (just as here in Germany), for the span of another generation, to indulge in the empty lamentation 'Oh, what dreadful people there are in the world!'

[*Weber assesses the relative strengths of various conservative parties and groups, including, amongst the more extreme, the 'Monarchist Party' and the 'League of Russian Men', and amongst the more moderate (*freikonservativ*) the 'Party of Legal Order' and the 'Union of 17 October'.*]

On 20 November, the Party of Legal Order[202] offered Count Witte help with strike-breaking in the threatened postal and telegraph stoppage. Such groups as these were joined by the moderate city duma and zemstvo members, the genuine bourgeoisie (bankers and big industrialists) and people who, like Krasovskii, took the view at the beginning of the zemstvo congresses that the demand should be for the attainment not of a constitution but of a legal guarantee of personal and press freedom – without, admittedly, being able to state what these would mean in practice without a constitution. What these groupings have in common beside recognition of the Manifesto of 17 October, to which as we know the old conservative civil servants responded with the butchery of the 'black hundreds',[203] and which they had sought to undermine, is undisguised religious indifference.[204] It is also true of them that they were for 'peace' at all costs and supported any measure that could bring this about.

The Petersburg 'League of Legal Order' endorsed the enfranchisement of the Jews, 'to calm them down'.[205] The Petersburg census voters, after a long debate, decided for the autonomy of Poland for the same reason. In other assemblies of census voters, contrary to the radical demand for separation of State and Church, the retention of instruction in the 'divine law' (catechism) was described as indispensable for the maintenance of order, and so on. So they will all finally be satisfied with anything the Tsar sees fit to concede to them.

Obviously, under the pressure of peasant and military revolts, the threat of a general strike and of the putschism which is prevalent in Social Democracy, the number of these people began to rise rapidly. And it was of course also the hope of the government, and especially of Witte, that anarchy would work in the interests of conservatism, and that, as Witte put it, finally 'society itself' would demand that order was established, and – may we add – a place be made for the slogan 'enrichissez-vous!'[206]

And this was indeed what happened.

Of course, this development took place at the expense of constitutional zemstvo democracy. The time of the zemstvo congresses was over, as Prince Dolgorukov remarked with resignation.[207] Indeed, the hour of the ideological gentry had passed, and the power of material interests resumed its normal course. In this process political idealism was eliminated on the left, as was, on the right, moderate Slavophilism, which was concerned with the extension of zemstvo self-government.

The eclipse of both did not cause Witte much grief. Nevertheless, it is in reality probable that Witte's wait-and-see policy has done the work for others or rather that he did not have the power to do anything else. In the eyes of the court he is no doubt regarded as essentially a place-man who is now indispensable because of the impression he makes abroad, especially on the stock markets, and also because of his intelligence. For there has never been any doubt about the attitude of elements in the government close to the *court*. The higher administrative officials of those regions in which, according to reports which are above suspicion and beyond dispute, the police have seized the initiative in organizing the civil war, have, in individual cases, been disciplined in order to placate foreign opinion, but, in the process, like our Prussian 'Canal Rebels',[208] they have been 'kicked upstairs'.[209]

Count Witte, however, made no serious attempt, and perhaps was unable, to break the ruthless obstruction of the provincial civil service, which, for the time being, refused to believe in the prospect of a lasting constitutional regime. If the liberals felt that to be a lack of 'honesty', then that was understandable but perhaps not quite accurate: 'a rogue gives more than he has'[210] – the impediment resided at a higher level.

Numerous measures taken by the Interior Ministry, which could be read about in the newspapers, could have no other *effect* than by turns to rouse the masses and then deliberately to slacken the reins until the Red Terror had been inflated so far that the time was ripe for the White one. It is simply *not* believable that this policy was *exclusively* the product of weakness and confusion. There was a need for 'revenge for the 17 October'.[211]

What this policy incidentally also produced and no doubt was supposed to produce, over a longer period, undoubtedly had to be the discrediting of all libertarian movements, especially bourgeois constitutional *anticentralist* liberalism, whose importance in public opinion and standing in the bodies of self-government have for decades aroused the hatred of both the reactionary and the rationalistic state bureaucracy.

Undoubtedly, if there should for a time be complete anarchy, liberalism would have even less reason for hope than in the case of a revival of autocracy, the precursor of which, under present conditions, would in any case be anarchy.

It has been said that the original sin of every kind of radical politics is the ability 'to miss opportunities'. But the same applies equally to every kind of ideologically orientated politics. When Vincke once refused to negotiate in private with the ministers of the 'New Era' about the Army Bill which was due to be brought in, on the grounds that this was morally unacceptable for a people's representative,[212] and likewise when in 1893 the liberals were just a few minutes too late in getting to the resolution which they passed nonetheless after the dissolution of the Reichstag,[213] both occasions were fateful turning points for the cause of liberalism. One is tempted to assume, and many of Witte's statements suggest this judgement directly, that a similar accusation must be directed against the liberals in Russia with regard to the policy of their party. I myself had prima facie this impression in the autumn.

But the more one thinks about the situation the more one is forced to surmise that the liberals understood what they had to expect,[214] more accurately than did Count Witte, to judge by his remarks.[215] The two examples cited concern doubtless 'sincerely' meant proposals. In the present case, however, even the 'most moderate' constitutional zemstvo liberalism was offered absolutely *no* 'opportunity', and it evidently did not lie in its power to change fate, any more than it was in the power of Bennigsen in 1877, who at that time, on far better grounds than our historians usually assume, refused the offer of a place in Bismarck's Ministry.[216] For, just as Louis XVI wanted on no account to be 'rescued' by Lafayette,[217] nothing seems more certain than that court circles and the civil service would rather do a deal with the devil than with zemstvo liberalism. Political hostilities within the same social stratum or between rival social strata are often the most subjectively intense.

On the part of the government the furthest 'step towards the other side' was the invitation by Count Witte to the Moscow Uprava to send representatives of the zemstvo party to him for consultation.[218] This took place on 27 October (Old Calendar) between Witte and the delegates Golovin, Prince Lvov and Kokoshkin.[219] The decisive difference of opinion at that time was that Count Witte wanted to leave it to the Imperial Duma, which was to include representatives of the working class, to introduce universal equal secret franchise, and in return for this expressly offered the prospect of his cooperation, whereas the delegates insisted on the calling of a constituent Duma based on that franchise, as the only means of securing peace.

However, behind this supposed difference, apart from the old mistrust of the zemstvo people, lay the fact, which was a hindrance to *any* un-

Bourgeois Democracy in Russia 107

derstanding, that at that time Trepov was still in power, that later Durnovo took his place and remained there, although respected persons accused him in open letters to the newspapers, giving details of the cases, of accepting money 'even if only in small amounts' (122–1500 roubles) for favours,[220] and that the required precise declaration of the Manifesto of 17 October *never materialized* in the strict constitutional sense.

Witte's assurance that he felt 'closest' to the Constitutional Democratic zemstvo party could not possibly be believed in these circumstances, especially after his 'confidential memorandum' of the year 1899,[221] which stressed the irreconcilability of the zemstvos with autocracy and thus frustrated the intended general application of the zemstvo system.

The situation of Russia 'cries out', it is true, for a 'statesman' – but the dynastic ambitions of 'personal rule' leave as little place there for a great reformer – if one were to be found – as elsewhere, here in Germany, for instance.

So much seems certain: never for a single moment has the *Tsar* had any genuine intention of reaching a lasting and sincere understanding with these men, whom just six months previously he had described in most unparliamentary language. If one accepts this 'factor' as 'given', then it is undoubtedly true that Russia is 'not ready' for meaningful constitutional reform; but the liberals cannot be blamed for this. Unless quite different 'guarantees' were given, any 'understanding' which the government might reach with zemstvo liberalism would be politically quite pointless. Its supporters could do nothing but 'keep their record clean' after they had discharged their 'mission' in the degree and sense in which this was possible at that moment. For the time being they may have to be content for this brilliant movement of zemstvo liberalism, of which Russia has as much reason to be proud as we Germans have to be proud of the Frankfurt Parliament,[222] to be 'consigned to history', at least in its present form. This would probably be better for it in the end than a 'March ministry'.[223] Only thus can 'ideological' liberalism remain, within its ideal sphere, a 'force' unassailable by outward violence, and only thus does it seem possible to restore the unity, which in recent times has been shattered, between the 'bourgeois' intelligentsia, whose power derives from property, a broad education and political experience, and the quasi-proletarian intelligentsia, whose strength lies in their numbers, their close touch with the 'masses' and their tenacious fighting spirit. This restoration of unity should be possible once the latter, as the disappointments which lie ahead of them may lead them to do, have discarded their current underestimation of the true significance of the 'bourgeois' element, against which they have an 'instinctive' aversion.

The further development of capitalism will put an end to 'populist' romanticism. No doubt its place will largely be taken by Marxism. But the work to be done on the formidable and fundamental agrarian problem cannot possibly be undertaken with the intellectual tools of Marxism, and it is this work which could reunite the two strata of the 'intelligentsia'. Clearly this work can only be done by the organs of self-government and for this reason alone it seems vital that liberalism continues to see its vocation as fighting against both bureaucratic and Jacobin *centralism* and working at the permeation of the masses with the old individualistic basic idea of the 'inalienable rights of man', which have become as 'boring' to us Western Europeans as black bread is for the person who has enough to eat.

These axioms of 'natural law' no more give *unambiguous* guidelines for a social and economic programme than they themselves can be produced *unambiguously* by any – least of all 'modern' – economic conditions *alone*.

On the contrary, though the struggle for such 'individualistic' values must take account of the 'material' condition of the environment at every step, the realization of these values must not be left to 'economic development'. 'Democracy' and 'individualism' would stand little chance today if we were to rely for their 'development' on the 'automatic' effect of *material* interests. For these point as clearly as they can in the opposite direction. Whether in the shape of American 'benevolent feudalism', the German 'welfare institutions', or the Russian factory constitution – everywhere the empty shell for new serfdom stands ready; it will be occupied to the degree that the pace of technical-economic 'progress' slows down and the victory of 'income' over 'profit',[224] together with the exhaustion of what remains of 'free' lands and the 'free' markets, renders the masses 'compliant'.

At the same time the growing complexity of the economy, partial nationalization or 'municipalization', and the size of national territory, creates ever new paper work, further specialization and administrative training – which means the creation of a caste. Those American workers who were *against* 'Civil Service Reform'[225] knew what they were doing. They would rather have been governed by upstarts of dubious morality than by a class of professional mandarins – but their protest was in vain.

In view of all this, let those who live in constant fear that there could be *too much* 'democracy' and 'individualism' in the world and not enough 'authority', 'aristocracy' and 'respect for office' or the like, set their minds at rest. Every precaution has been taken to ensure that democratic individualism does not enjoy unrestricted growth. Experience teaches that 'History' constantly gives birth to 'aristocracies' and 'authorities', to which anyone who feels the need can cling, either for their own benefit or for that of the 'people'. If it were *only* a question of the 'material' conditions and the complex of interests directly or indirectly 'created' by them, any sober observer would have to say that all *economic* indicators point in the direction of growing 'unfreedom'. It is absolutely ridiculous to attribute to the high capitalism which is today being imported into Russia and already exists in America – this 'inevitable' economic development – any elective affinity with 'democracy' let alone with 'liberty' (in *any* sense of the word). The question should be: how can these things exist at all for any length of time under the domination of capitalism? In fact they are only possible where they are backed up by the determined *will* of a nation not to be ruled like a flock of sheep. We 'individualists' and supporters of 'democratic' institutions must swim 'against the tide' of material constellations. Anyone who wants merely to go along with the latest 'developmental trend' had better give up these old-fashioned ideals as soon as possible.

Modern 'liberty' arose from a unique, never to be repeated set of circumstances. Let us enumerate the most important of them.

First, overseas expansion. In Cromwell's armies, in the French Constituent Assembly, in our entire economic life, even today, there wafts this wind from beyond the ocean. But no new continent awaits us; in a similar development to that which occurred in late antiquity, the peoples of the West are irresistibly pressing forward; this time, however, the advance is over the vast North American continent, and over the monotonous plains of Russia, so receptive to schematism.

The second factor is the peculiarity of the economic and social structure of the 'early capitalist'[226] era in Western Europe.

Thirdly there is the conquest of life by science, the 'coming to itself of Spirit'.[227] But rational control over external life has, though doubtless not before entirely annihilating countless 'values', today at least 'in principle' done its work: its universal effect under present-day conditions of business life has been to create uniformity of the external lifestyle by means of 'standardization' of production – and 'science', as such, can no longer create 'the universal personality'.

Finally, there are certain ideal values, which, emerging from the concrete historical peculiarity of a certain religious thought world, have, together with numerous particular political constellations and in collaboration with those (aforementioned) material conditions, gone to make up the particular 'ethical' character and the cultural values of modern man.

The question of whether any material development, let alone today's high capitalist development, could preserve these unique historical conditions, let alone create new ones, needs only to be put for the answer to be obvious. And there is not the faintest likelihood that economic 'socialization' could encourage the growth of inwardly 'free' personalities or 'altruistic' ideals. Do we find the slightest traces of anything of the kind amongst those who, in their own opinion, are borne along by 'material development' to inevitable victory? 'Correct' Social Democracy drills the masses in the intellectual parade-ground step and, instead of directing them to an other-worldly paradise, which, in Puritanism, could *also* claim some notable achievements in the service of this-worldly 'liberty', refers them to a paradise in this world, making of it a kind of inoculation against change for those with an interest in preserving the status quo. It accustoms its charges to the unquestioning acceptance of dogmas, submissiveness towards party authorities, to ostentatious mass strikes which achieve nothing, and to the passive consumption of the tiresome invective of their journalists, which is as harmless as it is ultimately ridiculous in the eyes of its opponents, but provides its authors with a comfortable living; it accustoms them, in other words, to a 'hysterical indulgence in emotion', which takes the place of economic and political thought and action. On this barren ground, once the 'eschatological' age of the movement has passed and generation after generation has clenched its fists in its pockets in vain or bared its teeth heavenwards, only intellectual torpor can grow.

Yet time presses, and we must 'work while it is day' (John 9: 4). What is not won for the individual now, or in the course of the next generations, in terms of the inalienable sphere of personality and liberty, as long as the economic and spiritual 'revolution', the much reviled 'anarchy' of production and the equally reviled 'subjectivism' continue undiminished, (and these things *alone* can take the individual out of the broad mass and throw him back on himself), will *perhaps* never be won, once the world is economically 'sated' and intellectually 'replete'. So it appears as far as our feeble eyes are able to peer into the impenetrable mists of the future of the human race.

However severe the setbacks in the near future may be, Russia is nevertheless finally entering the path of specifically European development. The mighty influx of Western ideas is destroying patriarchal and communist conservatism here, just as conversely the great migration of Europeans, and particularly East Europeans, into the United States is at work undermining old democratic traditions – in both cases in league with the forces of capitalism. In spite of tremendous differences, the nature of the capitalist economic development of the two 'communicating' reservoirs of population is in certain respects comparable, in particular, the absence of the 'historical' dimension and the 'continental' character of the virtually limitless geographical arena.

The greatest significance of both developments, however, lies in the fact that these are perhaps the 'last' opportunities for the construction of 'free' cultures 'from scratch'. 'Millennia had to pass before you came into being, and more millennia wait silently to see what you will do with your life.' These impassioned words of Carlyle, originally addressed to individuals, can, without exaggeration, be applied not only to the United States, but also to Russia, to some extent now, and probably more fully after another generation. And this is why, despite all the differences of national character and – let us be honest about it – probably those of national interests too, we cannot do other than to look with profound inner emotion and concern at the struggle for freedom in Russia and those who engage in it – of whatever 'orientation' and 'class'.

The coming system of pseudo-constitutionalism will itself ensure that their work is not without success. Certainly, as far as the *negative* side of the problem is concerned, the view of the 'development theorists' is correct: the current Russian autocracy, that is, the centralist police bureaucracy – particularly when, as now, it is victorious over the hated opponent – has, as far as one can foretell, no choice but to dig its own grave. There is no so-called enlightened despotism for it to fall back on in the interest of its self-preservation, and yet, for reasons of prestige, it must fraternize with those economic powers which, under *Russian* conditions, are the bearers of irresistible 'enlightenment' and dissolution. As Struve and others have rightly observed, the autocracy is not capable of solving any of the great social problems without thereby fatally wounding itself.

By the time these words appear in print they will no doubt already be out of date. Today no one knows how many of the hopes of the liberals that the foundations will be laid for a libertarian reform which will break down bureaucratic centralism *now* will still be alive and how many of them will, like a mirage [*Fata Morgana*], have dissolved into thin air.[228] Of course, there may not be an undisguised restoration. There is, in fact, almost certain to be some kind of 'constitution', granting and maintaining a greater degree of press and personal freedom.[229] For even the most devoted supporters of the old regime must surely have realized that the bureaucracy, if it bolts and bars all doors and windows, will itself be obliged to feel its way in the dark. Learning from the experience of others, they might conclude that pseudo-constitutionalism, when combined with some economically orientated 'policy of common interest' [*Sammlungspolitik*],[230] is a far more suitable instrument for holding on to power than crude 'autocracy'.

A certain degree of increased freedom of movement would then prove to be unavoidable and – coming after an arbitrary regime which succeeded, in one notorious incident, in driving people noted for their 'peaceableness' on to the streets in a frenzy, where they gunned down, not one of the 'leaders', but some wretched policeman – that after all is something to be thankful for in today's world. But the resolute and independently-minded elements of the social-reforming bourgeois intelligentsia would be politically and personally elbowed aside. The bureaucracy of the autocratic regime would still manage to harvest the fruits of its long-running demagogic policy of, on the one hand, fostering capitalism, and, on the other, strangling any ordered development of bourgeois independence and playing off the classes against each other. A constitutional and anti-centralist reform which lasted for any length of time and satisfied anyone, and in which the liberal intelligentsia took part, would perhaps be difficult *today* even if the monarch were to feel the calling and inclination to emerge as a liberal reformer. And the prospect that a group so hated by the bureaucracy should gain control is quite remote.

However, a victory for bureaucratic power interests such as looks almost certain to the onlooker *at the moment* (though it may take a constitutional form) would be no more the last word in Russia than the '*Landratskammer*' was in Prussia.[231] Even if the elections produce the most compliant 'people's representation', that will tell us nothing. Every peasant in the Empire will simply feel renewed hatred for the *Chinovniki* [see Glossary], though a blanket of silence may fall over the land.[232] For whatever may happen, the events, promises, and hopes of the past year are hardly likely to be forgotten. Every moment of weakness of this tightrope-walking mechanism of state can only bring new life to the movement. The alarming feebleness of 'spirit', which this supposedly 'strong' regime, despite the apparent refinement of its technique of government, has openly revealed, has surely etched itself in the mind of every section of the population.

Neither is it possible for the present system to change its *administrative* methods in the interests of its own security. It must also, following its political traditions, continue to give free rein to the *political* forces of administrative bureaucratization and police demagogy, which are undermining it and repeatedly forcing its economic allies, the property-owning classes, on to the side of its enemies. But the illusions and the nimbus with which it surrounded itself, hiding these developments from view, have been totally destroyed. It will surely be difficult, after all that has transpired between the Tsar and his subjects, for the system to maintain its dignity and to start playing the old game again in the same old way. All too great is the number of those who, having seen it revealed in all its nakedness, would simply turn to it with a smile, saying: 'Trickster! – You will conjure no more spirits.'[233]

Notes

1 [M–D] Weber is referring to S. Zhivago's review of the constitutional draft of the Soiuz Osvobozhdeniia, published in Paris in 1905: *Loi fondamentale de l'Empire russe*. This review appeared in the same supplement to the *Archiv für Sozialwissenschaft und Sozialpolitik* as Weber's essay. The two texts were published together under the heading: 'Towards an assessment of the current political development of Russia', as a supplement to vol. 22(1) of the *Archiv* in 1906.

2 [Weber] These remarks have been very hastily put together with the aid of the following sources: the newspapers available here (especially *Russ* and *Russkiia Vedomosti*, from time to time the *Novosti*, the *Yuzhny Kurier*, occasionally *Syn Otechestva*, *Nachalo* and *Novoe Vremia*) – which however were only available to me in a very incomplete form. Additionally I have used *Pravo*, *Osvobozhdenie* and the periodicals in the Russian Reading Room here [in Heidelberg] – the foundation of which is linked to the venerable personality of Ivan Turgenev, who remains unforgettable to me since the time I met him at the home of Julian Schmidt. Finally, particular thanks are due to Dr Th. Kistiakovskii, whose knowledge of affairs and people I ruthlessly and unsparingly plundered.

The exposition offers, of course, nothing but a poorly structured collection of notes, which is all that can be achieved under the circumstances. I am having it printed, despite the abnormally brief time available to digest the events, since even the most incomplete compilation may be welcome to some who are not able to follow events at all, and since our Russian colleagues at the moment have better things to do than to keep foreigners informed. However, I should only look ridiculous if readers were to see in it any pretension to 'expert knowledge' or anything other than a temporary substitute for the serious socio-political report which I hope will at some future date come from a Russian pen.

The compilation was made unexpectedly difficult – even for a piece of 'journalism' (note the inverted commas) – by the severing of all communication with Russia as a result of the postal strike which happened to be in progress throughout the period of writing. The time has probably not yet come for anything approaching an internal history of the [Liberation] Movement, and at the moment I do not have the material for it here: for the moment only notes in the form of a chronicle can be given, covering some stages of its outward course, the aims that have emerged and a provisional analysis of certain significant features of the general situation of which it must take account. I make no attempt here to go into the earlier history of the movement, with the exception of a few indications, if only for reasons of space. A 'history' of this memorable period will only be possible if those in Russia *now* make it their business immediately to start *collecting* all the reports, resolutions, circulars, press bulletins etc. concerning the individual events, especially *all* official statements of the associations, which are simply not accessible abroad.

3 [M–D] In the autumn of 1904 constitutional questions were debated at the congresses of the 'League of the Zemstvo Constitutionalists' and at the Zemstvo Congress, which met from 6 to 9 Nov. 1904 in St Petersburg. There is little information concerning the policy adopted by the City Dumas and their debates on constitutional questions. The organization of the City Dumas only began in late February 1905. [. . .] Unification of the zemstvos and city dumas [see Glossary] into one single 'bureau' took place in July 1905.

4 [M–D] From 20 to 22 July 1903, at a convention in the Black Forest, the first steps were taken towards the founding of the Union of Liberation (Osvobozhdeniia). Of the persons named in Weber's n. 6 the following took part at this 'Schaffhausen Conference': Ivan I. Petrunkevich, Prince Peter D. Dolgorukov, Nikolai N. Lvov, Prince Dmitrii I. Shakhovskoi, Fedor I. Rodichev, Vladimir I. Vernadskii, Sergei N. Bulgakov, Pavel I. Novgorodtsev, Ivan M. Grevs, Petr B. Struve, Bogdan A. Kistiakovskii, Sergei N. Kotliarevskii, Vasilii Ya. Bogucharskii, Dmitrii E. Zhukovskii, Sergei N. Prokopovich, Ekaterina D. Kuskova. See also the list in Shmuel Galai, *The Liberation Movement in Russia 1900–1905* (Cambridge, 1973).

5 [M–D] The Union was officially constituted at a meeting from 3 to 5 Jan. 1904 in St Petersburg. The 50 delegates came from 22 cities. In contrast to the 'Schaffhausen Conference', representatives of the 'legal' Narodnichestvo associated with the periodical *Russkoe Bogatstvo* also took part. The delegates elected a kind of central committee, which consisted principally of representatives of the Zemstvo Constitutionalists and the liberal intelligentsia. Cf. the wording of the statute in Terence Emmons, 'The Statutes of the Union of Liberation', *Russian Review*, 33 (1974).

6 [Weber] Petrunkevich was one of the longest-serving members of the Union in terms of age. An old liberal, as estate owner in the Chernigov province [*guberniia*] at the end of the 1870s he had associated himself with the resolutions for a constitution issued by the local zemstvo [M–D: Reference to the address by the Chernigov Zemstvo in the summer of 1878 to Tsar Alexander II, which demanded freedom of speech and of the press, the introduction of a social order on the basis of law, and an end to government influence on schools. Following a decree by the Governor, the address was not allowed to be read out in the meeting of the zemstvo. [. . .] Petrunkevich thereupon left Chernigov and worked with the zemstvo in Tver, which was known for its radical orientation.], was subsequently expelled from the whole of the Ukraine [Tr.: Weber actually uses the old name for the Ukraine ('Little Russia') *passim.*], then lived in the Tver province and, as son-in-law of the well-known big industrialist Malzov, became, unquestionably, together with Prince Peter Dolgorukov and N. Lvov, one of the financial pillars of the Union of Liberation. He is particularly suspected and hated both by the court and by the conservative press, viz. *Moskovskia Vedomosti*, *Grazhdanin* etc., who like to compare the Petrunkevich 'Dynasty' with the Romanov Dynasty. [Weber then lists some prominent members of the movement.]

Bourgeois Democracy in Russia 115

The Socialist Revolutionaries included, in *particular, Schreider and Peshekhonov, Annenskii* (an authority on zemstvo statistics), *Korolenko* (editor in chief of Mikhailovskii's periodical *Russkoe Bogatstvo*), N. D. *Sokolov* and others. [M-D: N. K. Mikhailovskii was regarded as the leading theoretician in the Narodnichestvo at the end of the 19th and the beginning of the 20th century. A. V. Peshekhonov, N. F. Annenskii and V. G. Korolenko were joint founders, at the beginning of 1906, of the 'Narodnosotsialistecheskaia Partiia' (People's Socialist Party), an offshoot of the PSR (Partiia Sotsialistov-Revoliutsionerov). N. K. Mikhailovskii had taken over *Russkoe Bogatstvo* in autumn 1892 and made it the organ of the 'legal' Narodnichestvo. After the death of Mikhailovskii (1904), Korolenko, who had been joint editor since 1895, succeeded him.]

Between the mid-1890s and the first years of this century, the 'Imperial Free Economic Society', founded by Catherine II, was infiltrated by a number of Marxists, and its chairman, the moderate constitutionalist Count *Heyden*, sheltered them from the authorities. In the end, though, it was 'silenced'. Count Heyden was not a member of the Union of Liberation, though he did belong to the zemstvo movement.

7 [M-D] On 8 Jan. 1904 Plehve dissolved the Tver Zemstvo and replaced it by a commission consisting of government officials. Ivan I. Petrunkevich and the other members of the zemstvo were expelled from the province of Tver.

8 [M-D] As early as 1903, in the course of investigations into 'secret links' with the Russian press, which in July 1904 were to lead to the suspects being put on trial in Königsberg for membership of a secret society, high treason against Russia and insulting the Tsar, Struve's home in Stuttgart was searched, and the address file of *Osvobozhdenie* confiscated. [. . .] In June 1904 the Russian Interior Minister Plehve directed a 'confidential question' to the German chargé d'affaires in St Petersburg, asking whether there was any possibility of banning *Osvobozhdenie* and deporting the editor. Although the royal Württemberg government refused to take any measures against Struve under the 'Württemberg legislation', Struve left Stuttgart and moved the journal's offices to Paris. Cf. Richard Pipes, *Struve: Liberal on the Left, 1870–1905* (Cambridge, Mass., 1970).

9 [M-D] Exact figures for the circulation of *Osvobozhdenie* could not be ascertained, and Weber's figures cannot be verified.

10 [Weber] *Struve*'s first major work, 'Critical Remarks on the Social Development of Russia' (1894), immediately focused public attention on him and was subjected to the most violent attacks from the 'Populists'. In 1897, with *Tugan-Baranovskii*, who will be well known to our readers, he took up the editorship of *Novoe Slovo*, which – hitherto 'Populist' – was the first unequivocally Marxist periodical in Russia. Others involved with it included Plekhanov, Ulianov (now usually called 'Lenin') and other Socialists. After eight months the periodical was suppressed.

11 [M-D] At the start of 1897 Struve took over as editor of *Novoe Slovo*, with Tugan-Baranovskii as joint editor; this had been founded in 1893, and may

be described as one of the first Marxist periodicals in Russia. After 10 months, in Dec. 1897, the journal was banned by ministerial resolution.

12 [Weber] Thus Prof. Khodskii (editor of the liberal academic periodical *Narodnoe Khaziaistvo*) founded the newspaper *Nasha Zhizn* to represent the views of the Union. At the same time, the publisher Iuritsyn founded *Syn Otechestva* and *Nashi Dni*; in a sense, these two were complementary, since when *Syn Otechestva*, which was edited, with the approval and support of Union members, by G. Schreider, who was both a member of the Union of Liberation and a Socialist Revolutionary, was temporarily closed down, *Nashi Dni* took its place. However on the question of the attitude to the Bulygin Duma, for example, Khodskii favoured participation, Schreider the boycott. After the October Manifesto, on 15 Nov., *Syn Otechestva* declared itself the organ of the Socialist Revolutionary Party. [M–D: It was on 17 Oct. 1905 that Tsar Nicholas II issued the so-called October Manifesto, in which 'civil liberty', improved voting rights, and the participation of the Imperial Duma (the parliament) in legislation were promised.] Meanwhile *Russ*, although under the direction of Suvorin junior, the son of the well-known nationalist editor of *Novoe Vremia*, has, in the latter months of this year, placed itself at the disposal of the Democratic Zemstvo Constitutionalists; and finally Miliukov has announced the transformation of the Petersburg *Birshevyia Vedomosti* into an organ of Democracy, under his editorship.

In Moscow *Russkiia Vedomosti*, to whose success Dr Iollos (well-known in Germany) contributed with his highly regarded 'Letters from Berlin', is very much in line with Struve's thinking.

[*Weber now lists some 'non-academic' periodicals, in particular:* the Marxist Obrasovanie *and* Pravda *(a monthly), the social-liberal* Mir Bozhii *('God's World'), the liberal 'idealist'* Voprossi Zhizni, *and the Socialist Revolutionary* Ekonomicheskaia Gazeta *and* Russkoe Bogatstvo.]

What immediately strikes the German reader about all these periodicals is their high degree of philosophical and especially epistemological content: and it is typical of the 'hunger for principles' which inspires these publications, and evidently its readers too, that editors and clientele can be distinguished, not only by their political orientation, but also very decidedly by the philosophies on which their epistemology is based. Windelband, Simmel, Avenarius and Mach, Stammler, Marxism etc. are each represented by at least one periodical which is consistently orientated towards it, while a whole series of other ones are equally consistent in their criticism. In Koshevnikov's *Pravda*, for example, a conflict arose which ended with Bogdanov's departure, because the latter, a socialist supporter of Mach, did not fit in with this Marxist ensemble. (The development of the various shades of neo-idealism will, it is hoped, shortly be critically examined in this journal by a qualified author.) [M–D: No such article ever appeared in the *Archiv für Sozialwissenschaft und Sozialpolitik*.]

Of course, this diversity, while pleasing in itself, has greatly furthered the fragmentation of the reform movement. The individual representatives of the liberal intelligentsia, in simultaneously contributing to numerous periodicals and newspapers, and in addition taking part in several political organizations with aims which are similar but not always quite identical, and which have the tendency (in spite of occasionally being run by the same people) to operate against each other, need to have a 'ubiquity' approaching that which Lassalle attributes to the bourgeoisie in this regard.

We must wait to see what influence the new conditions (freedom of the press, political activity) will have on the old type of periodical. Newspapers are the enemies of reading!

13 [M–D] Reference to the so-called Banquet Campaign in the autumn and winter of 1904. Numerous banquets, organized by the Union of Zemstvo Constitutionalists, were used as the occasion to put forward constitutional demands.

14 [M–D] The resolution of the Zemstvo Congress was drawn up by a commission. Prince S. N. Trubetskoi was responsible for the final wording. Together with Shipov he handed it to the Interior Minister Sviatopolk-Mirskii on 29 Nov. 1904. In its final session the congress had called upon all local zemstvo assemblies to include the resolution of the congress in its petitions.

15 [M–D] On 14/27 May the Russian fleet was totally destroyed in the Straits of Tsushima by the Japanese. The Zemstvo Congress, which was termed 'Coalition Congress', convened from 24 to 26 May 1905 in Moscow. The Constitutionalist majority and the Slavophile minority united in framing a resolution in which 'elected representatives' were called for, who, together with the Sovereign, should consider the consequences of war and peace, and decide on a legal order in Russia. The resolution was presented to the Tsar on 6 June 1905 by a deputation under the leadership of Prince S. N. Trubetskoi in Peterhof.

From 6 to 8 July 1905 a Zemstvo Congress again convened in Moscow. This concerned itself with the question of participation in the elections to the Bulygin Duma and with a constitutional draft. The attempt by the Interior Minister to ban this congress failed. However, it had to take place under the supervision of police officers. The term 'windbag' evidently related to the participants at the May Congress. In *Osvobozhdenie*, 73 (6/19 July 1905), p. 391, there appeared under the heading 'Vysochaishaia rezoliutsiia' the words of the Tsar: 'I hope that the congress does not take place. We have heard enough from these windbags.'

16 [M–D] From 12 to 15 Sept. a further congress of the zemstvo and city duma representatives convened in Moscow. In a resolution relating to the Bulygin Duma draft the participants of the congress demanded universal suffrage and effective control by the people's representatives over the budget and the administration. The Congress of the Zemstvos from 6 to 13 Nov. 1905

promised its support to Witte if he would remain true to constitutional principles (cf. reports in the *Frankfurter Zeitung*).

17 [M–D] In April 1904 Interior Minister Plehve refused to recognize the election of Shipov as Chairman of the Moscow Provincial Zemstvo on account of 'opposition activities'. The Moscow Zemstvo thereupon elected the radical Fedor A. Golovin as its chairman. Cf. Sidney Harcave, *First Blood: The Russian Revolution of 1905* (London, 1964).

18 [Weber] Most of the liberals listed as previously belonging to the Union of Liberation also belonged to the zemstvo congresses. [*Weber lists these men.*]

19 [M–D] In contrast to the Berlin National Assembly of 1848–9, in which economic professions were very strongly represented, in the Pre-Parliament, which prepared for the elections, and in the Frankfurt National Assembly, the 'Scholarly Estate' [*Gelehrtenstand*] (professors, clergymen, lawyers) played a major part.

20 [M–D] The National Social Association (Nationalsozialer Verein), after proving to be politically unsuccessful, was dissolved in 1903. Weber had at first taken part in the preparations for its foundation, but had then increasingly distanced himself from it.

21 [M–D] 'Third Element' (tretii element) is the term employed for the paid zemstvo employees, doctors, statisticians etc. The expression originates from the Vice-Governor of Samara, Kondoidi, who described the zemstvo employees as 'a new, third element in the life of the zemstvo'.

22 [M–D] The Soiuz Soiuzov (Union of Unions) was founded in May 1905 as an amalgamation of 14 unions organized according to occupational principles. To it belonged, amongst others, the Union of Academicians, the Union of Writers, of Grammar School Teachers etc. The 'Union of Zemstvo Constitutionalists' also joined the Soiuz Soiuzov. Miliukov was elected as the first chairman.

23 [Weber] Some light is shed on the relations of the two 'elements' to each other by the negotiations of the constituent assembly of the 'League of Zemstvo Employees' (*Pravo*, 19 (1905), pp. 1594ff). It was stressed that the conditions of work of these employees did not imply, as in a private enterprise, any conflict of interest between capital and labour, but was founded on the common work of both 'elements' towards the attainment of ideal goals. The elected zemstvo members were in general not interested parties, but *rentiers*, or economically independent people; criticism was directed against the frequent change of personnel amongst the elected members, on the one hand, and the hierarchical and bureaucratic organization of the employees, on the other. Demands were made not only for material improvements, but also for regular admission of representatives of the 'Third Element' with determining vote (this frequently happens already, and is one of the government's chief complaints), appointment by mixed committees of the uprava and the Third Element, dismissal only on the basis of *judicium parium* [M–D: The

Bourgeois Democracy in Russia 119

principle that each person may only be judged by his peers.] (as it would have been called in the Middle Ages), the right to a pension, and compulsory insurance.

24 [M-D] Osnovnoi gosudarstvennyi zakon Rossiiskoi Imperii. In French translation: *Loi fondamentale de l'Empire russe* (cf. above, n. 1).

25 [M-D] Since the middle of 1904 the Professors of Public Law F. Kokoshkin and S. Kotliarevskii, who belonged to the liberal camp, had been working on a constitutional draft, which appeared in Mar. 1905 under the title named in the previous note. The Zemstvo Congress in April 1905 also voted on this draft, and subsequently it underwent revision by S. A. Muromtsev and others. It then appeared in *Russkiia Vedomosti*, 180 (6 July 1905), and in September 1905 with the title: *Proekt Osnovnago Zakona Rossiiskoi Imperii. Vyrabotan kommissiei biuro obshchezemskikh s-ezdov* (Paris: Société Nouvelle de Librairie et d'Edition, 1905). Cf. Marc Szeftel, *The Russian Constitution of April 23, 1906: Political Institutions of the Duma Monarchy* (Brussels, 1976).

26 [M-D] See List of Parties and Associations.

27 [M-D] On the basis of the statute of 1 Jan. 1864 zemstvos were instituted in 34 provinces as self-governing corporations (see Glossary).

28 [M-D] At the First United Landtag of the Prussian Estates in 1847 the overwhelming majority of East Prussian estate representatives rejected acceptance of a state loan to accelerate the building of the East Prussian railway lines, which were designed to promote the economic development of East Prussia and its linking to the other Prussian provinces, in protest against the fact that periodicity had been denied to the United Landtag by the Prussian King Friedrich Wilhelm IV. In a contemporary pamphlet it was said that on this occasion the deputies of the province of Russia 'had, with unambiguous decisiveness, sacrificed material provincial interests to the higher political interest of the whole state.' Richard von Bardeleben, *Die Verfassungsentwicklung in Preußen und ihre neueste Phase* (Leipzig: Spamer, 1848), pp. 27f.

29 [Weber] And – as we must add – in spite of this, any objective observer will refrain from casting men like Plehve in the role of theatrical villain or sinister character. There is no question of that. The iron consistency of the *system* which they served, the rationalist government pragmatism of this 'enlightened' bureaucracy, quite naturally looked angrily upon the 'idle routine' and impractical 'stubbornness', the 'special interests', the 'lack of understanding' and egoism, the 'utopian dreams' of the 'intelligentsia' and self-governing bodies [zemstvos] and the 'sloganizing' of the press, as elements which constantly blocked and frustrated the uniting of the utilitarian imposition of happiness from above with the appropriate respect for authority required by 'reasons of state'. This system made life into a kind of 'hell' and helps to explain why the news of Plehve's murder sent quiet, unworldly scholars into a frenzy of joy. Anyone who saw that has no need of further grounds for 'criticism'. [. . .]

30 [M–D] Ever since their introduction in the year 1864 the zemstvos had played a part in the founding of primary schools and 'literacy' schools for adults. Up to the year 1914, when almost all zemstvo schools were taken into the control of the Education Ministry, the question of the financing of these schools and thus also of the exercise of control over them was fiercely argued between zemstvos and government. No evidence could be found for the 'prohibition' cited here.

31 [M–D] By the statute of 2 Apr. 1903 self-governing corporations were introduced in the 9 western provinces, whose members were appointed by the Interior Minister.

32 [M–D] i.e. the exercise of certain state rights is delegated to the zemstvos.

33 [Tr.] *Zweckverband* (German) An association comprising several parishes (*Gemeinden*), which carried out certain functions, such as collect taxes (cf. Meyers Lexikon, 1930).

34 [Weber] 'The Political Writings of M. P. Dragomanov', vol. I, pp. 279ff, now published by *Osvobozhdenie* (commissioned and funded by the 'Ukrainian Democrats'), with contributions from Kistiakovskii, amongst others.

35 [M–D] Reference to 'police socialism', which was particularly favoured by Interior Minister Plehve (1902–4), and was designed to bind the workers into organizations controlled by the government. This was supposed, on the one hand, to counteract the influence of the socialist parties and of trade union organizations amongst the workers, and, on the other hand, to play off workers and employers against each other when the need arose.

36 [Weber] A proclamation of the Kursk Marshal of the Nobility Count Dorrer, which was printed by the government printing press and read out from the pulpit of Trinity Church – published in *Russ*, 18 (14 Nov. 1905), p. 3 – accuses the Democrats of being eager 'not to let a single peasant into the Imperial Duma, as in England and France'. Frequently one can follow fairly closely the formation of the now typical alliance of police and civil service (from the nobility) with the leaven of the people, into the 'black gangs'. [. . .] The destruction of the brothels was undoubtedly due to the great number of pimps amongst these protection gangs (whose members are unquestionably paid by the supporters of the old regime), and not some upsurge of puritanical zeal, since the pimps see the brothels as 'competition', and consequently hate them. Furthermore those feared gangs do not consist by any means solely of mercenaries – there are also numerous 'volunteers' among them: e.g. the butchers of many larger cities, all kinds of other petty bourgeois, and finally many peasants. It is well known that whole villages turned out to besiege Moscow University. [M–D: The 'siege' of Moscow University – not only by peasants – took place in mid-Oct. 1905 at the climax of the wave of strikes.]

37 [Weber] Still an advance on the existing communal franchise in the cities to the extent that not only house owners but – as in the Petersburg Duma (thanks to Plehve) – tenants also have the vote.

38 [Tr.] See below, PC n. 1.
39 [Weber] Cf. the criticism by the Social Democrats of Lassalle's advocacy of universal franchise in the 1860s in the introduction to the (official party) edition of his writing (vol. 1, p. 124). [M–D: Edited by Bernstein, who was particularly critical of Lassalle's expectation that universal and direct franchise would also lead to a composition of parliament which corresponded to the social stratification of the population and thus eventually to the 'workers' estate holding state power in its hands'.]
40 [M–D] Motto of Emperor Ferdinand I (1503–64): 'Let justice flourish, though the world perish.'
41 [M–D] Could not be verified as a quotation from any particular person.
42 [M–D] Solovev's philosophical system aimed at the creation of a 'pure theocracy', the realization of divine humanity. The Russian nation had, in Solovev's conception, a universal mission, which should lead to the spiritual unification of humanity.
43 [M–D] Matthew 5: 39.
44 [M–D] See above, pp. 75f and 99ff.
45 [M–D] Since the constitution of 1879 in Bulgaria there had been universal franchise for the national assembly, to which one deputy was elected by 10,000 inhabitants. This parliament monitored the activity of the ministers and was the legislative organ.
46 Reference to Prince Ferdinand of Saxe-Coburg-Gotha-Kohary, who had been elected as King of Bulgaria by a National Assembly on 7 July 1887, after Alexander V. Battenberg had been forced by Russian pressure to resign in 1885. Weber is here alluding to the particularly unstable nature of this dynasty, which lacked national roots.
47 Such notions are, at present, wide of the mark, if only because in any critical comparison of the current achievements of the countries with parliamentary-democratic and those with 'personal' rule, the latter will always come a poor second, even in the area in which they ought to do best, namely, foreign policy. Only those who have seen the documents have the right to judge the achievements of our German diplomacy. But anyone can see that consistent leadership and the achievement of lasting successes must be impossible for our diplomats if their work is constantly disrupted by noisy intermezzi, speeches, telegrams and unexpected decisions by the monarch, resulting in their entire strength being spent in rectifying the situation which has thus got out of hand, unless indeed it resorts to indulging in these histrionics itself. [M–D: Weber is here alluding to the so-called personal rule of Kaiser Wilhelm II, who brought German foreign policy into disrepute by numerous independent initiatives, e.g. the congratulatory telegram he sent to the President of the Boer Republic, Paul Krüger, in 1896, and his after-dinner speech in Damascus in 1898.]
48 [Weber] The final party programme does not mention the Tsar, [M–D: Unlike the constitutional draft of the Soiuz Osvobozhdeniia, the Programme of the Constitutional Democrats of Oct. 1905 referred only in-

directly to the status in constitutional law of the monarch and to the structure of the state. Point 13 stated: 'Russia shall be a constitutional and parliamentary monarchy. The state structure of Russia is determined by the Fundamental Law.' The first sentence was added at the Second Party Conference in Jan. 1906.] but establishes only budget rights, legislative initiative, and the absolute necessity of the approval of the Duma for all decrees of any kind by the government, and the responsibility of the ministers. A resolution of the party congress demanded a majority ministry after the Duma had assembled. [M–D: In the resolution of the founding party conference of the Kadets (see Glossary), which was held from 12 to 18 Oct. 1905, point 7 read: 'The ministers are responsible to the people's assembly, the members of which have the right to put questions and the right of interpellation.']

49 [M–D] Bryce, *American Commonwealth*. A Russian translation appeared in 1889/90 entitled *Amerikanskaia Respublika* (Moscow: K. T. Soldatenkov).

50 [M–D] Proekt Osnovnago Zakona. At the April and July Congresses of the Zemstvos the constitutional draft of the Soiuz Osvobozhdeniia (cf. above, nn. 24 and 25) was slightly modified, and was published in Sept. 1905.

51 [M–D] See below PC: 233 n. 1.

52 [M–D] The congress, which ended one day after publication of the manifesto, on 18 Oct., passed a resolution in which it called into question the integrity of the government and stressed that the manifesto did not match expectations, especially since the Duma promised in it was not a 'proper (*pravilnoe*) body of popular representation'. The party still favoured the calling of a constituent assembly.

53 [M–D] See above, n. 1. In his criticism of the constitutional draft of the Soiuz Osvobozhdeniia, Zhivago commented that the 'mutual relations of the individual peoples had received barely adequate consideration'. He named especially Poland and Finland.

54 [M–D] The constitutional draft of the Soiuz Osvobozhdeniia was preceded by a Foreword by P. Struve, in which he took issue with the draft on the nationalities question, particularly with regard to Poland.

55 [M–D] After the Congress of Vienna in 1815 'Congress Poland' was united in personal union with the Russian empire. In Nov. 1815 it received a constitution in which executive and legislative were separated, and freedom of belief and of the press as well as the inviolability of the person were guaranteed. The Kingdom of Poland received an army of its own and Polish was established as the official language. The successors of Tsar Alexander I were obliged to swear an oath to the Polish constitution before their coronation in Warsaw.

56 [M–D] R. Luxemburg, *Die industrielle Entwicklung Polens* (Leipzig: Duncker & Humblot, 1898). This was Luxemburg's dissertation.

57 [Weber] This, however, is merely the consequence of the accumulation of army units on the western border.

Bourgeois Democracy in Russia 123

58 [M–D] See above, p. 46.
59 [M–D] i.e. of the Emperor of Russia and (since 1815) King of Poland.
60 [M–D] The problems of official languages and of the multilingual nature of the civil service in Austria-Hungary emerged particularly clearly in Bohemia as a result of the language decree of Baden in 1897. This laid down, among other things, that after a transitional period of three years all judges and civil servants must, before their appointment, be able to demonstrate a knowledge of both languages of the country in oral and written form. This bilingual requirement favoured the non-German nationalities and led to bitter rows both within and outside parliament, which brought the work of parliament to a standstill.
61 [M–D] Reference to the Bureau of the Zemstvo Congress.
62 [M–D] According to the Constitution of the United States (Art. 4, Sect. 34, para 1) states could either come into being by splitting off from existing states, or they could exist first as territories and then apply for admission as a federal state. In the latter case these states, when called upon to do so by the 'Enabling Act', had to agree on a constitution and present it to Congress for approval. Admission as a state then occurred by resolution of Congress. Cf. Karl Loewenstein, *Verfassungsrecht und Verfassungspraxis in den Vereinigten Staaten* (Berlin/Göttingen/Heidelberg, 1959).
63 In Nov. 1905 the 'Partiia pravovogo poriadka' (Party of Legal Order) extended its activities to the provinces. It regarded itself as a constitutional party, but demanded a strong state power and the preservation of unity and the indivisibility of Russia. The Petersburg group of the party joined the Octobrists in Jan. and Feb. 1906, whilst the rest of the party merely formed an electoral alliance with them.
64 [M–D] See above, p. 104.
65 [M–D] The (Hungarian) word *honved* means 'defender of the fatherland'. The word originally referred to the Hungarian volunteers in 1848. After the Austro-Hungarian settlement of 1867 it became the term for the Hungarian territorial army [*Landwehr*] (*honvedseg*), in which Hungarian was used as the language of service and command, whilst in the Imperial and royal army German was used as the language of command.
66 [M–D] As early as the end of Jan. 1905 a state of siege was imposed on Poland, and on 28 Oct. martial law was imposed on the 9 Polish provinces. This was lifted again on 12 Nov. 1905.
67 [M–D] See above, pp. 55 and 58.
68 [M–D] Reference to the 'Treaty of Pereiaslavl' (1654), whose constitutional significance is disputed, between the cossacks of Zaporog under their Hetman Bogdan Khmelnytskyi and Tsar Alexei Mikhailovich. The Tsar and his successors became supreme Heads of the Ukraine, which remained autonomous in administrative, financial and military respects. Cossack liberties and privileges, especially the right to elect the Hetman, were confirmed.
69 [M–D] See below, pp. 61f.

70 [M–D] In a conclusion, the programme was summed up in the following sentence: 'Since the decisions of the Union [of Liberation] were dictated by the prevailing political conditions at the time they were discussed, these decisions can only be regarded as binding as long as these political conditions remain unchanged.' The congress convened from 25 to 28 Mar. 1905 in Moscow.

71 [Weber] Since Dragomanov, attempts have constantly been made – as in a discussion of the Lithuanian question in the Nov. edn of *Russ* – to find criteria by which to establish when a nationality possesses a culture which confers on it the ethical claim to a special status. These would vary from case to case. Possession of a literature of its own is not enough for many Democrats – although, unlike scholarship, it is truly 'national'. Alongside possession of its own political press (which, when quality is disregarded, is a rather easy qualification) the decisive criterion may be the existence of 'bourgeois social classes', or possession of its own national parties, indicating the 'will' to maintain its own nationality. The principle of protection for minorities, while being recognized in principle, nevertheless tends, where the minority is an aristocratic cultural stratum like the Baltic Germans, to give way to the democratically reinterpreted principle: *cuius regio, eius religio* [M–D: In the Augsburg Religious Peace of 25 Sept. 1555, a ruler was permitted by Imperial law to determine the religion of his subjects. The formula, which was devised by the canonical scholar Stephani of Greifswald, is not found in the treaty text in that form.] i.e. to make it a duty to join the 'masses'.

72 [M–D] Reference to the policy of Germanization of the Polish part of the population, introduced in 1886, by the suppression of the Polish language and the increased settlement of German peasants and workers. This policy finally led to the growth of a Polish nationalist movement in the Prussian Eastern provinces.

73 [Weber] Events have shown that separatism is not thereby abolished. But considerable progress has been made towards unification of the *bourgeois* elements on the basis of the unity of the Empire.

74 [M–D] What is meant here by ABC Schools is probably the rural elementary schools which came into being on the initiative of the peasant communes after the Emancipation of the Peasants in 1861, and which were administered by the peasant communes.

75 [M–D] As early as the period of Ivan III (1462–1505) the 'ecclesiastical power tendency' under Iosif von Volokolamsk had been imposed, which formally aimed at subordination of the State to the Church, but in fact enforced the State's absolute domination over the largely powerless Church.

76 [M–D] Supreme organ of administration of the Russian Orthodox Church, instituted by Peter I in 1721.

77 [Weber] This concept needs to be qualified, when applied to the Russian Church. Even Ivan the Terrible did not dare to intervene in questions of dogma in the manner of the Comnenians [M–D: Byzantine Dynasty, 1081–

1185, which continually intervened in religious disputes.], and State influence on religious life is restrained out of consideration for the Eastern Community and the danger of schism. The Tsar would scarcely venture to imitate the practice of the *summus episcopus* and preach sermons himself, since he could not do this without offending the Church's self-esteem. [M–D: This is probably an allusion to the so-called sea sermons of Kaiser Wilhelm II, who used to preach himself on Sundays on his voyages when no clergyman was on board. In the view of contemporary Protestant church lawyers, the Sovereign, even in his capacity as *summus episcopus*, was not entitled to do this.]

78 [M–D] Stunda, Stundists: Protestant Free Church community, which came into being around 1860 in the Ukraine amongst German settlers. The term originates from the revivalist 'Bible hour' (German *Stunde*), which was conducted by lay people.

79 [M–D] The Chief Procurator of the Holy Synod (Oberprokuror Sviateishego Sinoda), in his capacity as state official, has supervised the activity of the synod since 1722.

80 [M–D] Since 1700 the Patriarchate had been vacant; in 1721 Peter I replaced it with the Holy Synod as supreme leadership of the Church. It was not until Nov. 1917 that the Patriarchate was restored in Russia.

81 [M–D] Reference to the priests, who were designated white clergy, as opposed to the monks (black clergy).

82 [M–D] The idea of Moscow as the Third Rome arose in the first half of the 16th century and under the reign of Ivan IV (the 'Terrible') became a firm part of the ideology of domination of the Moscow state. It was developed principally in the writings of the monk Filofei; he was convinced that the fall of Rome and Constantinople (the second Rome) was due to the lack of Orthodoxy. Only in the Moscow state was the Christian faith truly preserved. For this reason Moscow was the Third Rome.

83 [Weber] One should not simply generalize this phenomenon, nor measure the quality of the Russian priesthood against the very high standing of the Catholic clergy in Europe (e.g. in Germany). In the disaster districts during the starvation years the priests did much to help. [M–D: Reference to the great famine in Russia in the years 1891–2 which followed very bad harvests.] It is probably true to say that the masses value the priests' magical powers, which are indispensable for salvation from eternal punishment, without this affecting their opinion of the persons who exercise these powers, and, conversely, without their valuation of these magical powers being affected by the personal qualities of the priests. But even here there are considerable differences. At the first Pan-Russian Peasant Congress (to be mentioned later [M–D: see above, pp. 94f]) some speakers hit out at the 'greed' of the priests, although evidently the speakers included some sectarians. Here, as well as in many radical election meetings in the cities, the demand was voiced that the 'Divine Law' (catechism) should be removed from the list of compulsory school subjects, and, in the opinion of many,

replaced by natural science or taught as Jewish history. On the other hand, a very radical priest appeared at the second peasants' congress [M–D: from 6 to 10 Nov. 1905 the second Pan-Russian Peasant Congress convened in Moscow.] as elected representative of a number of villages. An address by 140 peasants from Kherson contained the proposal to pay the expenses of the war out of monastery property, which, it was said, 'belonged to the people'. 'Let the clergy make sacrifices for the government: during the war they only prayed, and not very zealously at that.' On the other hand one peasant representative at that first congress advocated treating the monasteries more favourably than private landlords with regard to expropriation of land, for they were 'communist' institutions and 'prayed for the people'. Others disputed this very vigorously: 'the monastery is a beehive, but the monks are drones living off the labour of others.' A middle view was to make a distinction between monasteries which provided an easy living [*Pfründenklöster*] and working monasteries, in which the monks earned their keep by the labour of their hands. [. . .]

84 [Weber] A group of anti-autocratic Christian Socialists opposed to autocracy, the 'Christian Fighting Brotherhood' (Khristianskoe Bratsvo Boryby), has recently been formed in Russia. [M–D: In *Osvobozhdenie*, 73 (6/19 July 1905), p. 386, it was stated that the Christian Fighting Brotherhood was a 'Christian socialist-democratic organization'.] *Osvobozhdenie* has published several statements from them, including (73 (1905), p. 386) a theoretical exposition of the tasks of the brotherhood, an 'Open Letter to the Bishops' and a 'Call to Fight'. No attempt will here be made to situate this movement, which formally is based on *Orthodoxy*, in the spectrum of uncommonly varied religious tendencies in Russia – if only because both their originators and the number and kind of their supporters are quite unknown to me. Nevertheless I should like to pass on some information on certain tendencies within the Church and on the effects of the activity of Gapon and the massacre of 9/22 Jan. 1905, which left such a profound impression. [M–D: On 9/22 Jan. 1905, a Sunday, a demonstration of workers led by the priest Gapon marched to the Winter Palace in order to hand over a petition to the Tsar. The army fired into the crowd and many people were killed or wounded.]

Historic Christianity, they say, in all its versions only ever preached and strove to fulfil one side of the doctrine of Christ: the Kingdom of God in the individual man, the Christian individual personality. It only ever asked what must be done in order to reach the Kingdom of God in the hereafter. It never asked: what was the this-worldly Kingdom of God – the Corpus Christi, as one would have said at the time in Western Europe – or the 'God of humanity', as 'sociologically' orientated authors put it? It thus encouraged the (in reality antichristian) idea of 'self-salvation' (*samospasenia*) of the individual by means of an essentially only inward transformation. But the apostles spoke not only of the sanctification of the flesh of the individual, but (2 Peter 3: 13) also of a new earth 'wherein dwelleth righteousness': the individual was not an 'atom' but a member of a great Individual, the Church, which was the 'objective Kingdom of God', and was called upon to overcome not only fleshly desires in his own personality but also in humanity, whose 'flesh' was represented by mutual economic, social and political relationships, and needed to be sanctified. Each individual had the duty to cooperate in this and thus to take part as effectively as possible in the social and political life of the (his) country, and here, in the sphere of life from which historic Christianity has turned away with the horror of the hermit, he had to realize the world-encompassing truth of 'Divine Humanity'.

The first fundamental task in Russia today, however, was the struggle against autocracy, whose claim to unlimited power was contrary to God's word to the effect that one cannot serve two masters, was indeed an infringement against the first commandment and was a blasphemous worship of a created being. For such power belongs to God alone. The events of 9 Jan. had shown that de facto the moral question 'Tsar or Christ?' still had to be answered, as long as the Tsar was legally enabled to command whatever he desired, including the shooting of innocent people. Conversations with officers are quoted as examples of this conflict.

To be linked with this struggle against the 'papist heresy' was the releasing of the Church from its involvement with the state, which had placed it in servitude to alien purposes, humiliated it, alienated Christ and forced it to 'gloss over disgraceful deeds, like those of 9 January'.

It was 'spiritually asleep' and was standing aside and resting, amid the immense developments of life, which it simply allowed to pass it by, justifying its indifference with 'formulas which had not changed for a thousand years'.

A change was only possible by renewed meditation on the command of 1 Peter 2: 9, according to which the clergy were merely members of the Church, whose lay members were all likewise called to the dignity of the royal priesthood. They must be re-installed in these rights, and the only canonical unit of the Church, the congregation, restored, the priest not sent into the congregation by the chancelleries of Petersburg, but elected by the congregation. The sobor [see Glossary] of the local priests should choose the arkhierei [see Glossary] from their members or from the monks, and the sobor of the arkhierei should choose the Patriarch in a similar way.

The financial affairs of the congregation should, in the interests of the dignity of the spiritual office, be in the hands of elected stewards, not the priests, and the upkeep of the Church gradually transferred from the State budget to the parishes: one should not wait until the State itself, as in France, gives up the Church budget. (These comments may reflect the views of the 'edinovertsi' [see Glossary], since lay administration and elected priests are today the foundation stones of the Raskol [see Glossary].) Only when thus liberated could the Church congregations provide the Church with the authority and power to Christianize life. This Christianization included the revitalization of the apostolic male and female diaconate and, above all, the struggle of the faithful against social inequality.

The inner freedom of the personality could only be attained in 'emancipation from everything that binds', especially from clinging to private property, after the model of the apostolic community. Monasticism existed within the Church today in 'too strong and thus harmful doses': it had suffocated the royal priesthood of the laymen and made the general Christian duty to fight against property-owning egoism a matter for one particular estate.

Admittedly, the apostolic precepts were only binding on believers: towards those who, as 'ungodly parasites', did not 'place their private property at the disposal of the congregation', but wished to use it for the exploitation of the destitute, one should not use propaganda, but struggle, which should be waged with the 'proven peaceful means' of the strike and of organization, 'and only with these means'. This struggle against the pressure of capital would thus be transformed from a 'grey fight for economic interests' into a 'divine action and religious duty'. The aim of the striving for healing of the 'body of humanity' was 'a woman clothed in the sun' (Revelation 12: 1).

The Brotherhood demands of the National Council, which should be convened, admission of lay persons to equal rights, rejection of autocracy, and the founding of the Church on its canonical unit, the congregation; it reminds the faithful in its Battle Cry that man ought to obey God rather than men and that, as He Himself said, Christ walked among us in the form of hungry peasants and workers: it was a grave sin for so-called Bunt People [rioters] to beat up or shoot such people, following the command of 'godless officials'.

Although views such as these, which are obviously of urban origin, may be gaining widespread currency, their radical tone should not deceive us into overlooking their *weakness* in 'ecclesiastical politics' when faced with the power of Church authorities, a weakness which resides in the alliance of such movements with certain social interests. This kind of movement does not lead, in hierarchical Churches, to an inner rupture with the Church authority: as with Catholicism, so too the Orthodox hierarchy knows how socially and politically to emasculate *anti*individualistic movements and to harness them for its own ends. The Catholic Church has been able to assimilate this kind of movement and many others, including ethical relativism, naturalistic and sociological ideals of 'development', and economic historicism.

A *purely* religious, biblical and *ascetic* movement, on the other hand, could be a serious danger for the Orthodox Church and thus for the authoritarian regime in a moment of outward weakness, but the age of fully developed capitalism offers little basis for this. [. . .]

All the problems of the regeneration of the Russian Church are obviously linked to Caesaropapism, whilst an additional factor is the peasant and

proletarian position of the white clergy, and their social opposition to the celibate black clergy, for whom entering a monastery is often little more than a formality, and for whom all the higher positions are canonically reserved. [. . .]
85 [M–D] Possibly an allusion to the fact that German Liberalism may have underestimated the conservative potential of Christian-social movements which proclaimed the principle of the 'social monarchy', movements such as the Christian Social Party of Stoecker, Wilhelm II's Court Preacher, in the late 1880s.
86 [M–D] P. Miliukov, *Ocherki po istorii russkoi kultury* (St Petersburg, 1902), ch. 2, pp. 394–401, esp. pp. 401f. Miliukov characterized the relationship of the educated Russian to 'religion' as 'indifferent'; ibid., p. 402.
87 [M–D] Reference to Konstantin Nikolevich Leontev, whose thinking concentrated on the necessity of theocracy; Leontev based his views particularly on Byzantinism, which he regarded as the true Christianity, in contrast to the Western Churches.
88 [M–D] James I, father of Charles I, based his rule on the theory of the divine right of kings. In his book 'True Law of Free Monarchies' (1598) he developed the conception of the 'absolute ruler, free of any control', who was not only 'God's Lieutenant' on earth and sat upon God's throne, but was even called God by God. Therefore neither the King nor his subjects could restrict autocracy. Charles I consistently appealed to these divine rights of the King.
89 [M–D] On 19 Oct. K. P. Pobedonostsev was dismissed as Chief Procurator of the Holy Synod and replaced by A. D. Obolenskii.
90 [Weber] Here there is a broad field of action for the priest. Cf. Belgium, where the cooperatives are at the heart of the clerical party, and Italy, where it used to be necessary to show your confession certificate before credit was granted.
91 [M–D] The Edict of Toleration of 17 Apr. 1905 guaranteed freedom of worship to non-Orthodox believers (with the exception of certain sects).
92 [M–D] Priests of the Old Believers movement (Starovery or Staroobriadtsy), described as Popovtsy, were ordained in the traditional way. This movement of Old Believers set up their centre on the so-called cemetery of Rogozhsk in Moscow in the 18th century.
93 [M–D] Reference to Gnostic sects, which possess divine knowledge gained through illumination and hidden from the masses. Only those who experience revelation of Christ by means of the required mystical initiation and ascetic exercises, and extinguish everything of the senses, attain the spirit (*pneuma*). Amongst the Gnostics are various Russian sects, including the Christovery (Khlysty), Skakuny and Skoptsy, who preached the dominion of the Holy Spirit.
94 [M–D] In the 16th century the Dutch Reformed Protestants called themselves 'Churches under the Cross' in the period of intense repression by the Spanish.

95 [Weber] Cf. Jellinek's well-known publication on 'human and civil rights' [M–D: G. Jellinek, *Die Erklärung der Menschen- und Bürgerrechte. Ein Beitrag zur modernen Verfassungsgeschichte* (2nd, expanded edn; Leipzig, 1904)]; my essay in this *Archiv [für Sozialwissenschaft und Sozialpolitik]*, vols 20(1) and 21(1) [M–D: Weber, *Die protestantische Ethik I* and *Die protestantische Ethik II* (both in MWG 1/9 and 1/18). English translation by Talcott Parsons (London, 1930)]; E. Troeltsch's exposition of protestantism in Hinneberg's collected edition 'The Culture of the Present'. [M–D: Ernst Troeltsch, *Protestantisches Christentum*. The book was not published until after the appearance of Weber's essay. Presumably Weber is referring to the galley-proofs provided for him by Troeltsch.] Struve was influenced by Jellinek's works, and frequently quotes from them. The relationship of the economic and political ethics of the Russian rationalist sects with Puritanism (in the broadest sense of the word) did not escape Leroy-Beaulieu and others. [M–D: According to Leroy-Beaulieu there were 'numerous analogies between the Old Believers and Puritanism'. A. Leroy-Beaulieu, *The Empire of the Tsars and the Russians* (3 vols; New York/London, 1905), vol. 3, p. 323.] But in some of these sects, especially the genuine 'Raskol', which is the largest of them, there are profound differences in their understanding of 'worldly asceticism'.

96 [Weber] The rift began at the Second Party Conference (1903) with a dispute over the journal *Iskra* edited until 1903 in Geneva by Axelrod, 'Lenin', Martov, Plekhanov, Vera Zasulich and 'Starover'. Only Plekhanov, Martov and Lenin were re-elected. There was the keenest antipathy between the two latter both personally and with regard to party organization (Lenin was a 'centralist'), and tactics (Lenin was regarded as a 'Jacobin', Martov as a 'Girondist'), whilst Plekhanov attempted to mediate, but finally sided with Martov. Lenin thereupon resigned and founded *Vpered*, but Plekhanov also left the *Iskra* editorship in 1905 and then, on his own, published only *Dnevnik Sotsialdemokrata* (one and a half sheets of octavo per issue, appearing at irregular intervals), described as 'above party'.

97 [M–D] The 'Pervaia obshcherusskaia konferentsiia partiinykh rabotnikov' met in Apr. 1905 in Geneva, organized by the editors of the Menshevist *Iskra*.

98 [M–D] Since the party split in 1903 *Iskra* was the organ of the Menshevist faction of Russian Social Democracy. *Vpered* was founded as the organ of the Bolsheviks in Dec. 1904 and a total of 18 issues were published illegally in Geneva between 22 Dec. 1904 and 5 May 1905.

99 [M–D] The Third Party Conference of the RSDRP, in which only Bolsheviks took part, convened from 12 to 27 Apr. 1905 in London. The first issue of *Proletarii* appeared on 14 May 1905. A total of 26 issues of this paper appeared up to 12 Nov. 1905 in Geneva.

100 [Weber] The Lenin group was at first reluctant to make any formal changes to the programme, in spite of its resolution. Not until Dec. was it proclaimed that the passage on the 'obrezki' would be deleted, and replaced by

Bourgeois Democracy in Russia 131

'support for the revolutionary measures of the peasants up to and including confiscation of land' (including private land), 'autonomous organization of the village proletariat' and 'irreconcilable enmity to the village bourgeoisie'. [M–D: Demands for 'confiscation' and for 'autonomous organization of the rural proletariat' had already been made in the resolution at the Third Party Conference in Apr. 1905. In this there was also mention of the 'unbridgeable gulf' between rural proletariat and village bourgeoisie.]

101 [M–D] Evidently a reference to the disputes at the Pan-Russian Conference of Journalists; there was a confrontation over the agrarian question at that conference.

102 [M–D] This term evidently refers to the Menshevist wing of Russian Social Democracy, with which Plekhanov sympathized after the rift in the party which occurred in 1903.

103 [Weber] The reasons reflect the ambivalent ['two souls'] character of Marxism, as shown e.g. by Marx's own attitude to the Paris Commune [M–D: In the 'Second Address of the General Council on the Franco-Prussian War', written in Sept. 1870, Marx warned against a new uprising after the setting up of the French Republic. 'Any attempt to overthrow the new government, with the enemy almost at the gates of Paris, would be desperate folly.' Marx, *Der Bürgerkrieg in Frankreich* (3rd Gn edn; Berlin, 1891), p. 25. Writing *The Civil War in France* after the suppression of the Paris Commune, Marx represented the Commune as a model of the dictatorship of the proletariat, ibid. pp. 45ff.]. Sombart has recently called attention to this [M–D: Werner Sombart, *Sozialismus und soziale Bewegung* (Jena, 1905), pp. 65ff. Sombart speaks of 'two natures, two conceptions of the essence of social development in Marx and Engels'.]; but in the case of Russia certain intellectual traditions and the existence of the village commune, acting as a kind of sounding board, play their part as well.

104 [M–D] In the dispute between the two wings of Russian Social Democracy August Bebel frequently tried to mediate. The proposals he made in Feb. 1905 were rejected by Lenin in a letter dated 7 Feb. 1905.

105 [M–D] Herzen rejected the view that there was a general historical law of development. He believed that, thanks to the conditions provided by the mir system, the Russian social order could move directly to socialism without passing through the capitalist stage of development.

106 [M–D] 'This being with itself of Spirit, this coming-to-itself of the same can be seen as the supreme, absolute goal.' Hegel, *Vorlesungen über die Geschichte der Philosophie*, vol. 1 (Berlin, 1940), pp. 35f. In the law of stages developed by Petr Lavrov, the most important theorist of the Narodnichestvo, the highest stage was regarded as that of 'convictions', which make possible political action, a theory based on Hegel's self-unfolding [*Selbstentfaltung*] of Spirit. Cf. Klaus von Beyme, *Politische Soziologie im zaristischen Rußland* (Wiesbaden, 1965).

107 [M–D] In mid-Oct. 1905 the 'Social Democratic Federal Council' was formed, and was based at first in St Petersburg, then also in Moscow; its

Bourgeois Democracy in Russia

task was to coordinate the activities of the Bolsheviks and the Mensheviks. It was supposed at the same time to smooth the path for a unification party conference.

108 [M–D] This is presumably an allusion to the orthodox course of the Social Democratic leadership, in particular that of August Bebel, who, while in practice encouraging revisionism, emphasized, on the other hand, the revolutionary goals of Social Democracy.

109 [M–D] A total of 28 issues of *Novaia Zhizn* appeared between 27 Oct. and 3 Dec. 1905. Only from no. 21 did its masthead include the words: 'Rossiiskaia Sotsial-Demokraticheskaia Rabochaia Partiia. Proletarii vsech stran, soediniaites'! [Russian Social Democratic Workers' Party. Workers of the world, unite!] A total of 16 issues of *Nachalo* appeared between 13 Nov. and 2 Dec. 1905. This paper bore the same imprint.

110 [M–D] When both papers published the 'Financial Manifesto' of the Petersburg Soviet of 2 Dec. 1905 (see below, n. 127), both *Nachalo* and *Novaia Zhizn* were banned.

111 [M–D] In the Grand Duchy of Baden the 'Centre Bloc' was formed after the elections of 1905, consisting of National Liberals and Progressives [*Freisinnigen*]; the bloc was supported in parliament by the Baden Social Democrats against the Centre Party (Zentrum) and the Conservatives. The Berlin Party Central Office severely censured this strategy in the party press.

112 [M–D] See above, pp. 80ff.

113 [M–D] See above, p. 41.

114 [Weber] In other ways too this behaviour is quite familiar to us. *Nachalo*, which appeared under Plekhanov's joint editorship, demanded 'revolution' and furiously attacked the 'bourgeois' liberals because they would not support it – knowing that the masses have a very concrete image of 'revolution'. If the 'masses' let fly and the putsch fails, and a thousand youthful ideologues are left lying on the streets to no purpose [M–D: Reference to the Moscow uprising of 7 to 17 Dec. 1905. Weber's date is based on the Western calendar.], as they are today (27 Dec.), then the uprising is declared to be an 'unfortunate bit of thoughtlessness' and the view is espoused that revolution can only succeed when it enjoys the sympathy of the bourgeoisie. Should the 'masses' now ask, in surprise, what then the demand for 'revolution' means, they would hear, to their astonishment, that it means something extremely abstract, far removed from what they had understood by it: if only they had listened to orthodoxy, instead of the Socialist Revolutionaries or the Leninist heretics! In this way the apologist of the miracle, when cornered, takes refuge in the idea that the true, and finally the only 'miracle' is – 'historical development and the everyday'.

We should not assume that such ambiguities necessarily arise from disingenuousness. Plekhanov said the same thing in the Nov. issue of his *Dnevnik* (3, pp. 16 and 21) and recalled the 'readiness to fight' of Minister Leboeuf in 1870. [M–D: The French Minister of War, Marshal Leboeuf, declared in July 1870 that the French army was 'ready and willing' for war.]

Bourgeois Democracy in Russia 133

At the moment, he said, the aims of the workers and the bourgeoisie coincided. His own attack, and the resolution which demanded the 'discrediting' of the liberals, were only due to the fact that Struve was still regarded as a 'Marxist'.

That is it, then: sectarians are like men of the cloth: the Calvinists in Holland did not persecute either the Catholics or the Baptists as fiercely as the 'remonstrants'. [M–D: The doctrine of the remonstrants or Arminians (named after Jacob Arminius), set down in 1610 in the 'remonstrance', was directed in particular against the Calvinist doctrine of predestination. In the Synod of Dordrecht in 1618–19 it was condemned as heresy. Between 1619 and 1630 severe persecution of the remonstrants took place.] Besides, Plekhanov, now that he had to carry the whole crowd of ranters (of both sexes) with him, no longer had the power to deny his editors their craving for slogans and strong words. Today the 'intelligentsia' in the party is powerless against such servility.

115 [M–D] The Petersburg Soviet (Soviet Rabochikh Deputatov, or Council of Workers Deputies) met for the first time on 13 Oct. 1905. On 3 Dec. the executive committee of the Petersburg Soviet and about 200 deputies were arrested before the meeting of the soviet.

116 [Weber] The Shidlovskii Commission 'to investigate the causes of discontent among the workers' proposed election of 15 deputies of the employers, and of 54 deputies of the workers of individual branches of big industry, from workshops employing more than 100 workers, for the purpose of negotiation under government representatives. On 27 Jan. (Old Calendar) the Petersburg manufacturers refused to participate, saying that industry was 'not a welfare institution', and that they 'conceded to workers whatever was possible anyway'.

117 [M–D] See above, pp. 94–8.

118 [M–D] Khrustalev-Nosar was arrested on 26 Nov. 1905. He was one of the worker deputies in the commission of Senator Shidlovskii. (See Weber's n. 116.)

119 [M–D] See n. 22 above.

120 [M–D] See n. 180 below.

121 [M–D] Count P. M. Tolstoy was one of the organizers of the 'Soiuz sluzhashchikh v pravitelstvennykh uchrezhdeniiach' (Association of Employees in Government Institutions); in Nov. 1905 he was relieved of his post.

122 [M–D] The Fourth Congress of the Union of Unions was originally supposed to have met from 10 to 12 Dec. 1905. Owing to the political circumstances it had to be held from 14 to 16 Jan. 1906 in Finland instead.

123 [Weber] Some of these were not without an element of tragicomedy: the members of the Petersburg Conservatoire, for example, united in declaring that the 'music of the future' (*sic*) should not, as now, be debased by the 'bourgeoisie' (only?!) in cabarets and operettas (report in *Russ*).

124 [M–D] The Soiuz Osvobozhdeniia merged in Oct. 1905 with the Zemstvo Constitutionalists to form the Constitutional Democratic Party.

125 [M–D] The programme of the Constitutional Democrats does not contain these demands. However, at the end of the Founding Party Conference the party published a declaration in which it demanded the calling of a constituent assembly (see n. 52 above).
126 [M–D] See above, p. 72.
127 [M–D] This is the 'Finance Manifesto' of 2 Dec. 1905.
128 [Weber] Admittedly, at the moment without success. In the press (e.g. in *Russ*, 19 Nov. 1905) an appeal by the 'Gapon Organization Group' to the 'comrades' was published, urging them to resume their activity. However, the Socialist Revolutionaries immediately condemned Gapon to death as a 'traitor and government agent'. [M–D: In the late autumn of 1905, Gapon returned to Russia after a fairly lengthy stay abroad, and made contact with Witte and later with the tsarist secret police, Okhrana. At the same time he maintained relations with the Socialist Revolutionary Party (PSR). There is no evidence for any 'official' condemnation of Gapon by the party.] At the moment he is abroad. Meetings of his party comrades are disrupted either by the police or by 'correct' Social Democrats. The assessment of Gapon seems to be unfavourable abroad too, which is scarcely justifiable as far as his character is concerned. At any rate the view of the Socialist Revolutionaries, as the socialist press showed, is not shared on all sides, in spite of bitter opposition. There is scarcely any doubt that he was unfairly treated by the autocracy. The allegation that he pursued other than sincere 'Christian Social' aims is by no means proven. One only has to think of the harm that many a 'loyal, royalist' Christian Social ideologue has done to the workers' movement in our own country. [M–D: Allusion to the Christian Social Workers' Party (later Christian Social Party) under Adolf Stoecker, which was founded in 1878 with the aim of keeping the workers away from Social Democracy.]
129 [Weber] Compulsory insurance, compulsory arbitration courts, the principle of the 8-hour day, etc.
130 [M–D] Reference to the attempts of the chief of the tsarist secret police, S. V. Zubatov, to influence and organize the workers, in the years 1900–3, by state-directed measures. These measures, known as Zubatovshchina, were at first approved by Interior Minister V. K. Plehve, who, however, after strikes and rioting, ended this 'police socialism' in 1903.
131 [M–D] Presumably Weber is referring to the subsidies by Okhrana (the tsarist secret police) for the building of the clubhouse of the Gapon organization in the Vyborg district of St Petersburg.
132 [M–D] See above, p. 45.
133 [M–D] See List of Parties and Associations.
134 [M–D] See above, p. 104.
135 [M–D] See List of Parties and Associations.
136 [Weber] Odessa, Kharkov, Vilna, for example.
137 [Weber] A dvornik (often quite a large number of them) is clearly essential in the big blocks of flats, if only to carry in the firewood. Meetings of the

Bourgeois Democracy in Russia 135

Union of Dvorniks in the capital cities are now protesting against having to assume police functions.
138 [M–D] Preface by Peter Struve, in *Loi fondamentale*, pp. xiiif.
139 [M–D] Cf. above, nn. 24, 25.
140 [M–D] Cf. above, p. 61.
141 [Weber] By 'village commune' we mean the 'strict' village commune system, in which the individual does not inherit his share (arable land etc.) from the family, but the commune assigns it to him (by redistribution).
142 [Tr.] Village community in which land is held in common.
143 [M–D] Under the law of 19 Feb. 1861 the peasants were obliged to fulfil their tax liabilities under the common responsibility of the commune. This communal liability was repealed on 12 Mar. 1903. Weber almost always dates this law as 1904.
144 [M–D] The peasant communes had the right to issue passports to their members. Peasants were not permitted to leave their home district without a passport. The Soiuz Osvobozhdeniia demanded the abolition of this compulsory passport.
145 [M–D] Gerhart von Schulze-Gävernitz, *Volkswirtschaftliche Studien aus Rußland* (Leipzig, 1899), and V. G. Simkhovich, *Die Feldgemeinschaft in Rußland* (Jena, 1898).
146 [Tr.] Russian peasant. The word is in the diminutive form, as under old Russian law peasants were regarded as minors.
147 [M–D] In 1879 the grouping 'zemlia in volia' split up into the groups 'chernyi peredel' and 'narodnaia volia'. Whereas the former rejected political terror and aimed to achieve social revolution by propaganda, the latter preached terror as a means of achieving its own revolutionary goals.
148 [M–D] Reference to the theories of the American social reformer Henry George (1839–97), who, in his principal work, *Progress and Poverty: An Inquiry into the Cause of Industrial Depressions and of Increase of Want with Increase of Wealth; The Remedy* (San Francisco, 1879), stressed his belief in the 'natural right' of each person to land. George advocated the nationalization of land, and demanded the replacement of land rent by the single tax.
149 [Weber] *Both* terms are, however, evidently quite fluid, and in fact the transition between reactionary Slavophile on the right to terrorist on the left is a gradual one. Even the unpolitical 'Narodnik' Vorontsov has endured perhaps a dozen house searches, and Mikhailovskii was always regarded, on account of personal relations to 'narodnaia volia', as 'suspicious'. All they had in *common* was their opposition to the modern forces of (1) bureaucracy, and (2) capitalism.
150 [M–D] The Partiia Sotsialistov-Revoliutsionerov was created in the early 20th century by the union of regional groups of the Narodnik tendency with exile organizations. Although there were points of continuity in both the personnel and the programme with the organizations of the Narodnichestvo of the 1870s and 1880s, the party was a new foundation. The first draft

programme was in 1904; the first party conference took place from 29 Dec. 1905 to 4 Jan. 1906.

151 [Weber] The recent draft of a 'theoretical section' – these seem indispensable for Russian radicalism – of the *tactical* programme of the PSR includes the following points: Alongside the factory workers the 'lower strata' of the 'intelligentsia' and the commune peasantry are regarded as potentially the most rewarding targets for agitation; less so the 'higher intelligentsia', because it is 'classless', or the 'Lumpenproletariat' (most of the terms of extreme radicalism are German imports). The party does not disdain any, 'even the most peaceful', means. 'Terror' can never be the sole means of struggle; 'viewed in historical perspective' only the ages of heroes (cf. Carlyle!) with a particularly 'revolutionary atmosphere' give birth to the heroes of terrorism. These eras are followed by others in which 'Tolstoyism' and 'ultra-evolutionist socialism' rule. 'Centralized terror' against persons guilty of particular lawlessness and oppression may induce the government to transfer power to the 'general Zemskii Sobor (popular assembly)'. However, the party wages no struggle against means of production and leaders of industry, except when they act as instruments of oppression. Nothing can be hoped for from parliamentarism alone, on account of the 'inertia of the masses'. A merger with the Social Democrats is possible in spite of their very different agrarian programmes, with the exception of those of the *Iskra* orientation. Likewise temporary alliances with the progressive liberals are called for in the common struggle against autocracy, which is now to be given priority over all else.

152 [M–D] A. V. Peshekhonov replied to the open letter from Novotorzhskii with the article 'Obshchina i gosudarstvo'. In the following, Weber refers to this reply from Peshekhonov and also in some places to an article by Peshekhonov in the same issue of *Russkoe Bogatstvo*: 'Agrarnaia reforma s tochki zreniia rynka' (Agrarian Reform from the point of view of the Market), *Russkoe Bogatstvo*, 8 (Aug. 1905).

153 [Weber] *Russkoe Bogatstvo*, 8/2 (1905), pp. 116ff. In fact, this proposal merely meant a reinforcement of the legislation of 1893, which subjected the mir, which had hitherto been sovereign, to police control. [M–D: The law on the land captains (Zemskie Nachalniki) of 12 July 1889 introduced supervision of the obshchina by the Zemskie Nachalniki.]

154 [M–D] On the Single Tax, see above, n. 148.

155 [M–D] Essentially, Weber is here repeating Peshekhonov's answer to Novotorzhskii. Peshekhonov, 'Obshchina i gosudarstvo', pp. 147–59.

156 [M–D] 'Partisan hatreds and affections shroud/His character, as history portrays it.' Friedrich Schiller, *Wallensteins Lager*, Prologue. [Tr. F. J. Lamport, 1979. Harmondsworth: Penguin.]

157 [M–D] Reference to the strict centralization which the Convention Government in France carried out by means of the constitutional order of 14 Brumaire of the Year II (4 Dec. 1793).

158 [Weber] One of the principal objections made by the Socialist Revolutionary

Bourgeois Democracy in Russia 137

organizations against the Social Democrats is their centralist tendency, cf. e.g. point 7 of the resolutions of the Grusian Social Revolutionary Party in *Revoliutsionnaia Rossiia*, 46 (5 May 1904), p. 9.

159 [M–D] The demand for extension of the nadel was principally made by agrarian experts close to the Constitutional Democratic Party. It related in particular to the expansion of the so-called dwarf nadels mostly to bring them up to a level which made possible subsistence economy.

160 [M–D] Reference to the Land Law Act 1881, which created state land commissions in Ireland which calculated the level of rent and fixed it for 15 years. The law also provided that in the case of rent increase both tenant and landlord had the right to apply for the establishment of a fair rent. This rent, established by the court, was also valid for a period of 15 years.

161 [M–D] See above, p. 58.

162 [Weber] The social movement in the countryside is much less well developed in those areas where large capitalist farms have completely dispensed with peasant work and merely operate with freely hired and *not* local workers. It is like this with the completely proletarianized workers of e.g. the western provinces. For them there has existed since 1886 – in contrast to common law – a system of labour law, including sanctions for contract breaking, with only very limited opportunity to appeal to the public courts. Nevertheless, in contrast to the wild insurgency character of the old 'Bund' movements, they have achieved the beginnings of a socialist organization, which, in spite of its weakness, seems to have managed to intimidate the owners to a certain extent. Whereas the Congress of Landowners in Moscow in 1895 rejected the idea of a labour office (which was to serve primarily as a 'job centre') out of hand, rejected all hygiene controls and all attempts to interfere in labour relations, even by voluntary activity, last summer the landowners (in *Nasha Zhizn* of 19 Aug.) proposed the creation of an inspectorate on the model of the factory inspectorate. By contrast, however, the Moscow Congress of Landowners in Dec. 1905 was highly reactionary.

163 [M–D] See above, p. 90.

164 [M–D] Acquired rights (*iura quaesita*) are those subjective rights which have been acquired by special legal title and not merely as a result of natural freedom.

165 [M–D] *Glebae adscriptio* ('bound to the soil') is the term for the legal status of the unfree peasant who represents a legal and economic unit with his land. Binding to the soil was established in the so-called *ulozhenie* (see Glossary) of 1649.

166 [M–D] Reference to the reform of the administration of state peasants, which Count Kiselev, who was Domain Minister from 1837, carried out. Particularly by means of the law of 30 Apr. 1838 (the text of the law runs to more than 150 pages) the rights of the village commune, which hitherto had for the most part not been codified, were either abolished or buried under a bureaucratic apparatus.

167 [M–D] The quotation could not be verified. The reference is to the demand made by peasants, the political parties of the centre and left, and officers of the state, that peasant farms should be provided with state land or land expropriated from the big landowners.
168 [Weber] No one has stressed this more strongly than Witte in the 'special discussions' on the 'needs of the village economy'.
169 [M–D] Reference to Tsar Alexander II, who was responsible for the Peasants' Emancipation in 1861. Some of the Russian peasantry believed that the Tsar had promised all the land to the peasants, but that the landowners and the bureaucrats had deprived them of it.
170 [M–D] The law of 14 Dec. 1893 abolished Art. 165 of the Redemption Law of 1861. It eliminated the previous right of the peasant to leave without the consent of the village commune and thus also the possibility of managing the land as private property after paying the full redemption sum. Leaving the obshchina thus became impossible again. Additionally, peasants were banned by this law from selling their land.
171 [Weber] The (orthodox) *Social Democratic* Party Programme of 1903 (point 2) strictly opposed agrarian communist ideas, by demanding the 'abolition of all laws which restricted the peasant in his control of his land'. For unless there is an ambiguity in the expression 'his' land, this demand in *effect* means dissolution of today's obshchina. In line with this, the programme stated that 'obrezki' (point 4) should be returned to the 'village societies'. The neutral term 'obshchestvo' (society) was substituted for the technical term 'obshchina'.
172 [M–D] In his article 'Ocherki nashego pereformennago obshchestvennago khoziaistva', which appeared in 1894, Struve advocated both the granting of individual rights for the peasants and the creation of independent peasant farms.
173 [M–D] The office of land captain was created by the law of 12 July 1889. Land captains had administrative and legal functions in the village, were appointed by the government and supervised all decisions of the obshchina. They were normally recruited from the local nobility.
174 [Weber] The village *uriadniki* [village policemen], created by Plehve, of whom there were several tens of thousands. [M–D: Reference to the decree of 5 May 1903, which provided for the institution of a 'politseiskii uriadnik' for each volost, i.e. a rural police officer.]
175 [Weber] In the petitions of the peasants one not infrequently finds the desire that the Tsar provide a good newspaper in which 'only the pure truth' should appear.
176 [Weber] The Novgorod peasants also demanded (according to newspaper reports in Dec. 1905) the replacement of the uezd (district) uprava by the volost assembly (which would be free of the control of the Zemskiie Nachalniki) and an uprava to be elected from it. They were particularly keen on this 'smaller zemstvo cell'.
177 [M–D] Since the village commune administered the overwhelming majority

Bourgeois Democracy in Russia 139

of its affairs itself, it continued to have the right to assemble, and to vote on the tasks for which it was responsible, even after the Peasants' Emancipation of 1861.

178 [Weber] As far as the history of this organization is concerned, the initiative seems to have come from those sections of the radical intelligentsia in Moscow who had formed the Union of Unions. It was in response to attempts by some Moscow Slavophiles (including Samarin), with the aid of rural officials, to found an antiliberal peasant organization in 1905. These attempts failed at the time, it appears, but the peasants and the intelligentsia from the Province of Moscow got wind of them, and held a congress in May to plan the campaign for the 'Pan-Russian' Congress.

179 [M–D] Between July and Nov. 1905, the Pan-Russian Peasant League (Vserossiiskii Krestanskii Soiuz) succeeded in setting up a network of local organizations in almost the entire European part of the Russian empire. The centres of agrarian unrest in 1905–6 were particularly in the central Black Earth district, the Volga district and the Ukraine.

180 [M–D] Reference to the rescript to Interior Minister Bulygin of 18 Feb. 1905, which gave to individuals and organizations the right to hand in petitions to the relevant ministers, or to the Council of Ministers.

181 [Weber] The franchise was to be for those aged 20 upwards and also for women (the right to vote was agreed unanimously, on the grounds that the men in Russia were often away and women were the only reliable opponents of alcohol – the right to stand for election was passed with 5 votes against, one of the objectors wishing only to except married women).

In view of the usual barbarous kind of treatment of women by the peasants and the volost courts (authentic material to be found e.g. in *Sbornik Pravovedeniia*, 1 (1893), pp. 268f) the 'authenticity' of this example of women's emancipation among the peasants seems somewhat 'doubtful'.

Only in the strata of the intelligentsia has the free position of the Russian woman before the law led, under common pressure, to that comradeship of the sexes which in our country raised the woman actively participating in the struggle to a position which is comparable to that of the American woman and is far above that of the German *Hausfrau*, with her indifference to general public affairs. This is expressed also in the custom, widespread in these circles, of entering marriage without any legal formalities, in order to avoid the intervention of the Church and the 'sacramental' character of the relationship, which is indispensable for the Orthodox. Socially, free marriage has parity of esteem with legal marriage and is regarded as equally 'sacred'; the children (according to the law, illegitimate) are cared for under the terms of the will. Only those aspiring to ministerial office may find – under a bigoted monarch – that this form of marriage is an obstacle, as a case under Alexander III showed. [M–D: Weber may be referring here to P. N. Durnovo, who was then police chief and subsequently became Interior Minister under Witte. Durnovo was dismissed by Tsar Alexander III for having an affair.] In any case, free marriage is not infrequently legalized at a later date, especially amongst the nobility. (A detailed account by a Russian author would be welcome.)

The Union of Liberation was divided over the question of votes for women, Struve, for example, being opposed to it. Zemstvo liberalism rejects it for reasons of *realpolitik*. The division of opinion was reflected in the programme of the Constitutional Democrats also. [M–D: The demand for votes for women contained in the programme of the Soiuz Osvobozhdenia was declared to be 'not binding', since a minority was against it. Similar wording was used in the programme of the Constitutional Democrats of Oct. 1905. This passage was deleted at the Second Party Conference of the Kadets, yet there remained a minority within the party, including P. Struve, that was against women's suffrage.]

182 [M–D] Ever since the outbreak of agrarian unrest the local and regional organizations of Russian Social Democracy had supported the actions of the peasants, i.e. strikes, the burning down of farmhouses, occupation of land etc. Both Lenin and Plekhanov had supported revolutionary measures on the land, as e.g. Lenin's speech at the 3rd party conference of the RSDRP on 19 Apr. 1905.

183 [Weber] As already stated, the Social Democrats had abstained in the ballot at the (essentially Socialist Revolutionary) Pan-Russian Journalists' Congress, when nationalization of the land was demanded. Their view at the time was that failure to 'socialize' the means of production meant handing over the land to the bourgeoisie. [M–D: The Congress of Journalists convened from 5 to 8 Apr. 1905 in St Petersburg. The resolution on the nationalization of land was passed by 54 votes to 31.]

184 [Weber] Kautsky's own proposal was: general formation of village co-operatives, which should be provided with capital, evidently from public funds. Whether this proposal can be regarded as 'orthodox' is up to orthodoxy to decide. [. . .] In *Pravda*, 9 (1905), pp. 256f, Maslov [a Menshevik] (quite rightly) severely criticizes the petty bourgeois programme of the Young Populists: 'Division is division' – i.e. an ethical, not a developmental principle. Nationalization, however, ever since Kautsky argued that it strengthened the power of the state, has been discredited amongst all Russian Marxists. Maslov himself will propose only the 'takeover' of farmland by the *local* communities, zemstvo and provincial government, i.e. essentially something similar to Peshekhonov, to whom, however, he noisily claims superiority. In this way the (indispensable) development of agricultural capitalism would not be restrained, and the ground-rent derived from those farms which yielded any such – and the peasants did not own such farms – would be confiscated and given to the communes, which would do more for the relief of the masses than any amount of income tax.

185 [Weber] If our brothers in the factory want to go on waiting, let them – we can wait no longer, was the answer.

186 [Weber] Consistent 'natural law' simply reverses the principle of 'acquired rights'.

Bourgeois Democracy in Russia 141

187 [M-D] Allusion to the successful mobilization of the peasants by the 'League of Landowners' for an economic policy serving the interests of the agrarian aristocracy.
188 [M-D] Weber is here probably alluding to the fact that the village priests cultivated the land belonging to the Church for their own subsistence. The clergy continued to form a self-perpetuating estate in spite of the reforms of 1869.
189 [Weber] According to press reports, in a number of eparchies (e.g., as far as I can recall, in Saratov and Ekaterinoslav) assemblies of priests have declared that they support the Constitutional Democratic programme.
190 [Weber] Press reports (cf. e.g. *Kievskie Otkliki* of 6/19 Dec., p. 5) show that the Third Element always jointly edits the peasants' 'prigovors' and constantly advises them, in defiance of admonition by the zemstvo upravas.
191 [M-D] In contrast to the 'Bulygin Draft' of 6 Aug. 1905, the electoral legislation of 11 Dec. 1905 extended the franchise considerably, to include workers, non-Russian nationalities and considerable sections of the urban population. It did, however, retain the system of indirect census election (i.e. by wealth qualification).
192 [M-D] The electoral law laid down that the representatives were to be elected to the next highest curia, or, as the case may be, to the Duma, from the membership of the delegates or electors. Arts 38, 49 and 50 of the Electoral Law of 6 Aug. 1905.
193 [M-D] Weber is referring to the practice in numerous American States of nominating candidates for political offices (Governors, Delegates, Senators etc.) from within the legislative bodies. This pre-election 'from their own membership' also occurred in the elections for these legislative bodies themselves. They took place in semi-official meetings of the members of the state legislatures, the 'Caucus'.
194 [Weber] This is consistent with the view of Leo Tolstoy, who still exerts a powerful influence. For him, the constitution, personal liberty and the like are, basically, Western abominations, or at best matters of indifference. On the other hand, he has now discovered Henry George, and he has recently proclaimed, in an article in *Russkaia Mysl* on 'the great sin' (*velikii grekh*), that the latter consists simply and solely in private ownership of land, after the abolition of which everything else would fall into place. Of course he holds fast to his view that all work other than peasant work is simply contemptible. [M-D: Tolstoy, 'Velikii grekh', *Russkaia Mysl* (July 1905), pp. 247–66.]
195 [M-D] This relates to the manifesto and ukase of 3 and 25 Nov. 1905, which (1) reduced redemption payments by half from 1 Jan.; (2) facilitated land purchase by means of cheap loans from the Peasant Bank; and (3) placed 50 million roubles at the disposal of the Peasant Bank. At the same time the Tsar placed 4 million desiatins of land at the disposal of the Peasant Bank, and set up a commission under the leadership of Goremykin to consider

measures to increase the prosperity of the peasants; the possessions of the big landowners were, however, to remain untouched.

196 [Weber] This expression is very popular in Russia at the moment. Not only Democrats and land reformers but also Socialist Revolutionaries and Young Populists want to be 'realnye politiki'. Should this fine-sounding expression be somewhat devalued in Germany on this account, I would regard this as no great loss, given present developments in Germany.

197 [M–D] There was an armed uprising in Moscow from 7 to 17 Dec. 1905 mainly carried out by the Moscow Soviet. The struggle, which was supported by only some of the workers, failed on account of the loyalty of the military and the weakness of the forces of the insurgents.

198 [M–D] It is commonly accepted that foreign financial interests, principally French, tried to put pressure on the Tsar to permit a constitution, in order to prevent further intensification of the revolutionary development. We do not know to what extent foreign financial circles exercised any direct or indirect influence.

199 [M–D] Shortly after the announcement of the Manifesto of 17 Oct. 1905 Witte said to journalists that there was now no longer any autocracy in Russia. On the other hand, in early Jan. 1906 he announced that the Manifesto of 17 Oct. had changed nothing regarding autocracy. However, this latter statement was immediately denied.

200 [Weber] The course of the Moscow uprising, which is now raging, shows this. [M–D: see above, n. 197.] Only in the tragic event of a *European* war would the autocracy finally be destroyed.

201 [M–D] Reference to the policy of the Social Democratic Party leadership, which firmly rejected any cooperation with the bourgeois parties.

202 [M–D] The Party of Legal Order (Partiia pravovogo poriadka) was founded on 15 Oct. 1905 by members of the Petersburg City Duma.

203 [M–D] Immediately after the issuing of the Manifesto of 17 Oct. 1905, between 18 and 25 Oct., there were major Jewish pogroms, especially in the south-western provinces, in which some government officials, as well as police and gendarmerie were quite heavily involved, both as participants and as organizers.

204 [Weber] This should not be taken to imply that sceptical bureaucrats like Pobedonostsev and Plehve, or journalists like Gringmut and Pikhno, or the Counts Sheremetev amongst others, are in any sense personal 'believers'. But, like Prussian conservatives of today, 'officially' they are, and that of course 'suffices', as it does here.

205 [Weber] The electoral law makes no distinctions of religious denomination.

206 [M–D] Statement by the French Minister Guillaume Guizot (1787–1874) in the French Chamber of Deputies on 1 Mar. 1843.

207 [M–D] Cf. the report in *Frankfurter Zeitung*, no. 350 of 18 Dec. 1905, in which we read: 'Prince Paul Dolgorukov said to the correspondent: "There is little hope that the zemstvo congress will meet; the time for such meetings is past." '

Bourgeois Democracy in Russia 143

208 [M–D] On 19 Aug. 1899 20 provincial officials in the House of Deputies voted against the bill in which the building of the 'Mittellandkanal' (a major east–west link) was proposed; the bill was thereby defeated. On 26 Aug. 1899 these officials were 'suspended' by 'Supreme Decree', though in the course of the following year many of them were reinstated – in higher positions.
209 [M–D] Thus e.g. Governor Kurlov (Minsk) and the City Captain Neidhart (Odessa) were removed from their posts for taking part in the Jewish pogrom in Oct. 1905, though criminal proceedings were soon dropped. [. . .] After a certain time they were promoted.
210 [M–D] German proverb.
211 [Weber] It is simply inconceivable that the present Minister of the Interior should lose his nerve in such a way. Durnovo, as police chief, has shown himself to be notoriously efficient in both combating and provoking revolts. The apparently typical nervousness, or even neurasthenia, of large sections of the Russian intelligentsia, which was and is not merely the consequence of an inevitable 'psychological sensitivity' but simply of the conditions under which the police force these people to live, have made the task of the police bureaucracy a fairly simple one. Note 114 above shows that the Leninist group, on the other hand, and a section of the Socialist Revolutionaries, have been *planning* the foolish revolt for a long time.
212 [M–D] It is not clear what Weber is referring to. In fact, in Aug. 1862 the leader of the Old Liberal fraction in the Prussian House of Deputies, Georg von Vincke, negotiated with the Trade Minister, von der Heydt, about a compromise in the matter of compulsory military service, though without any tangible result. The Prussian constitutional conflict, which led to a fateful defeat for Liberalism, could not be prevented. Weber might be thinking of a statement by Vincke in the Prussian House of Deputies on 12 Aug. 1862, in which he stated that 'confidential information from Ministers which could not be made use of in public', must ultimately be politically ineffective. Weber here interprets this declaration, however, to mean that confidential contacts with ministers were not permissible for a deputy.
213 [M–D] When the Army Bill was introduced in 1893, the German Progressive Party [Deutsch-Freisinnige Partei] could not agree to the compromise motion which the Centre Party Deputy, Huene, had negotiated with the Government of Caprivi, although Caprivi had announced that the Reichstag would be dissolved if the compromise fell through. The German Progressive Party thereupon split into the Progressive People's Party [Freisinnige Volkspartei] and the Progressive Association [Freisinnige Vereinigung]. After the Reichstag elections the Progressive People's Party then did after all vote for the Army Bill in the new Reichstag.
214 [Weber] This should *not* be taken to imply that the liberals have made *no* 'tactical' errors. All that can be confidently asserted is that such errors are not apparent to the foreign observer. Of the resolutions of the October Congress of the Constitutional Democrats, that concerning the general

strike is doubtless of only rhetorical significance; but compared with the dreadful fog of sloganizing of the tsarist 'manifestos' it is almost refreshing. And certainly the 'holy' entreaties of Mr Gringmut and the conservatives in the Moscow Vedomosti cannot stand before God or man.

215 [M–D] In Oct. 1905 Witte negotiated with various representatives of the Zemstvo Congress and representatives of the Constitutional Democrats concerning their joining the cabinet. Amongst the liberals Witte's conduct of the negotiations aroused the impression that further reforms were conditional on the liberals' agreement in principle to the Witte Government's policy. As they were not prepared to accept these conditions, they broke off the negotiations. Finally, in a written declaration, Witte expressed the view that the government did not need the parties, since the parties refused to cooperate in saving the fatherland.

216 [M–D] In late Dec. 1877, in order to secure the support of the National Liberals for the reform of the customs and finance policy of the Reich, Bismarck offered Rudolf von Bennigsen the office of Prussian Interior Minister, coupled with the Reich Interior Ministry. Bennigsen, who feared isolation within his party if he were to join the leadership of the Reich on his own, asked for the Finance Ministry instead and also demanded that two further National Liberals, Forckenbeck and Stauffenberg, be invited to join the government. Bismarck, seeing in this the beginning of a parliamentarization of the Reich constitution, thereupon broke off negotiations with Bennigsen.

217 [M–D] In 1789 the Marquis de Lafayette had handed the draft of the Declaration of Human Rights to the National Assembly, and was commander of the National Guard after the storming of the Bastille. He advocated a constitutional monarchy.

218 [Weber] Of the zemstvo representatives who were brought to the ministerial discussions on extension of the franchise in late Nov., Guchkov and Prince E. Trubetskoi were the most 'radical'; the rest were 'liberal' Slavophiles.

219 [M–D] The meeting between Witte and the zemstvo representatives did not, as Weber states, take place on 27 but on 21 Oct. 1905.

220 [Weber] There are also detailed accounts, provided in private by completely trustworthy sources, of specific cases. Although Durnovo obviously *cannot* deny before the courts the accusation made in public meetings, he has just been decorated and promoted. [M–D: In Oct. 1905 Durnovo, who had been deputy Interior Minister since 1900, was given the post of Interior Minister in Witte's cabinet.] It is the strength – *and* weakness – of tsarism compared with 'ideologues' that it, unlike them, can and does make use of 'gentlemen' like this. Tsarism as we know it cannot do without the crafty peasant tricks of such loyal men for a single moment, and the Tsar *must* therefore shake hands with people to whom any self-respecting 'citizen' would not give the time of day.

221 [Weber] This memorandum, in the 2nd edn (Stuttgart: Dietz, 1903), published with two forewords by Struve, gives the most striking insights into the

substance and *form* of the 'inner life' of the central Russian bureaucracy. [M–D: Witte's 'confidential' memorandum of 1899 was independently published outside Russia by P. Struve, after it had been leaked to the Soiuz Osvobozhdeniia. (Witte, *Samoderzhavie i Zemstvo.*) It was evidently attacking the plans of the Interior Minister, I. L. Goremykin, who wanted to introduce provincial zemstvos in the western provinces too. Witte's firmly held view was that local representative bodies were incompatible with the existing political system. Goremykin resigned in October 1899. The new Interior Minister was D. S. Sipiagin.]

222 [M–D] Reference to the National Assembly in the Frankfurt Paulskirche 1848–9.

223 [M–D] On 29 Mar. 1848 in Prussia the Conservative ministry of Arnim-Boitzenburg was replaced by the Liberal ministry of Camphausen-Hansemann, which, in order to maintain itself in power, attempted to achieve a compromise between the ideas of the King and bourgeois Liberalism, with the aim of getting a moderate constitution while at the same time retaining the prerogatives and absolute right of veto of the Crown.

224 [Tr.] Weber is here contrasting unearned income with profit derived from rational, commercial enterprise.

225 [M–D] Reference to the opposition not only of the American workers, but also of the farmers, to Civil Service Reform ('Pendleton Act') of 1883, which laid the foundations for a professional civil service.

226 [Weber] What should be understood by this has, in my opinion, been clearly stated by *Sombart* in all important aspects. [M–D: W. Sombart, *Der moderne Kapitalismus*, vol. 1 (Leipzig, 1902), pp. 71f and 423ff.] There are no 'final' historical concepts. But the vanity of today's writers, who treat someone else's terminology as they would his toothbrush, is something I will have no part in.

227 'This being-with-itself of Spirit, this coming-to-itself of Spirit can be seen as the supreme absolute goal.' Hegel, *Vorlesungen über die Geschichte der Philosophie*, vol. 1 (Berlin, 1840), pp. 35f.

228 [Weber] Now that newspapers are at last beginning to reach Germany again, a little more light is beginning to be shed on the picture. Election agitation is getting under way. Interest in the elections is variable, e.g. in Moscow it has been very weak, as the small number of registrations to the voting list shows; in Petersburg, of 150,000 entitled to vote about 22,000 have registered, and of these very many only after being requested to do so by the authorities. The 3-week period allowed for registration since the announcement of the new electoral law was suspiciously short; in Moscow (and elsewhere) press reports suggest that those entitled to vote believe that registering is punishable as a political act! Now, at the eleventh hour, when it is probably too late, even the Social Democratic Party is urging the comrades to apply for registration. The three 'monarchist-constitutional' parties, which evidently enjoy the protection of the government – the 'Party of Legal Order', the 'Union of 17 October' and the recently founded 'Party of Trade and

Industry' [on these see List of Parties and Associations] (which quite ruthlessly forces workers and employees to join (cf. *Russkiia Vedomosti* of 4 Jan., pp. 3 and 4)) – have formed a cartel, under the leadership of Gushkov and Shipov. (We intend to report on their programme after the elections.) On the other hand, the government is taking every possible action against the Constitutional Democrats: not only are their election meetings prohibited where possible, but for a time all their newspapers, with one exception, were suppressed, and the majority remain banned today; e.g. in Kiev a new edition of one of their newspapers was prohibited because of its federalist programme. Putting up posters for the party is prohibited even in Petersburg, a prohibition which does *not* apply to other parties. In Kostroma the election of an Old Believer as elector was declared 'prohibited' (the Congress of Old Believers has since, on 4 Jan., issued an appeal which stresses loyalty to the monarchy, but otherwise, even in its policy towards the peasants, has approved a programme which is essentially the same as that of the Constitutional Democrats). A congress of the Marshals of the Nobility and likewise a zemstvo congress – both on the agrarian question – are planned. A congress of the Constitutional Democrats has just been opened. Negotiations are at last about to begin between the Union of Unions and the zemstvo left on a common procedure. The government is proceeding ruthlessly against those trade and professional associations which adopt a political stance and against politicians sympathetic to them; e.g. the Rector of the University of Kharkov, Prof. Reinhardt, has just been arrested. [M–D: In late 1905 and early 1906 many of the Russian provinces were under emergency law, and there were numerous arrests, some of them completely arbitrary, of opposition politicians.] Arrests and disciplining of members of the Third Element are reported everywhere on a massive scale. [M–D: On 16 Dec. 1905 Interior Minister Durnovo issued a circular in which he instructed all the appropriate authorities to arrest teachers, doctors etc. who were hostile to the government.] In Moscow, the election of representatives of the Union of 17 October is regarded as likely in all but two constituencies, and in Petersburg too the Constitutional Monarchist parties are reckoned to have the best chances.

229 [Weber] A semi-official communiqué (*Novoe Vremia*, 4 Jan., p. 2) has announced the transformation into an 'upper house' of the Imperial Council, a pool of ex-ministers and other high dignitaries (about 70), which was created by Speranskii under Alexander I for consultation on the 'laws', but had been ignored for years by the 'enlightened' bureaucracy (Witte in particular). The following will now also join the council: 51 provincial representatives, elected by the zemstvos or, in their absence, by the electoral assemblies of the Imperial Duma; 18 representatives of the corporations of the nobility; 12 representatives of the stock exchanges, chambers of commerce etc.; 6 representatives of the Holy Synod (3 'white', 3 'black' clergy); 6 elected representatives of the Polish provinces. It should have equal rights with the Duma, but no 'question' which had been rejected by

Bourgeois Democracy in Russia 147

the latter should be allowed to go to the Imperial Council. (The Manifesto of 17 Oct. used the word 'Law' – *zakon* – a fairly narrow term.) Otherwise there were to be negotiations by committees about differences of opinion in the two bodies, but where they could not agree the Tsar would have the final decision. Thus the Duma has *no* budget rights, *which the German capital market should note*. This disappointment has led even the committee of the united 'Constitutional Monarchist Party' to adopt a 'defensive' attitude to the government.

230 [M–D] The Prussian Finance Minister Johannes von Miquel, in his programmatic speech of 15 July 1897 in Solingen, introduced a plan for 'Sammlungspolitik', i.e. the harmonization of the interests of industry and agriculture, with the aim of stabilizing the existing political system in the German Reich. The term itself was coined by Miquel on 23 July 1897 in a speech before the Prussian Landtag.

231 [M–D] Term for the Prussian House of Deputies in the age of Manteuffel (1850–8), in which sat numerous *Landräte*, who had been invited to be candidates by the Prussian Government. Moreover, with the help of the *Landräte* the Prussian Government had succeeded in so influencing the election that it was able to secure a majority. [Tr.: At that period a *Landrat* was a kind of Royal Agent, nominated by the local nobility, but answerable only to Berlin.]

232 [Weber] Let the German 'bourgeois', who is expected to invest capital in Russian government stocks, take careful note of that. The list of arrest warrants and bans on assembly is *infinitely more important* for his business interests than the financial reports 'embellished' with the aid of Russia's foreign credits.

233 Friedrich Schiller, *Der Geisterseher*.

2

Russia's Transition to Pseudo-constitutionalism

The General Policy of the Interim Ministry

The two months following the issuing of the October Manifesto[1] and the formation of the Witte Ministry were a period of extreme confusion and continual uncertainty, a chaos of spontaneous claiming of freedoms and rights, at which the government looked on aimlessly, unsure of how to react. The flaring up and suppression of the Moscow uprising[2] and the collapse of the third general strike[3] (which was linked to it) mark the resolute turning of Russian domestic policy towards the severest reaction. This gives what is, in itself, a foolish putsch a historical interest. Quantitatively, the furious civil wars in the Baltic provinces and in the southern central provinces[4] were perhaps more significant, and qualitatively the troop mutinies at Kronstadt and Sevastopol were far more serious – yet the renewed subjugation of a few blocks of streets in Moscow was of a far greater 'moral' significance in itself and had far greater political consequences.

Let us first recall the events themselves.

Leading the strike movements during the whole of the autumn of 1905, which were immeasurably more powerful than expected, was the Petersburg Council of Workers' Deputies (Soviet Rabochikh Deputatov, or SRD). It was first created at the time of the typographers' strike in September by the typographers themselves and was originally intended only for them. At the beginning of October their organization was imitated by other categories of workers, who then united with the printers' delegates. The composition of the council was based entirely on the scheme of workers' representation which had been designed by the government itself: the representatives were elected by workshops, at first one to every 20 members, and finally, in October, one to every 500. When the great political strike,[5] which led to the constitutional manifesto, broke out (15 October), the number of workers under the leadership of the council rose to 113,000 within two days.

There followed in numerous provincial cities the furious counter-revolution of the 'Black Hundreds',[6] which demonstrated for all to see the need for the workers to stick firmly together. In Rostov-on-Don, Kiev, Ekaterinoslav, Kharkov, Moscow, Saratov, Smolensk, Krementshug, Belostok, Taganrog, Novorossiisk, Baku and Krasnoiarsk similar associations were formed at breakneck speed, which kept in touch with the Petersburg group by correspondence. Soon after the victorious conclusion of the October strike the Petersburg SRD was drawn, rather reluctantly, into the movement for the eight-hour day by the workers, acting, at first, on their own initiative. On 29 October the introduction 'by revolutionary means' of the eight-hour day was made binding for Petersburg factories, to be effective from 31 October, by resolution, that is to say, by unilateral declaration of the workers. In fact it was only achieved in 29 factories; the others remained intransigent. In the meantime, however, the first signs of reaction had begun to appear in government circles.

In the press it had become known that the Tsar had adamantly refused to lay aside the title *samoderzhets* ('autocrat'), contrary to Witte's assurance (well authenticated in spite of his denial): 'Henceforth there will be no more autocracy in Russia.' More significant than this was the imposition of martial law on Poland on 28 October, eleven days after the manifesto, the motives and origin of which are mysterious and cannot be explained at all by semi-official talk of local 'revolutionary actions' of the kind that have been going on in Poland for years. Poland replied with a general strike, which, however, at least as far as the railway was concerned, was over by 4 November, almost at the same time as the sympathy strike in Petersburg decreed on 2 November by SRD *began*. The latter now went completely awry; on 7 November the SRD had to end it, and on the 12th had to rescind even its decree regarding the eight-hour day.

In the meantime D. N. Shipov and Prince E. Trubetskoi had refused the portfolios offered them in Witte's Ministry.[7] A rather disparate team of ministers remained. Trepov had left the Ministry of the Interior, Durnovo had taken over the department, at first as 'caretaker'. Soon after the issuing of the very vaguely worded Agrarian Manifesto (3 November) the first peasant unrest began, which was answered by the imposition of a state of 'enhanced protection', whilst on the other hand, as a concession to the liberals, martial law in Poland was – partially – lifted.

Anarchy slowly spread. Nothing was heard of any steps to fulfil the promise to call the Duma on the basis of the extended franchise. Everything seemed uncertain. On 14 November came the arrest of the board of the Socialist Revolutionary Peasant Congress in Moscow for recommending tax obstruction (under certain circumstances), whereupon the committee of the congress formed an alliance with the SRD. On 15 November a congress of delegates of the postal and telegraph employees met in Moscow. On the grounds that those in question were civil servants, the police and military broke up the congress, but not before a strike had been called, which, between 15 and 19 November, spread to every other city, cutting them off from each other and from the outside world. No sooner had it begun to crumble (from 1 December), than the chairman of the SRD in Petersburg, Khrustalev-Nosar, was arrested, on the grounds that the council had been involved in this postal strike; there followed on 1 December the manifesto of the SRD and of its ally the Peasant League, also signed by the Social Democratic Party, which called for refusal to accept paper money, withdrawal of assets from the savings banks – in fact, according to official figures 140 million roubles were withdrawn – and, with equally great success, for an end to all payment of taxes and dues. The response was the arrest of the entire SRD in Petersburg. Thereupon the Moscow SRD seized the leadership and declared a general strike in Moscow for 7 December. On the same date the Pan-Russian Committee of Railwaymen declared a general rail strike. Both strikes spread quickly and reached their climax between 9 and 12 December. By the 19th they were over. At *no time* did they equal the geographical extent and numerical support of the victorious political October strike, although this time the powerful organizations of the peasants, railway workers and postal and telegraph workers as well as the numerous Councils of Workers' Deputies had the leadership in their hands.

This example is evidence of what the power of an 'idea' which *unites* the classes, and the cooperation of broad strata of the bourgeoisie, can achieve and *how little* – one may regret this or not – the 'strong arm', at whose bidding 'every wheel is still',[8] can achieve without that uncertainty in the established cadres of the existing social order which is brought about by such cooperation amongst bourgeois elements.

Non-proletarian elements and, in particular, the assorted crew of ideologues and dilettantes who romanticize the revolution, did not begin to rally to the cause of the revolution until the general strike in Moscow turned into a revolt, the Social Revolutionaries having long toyed with the poetic term *vooruzhennoe vostaniie* ('armed revolt'). This perfectly suited the book of the military leadership, this time under the ruthless leadership of Dubasov.

On the night of 9 December in Moscow the first revolver shots were fired at the military, who were surrounding a meeting, whereupon barricades were thrown up and for ten days there was an at first rather uncoordinated deployment of artillery, shelling of houses from which someone or other had fired, and a general shooting at anyone who was armed or otherwise suspect, all of which only ended with the arrival of the Semenov regiment from Petersburg to reinforce the 6,000-man garrison, which systematically encircled the remainder of the revolutionaries (19 December).

The figures for the hospitals in the period from 7 to 17 December show 548 dead, and 1,065 wounded; many of the slightly wounded escaped, some even to German universities, but apart from that there are no figures for the last days or for the prisoners who were simply shot out of hand in large numbers. The number of effective fighting men cannot be established, since some of them were only casual combatants. The maximum number actively taking part in the battle *at any given time* must have been around 8,000.

It was certainly no surprise that the troops remained loyal, faced with such an unplanned and hopeless uprising, especially in view of the grim tactics which the official organ of the SRD, *Izvestiia* (11 December), recommended: form small detachments (up to a maximum of four), lie in wait, and open fire on full columns of troops when least expected. It *was* a pleasant surprise for one important element in Russian constitutional development – the foreign *stock exchanges*. In order to understand the behaviour of the Russian government it is essential to bear in mind that Russia is a debtor state. It is quite correct to say (as the reactionaries maintain) that 'the Jews' forced through, brought about by stealth or at least helped to construct the Russian constitution; not, of course, the dreadfully abused inhabitants of the Russian ghettos, but their (in some cases) ennobled cousins in high finance in Berlin and Paris, who are entrusted with the control of the prices of Russian government stocks. This could be very clearly observed too in that period of violent reaction which accompanied the suppression of the revolutionaries in Moscow and the subsequent overthrow of the uprisings in the Baltic provinces and in the inland provinces. The Manifesto of 17 October should have had a calming influence. It had no such thing. The prices of government stocks fell again. On the other hand the bloody tragicomedy in Moscow tended to push stock market prices up: the holders of Russian government stocks wished for 'order', and Count Witte uttered ambiguous words about the possibility of 'retracting' the Imperial promises. This 'kite-flying', however, was itself not always well received. For days on end, from the beginning to the middle of January, *Novoe Vremia* received telegraphs from London indicating, no doubt correctly, that the banks regarded Russia's credit-worthiness as assured only if a 'constitutional' form of government were introduced.

From abroad, then, caution was demanded, and the reactionaries now became aware of this. On 23 December (Old Calendar) the Tsar received, for the second time, a deputation of 'Russian people'. Passionate speeches against severing the bonds between Tsar and people, the overthrow of a centuries-old order, and the ending of the absolute power of the Sovereign finally even appeared to inflame the feeble passions of the Tsar himself. In lurid phrases he spoke of 'the truth coming soon, very soon shining its light over the Russian earth' and the like. With enthusiasm and delight the deputation passed this on to the papers, for the consolation of all true Russian hearts – and straight away came the semi-official announcement that the deputation stood accused of unauthorized publication of a court report. Witte's comments on how out of place such romantic motions were, when the coffers were empty, had evidently sufficed to cause His Divine Grace, having held his head up a little too soon, to bow it again and henceforth to remain in a more appropriate state of subordination towards the impersonal but ineluctable power of the money market. This was shown in a number of ways: for example, it was officially denied that police officers had taken part in anti-Jewish pogroms in late autumn and winter, but when shortly before Easter the big loan was due to be issued,[9] the authorities felt constrained to make the provincial officials personally responsible for any such riots by a decree which was indeed unambiguous, not to say draconian. The result was that absolutely no such disturbances occurred. However much they had 'compromised' themselves, writers like Gorky, who were well known abroad and whose unduly harsh treatment could make a bad impression there, were able to enjoy a very much better fate than those who lacked his reputation.

Thus, in the light of the financial situation, the government was obliged to engage in some 'double accounting' in domestic policy. It was abundantly evident, and emerged clearly on every occasion which allowed it, that the Tsar himself *never* sincerely intended the transformation of Russia into a constitutional state [*Rechtsstaat*], with what the October Manifesto rather naively termed '*real*' guarantees of personal rights; for the Tsar there were only police interests. That chimed in perfectly with the interests of the old-style police bureaucracy, and the policy of ruthless repression was no doubt intended to demonstrate 'strong government' for the benefit of the foreign stock exchanges. On the other hand, however, the repeated fruitless sending of finance officials abroad showed that in spite of everything the bankers still felt they had to insist that the Duma should really be elected (and convened) before they would consider providing any large-scale loan. The constitution had to be implemented and the commitments of 17 October formally observed to the extent that the foreign audience which the bankers needed to impress was at least shown the outward appearance of 'constitutional' guarantees.

The attempt therefore had to be made to reconcile the domestic 'bourgeoisie' with the interests of the government, and to look for parties which would represent these interests in the Duma and help them to secure victory in the elections. Complications arose, however, through the fact that whereas supporters of a decidedly liberal transformation of the state occupied positions (mainly lower, but also higher) within the bureaucracy itself, right up to the Imperial Council and the Ministry, as well as within the army, on the other hand the period of the demagogic Plehve regime had aroused the deepest antagonism and a mistrust amongst 'bourgeois' circles which was hard to overcome.

One could only hope – and this was Witte's standpoint – that the red terror of the general strikes, uprisings and peasants' revolts would prove stronger than all these recollections. Within the bureaucracy and the army, however, the wheat had to be slowly but systematically separated from the chaff, at least in the higher positions, now that the attitude of the Tsar was clear. The Democratic Agriculture Minister Kutler and the centrist Trade Minister Timiriasev left, one after the other. Since the December uprising the Minister of the Interior, Durnovo, had been the Tsar's principal spokesman. The feverish activity of his ministry during January and the early part of February was in marked contrast to the other ministries.

He personally led the policy of repression, though this business was much facilitated by the fact that most provincial governors regarded it as a sport, conscious that the more they distinguished themselves in this, the more they would please the Tsar. For them there was no law; officials like Neidhardt (Odessa) and Kurlov (Minsk), whose prosecution had been demanded by the Senator charged with overseeing their activity, were pronounced immune from prosecution by the First Department of the Senate at the urging of the Minister of the Interior (who was present *in person*), since 'their actions had been in accord with the intentions of the government'. The zealous governors did not even react to warnings or prohibitions by the ministers, especially Witte, or in individual cases even Durnovo; in one particular instance a minister in council declared by way of excuse that the governor had clearly taken the view that he was required to obey only the Council of Ministers, and not one of its members: in the matter of administrative arbitrariness, Russia in January fell de facto into regional satrapies.

A press report – details not fully authenticated – asserts that in a Council meeting Witte urged limitation of the policy of repression and especially of the uncontrollable tyranny of the officials; to which Durnovo replied that in that case the time had come for him to go, a reply which was met with an icy silence. Some days later, however, a discussion between them led to an 'understanding'. In fact it was only another humiliation for Witte. He did manage to get his position as Council president *formally* recognized, so was officially informed of departmental decrees; in reality, though, things remained as he occasionally declared, namely that Durnovo was all-powerful, and if he wanted him (Witte) hanged he could arrange that at any time.

The first disciplinary action of the bureaucracy, which was regaining its strength, was the change in police organization, and the purges of postal, telegraph and railway employees – which we shall not go into here – while at the same time salaries were considerably increased. An extra 3 million roubles was set aside for the police (in addition to the 21 million roubles already being spent on the police).

Then the *army* had to be tackled. I cannot check the accuracy of newspaper reports about the *number* of generals and colonels (over 300) who were dismissed in the course of the three months from 1 December to 1 March. Nevertheless for a long time the major newspapers were full of the declarations (published as late as January) of assemblies of officers that they stood by the Tsar, though on the basis of the Manifesto of 17 October, alongside other declarations advising against any politics in the officers' mess, and other declarations expressing support for these positions etc. About mid-January – according to newspaper reports, which, to my knowledge, have not been disputed – a cossack regiment declared that it stood on the ground of constitutionalism according to the Manifesto of 17 October, and protested against being used for police purposes. The government itself, however, by encouraging supporters of the 'League of Russian Men'[10] in the officer corps, gave a boost to the role of politics and thus also to hypocrisy, which, according to all historical experience, is bound to have worrying consequences for the government itself.

But to stop at the officers was impossible. Apart from the guards, who had already been thoroughly purged, the government had to be sure of the loyalty of the cossacks. That could no longer be taken for granted, now that protests had been heard from their number against the use of the army by the police, and especially since economic changes had threatened to undermine the very foundations of the cossacks' way of life. No fundamental changes could be made in a hurry, but something had to be done immediately. The government resorted to the remedy applied by the Roman Emperors in the declining years of the Empire:[11] generous gifts for service in the civil war. The government, though living on credit, applied to distribute in cash to these pillars of the monarchy no less than 7.5 million roubles (over 17 million marks), 100 roubles for every cossack, a sum which the Imperial Council reduced by about 1.6 million roubles. A number of cossack regions, if we may here anticipate, answered this demagogic measure by voting for *Democrats* in the elections! After the opening of the Duma, cossack deputies bombarded each other with letters to the newspapers (for example in *Novoe Vremia*, no. 10825, and elsewhere) for and against a public statement by one of their number directed against the maintenance of special cossack military service. The *atamans* [see Glossary] among them were indignant at this, but evidently the common people amongst the cossack electorate were not so at all.

By now the reservists were beginning to arrive home from Manchuria. Finding that the assurances which had been given them regarding provision for their families left at home had not, in most cases, and for typically Russian bureaucratic reasons, been honoured, they were furious and threatened to turn against the government. The government had to dig deep into its pockets again, without achieving anything other than to strengthen the conviction of the masses that this state mechanism could only be made to do its duty through fear. The improvements ordered for the standing army in the provision of meals etc. forced out of the government by mutinies, had similar results. Nevertheless, for the foreseeable future, now that there was no expectation of a repetition of such unplanned and pointless revolts as those in Kronstadt and Sevastopol, the army would be at the government's disposal.

After suppressing the peasant uprisings, the government started to make use of the available instruments of power. On 1 March – according to figures published in *Pravo* – 8 provinces in their entirety, and 18 partially, were in a state of 'reinforced protection'; 5 provinces in their entirety, and 10 partially, were in a state of 'extraordinary' protection; and 17 (!) provinces in their entirety, and 22 partially, were under *martial law*'. Only 27 out of a total of 87 provinces and 'territories' of the Empire were in a normal state, whilst in two-thirds of the Empire the regular administrative principles had been more or less drastically altered, and in about two-fifths there was martial law. It is worth noting that similar conditions prevailed at the time of the 1871 elections in France,[12] and this should be borne in mind when considering the significance of the Russian elections as a picture of the Russian people. It should also be remembered that the government left no doubt that the return to normal conditions was *dependent* on the political 'good behaviour' of society at these elections.

No great purpose would be served in describing the 'White Terror' here in detail.[13] The scope of it can be gauged from the fact that a series of changes in the legal constitution were necessary merely to create the *physical capacity* for the required number of sentences. In the course of January and early February the prisons became so overcrowded that the administrations frequently turned to the zemstvos to ask for more accommodation, a request which was regularly turned down. The greatest possible increase in 'administrative banishments' – internment in distant provinces *without* a court hearing and sentence and totally without recourse to law – was no more able to solve the problem than the executions by firing-squad, in areas with martial law, carried out on the spot often on official instructions for certain revolutionary or 'suspicious' actions, *without* even the formality of a trial.

The prison authorities often exercise restraint in their treatment of 'politicals', sometimes going beyond what is strictly permissible, for they are reluctant to face the trouble which the determined solidarity of these people can cause them. Equally, for the Russian revolutionary, once arrested, the shedding of the terrible burden of responsibility for his cause and the ending of the continual mental tension, at least at first, provides some physical relief, and *short* gaol sentences are regarded as 'a holiday'. However, this time, with the bitterness on both sides and as a result of the general conditions in the overcrowded prisons, there have been numerous instances of suicide attempts or nervous breakdowns among prisoners, or hunger strikes directed against the administration in protest at barbarous and degrading treatment of both men and women by officials.

It seems quite impossible to establish the *number* of those who, without trial, were shot, imprisoned or banished – estimates in the press vary for the two last categories between 17,000 and 70,000. More important for a political assessment of the developments is the question of what was *achieved* by this regime. Large-scale uprisings were of course put down wherever they occurred. The mass burning of farms ceased, after losses which can only be very roughly estimated (for 17 out of 61 European provinces the figure was *officially* put at 31.3 million roubles, and in Saratov at a maximum of 9.5 million roubles). The insurance companies refused to pay up, citing the war clause, – in glaring contrast to America after the San Francisco earthquake. But as late as April, faced with the renewed threat of peasant unrest, a re-garrisoning of 159 infantry bat-

Pseudo-constitutionalism 157

talions and an equivalent number of other arms of the service had to be undertaken, at a cost of several million roubles.

'We shall not only destroy the revolution, we shall pulverize it,' Durnovo had said.

To instil salutory fear into the bourgeoisie, *Pravitelstvennyi Vestnik* published weekly a list of revolutionary brutalities, a list which was inevitably incomplete. For the period from January to May no diminution is evident, and the same is true for the regular daily report of between a half and one column in length, headed: 'Disturbances', in, for instance, *Novoe Vremia*.

In the month of April, up to the start of the Duma, there were the usual number of executions, while the number of political assassinations remained at a daily average of about five – though of course varying from day to day. Tagantsev announced in the Imperial Council (27 June) that whereas from 1863 to 1903 15 death sentences had been pronounced, from 1 January to 1 June 1906 there had been 180. This number can only refer to the 'regular' courts.

It cannot of course be known for sure how many of the bank raids really served the purpose of obtaining money for the purposes of the revolution. In March and April they reached epidemic proportions, after the undoubtedly political, unprecedented robbery of 850,000 roubles in cash had been successfully perpetrated at a Moscow bank; the culprits were never discovered.

The highest officials did succeed in protecting themselves personally against attempts on their lives, as did most of the middle-ranking ones, and only a mere dozen governors or their deputies fell victim to class revenge. But the lower ranks had to risk their lives in daily battles. Of the higher officials, as far as I am aware, only those who were proved to have been guilty of acts of cruelty beyond the requirements of the law, or those who were denied justice, were executed. The revolutionaries reacted promptly when the poet and publisher of *Russkoe Bogatstvo*, Korolenko, in an open letter, pilloried the shameful violation of the human dignity of peasants, of which State Councillor Filonov was said to be guilty, just as – according to press reports – the *wives* of a cossack officers' corps accused the cossack officer Abramov of indecent assault on the assassin Spiridonova.[14] A special law against the propagation of 'false' reports about actions of officials was passed, in an attempt to protect the latter against such public appeals.

Whilst on the one hand the government had no success in curbing the murders or the bomb attacks, they no longer had any visible intimidating effect on the practice of administration: chronic civil war simply raged in the form of the most dreadful guerrilla warfare: no mercy was shown by either side, and innocent people were killed without compunction. Every bomb that went off killed some who were quite uninvolved; the troops regularly replied to a shot or a bomb, if they themselves had been hit or just happened to be in the vicinity, with a salvo fired blindly into the throng of passers-by. It was only after the elections, at Easter time, when subscription of the loan was due to begin, that measures began to be taken, for the sake of making a good impression, to relieve the quite intolerable overcrowding of the prisons by numerous releases of 'politicals', who had been held *without charge*, in some cases for four to five months. In the meantime, faced with the resolute efforts of the prisoners, the prison administrators moderated their severity to the extent of negotiating compromise agreements with committees of prisoners regarding what privileges they should be allowed.

Analysis of the General Political Legislation of the Interim Ministry

Alongside these attempts to control the *kramola* [uprising], which, though carried out with great barbarity, were still not really successful, and which were undertaken in the interests of self-preservation and in order to restore credit-worthiness, attempts were also being made to create institutions which would give the outward impression abroad that the Manifesto of 17 October was being carried out, though without seriously jeopardizing the power of the bureaucracy.

The Manifesto had promised:

1 the granting of 'effective' (*deistvitelnaia*) inviolability of the person, freedom of conscience, of speech, of assembly and of association;
2 extension of the franchise, of which we shall have more to say later;
3 implementation of the principle that no law should come into force without the consent of the Duma, and of the principle of actual participation of the Duma 'in the supervision of the legality of the actions' of the state authorities.

It is worth while looking a little more closely at the implementation of these promises by the old regime, which continued to function until the Duma *actually assembled* and which made the feeble old Imperial Council, which is normally so sluggish, go on working in feverish haste right up to its formal closure (17 April/1 May 1906). Let us also analyse rather more closely, with the aid of documents from the last two years, the fate of the individual 'liberties' which are being fought for with a desperate tenacity reminiscent of the age of Charles I.

Pseudo-constitutionalism

We shall begin with the liberties promised under point 1 of the Manifesto.

(1) Of these, *'freedom of speech'* was the one which automatically imposed itself on the government's attention. After the manifesto, the press de facto gained complete freedom from censorship. The required submission of copies for checking did not take place, the circulars in which in the hitherto customary manner certain subjects were put out of bounds were simply ignored, and the government did not dare to intervene. Only the republican provocation by the newly founded socialist press – incredibly foolhardy in view of the existing power situation – caused it to intervene, in the interest of self-preservation, and the exhaustion of the masses due to the fruitless second general strike in November gave it the courage to take a first step in the direction of reaction.

The 'temporary ruling on the press' of 24 November/7 December 1905 abolished preventive censorship for the majority of periodicals, namely for those published *in the cities* (No. I), made the press exclusively subject to the courts in cases of infringement of the law or of the suspicion of such (Nos II, IV), abolished the concession requirement for newspaper publishers (No. III), did away with the right of the Minister of the Interior to prohibit the treatment of certain subjects 'of state significance' in the press (No. V) and, where there was an intention to start a new journal, introduced officially the *iavochnyi poriadok* (requirement to give notice [see Glossary]) in place of the concessionary system. But this is nothing but a sham, for the ruling requires that with the notice, as well as other information, a 'programme' of the newspaper or journal should be handed in (No. VII. 1) and gives the authority the right to prevent publication by refusing a certificate, should the programme conflict with 'morality or the law'.

Since the newspaper may not appear before issue of the certificate, in practice the way is open for complete arbitrariness. In fact in this way very many newspapers have been suppressed for 'antigovernment' orientation; for example the *word* 'socialist' is evidently enough to ensure rejection, and likewise publications favourable to the Ukraine are not permitted, on account of their programme etc. I am at the moment not aware of the attitude taken by the Senate, to whom complaints may be made. Moreover one copy of each issue must be delivered on publication (No. VII. 8), whereupon, should 'indications of a criminal act' be found in it, it can be seized, and moreover – a worsening of the existing situation – this can now be authorized not merely by the censorship committees made up of fellow professionals, but by individual officials, and, furthermore, without any time limit within which a decision of the court must be obtained, provided the period of the seizure has not expired (it must simply be carried out 'without delay', No. VII. 11). *Except for all newspapers not published in cities,* censorship was maintained for court news, and for the proceedings of meetings of the nobility, of the *city* dumas and zemstvos, and also – very significantly for the *election campaign* – for *advertisements* (Art. 41 of the censorship statute, No. XI of the regulations)!

[*Weber refers to other restrictions on the press and on booksellers, largely through various strategems of censorship and criminal prosecution.*]

[Despite this,] as a glance into the newspaper advertisements or in *Knizhnii Vestnik* shows, at the moment Russia is positively flooded with translations of foreign, especially socialist literature, which are astonishingly cheap, because in the absence of copyright protection for foreign authors everything is imported illegally. The editions of the well-known socialist works frequently run to 30,000 copies and are coming on to the market one after another. One can see what intellectual fare is being voraciously devoured by looking, in particular, at the sphere of ethics. Primitive products like Kautsky's *Ethics* or Anton Menger's latest book, which in Germany is disdainfully dismissed as mere childishness, have the most tremendous success in the bookshops. The appetite for radical literature seems virtually insatiable. Even the most extreme measures of repression and confiscation imaginable would not be able to reverse the widespread ownership of these writings, which runs into hundreds of thousands of copies. Only harassment of all kinds, which only succeeds in stirring up renewed hatred for the regime, is possible here, and it is widely practised.

(2) Of the liberties promised in the Manifesto of 17 October the '*freedom of conscience*' had to some extent already been conferred by the ukase of 17 April 1905. This 'Edict of Toleration' was itself based on the thorough deliberations of the Committee of Ministers (25 January, 1, 8, and 15 February 1905), which had been necessitated by the ukase of 12 December 1904, point 6, in which, as the published extracts from the minutes clearly reveal,[15] the views of the *Metropolitan of Petersburg,* Antonii, carried the greatest weight, whilst the Chief Procurator of the Holy Synod, Pobedonostsev, had to concede more than usual.

Force, the Metropolitan had explained, was at variance with the nature of the Orthodox Church, and, appealing to Titus 3: 10 and Matthew 18: 17, he had pointed out the intolerable situation in which servants of the Church were placed by the duty laid upon them by Art. 1006 of the penal code to cooperate with the 'secular arm' in cases of apostasy or heresy. The committee therefore decided that force was not to be applied at all in cases of change of faith, and that where someone wished to transfer from one Christian faith (including the Orthodox faith) to another, the principle of complete freedom of choice of confession must apply.

Only apostasy to non-Christian faiths (Muslim and Jewish were named) must continue to entail civil and legal consequences, given the Christian character of the state and the rarity of the occurrence. These consequences arose from the impossibility of the state's legally recognizing the procedure. Even here, though, there should be no violent repression.

The question of mixed marriages was discussed in great detail and the opinion of the Metropolitan was accepted. This was that the existing regulation should be retained (namely that where one of the parties to the marriage was Orthodox the children were to receive an Orthodox education – no special arrangements by parents were permitted) 'since the admissibility of mixed marriages was itself a concession to the state' and after all the children were at liberty to leave the Church on reaching the age of majority.

The 'Raskol' ('Old Believer' schismatics separated from the official Church in the seventeenth century [see Glossary]) had suffered under the harsh legislation which in 1874 created special registers for them; but then in 1883 – under Alexander III, who was more sympathetic to their cause – their communities were granted civil recognition and their ritual was officially recognized. The consequent lessening of the Raskol's opposition to the Orthodox Church was one of the Metropolitan's main arguments for the removal of the remnants of the old legislation discriminating against it.

The position of the 'sects' was more difficult, not least because the *concept* lacked any legal or customary definition, and furthermore because even in the last century legislation had varied in its attitude towards them. The law of 1874 concerning church registers had, according to preliminary discussions, been intended to include them, but did not in fact do so, and the law of 1883 certainly did not, and thus they were subject to the arbitrary rule of the administrators. The 'Stundists' were *prohibited* from holding prayer meetings, first in 1878, then by ministerial decree of 4 July 1894 (confirmed by Supreme authority). What was worse, the administration, not appreciating the character of the 'Stundists', extended this ban to cover sects of all kinds, lumping together the Stundists (pietistic Protestants) with every kind of other sect (e.g. the 'pneumatic' Dukhobortsen.[16]

The Committee of Ministers recommended the abolition of the decree of 1894 as ineffective and also unnecessary, since the nature of Stundism was now better known. The committee also proposed to categorize the entire recognized religious communities, both those which were not Orthodox and those which had not previously been recognized, like the Lutheran Church, no longer, as before, according to their degree of 'harmfulness', but in groups as follows:

1 Those who accept the fundamentals of Orthodoxy but differ from it in their ritual: these should from now on be known as Staroobriadchiki (Old Ritualists).
2 Rationalist and mystical sects (to be tolerated).
3 Superstitious doctrines: not to be tolerated, because they conflicted with the moral foundations of the state; profession of these should continue to be an offence (this category unquestionably included the Skopchi;[17] but the question of which other sects were to be included was left to be determined 'in practice'). [. . .]

The most important amendment of the ukase of 17 April 1905[18] was the regulation (No. I), according to which, in future, apostasy from the Orthodox Church to another *Christian* faith – that is, not formal apostasy from Christianity altogether – should entail no personal or civil disadvantages for the individual at all, who should henceforth be treated as belonging, on attaining majority, to the faith community chosen by him.

[*Weber writes of the penalties that apostasy from Orthodoxy had previously attracted.*]

If one compares the decree of 14 March 1906 with the edict of amnesty for crimes of religion, which was issued on 25 June 1905 (*expressis verbis*) *as a result of* the ukase of 17 April 1905, it is clear that the group of religious offences now finally eliminated is not identical with the group of those embraced by the amnesty, but is in fact considerably smaller. The regulations against publicly propagating 'heresies' are likely to cause a recrudescence of all the old persecutions of the past: only proselytizing by the small *sects* from person to person is in fact protected.

[*Weber describes the disappointed response of the 'Old Believers' (see Glossary) to the decree of 14 March largely because the religious crimes of conversion and propaganda remained in existence.*]

(3) The Edict of Toleration (No. XIV) instituted the principle of religious instruction in the *mother tongue* by clergy of the appropriate community and, in the absence of that, by secular teachers of the same community.

The December edict of 1904 had held out the prospect of a review of language legislation. This promise of a general revision of language legislation led to changes more far-reaching than any of the other promises made.

On 1 May 1905 came the approval for the ministerial report regarding the use of the Lithuanian and Polish languages in the 'Western Raion' (the nine provinces of Belorussia and the Ukraine and the Polish–Russian border areas) in the internal affairs of private companies, except for those concerned with officially controlled accounting and record-keeping; also approved was the use of the mother tongue as *object* of instruction (not *language* of instruction) in the two-class and higher schools.

In the course of the first months of the year 1906 Polish was introduced as language of instruction in the 'Tsardom of Poland', and German, Lithuanian and other local languages were introduced in *privately* funded schools in the Baltic provinces (except that Russian geography, history and literature were still to be taught through the medium of Russian).

[*Weber sketches the regime's electoral policy in regard to various nations under its sway, notably Poland and the Baltic provinces.*]

(4) The issue of *academic freedom* in the fourfold sense: university autonomy, freedom to teach, freedom to learn, and freedom of student life, has been a tremendously important one over the last 20 years. But it is equally clear that since the great student strike of 1899,[19] which was in protest against police brutality towards peaceful students (whom the police suspected of intent to demonstrate), the genuinely 'academic' aspect has played a less significant part than it did previously. For the unrest which has arisen year in year out has only an indirect and loose connection with questions of 'academic freedom' in the German sense of the word.

The hitherto undisputed right of the entire body of professors to elect the Rector, and of the faculties to elect the Deans – subject only, as with us, to regular confirmation by the Ministry – was taken away from the Russian universities by Alexander III in 1884: academic functionaries were *appointed*, and the hitherto existing academic court, consisting of elected professors, was abolished and replaced by an office consisting of the appointed dignitaries (Rector, Dean) plus the similarly appointed 'Inspector', who was no longer subject to the Rector, but to the State Registrar (*popechitel*).[20] De facto then the hitherto obligatory formal legal procedure was abolished in favour of purely administrative decrees, analogous to 'banishment by the administrative route'. The 'Inspector of Students' became at one and the same time judge, public prosecutor and chief detective for the university, the caretakers were at his disposal and with the aid of their information he prepared the lists of unreliable students to hand to the registrar, who then 'dealt with' them. Almost up to the end of the century the filling of professorial chairs – contrary to the situation prior to 1884, when the right to propose these had existed in all cases – was by unilateral appointment, the curriculum was drawn up by the government, and there were even constant attempts to interfere with the freedom of teaching by prescribing a certain 'Russian spirit' in the lectures.

These processes seriously discredited the professorial body in the eyes of students – but it was not so much this as the banning of any corporate student life which formed the starting-point for the incredibly powerful and successful revolutionary spirit in the universities. Although student associations (indeed any corporate activity) were prohibited by the ministerial ruling of 1885, they came into being nevertheless, since the huge dimensions of the Empire and the poverty of most of the students rendered it imperative to meet their material needs, by means of aid funds, sickness funds, information offices of all kinds, and, as would be the case anywhere else, places where the individual, thrust into a completely strange world, could meet and join with others. Of course, the *official* support system, which was unreliable and, moreover, functioned as an arm of the political police, was shunned by all self-respecting students.

The student associations [*Landsmannschaften*] which thus inevitably arose began, in the 1880s, to take on the character of *secret* organizations, since open ones were banned or made subject to quite humiliating conditions. At the end of 1896 the 'Federal Council' of Moscow University comprised, according to official figures, almost half the student body. Once a technique of clandestine communication between the individual universities, and secret organs of association, had been created, then – despite individual interventions, arrest etc. by the authorities – suppression of this illegal student autonomy proved to be an impossibility. The associations, for their part, terrorized the universities, kept watch over every unwelcome move by the professors, administered rebukes – often publicly in the lecture hall – and interrupted classes; no way was found to break their power.

The government now began to relent a little; it restored the professorial court, and began to fill posts on the basis of proposals – but it was too late. The professors refused to act as a political court, and in any case the government soon deprived them of this function, and confined their authority to matters of discipline.

The clandestine student associations began to be drawn into the radical Russian parties, which were now being reorganized. These associations

Pseudo-constitutionalism 165

became increasingly detached from the ground of particular academic interests; concessions in the sphere of 'academic freedom' *alone* could no longer satisfy them, indeed each of these was regarded rather as a sign of government 'weakness' and as a stage in the political struggle.

In vain did Vannovskii [Minister of Public Information, 1901-2] try, during his short regime, to make concessions, by giving permission for meetings of individual year groups, attended by professors. Even the demand to allow 'General Assemblies' of *all* students (which he refused to grant) would not have restored peace, for in recent years the students were claiming 'right of assembly' in the university only in order to be able to organize a place of asylum for *political* meetings which were out of reach of the police, with attendance by *non*-students as well, to serve the cause of the universal liberation movement. Every imaginable device was set in motion against these activities, but in vain: academic life simply could not pursue its course without lecture halls becoming venues for political demonstrations. As soon as professors attempted to prevent this happening, it became clear that they no longer enjoyed any authority over the students. Strikes had been taking place since autumn 1904; from 9 January 1905 the strike became total, and has lasted for a year and a half without a break, during which time the universities have remained closed.

The liberal professors formed the Academic League (Akademicheskii Soiuz), which then joined the radical Union of Unions (Soiuz Soiuzov). The government resorted to extreme measures: after numerous professors, including some of the outstanding representatives of Russian scholarship, had been dismissed, and a few arrested, it officially *threatened* the dismissal of *all students and all professors* in the universities concerned, if regular duties were not resumed in the autumn of 1905, and imposed detailed curricula on the faculties as well as prescribing the content of teaching and lectures course by course.

This amounted to a lock-out in the grand style and an attempt to treat university studies on the same level as the middle schools. It was perfectly clear that the autumn semester (officially 20 August until 10 December) would *not* begin under these circumstances. Then suddenly the government lost its nerve, and almost immediately after the official date for the start of the semester published the ukase of 27 August 1905, which abolished the ruling of Alexander III and decreed that the Rector and his 'aide' as well as the Deans would be elected by the Council (i.e. the assembly of professors) or, in some cases, by the faculties (No. 1), and confirmed by the government.

The Council (or 'Great Senate', as we would call it) had the right and duty to ensure 'the ordered course of university life'; in the case of disorder it was obliged to request a suspension of studies (2b), the

'Inspector' was subordinate to it (2c), and the professorial court remained as the only disciplinary body for the students (2d).

The step taken was half-hearted and unclear: for example, the disciplinary court had already been restored in 1902, as previously mentioned; a 'confidential circular' had, however, transferred the handling of 'mass disorder' to the (appointed) Rector *alone*; the rights which were granted to the 'Council' were not enumerated, but (2a) there was only general mention of 'measures' which he himself should take or should direct to be taken by elected commissions, in order to ensure the ordered course of academic life, and so on.

Of course there was no mention of renewal of academic life. The events of October threw everything into turmoil; the universities opened up, but only in order to serve as open forums for radical assemblies. Now the government did nothing more. It hoped the students' hardship would wear them down. Not until after the Duma elections did Moscow University undertake to open its lecture halls (in April); the student movement then called upon the students to leave politics to the Duma and re-enter academic life. In the meantime, following the December events, the 'Academic League' of professors had left the Union of Unions. In fact, in spite of strong protests and heated debates in the student meetings, they did manage to organize a fairly large number of lectures, though the attendance at these lectures was at first poor. At the same time a 'summer semester' was introduced into the Russian academic year whereas previously there had been two semesters, one from 20 August till 20 December, and one from 15 January till 31 May, which in fact contained scarcely six months of effective work. Elsewhere, however, e.g. in Kazan, the boycott of the universities continued.

In the meantime, the question of the re-ordering of university life had been discussed by the Academic Congress, which took place, at the instigation of Education Minister Count Tolstoy, in January 1906. The Congress decided to 'finish the job' by drawing up a draft of statutes: a reform draft, sent by the Education Minister some time before the meeting of the congress, was rejected *in toto* without debate before the actual discussions had begun, and can therefore be left aside here.

The deliberations of the Congress concerned the questions of (1) 'autonomy'; (2) the manner of the filling of professorial posts; (3) the situation of 'Privatdozenten'[21] and other teaching staff not on the establishment; (4) academic degrees; and finally (5) student 'academic freedom'.

In the question of autonomy the congress took as a basis the formula accepted throughout Russia on the relations between 'self-government' and state supervision: supervision only over the *legality*, but not over the *appropriateness* of the official actions of the autonomous corporations. Thus the *final* decision on all matters relating to the teaching and economic administration of the university was to be in the hands of the 'Council' (consisting of professors); there was also to be an end to the office of state registrar, and restriction of the position of Rector to that of an executive officer for the Council. Confirmation by the Minister should only be required for the election of the Rector and of the full professors – this was opposed by a significant minority – and was to be limited to a purely *formal* check on the correct procedure in the conduct of the election, within two months after its completion. The university, or the faculties, should be in sole charge of 'Habilitation'[22] and employment of all other 'Dozenten'[23] and other academic staff as well as the entire administrative staff of the university.

Given this attitude to the question of the formal *right* to fill posts, the task of ensuring that the right appointments were made was all the more urgent, given the danger of nepotism. Opinions were divided over the procedure for appointing to a chair: 'competition' or 'proposal'? Should the main weight of decision fall in the faculty or in the 'Council'?

[*Weber rehearses the various positions on this, including use of the ballot.*]

These details have only been cited here in order to illustrate the faith of Russian colleagues in the efficacy of a good *balloting system*, even where *personal* qualities are concerned – one can only wish that they abandon their special esteem for the efficiency of the 'Council' ('Great Senate' as we should say). As far as I understand the procedure of appointments by means of such a sizeable assembly, the Council is quite useless when it comes to making sound decisions on such questions as the academic qualities of a scholar in a particular *subject*, and should only be set in motion by the direct *request* of a certain minimum number of faculty members.

Against the vote of the faculties – however far from 'infallible' they invariably are – there should only be a *veto*, never a right to impose a choice, and this should be given to a body which is preferably not too large (such as the proposed administrative committee – or 'small senate', as we should say[24] – which it is suggested should consist of Rector, Pro-Rector, Deans and two elected members from each faculty), if, as in Russia, one has reasons for not entrusting the task to the government.

True '*academic freedom*', in the sense of – as far as human frailty permits this – the consideration of only the scholarly qualities (and teaching ability) of the candidate, cannot be attained by ballot in a large assembly of mainly not well-informed members any more than it can be by intervention of political party patronage or bureaucratic bodies loyal to the state.

For the 'Dozenten' (Extraordinarien,[25] to use German terminology),[26] on the other hand, election by the Faculty (by selection with or without competition) and confirmation by the 'Council' (the only correct method) has been accepted, for the reason that – in the majority view – these 'younger teachers' should not belong to the 'Council' of the University. It is, however, precisely with this question that the most vigorous debates, press controversies, petitions and protest meetings of Extraordinarien and Privatdozenten have been concerned. As regards the Extraordinarien (or Dozenten), their participation in all affairs *other than* proposals for the election of professor, was accepted by *determining* vote.

There was doubt only on whether they should be authorized to participate, possibly by means of deputies to be elected by them, in the discussions of the 'Council' (Great Senate) and possibly on the question of whether their role should be advisory or with powers of decision. The same question was posed for the other categories of university teachers, i.e. those *not* part of the establishment: Privatdozenten, assistant lecturers, pathology assistants etc. It was connected with the whole question of the future position of the Privatdozent.

[*Weber expands on this, particularly in regard to the qualification to be required for Privatdozenten and the precarious position of the latter in the Russian system of higher education.*]

The nature of the organization of the teaching, the planning of the curriculum, compulsory courses and examination subjects – which has been hitherto the duty of the Education Minister after taking advice from the Faculty – is to be left to the Faculty, with confirmation by the 'Council'. The important questions of teaching method which remain unresolved cannot be dealt with here. Admission of women to Dozent posts, cancellation of the Chair of Theology and its replacement by the History of Religion have been accepted without question. The formation of student associations is to be subject to the general laws of association, and only assemblies of academic student associations with statutes approved by the 'Council' are to be held in university buildings. The 'Inspector of Students' is to be abolished, and the disciplinary court, with the right of relegation as the severest sanction, is to be restored.

The attitude of the Teaching Administration towards this array of proposals remains to be seen. I will say nothing further about the reason why experts in both German and American university affairs are somewhat sceptical about the prospects for success of some of these proposals, which in theory are excellent almost without exception.

(5) The *Freedom of Association* promised in the Manifesto failed right from the start to keep pace with the actual developments of the year 1905.

[*Weber deals with this at some length, indicating how freedom of association for professional bodies and trade unions is continually undercut in practice by government restrictions and prohibitions.*]

(6) The first, meagre beginnings of guaranteed 'freedom of assembly' were brought to Russia by the Bulygin Electoral Law, which introduced, *in the cities*, 'preparatory' assemblies of those enfranchised within one electoral body (voters, delegates and electors), the police being excluded; the assemblies were to be under the chairmanship of the electoral commission (i.e. either the Marshal of the Nobility [see Glossary], or the Mayor or his deputy). The sole purpose of these assemblies was to consult on the *person* of the candidates for election.

The ukase to the Senate of 18 February (rescinded at the time of the issuing of the Bulygin Duma Law) did not give the right to assembly, but only the right of *petition* (which had existed for private individuals since 1811, though denied to the self-governing bodies).

As this was of course insufficient for electoral campaigning which would at least outwardly guarantee political success, the '*ancien régime*' issued a 'temporary' ruling on assembly, dated 12 October 1905, which, published together with a relatively liberal instruction regarding its execution from Treptov, introduced the *iavochnyi poriadok* at least formally, as a *general* rule for assemblies.

The 'temporary' *Law of Assembly* of 4 March 1906 is merely a revision, in part retrograde, of that ruling. It no longer recognizes any distinction between town and country but distinguishes between:

1 *Private* meetings, which neither require prior permission nor need to be notified to the authorities. This category also includes assemblies of legally constituted associations, *provided* no persons other than active association members – i.e. neither guests of honour nor, for example, *emissaries from other associations* – are present;
2 *Public* meetings, i.e. (a) those *attended by persons unknown to the organizer, or* (b) meetings held in theatres, concert halls, exhibition halls, premises of public corporations, or in rooms specially prepared for assemblies or hired for that specific purpose, whether or not they are, for example, private dwelling rooms. This is enforced whether or not section (a) applies, and however many people are present.

Thus the only meetings which are *not* public are meetings in *private* rooms which are *neither* specifically designed as meeting rooms, *nor* hired for the meeting, and where all participants are *personally* known to the organizer. Furthermore, 'public' meetings – and this is of tremendous importance for the electoral movement in small towns and in the country – are *banned* in restaurants (III. 4 of the Law); in educational establishments they are only permitted according to the relevant statutes, and open-air meetings are only permitted with the permission of the governor – which is important for villages.

The authorities must be notified of every 'public' meeting three days in advance, with notice of the subject under discussion and, if an address is to be given, the name of the speaker; the police must be allowed access to the meeting. Meetings can be *banned* if they are a 'threat to public order'; they can be *terminated* if they 'depart from the subject they should be dealing with', or for other reasons; where 'words are used which incite one section of the population against another section', where 'order is disturbed' by inflammatory calls or utterances – all reasons which permit a party loyal to the government or *agents provocateurs* working for the police to put a stop to any meeting of government opponents.

In fact the law has become a pretext justifying absolutely any arbitrary action the authorities feel inclined to take, actions similar to those we have recently experienced in a number of German states with similar laws.[27] 'Congresses' – the concept is not defined any more closely (III. 17) – require the permission of the minister, and their public meetings are subject to the general rules. 'Preparatory meetings' of Duma voters, which, where participation is limited to *those entitled to vote*, are expressly *excluded* from police supervision by the electoral law of 11 December 1905 (XII. 1–6), are treated rather ambiguously (III. 16. V). The law (No. IV) is only invalid for meetings of delegates – as well as for religious meetings and for *traditional* processions (That is, not for newer ones, such as those organized by the sects).

(7) The 'actual' inviolability of the *person* and of the *home*, promised in the Manifesto of 17 October, has *not* been realized: there was no sign of a law at the time the Duma met. As early as 25 November 1905 a decree from the Ministry of Justice mentioned that the Tsar, in the Manifesto of 17 October, had held out the prospect of a 'significant *reduction*' of administrative banishments in favour of judgements of the court. Even that did not in practice occur; on the contrary, banishments flourished as never before.

There has been no mention of abolition of the emergency laws. True, a 'special commission' looked into the question of the protection of 'the

Pseudo-constitutionalism   171

inviolability of the person' – but in February discussion of this was 'postponed' for an indefinite period (*Russkiia Vedomosti*, 14 January). At the end of March, after the election, the question re-emerged in a different form. A commission report (cf. *Russkiia Vedomosti*, 81/3) on changes to the 'emergency laws' proposed at first the creation of a *list* of 'persons endangering the security of society', who, after a *legal* 'warning' and sentencing (by the local courts) were to be placed under police surveillance. For persons declared 'highly dangerous to society' house arrest should be retained. This latter disciplinary measure was to be imposed by the 'prisutstviie' [office; see Glossary] of the governor, or of the city captain, representing the state, with the participation of a minority of three zemstvo or Duma members (of whom two would have to be present for decisions in the meeting to be binding).

In this way the authorities evidently hoped – and this was not a bad idea – to interest the propertied classes (who were dominant in those self-governing bodies) in the banishments and to get them to take some *responsibility* for them. How little their participation was intended as a *guarantee* [of fairness] is clear from the fact that complaints – naturally on the part of the police as well – were to be made to the notorious first department of the *Senate*.

The inevitable abolition of the old *passport* system, in the view of the commission, relieved the police from '*paperwork*', with the result that they could now be expected to carry out effective *personal* surveillance of *all* persons placed under their supervision. To imagine that 'confidence' between 'society' and bureaucracy could be created in this way is typical of the representatives of the old regime.

There was, by the way, no mention of any habeas corpus legislation and it goes without saying that this regime could not, in the interests of self-preservation, be prepared in *any* circumstances to concede it. Such legislation assumes the existence of bodies with *constitutionally* guaranteed independence, which can exercise effective control of the administration, just as, conversely, any true 'constitution' must produce habeas corpus legislation as its first-fruit.

The Interim Ministry of Count Witte and Durnovo, by contrast, was guilty of weakening even that legal protection of the 'person' which *did* previously obtain. We have already briefly mentioned the changes in the personnel of the courts and all kinds of other changes in who is responsible for what (extension of activity of individual judges);[28] the details need not concern us, and would presuppose a discussion of the entire judicial system.

We should like to stress only the extension of competence of *Schöffengerichte*[29] (courts to whose proceedings, according to Art. 1105–6.2

of the penal code, representatives of the estates can be co-opted) to include the offence, newly created by the Supreme Decree of 9 February 1906, of *possession* of explosives, which, if no innocent use can be proved, will entail sending to an institution of correction for up to 15 years; also, especially, the newly created offences of actual or (when aimed at a *civil servant*) *putative* attack on or resistance to the state power; and a whole series of other offences of riot and violence, especially against property, enumerated in the Imperial Council's report (confirmed at the Supreme level) of 18 March 1906 No. II.

What is iniquitous about these changes is the fact that these offences, which are to a high degree *class* offences, are to be dealt with by *class*-based courts, in which the judges are people whose class interests are affected by them, a fact which must be tremendously significant, especially in view of the quite incredible haste with which the courts are expected to operate.

Also worthy of notice is the Supreme Decree of 13 February 1906, which issues threats against (1) the dissemination of 'obviously false assertions' regarding the activity of the authorities, which provoke people to assume a hostile attitude towards them; and (2) the 'incitement to hatred between the different sections and classes of the population, between the estates or between employers and workers' by the spoken or written word (i.e. a covert form of the anti-socialist law).

It would be extremely tedious to give an account of the effects these additions to the already existing laws have had. The feature which remains most incredible for everyone with a sense of justice, of whatever party standpoint including the most authoritarian and conservative, is the brazen effrontery of the government, which has ignored the promises of 17 October, and has not only maintained and continued to practise, but also, to a degree that can scarcely be overstressed, intensified, the principle of *arbitrary administrative decree* over the person of the 'subject' [*Untertan*] by means of restrictions on freedom of movement, exile to distant regions of the Empire, and mass 'deportations'.

A decree of Minister Durnovo of 30 November 1905 stipulated that the governors should, where 'notorious agitators' had been *released by the courts*, arrest them and have them deported (point 3), that in doing this (point 4) 'no account should be taken of any protests from associations and delegates', and that (point 7) 'absolutely no hesitation was permissible in carrying out the intended measures'. Telegraphic reply using the words 'is being carried out' was demanded at the end of the decree.

As if this were not enough, at the same time as the authorities were beginning to break up the peasant obshchina – as will be described later[30] – they were using the most medieval of all their rights: the right to deport to Siberia by resolution of the commune those members who were unacceptable and had been punished. To achieve this, state subsidies towards transport costs were increased by special decree.

It scarcely needs mentioning that nothing was changed regarding the *passport* regulation, whose unsuitability for the purposes for which it was intended had been obvious for a long time; the authorities (for example) had considerable difficulty in bringing back into the country those who had fled abroad for their lives (for fear of the peasants) and who had failed to acquire the necessary passport. A special ministerial instruction was required for this.

In sum, then, we can see that in *all* areas, any 'liberties' that had been *legally* realized at the opening of the Duma were, with very few exceptions, the work of the *ancien régime before* the Government of Witte, having been created out of fear of enraged public opinion, as a result of the loss of prestige in the war and in the hope of somehow winning over the property-owning classes to the side of the bureaucracy, *without* placing any curbs on the unlimited power of these elements in the future. *After* the institution of a legislature had been promised in the October Manifesto, the Interim Ministry did nothing more in the direction promised, but, employing every possible legal trick, it placed the right of 'iavochnyi poriadok' for the press, associations, assembly, and religious affiliation (which had been formally conceded) back under the arbitrary control of the administration, and in particular it did *nothing* to remove the completely arbitrary powers, which are bound by no legal limitations, over the person of the citizen.

One can only ask what one is to make of a situation in which *on the very day* when such tremendous anger erupted in the Duma during the address debate, and amnesty for so-called political criminals was being demanded, when prison administrations were powerless to prevent declarations and *greetings telegrams* from the prisoners from reaching the Duma, and every village in the entire Empire was waiting for a decision, the stark news was published in the press that a transport of 240 prisoners, of course without trial or sentence, was 'standing ready' at Petersburg prison for administrative deportation.

The machinery grinds on as if nothing has happened. And yet things have been done which cannot be undone. The insincerity by which liberties are officially granted, and at the moment when one is about to avail oneself of them, are taken away again with the other hand, *must* become the source of constantly repeated conflicts and fierce hatred, and be far more provocative than the old blatantly crushing system of repression. You cannot play a game of tag with a nation's political liberties, by holding them out to it as one holds out a ball to a child and, when it reaches for them, making them disappear behind your back. It is the same with the '*constitution*' which the Manifesto of 17 October promised, however many provisos accompanied the promise.

Before we turn now to the treatment of this promise by the bureaucracy, we must recall that in those October days the leader of bureaucratic rationalism, Witte, extracted from the Tsar, as well as the ambiguous constitutional manifesto, with its obscure promises for the future, a change in the concrete machinery of the so-called autocracy which came into force *immediately* and which changed its essential nature once and for all.

Completing the Bureaucratization of the Autocracy

The peculiar character of the Russian state system was formally expressed up to October 1905 in the highest sphere of state life in two externally perceptible 'omissions': 1. the lack of the ministerial countersignature on Imperial decrees and 2. the absence of a 'Ministerial Cabinet' in the West European sense.

Up to the Fundamental Law of 23 April 1906, which decreed the *skreplenie* [counter-signature], Imperial decrees, ukases and laws were either signed by the Emperor, or they bore the words: 'on the original there is noted by his most personal hand: "so be it (byt po semu)," ' or at the end of the ministerial report or the Imperial Council report (which was usually closely argued and contained reasoning and decree alongside one another), was appended the remark that the Emperor had approved the report at the Supreme level on such and such a date. The personal ukases and manifestos and all laws generally made great play, in the introduction, with all kinds of fulsome remarks the Monarch is supposed to have made, as the custom was in early nineteenth-century Prussia. This really should cease, but shows no sign of doing so.

The first decree sanctioned *after* the meeting of the Duma – that of 8 June (extension of the state of siege in Moscow) – bore no countersignature. After complaints by the press there followed a communiqué in *Pravitelstvennyi Vestnik* (17 June), which said that the *Senate*, whose task, even under the *ancien régime*, it was to examine the authenticity of decrees before publication, should also examine the regular *skreplenie* – the meaning of the word lies somewhere between 'confirm' and 'certify'. It was thus a kind of counter-signature in private, in order to avoid any similarity with 'the West'. Moreover, in the case of laws, it is not the 'skreplenie' of the ministry that is stipulated, but – since they are pre-

Pseudo-constitutionalism

sented directly to the Tsar by the President of the Imperial Council after being passed by the two chambers – that of the State Secretary (Art. 65 of the definitive Imperial Council Order of 24 April 1906). This means that here too the intervention of the 'competent' minister is *formally* excluded.

Clearly, these are purely respective amendments to the ukase of 21 October 1905 (to be discussed below). However, in spite of these small, subtle changes a situation has been created by this ukase which cannot de facto be reversed, and by means of which, even before a 'constitution' has come into being, the manner by which the laws are made has at least *begun* to change, and the way in which the highest organs of state interconnect really has changed in the most far-reaching way.

The Slavophiles of conservative leanings were almost more shocked by the reorganization (by ukase of 21 October 1905) of the Council of Ministers, and its growing similarity to a 'cabinet' with a Prime Minister at its head, than by the creation of the Duma as the law of 6 August required, or even by the agreement that no law should come into force without the Duma's approval.

Hitherto, alongside the Imperial Council, which consisted of members nominated for life, usually former civil servants, often dependent and occasionally half senile 'former luminaries' who had to approve every 'law', there had been two institutions: (1) the Committee of Ministers; (2) the Council of Ministers.

The former consisted not only of the respective ministers, but also of various other civil servants, and its 'President' was a figurehead who until recently was not even in charge of an office and needed none. His business was not highly political resolutions, but rather (1) dealing with certain current interdepartmental business; and (2) particular tasks assigned to him by law, such as the granting of concessions to limited companies, and the like.

The Council of Ministers, on the other hand, was, in Prussian terminology, a Crown Council, presided over by the Monarch or, if he desired 'more detailed discussion of any subject in his absence', by the most senior minister present. It was called by Imperial command, and its function was to discuss changes in the law and other important political decrees issued by a department, and to make resolutions based on the reports of the ubiquitous 'special commissions', which debated concrete problems of general political significance; the Council might also have to deal with other matters determined by the Monarch. It consisted of all Departmental Ministers *and others* chosen on an ad hoc basis by the Monarch; the Secretary of the Imperial Council was also a member. There was neither a Prime Minister, with the right to exclusive control over the presentations made by his colleagues to the Monarch, nor any regular discussions within a State Ministry, as practised in Prussia, for example. Except in the cases in which the law or the command of the Monarch determined otherwise, the relationships of a Department [to the Council] depended on the personal whim of the Departmental Ministers and their relationships to each other.

The result was a condition which could without too much exaggeration be characterized as the Empire falling into a multitude of *Satrapies*, which corresponded not to regions, but to Government 'Departments'; they were constantly in dispute and alternated between a state of war and a painfully achieved cease-fire, between alliances and renewed intrigues. When a state of war prevailed between these potentates, massive volumes of state papers, at times hundreds of pages long, were used as missiles. To produce these volumes, the attacking Department, or the one under attack, employed scholarly assistants, not infrequently trained in Germany, to pore over every imaginable piece of legal, economic and historical literature, both domestic and foreign. In the cases where these papers can be examined, they afford enthralling, and at times even, if not exactly entertaining, at least factually quite informative reading.

Not infrequently, experts, Russians and others, have answered *in the affirmative* the question of whether the interests of the country were in good hands, for the very same reasons as they have deemed the corruptibility and idleness of some strata of the Russian civil service a positive virtue. Immersing oneself in the Russian complex of rules within and outside the 16 volumes of the *Svod*[31] is bound to convey the impression that any attempt to take seriously this morass as effective valid *law* must not only make life impossible for the 'modern' person, but, just as the 'technical obstruction' practised by railway workers in Italy succeeded in doing, reduce this whole complex itself to absurdity.

Purely from the standpoint of individual freedom of movement of 'bourgeois' circles, any restriction which the 'system' of the autocratic regime imposed on itself, any channel – to use the words of Leroy-Beaulieu – however dirty, out of which escape from the net of this dreadful bureaucratic rationalism remained a possibility, could be regarded as protection of the human dignity of the subject. The profoundly hated civil servants were, not by chance, the 'pedantic' Germans, who honestly believed in the 'sacred' nature of the 'rules' to which this 'system' gave birth, or incorruptible centralist rationalists in the grand style like Plehve. The old patriarchal autocracy was only technically workable as a system of idle routine which actually 'governed' as little as possible.

Pseudo-constitutionalism 177

The ukase of 21 October 1905 meant the demise of what still remained of 'autocracy' in the old sense and the definitive setting up of the centralized rule of the modernized bureaucracy. Between the Monarch and the Departmental Ministers there now stood the 'Council of Ministers' and its president, who is always himself a Minister, though perhaps without portfolio (No. 3).

This can be compared, here in Germany, with both the well-known dispute between the Monarch and the Minister President on the occasion of the dismissal of Bismarck[32] and the events at the time of the creation of the *first* 'cabinet' in Prussia in 1848 (more details of which have recently emerged) and the attitude of Friedrich Wilhelm IV towards it.[33]

Participation of persons called ad hoc by the Monarch, and that of the Imperial Council Secretary, in the meetings of this Council of Ministers (henceforth to consist only of the Departmental Ministers) ceases; only the Prime Minister may ad hoc invite other experts to take part with advisory vote (No. 9).

The Monarch *may* preside over the Council of Ministers, but this is regarded as the exception (No. 5). The Prime Minister alone presents to the Monarch the resolutions of the Council of Ministers requiring confirmation at the Supreme level (No. 7); he also gives an account of all differences of opinion arising in the Council of Ministers which remain unresolved (No. 16). He has the right to demand from all Departmental Ministers the explanations and reports which seem necessary to him, and all reports of the Departmental Ministers to the Monarch must first be brought to his attention (No. 17); he also has the right to be present when these are presented. He is called to represent, possibly alongside the Departmental Minister, every department in the Imperial Council and in the Duma. Alongside the Minister he has the right to take a matter before the Council of Ministers (No. 11). Every matter that comes before the Imperial Council and the Duma *must* be brought to the Council of Ministers (No. 12), and no matter having 'general significance' may be dealt with by the Departmental Head without passing the Council of Ministers (No. 13), though in matters regarding the Imperial Court and the appanages, the defence of the state, and foreign policy, this is restricted to cases where the Departmental Heads regard it as necessary (No. 14).

Proposals for filling the upper positions in the Central and Provincial administration must be brought to the Council of Ministers by the Departments, with the exception of the Departments of the Imperial Court and the appanages, the army and the fleet, and the Diplomatic Service. The former '*Committee*' of Ministers has been dismantled bit by bit and lost the final remnant of its powers when the Duma was called.

Anyone can see at once what has here been created: the definitive bureaucratic rationalization of autocracy over the whole area of domestic policy, which today really calls for the *expert*, and that means, given the deficiencies of local government: *exclusively* the bureaucrat.

The Tsar is informed of internal political questions only after they have been digested by the Prime Minister and Council – even an Autocrat endowed with a more robust personality than the present Tsar would be in the same position. The bureaucratic interests in the Council are united to form a powerful trust; to employ the image applied to the high turnover of ministers in the French parliament, the Tsar is nothing but a skittle-player who, if he *wishes to*, may knock down 'all nine', but then has to set them all up again himself, like the skittle boy. Thus it was the *Prime Minister*, Count Witte, who issued the invitation to liberal politicians to join 'his' cabinet, quite in the Western European manner, and, although they all refused, almost the entire ministry was re-formed.[34]

Since the Imperial Council too, as will be mentioned later,[35] has been transformed into a parliamentary body, and is therefore incapable of giving confidential *advice* to the Tsar, the *only* 'item of clothing' – to use Bismarck's language – remaining to the Tsar is the Council of Ministers.

The resulting defencelessness of the Monarch in the face of the bureaucracy is of course not diminished by the fact that in any number of individual cases he may decide to act ruthlessly *against* the Council – an action which can have quite considerable political consequences: he is removed from the rhythm of 'service' and his activity is, in the nature of things, condemned to be *unsystematic*, whilst on the other hand the maxim that 'the *machine* never tires' still applies. He used to be a beneficiary of the war of the departmental satrapies; now he is de facto essentially restricted to a power of *veto*, as far as the area of the activity of the Council stretches; even if he forms a private 'subsidiary government' consisting of the Grand Dukes or other 'confidants', as allegedly is the case, his intervention is either directed by the interests of certain cliques or is completely fortuitous. In a system of *pseudo*-constitutionalism, however, the monopoly position of the Council would necessarily become inflated to monstrous proportions, and the ministers, with a shadow parliament fabricated by their administrative machinery and bereft of any securely based influence of the *law*, would simply do as they pleased.

The situation could develop quite differently if the 'constitutional' system were fully implemented *in law*; for then the bureaucracy could be dependent on the Monarch *against* parliament and would have a *common interest* with him. Strange as it may sound, this would be the surest way for the Monarch to remain de facto *master* of the bureaucracy.

Although few general principles can be put forward in these matters, which are, in the nature of things, constantly 'in flux', they do help to explain the (in practice often much stronger) position of monarchs who are constitutional in the strict *formal* legal sense (Prussia, Baden). Indeed, the purely *parliamentary* 'Kingdom of Influence' can, *precisely because of* its deliberate moderation, carry out a measure of positive systematic work in the service of its country that is not attainable by the 'Kingdom of Prerogative'.[36] This is because dynastic vanity or inflated self-esteem, which can so easily be mobilized by the legally recognized existence of his Crown prerogatives, lead the monarch towards personal ambitions which cannot, without serious harm being done, be reconciled with the reality of the modern state, where there is no place for the dilettantism characteristic of Renaissance rulers. Whatever the ultimate fate of the 'constitution', it will be fascinating to discover which path the tsardom will take.

Shipov's proposal, which is at heart a Slavophile one, of April 1906, is that the Imperial Council should comprise merely or predominantly representatives of the zemstvos and similar corporations and then – in contrast to the innovation which now exists, and which we shall be discussing shortly – to leave it in existence, but *solely* as a body directly *advising* the Tsar, independent of the Duma, which participates solely in a legislative capacity.

This proposal rests, *theoretically*, on a partially correct notion: since the laws of 20 February 1906, the Imperial Council has become *nothing but* a brake for the Duma and exists only in the interests of the *bureaucracy*, which by law has the absolute voting *majority* within it. There is not the slightest support within such a body for the Tsar, since it acts and resolves according to the rules of parliamentary business. On the other hand, a purely advisory, *not too large* body, with which he was in direct communication, could – the theory evidently assumes – not only be more *influential* for 'positive' work (because of the circles represented in it), but could even give the Tsar, provided he knew how to make use of it, strong support against the bureaucracy. However, given the lack of 'intimacy' inescapable for a body which necessarily comprises *at least* 60–80 members, the likelihood of it succeeding must be highly doubtful.

However that may be, it is certain that the order created by the ukase of 21 October represented the apogee of Witte's bureaucratic power. He did not succeed in truly capitalizing on the position of Prime Minister he created for himself: as in the 'Miquel case'[37] here in Germany, it was shown that, armed *only* with intellect, however powerful the intellect may be, and *entirely* without what is called 'political character', a man of boundless ambition (as both statesmen were) will finally succeed only in sacrificing everything to gain a portfolio – only to depart without honour from the stage.

After remaining in office until he had satisfied the *stock exchanges* and obtained the loan, he disappeared from the scene; even the securing of the loan was perhaps not quite the success he had been aiming for. Instead of challenging Durnovo in cabinet in January, when he was still indispensable, he gave in to this individual, the only corruptible member of the Council, condemned himself to be totally lacking in influence, and surrendered himself to the hatred and contempt of 'society', without gaining the confidence of the Tsar; he also virtually ruled himself out as a future 'saviour'. However we do not wish to talk about Witte personally. What is certain is that if the rationalization of bureaucratism in Russia continues to spread into lower levels too, this will strike at the roots of all Slavophile ideals.

It will also provoke a permanent state of war between 'society' and bureaucracy. *Novoe Vremia*, using the particularly tasteful slogan '*noblesse oblige*', is, to my knowledge, the only important journal to call upon Count Witte to stay on. Apart from the civil service, only the big capitalist entrepreneurs and the banks would be happy to accept the dominance of the bureaucracy (which merely pays lip service to constitutionalism), and then only on condition that a free hand be given to money making and that the practice of *zubatovshchina* [see Glossary] be ended.[38]

Now, however, the bureaucracy has so enmeshed itself in the web of its own *electoral* laws that it has been unable to help these favoured groups: for example, the Trade and Industry Party[39] (as we shall see,[40] the representative of the bourgeoisie in the strict sense of the word) has only achieved the election of a *single* member.

The whole of the rest of Russian society stands as one man *precisely* against the development of the old autocracy into a modern rational bureaucracy, whatever party standpoint it may otherwise take. The Red Terror may temporarily scare the wealthy into seeking shelter beneath the bureaucracy, but we shall soon find – and this is the interesting thing about developments at the time of the Interim Ministry – that even this is not able to force Russian society to submit to the system of 'enlightened' (i.e. bureaucratically rationalized) absolutism, a system which is the logical consequence of the technology of modern bureaucratic work. It is rather the case that the gulf has widened to such an extent that, with the final destruction of the patriarchal ideals of the Slavophile theory of the state, *legal* restrictions on bureaucracy could only be avoided at the cost of chronic civil war. As we have already seen,[41] the interim regime was not even capable of keeping the peace.

We shall now proceed to examine the extent to which the regime honoured its promise to share legislative power.

The 'Constitution'

[*Weber critically reviews the constitution of the forthcoming First Imperial Duma, as expressed by the Manifestos of 6 August 1905 and 20 February 1906. Amongst other things, he finds that the powers of the Duma are too restricted, since bills require the approval of ministers or the Tsar himself.*]

The constitutional rights of the Duma are, from the start, very severely restricted by the continued existence of the *Imperial Council*,[42] whose members are merely *appointed*. [. . .] The provision of the Imperial Council, formerly a purely advisory body, with the same rights as the Duma, seems – not only to Democrats, but also to moderate Slavophiles like Shipov – to be an infringement of the 'spirit' of the Manifesto of 17 October. True, the Imperial Council has been expanded to include members to be elected from amongst the nobility, the clergy, the zemstvos, the universities, and from trade and industry, but the Emperor has been allowed to appoint members *equal in number* to all of these, and the President of the Imperial Council, *appointed* by him, has the casting vote. The fact that the appointed members of the Imperial Council may remain in membership as long as they wish, and it is therefore not possible, for example, for some Duma ministry to replace them with members of its own choice,[43] amounts to *formal* obstruction of the progress of legislation by means of the *appointed* bureaucracy of the Imperial Council.

Looked at in the cold light of day, the whole of the authority vested in the Duma proves to be in fact only a slight change in the law of 6 August, insofar as the Duma – as well as the expanded Imperial Council – has been granted a *veto* against new 'laws' purporting to be *permanent*. The entire relationship between government and people's representation presupposes that it is axiomatic that *the representative body of the people is and always will be the natural enemy of the state power.*

It is immediately clear that the familiar view (often attributed with much indignation to the Democratic movement, especially in Germany) that the government is the natural enemy of 'the people', would have been the *only possible* reaction – were it not for the fact that the masses have already been forced to this conclusion by the behaviour of the bureaucracy over the last decades. [. . .]

Clearly, the following points have been left unanswered:

1 The question of *which* regulations are counted among the 'Fundamental State Laws' and are thus *outside* the initiative of the parliamentary bodies. [. . .]

2 Also left open is the question of *how* the *budget* is to be set and what rights should be granted to the parliamentary bodies in this. [. . .]
3 Although not directly stated in the law, there remains a doubt as to whether the Crown should retain the right to grant privileges and the right to impose emergency laws. [. . .]

The other constitutional acts formed a chain of further disappointments.

First, there was the ruling of 8 March 'concerning deliberations on the *state budget*, and the allocation of those expenses from the state treasury which are not provided for in the budget'. The ukase containing the ruling decreed that the two legislative bodies should be placed *on an equal footing*: the budget should pass through each of them at the same time before 1 October. By that time the following were to have already been presented: [*a list of the various items of expenditure follows*].

The budget is set (No. 3) according to 'legal paragraphs' (for revenue) and according to 'numbers' (in parentheses: 'principal subsections') for expenses; in other words, modern constitutional demands for 'specification of the budget' have been *rejected*: the very point at which Bismarck, at the outset of his Government, immediately agreed to compromise in the dispute with the House of Deputies.[44] The budgetary items are *leges saturae*,[45] to employ Roman terminology.

Both bodies debate the budget at the same time, in the committees set up for the purpose, which may tackle the budgets (which are already available) before the opening of the session (No. 2 of the ruling), and they must have concluded their deliberations by 1 December (No. 10). Differences of opinion between them must be referred to a joint committee comprising members from both bodies, from where the budgets return to the Duma for debate (Nos 9, 11). The same happens to all motions of either one of the bodies which propose amendments to laws and decrees affecting the setting of budgets or which propose the inclusion of new items. Should a difference of opinion remain between the two bodies, then the figure which comes closest to the level of the previous budget item is entered (No. 12). If the budget has not come into force by the beginning of the financial year (1 January) – whether because the parliamentary bodies have not completed their work on it or because the Emperor has not signed it in its final form after debate – then the previous year's budget, with the changes resulting from valid laws, remains in force, and is remitted in twelve monthly instalments by the appropriate ministry (No. 13).

It goes without saying that these regulations alone are enough to destroy the vital nerve of any constitutionalism – the right to approve *expenditure*, to say nothing of the 'approval of *revenue*' (in the parliamentary sense of the word). The Duma can only prevent an *increase* in particular budgets *over and above* the previous budget through the Imperial Council (the majority of which consists, as required by the law, of appointed members, and in which the chairman – also appointed rather than elected – has the casting vote), and it can only influence the revenue side of the budget by refusing to approve *new tax laws*. The price of brandy, the level of tariffs etc. are, of course, at the discretion of the administration.

Point No. 4 of the Budget Law excludes from parliamentary consideration credits for the Imperial Court and for the Imperial family, the former being as stated in the 1906 budget, the latter as determined also by other rulings which may become necessary. What is more, even the expenses of the Personal Imperial Chancellery, and the Chancellery for Petitions, and, in particular, extraordinary expenditure not provided for in the budget, are excluded, provided they do not exceed the budget items for 1906 (No. 5).

Additionally, the parliamentary bodies are not permitted to reduce any expenditure on servicing the state debt, any 'obligations of the state correctly assumed', or indeed any items instituted on the basis of valid laws, decrees, statutes and tariffs. And to cap it all (No. 16), in the case of '*urgent*' expenses the Council of Ministers can allocate the credits required outside of and even *during* the session, and is obliged merely to provide the Duma with a special report giving reasons. The ministry is *even relieved of this obligation* in cases where *observance of secrecy* regarding the reason for the allocation is necessary. Finally, in time of war the entire Budget Law is set aside and is replaced with the ruling of 26 February 1890.

We can see that this Budget Law is a farce, and it would have been more honest to allow the Duma only *advisory functions* with regard to the budget and to establish that new dues and an increase in the ordinary expenditure above the level of the last budget should only occur without its approval for the purposes of the Imperial family or on the basis of obligations of the state validly entered into, plus any increase in extraordinary peacetime expenditure deemed necessary by the Council of Ministers. For that is the essence of this law. [. . .]

In fact, it became evident that the government itself was determined to demolish even this last barrier to arbitrary bureaucratic control of the budget and to transform into a dead letter not only the participation of the Duma in the establishment of the budget but also the promise of 17 October that no law should come into force without its approval.

[*Weber gives a critical account of the Fundamental State Laws, which were finally introduced just two days before the opening of the Duma.*]

The *codification* of this caricature of the powerful idea of constitutionalism may in the long run have a quite different effect to that hoped for by the codifiers. This bureaucracy, which, however efficient many individuals may be and however refined its technique, shows a complete lack of *political* skills, is seeking to use its Eastern wiles and peasant cunning to close any gaps in the *legal* net, so that parliament becomes ensnared and trapped in it.

But just as 'hypocrisy is the homage paid to virtue by vice', the express codification of such a profoundly false pseudo-constitutionalism is an equally profoundly humiliating homage paid to the constitutional principle by the 'idea' of autocracy. In the long run it harms not the respect in which this principle is held, but rather the authority of the Crown, which evidently allows itself to be coerced into granting 'concessions' to a system which is inimical to its [the Crown's] vanity and its desire for sycophancy, instead of openly and honestly *putting the system to the test*.

Of course, such an 'honest experiment' might actually lead to mere rhetoric, to a failure to recognize the 'opportunities' afforded by the present stage of development and to attempts to establish pseudo-parliamentary domination by cliques. *If this were to occur*, and if this ancient Crown, sanctified by a religious reverence which, in spite of everything, is still deeply rooted in the consciousness of the masses, *then* pronounced the experiment a failure and trod formal justice underfoot, it would at least have had, as well as bayonets, the power of 'ideal' forces on its side, however 'illusory' they might be. Its reputation would have emerged from the struggle strengthened at the expense of its really dangerous opponents for a long time to come. Now, where every movement of parliament runs up against legal barbed wire, the situation is evidently precisely the opposite: parliament is in a position to convince the masses that the experiment of ruling with the *Crown* has 'failed'. If parliament were then to be broken up and, with violence and deception, a *Landratskammer*[46] forcibly set up, the '*idea*' of tsarism would pay the price.

Analysis of the Electoral Law of the Duma

The Bulygin Electoral law (Electoral Order of 6 August 1905) was based on the idea of representation by class and 'estate', which was constructed in a rather complicated way, based on the existing zemstvo electoral system.

Pseudo-constitutionalism

Within each constituency – which was normally equivalent in size to a province – there should be two separate meetings for the election of electors: firstly the representatives of private landowners (those with large landholdings do this in person, those with small ones – holding up to a tenth of the large – by means of delegates), secondly the representatives of urban house owners and, with them, of all kinds of 'moveable' wealth, i.e. trade and industry capital and 'moveable' wealth associated with particularly valuable dwellings.

There was also a third class entitled to choose electors, namely the peasants (in the *'estate'* sense of the word, that is, those entered in the peasant tax lists). With regard to the election of deputies, the 'peasants' were granted the privilege of sending one of their number from each district to the Duma. They then, together with the electors of the two other classes, elected the remainder.

In the urban and rural census classes, the census was calculated in such a way that ownership to the value of 30,000–50,000 roubles or an income to the level of at least 3,000 roubles was necessary to satisfy those conditions (payment of certain taxes, minimum extent of land ownership) to which the right to one's own vote at the election of the electors was tied: the small landowners in the rural areas (*only* there) had, as already stated, the curial franchise.[47] So not only the proletariat (other than the peasant proletariat) but also the 'lower middle class' (craftsmen, middle-ranking civil servants), and above all the *intelligentsia* – which was not endowed with any considerable land ownership – were excluded. The latter exclusion was achieved by setting up the principle (directed against popular 'leaders') of election 'from within' the (*local*) electoral body itself, by prohibition of double candidature, and other provisos. Thus it was hoped to combine the interests of property owners and peasants (the peasants were seen as amenable to authority), on the one hand, with the interests of the bureaucracy on the other.

Electors representing 'moveable' wealth were always bracketed together with the two other classes and only a number of larger cities were classified as autonomous constituencies. Large landowners and peasants were therefore to share power, whilst a warm corner was to be held in reserve for the 'bourgeoisie' in the specific sense of the word, and for the 'house-owning agrarians' of the cities. [. . .]

The Manifesto of 17 October promised extension of the franchise to the classes hitherto unrepresented by this system – and this threatened to thwart all this ingenuity. However, the bureaucracy tried craftily to turn the effects of the great extension of the franchise, which it was compelled to accept, to its own advantage, by diverting the stream of new voters almost entirely into a single channel, namely into the class of voters representing *moveable* wealth, which was in a hopeless minority compared to the two electoral classes of the rural landowners and the peasants. The number of voters representing moveable wealth was increased at least *twentyfold, whereas the number of delegates representing them remained the same.*

[*Weber then examines in great detail what he refers to as the 'legislative product of this simple trick'.*]

If in the autumn of 1904, before the fall of Port Arthur, or at least instead of the rescript [addressed to Interior Minister Bulygin] of 18 February 1905, which had quite obviously had to be wrested from the Tsar and had been kept quite vague, a 'constitution' with census or class franchise had been imposed and immediately come into force by announcement of an election and calling of the people's assembly, then the creation of a 'grateful' bourgeois Duma, ready for far-reaching compromise, would have been the likely outcome. Dynastic vanity and the interests of the bureaucracy caused the chance to be lost. If at least the elections for the Census Duma of the Bulygin draft had been announced at the beginning of August, and the time for its first meeting been made known, then there was just a chance that there could have been a parliament with which Witte could have governed, thanks to the reputation he had gained. However, the October strike intervened, and then, after the Manifesto of 17 October – a pure and patently shameful personal defeat for the Tsar – all opportunities were on the side of Democracy.

From the *egoistical* standpoint of the bureaucracy, 'biding one's time' was now the 'tactically right approach', if it *sought* pseudo-constitutionalism and not an 'honest' constitutional policy. When, however, the December events and the peasant riots had had their effect, that would have been the moment for it to act. If at that moment it had been in possession of an electoral law and of the electoral registers and had thus been in a position immediately, and of course on the basis of a political understanding with the leading circles of 'property', to hold elections, then it can be safely assumed, with a very high degree of probability, that the result would have been significantly more 'favourable' than two months later. Instead, the government hesitated, as we have seen,[48] in the hope that this 'cup' might pass it by; the *mechanism* of the elections also played its part, with the result that several months more passed before the most important of the elections could take place. This lengthy delay frustrated all the hopes that had been placed in this law.

If the government had expected the law to reduce the heat of electoral agitation or the exclusive significance of the party system, it was doomed to disappointment – in spite of the foolish boycott by the extreme left.

Pseudo-constitutionalism 187

Not only, as previously shown, were the rewards for party discipline *very high*, but also the *lengthy duration* of the electoral campaign (connected with the complexity of the system) was bound to cause agitation to rise to boiling point, at least, where this had not simply been suppressed – and such suppression proved more difficult than expected.

The peculiar feature of the current Russian development is that every phenomenon of Western European economic and state 'civilization' is suddenly and abruptly irrupting into a society which – with the exception of the highest stratum – is still archaic. The weakening of the restrictions on clubs and societies has not only unleashed the tremendous flood of trade and professional associations, but there have also arisen on Russian soil the equivalents of such monstrosities of our German culture as the 'League of Landowners', a 'Central Association of Industrialists', and various 'protective associations' against the Red Terror; there is even an 'Association of National Liberal Youth' (if one may equate the 'Union of 17 October' with the German 'National Liberals') with a fine clubhouse in Petersburg, and there are special 'Women's Leagues' (with such groups as the Women's Union of Legal Order of Petersburg being especially popular with the reactionaries).

All the parties organized, as a form of publicity, supposedly 'merely' academic 'informative' lecture evenings of every conceivable kind, they set up questionnaires such as that of the 'Constitutional Democrats' on the agrarian question and land shortage amongst the peasants, and they founded Peasant Leagues, such as the Peasant League of the 17 October, or the League of the People's Peace (for which Durnovo was responsible), they took an interest in all kinds of cooperatives, founded – if not officially then at least semi-officially – a great many soup kitchens, which, if the founders were of 'leftward' leanings, were constantly banned by the government (and thus served as an even better free advertisement), they concerned themselves with the founding, counselling and influencing of trade unions, founded 'neutral' workers' newspapers, and – last but not least – they managed to look as if they were interested in the Church and the movement taking place within it.

There is little point in attempting to enumerate the newly founded newspapers in the principal and provincial cities – all of them struggling against determined attempts to ban them – and to report on their fate. They have been dealt with in the frequently extensive 'Press' rubric in every edition of (for example) *Novoe Vremia* since October.

The journeyings hither and thither of the various 'leaders' and especially of the academic and scientific authorities of the parties – the year and a half long holidays enforced by the student unrest gave them a wonderful opportunity for this – almost bordered on frenzy, to judge from press reports, and bearing in mind that various 'university extension courses' were running at the same time. The number of election meetings held by the Democrats was put – by opponents – at 200. More significant, however, was the number of meetings, lecture evenings and courses (especially those run by the left) which were cancelled, thanks to the right of the local authority (the governor) to impose a ban. This ban was sometimes used against moderate parties too. These cancelled meetings were no less useful for party agitation than those that actually took place; indeed they were more so. It should come as no surprise that, in the eyes of both the urban masses and the peasants, whatever the bureaucracy banned must necessarily be something excellent that it wished to withhold from 'the people'.

By banning these meetings the authorities were effectively protecting agitators from additional nervous strain – especially necessary for our Russian colleagues, whose work rate is far higher than the German professor, accustomed as he is to a more leisurely pace.

Alongside the *tours de force* in public speaking, there was a great deal of journalistic activity, and again it is unbelievable what a flood of articles, each based on comprehensive, though irreconcilably conflicting statistical calculations, especially on agrarian questions, were exchanged, not only between the different party factions, but also, in a continual cannonade, *within* one and the same newspaper between party comrades from university circles. In these circumstances a ban on a meeting was a blessing for the speaker, who was by then half dead, and moreover it provided the most effective possible advertisement for the party in question, often a much better one than the lecture itself could have done and, what is more, *free of charge*. And that really meant something in this electoral system. For even the costs of the electoral campaign were, relatively speaking, disproportionately high. Even the government's expenses must have been very significant. An ad hoc system of electoral registers for individual elections was adopted, in contrast to France and England but consistent with Germany. This was naturally unavoidable in any case on this first occasion, but will in future be required by law.

Part of the work was apparently left to the electorate themselves, since registration depended on them making an application. This in turn meant that officials had to check the right of these individuals in each particular case, instead of preparing a list and periodically amending it on the basis of police registration lists and then leaving correction of these lists to the voters themselves at the time of the election – or, as in countries with a developed party system – leaving it to the party functionaries.

As a result of the shortness of time permitted for complaints, the work was enormously compressed. As previously mentioned, a register had to be drawn up for each electoral category; where a voter belonged to several categories within the same constituency (excluding the workers' special franchise), plural registration had to be eliminated; not only the approximately 7,000 electors but also the vastly greater number of 'delegates' of the peasants, small private landowners and workers, and, with regard to the latter, the numbers of workers in each factory had to be registered and the numbers checked. Clearly, then, in spite of the absence of any electoral registers for the peasants, the work was extremely laborious and expensive. It can easily be imagined what significant costs such a complicated electoral method must impose on the parties.

Amongst other reasons it is also the desire to simplify the election campaign and to conduct it with lower costs – both intellectual and material – that has caused the press and the best organized parties – socialist and clerical – in the west of the country to urge the replacement of the indirect by the direct vote.

The interest of the masses in the election and thus the effectiveness of 'demagogy' can be increased with much less expenditure by means of the direct form of election than by means of the indirect, and the elections in Baden, for example, have shown that direct election – other things being equal (which was more or less the case here) – has a tendency to produce *different* results, here more in favour of *reactionary* demagogy, from those associated with indirect election. However, this presupposes that the electorate has 'normal' relations with the state, that is to say, that concrete questions, not the social and political foundations of the state, are under discussion.

Under circumstances like those in Russia such 'normal' relations would be inconceivable for another generation. The bureaucratic regime of *today* must first stand down, enabling the rise of a stratum which is safe from the arbitrary barbarity of the police, and whose needs are 'satisfied', before the West European bourgeois electoral psyche can emerge.

It is difficult to say what effect the system of election had on the *peasants*. It is very hard to guess what their *subjective* attitude to the elections would have been in a direct election system, with rural electoral districts which would have had to be *at least* as large as an average Prussian government district.

Their general attitude was that in principle one deputy must go to Petersburg from *each village*, in order to achieve anything useful; petitions arrived at the ministry in which the peasants declared themselves willing to send a dozen instead of just one for the 10 roubles of daily expenses which were allowed to the deputy, since the amount was quite adequate and it was also unfair to let one individual 'earn' so much. In the case of an election system organized on the model of the Reichstag franchise, the attitude of the peasants would have been hard to predict, even though, even in the eyes of quite hard-headed reporters, the development of their (still very primitive) 'political thinking', that is, their adaptation to the whole thought process which the idea of the modern 'representation of the people' presupposes, has in many areas been quite rapid.

[Under a direct election system] they would have had to follow the 'slogan' of some unknown figure, and it is *by no means* certain that the reactionaries would not then have gained their votes. A deputy who was not elected purely by *peasant* votes would be regarded with suspicion by the peasants, and support for a Duma elected according to party slogans and instructions of party committees would undoubtedly be far weaker than that enjoyed by the present one.

One factor should not be overlooked: the number of 'intellectuals' from amongst the peasants themselves was considerable, and the course of the elections showed that the peasants were perfectly willing to vote for them.

Indirect election 'from their own ranks' gave the local police more control over the election process. However, under Russian conditions, the effect of this, coupled, ironically, with the demagogic principle 'only real peasants to the Duma!' (implicit in the electoral law), was undoubtedly to strengthen the antibureaucratic feelings of the mass of the peasants. Of course, even without pressure from the government, the peasants would have voted in accordance with that slogan. But while the government was able to depress the average intellectual level of the deputies, owing to the formalism through which it attempted to exclude the intelligentsia, especially the feared 'Third Element',[49] from election by the peasants, and by means of its filter system, it could *not* thereby affect the candidature of the class most dangerous to it, the 'peasant intelligentsia'; in fact, it only strengthened its position.

As long as they did not exclude themselves from participation in the elections by joining in the foolish boycott, there was nothing the police bureaucracy could do against them except use force, and such force, where it was employed, only served as *publicity*. Arrested peasant delegates telegraphed the police from prison to thank them for what they had done for their election – and they had good reason to do so, as it turned out.

In general, the application of force by the police, wherever it occurs, offends the Russian peasant's sense of justice, although, and partly because, he is accustomed to yield to it outwardly, in probably a greater measure than in other countries; for he sees in it nothing whatever 'moral', nothing but the purely 'random' and senseless brutality of power, which is in the hands of people who are his sworn enemies.

In this case, the only question was whether that obstinate and taciturn feeling for justice or the fear of the police would prove the stronger motive at the election. The government assumed the latter, and one must concede that in this respect at least it 'did its part'.

A decree of the Minister of the Interior to the Zemskiie Nachalniki [see Glossary] on the occasion of the election, published first in *Rech*, then in *Pravo* (no. 9), which was at first regarded by the Democratic press as apocryphal, but whose authenticity is beyond dispute, laid down, *inter alia* (no. 6), that in the *polling stations* 'the names of persons who might not stand as candidates *on account of their undesirability (!)*, be posted and, should voters nevertheless wish to vote for them, they were to be told that such elections would be deemed to have been *incorrectly (!)* run, be impermissible and be challenged. Furthermore (no. 7), should agitators 'attempt to turn the election meetings into committees for the redistribution of the land', not only should the armed forces immediately intervene, but also (no. 5), people known to be 'undesirable' should be kept away from the polling stations by force. The zemskiie nachalniki, moreover (no. 2), must 'educate' the peasants in private regarding the elections and employ trustworthy people (no. 3) to report any suspicious conversations or if they hear of any promises being made [to influence the vote]; they must then take measures as instructed.

After such precautions, the election débâcle came as a shock to the government and was equally surprising for its opponents. Viewed objectively, it was such a remarkable phenomenon that its principal features seem worthy of interpretation.

The Social and Political Background to the Election

When the election campaign began, the prospects for democracy were, to all appearances, extremely poor. The Socialist Revolutionaries, both the official party and the 'Jewish League' [*Bund*], as well as the free organizations, especially the Union of Unions, had boycotted the Duma, and official Social Democracy did likewise. The peasants were barbarically punished and forced to beg for pardon – often whole villages were made to kneel. The zemstvos received huge numbers of petitions from village communes, retracting the resolutions which had been inspired by the Peasant League. Registrations to the electoral lists in the cities from the broad lower electorate, which was qualified by virtue of ownership of an independent dwelling, at first came in only slowly and in small numbers.

The power of the revolutionary mood seemed to be broken. The resolution which Socialist Revolutionaries, Social Democrats and Constitutional Democrats had jointly passed, to observe 9 January as a general day of mourning, was, at least on the surface, a fiasco: *Novoe Vremia* found to its satisfaction that the appearance of the city and attendance at theatres and restaurants were normal.

Almost all the leaders of the radical associations of workers and peasants, and anyone in the slightest degree suspicious in the country areas, was under arrest. The trade and professional associations,[50] which had suddenly begun to flourish, the bearers of the radical movement, had been dissolved; and even if the government, acting in a more unprejudiced fashion than our blinkered Puttkamer regime,[51] treated the actual trade unions with more restraint, yet the terrible pressure on industry still created an astonishingly numerous reserve army of unemployed, so that those factories in which work had been resumed were able, with the greatest of ease, to undertake a thorough 'filtering' of the work-force. The mood of the proletariat became despondent, and it seemed on the point of completely forfeiting even the purely economic fruits of the revolution.

Factories everywhere, if they were working at all – some remained closed until April – began to extend the working day, and it seemed as if the workers had gained nothing from the revolution but the right to the polite form of address (*vy*) instead of the familiar form (*ty*).

However, under Russian conditions, this economic pressure did produce one result which is closely linked to agrarian communism. Only a small, though significant, section of the reserve army of the unemployed remained in the cities; the rest streamed back to their home villages, and the agitators and socialists, who had been 'filtered out', now became propagandists of radicalism among the peasants. The workers' movement itself, however, in spite of the difficult situation, sprang back to life again in a quite astonishing and perhaps unprecedented manner, despite the forceful way in which their leaders had been made to feel the 'iron fist' of the authorities.

[*Weber describes the cooperative movement and other experiments in worker participation.*]

Those workers that take their stand on 'correct' socialist ground reject these experiments and, as a substitute for political activity, cultivate the trade union movement.

This movement is headed, as always, by the typographic trades, the only ones to be expanding, perhaps because of the political excitement and unrest. In Moscow, in the last week of March, the chairman of the League of Print Workers reminded all members that their membership would lapse if they failed to pay their subscriptions; about 2,000 paid immediately. These subscriptions were chiefly used to put the principle of class solidarity into effect on a grand scale. In practice this meant primarily unemployment support (without distinction of occupation).

The Bookbinding Association set up 40 soup kitchens for the unemployed, and the association of railway workers used its entire funds on these. The Bureau of Trade Associations in Moscow resolved to deduct regular monthly sums from wages for the benefit of the unemployed. The associations of newspaper printers, who hitherto had not enjoyed a rest day on Sunday, began to wage a determined struggle to achieve this, which was frustrated by the resistance of *Novoe Vremia* in Petersburg. However, they continued their efforts.

The strength of the Association of Bricklayers grew again as spring approached. In the Moscow building trade the employers attempted to reach an agreement with the workers on a mutual accident insurance. In Petersburg the original workers succeeded in rapidly driving out the blacklegs, when at the beginning of March the big factories resumed (*Novoe Vremia*, 10762/4). In June the typographers succeeded in forcing the employers to almost complete surrender, including getting them to pay 'war costs' (half-wages for the period of the strike; *Russkiia Vedomosti*, 146/4).

One can read in the *Torgovo-promyshlennaia Gazeta*, no. 158, of the unusually painstaking preparations made by the Moscow printing workers in the face of the threatened lockout – perhaps the *first* in Russia. These preparations included localization of the struggle to the firms belonging to the Employers' Association, precautions against the possibility that orders might be passed to outside branches, the organization of the unemployed on the one hand and of those locked out on the other, with careful consideration being given to relative voting strengths, prevention of any workers being brought in, the removal of the reserve army to their home villages (notice here the effect of the agrarian social order [*Agrarverfassung*]!), mode of negotiation with the managers, measures to gain the sympathy of the public (in relation to the strike of printing workers), and so on. Issue 161 of the same journal sets out the basis on which, it appears, an agreement was reached with the Employers' Association (the managers have in particular conceded the recognition of the trade union and agreed to consultation on both labour *and political* matters within their workshops).

At the end of April the Bureau of Trade Associations sent out, at the same time as calling a pan-Russian delegates' congress, a programme, which declared that discussions should be held on: (1) the state and public institutions as employers; (2) occupational statistics; (3) the eight-hour day; (4) unemployment; (5) trade union law; (6) national trade unions; (7) relationship of the trade unions to the political struggle.

We shall have to await the congress in order to gain a true picture of the state of the movement. An answer to the last question should be of the greatest interest. Could it mean revival of revolutionary sindacalism?[52] Strictly neutral trade unions or official relations with the party leadership? Two Social Democrat delegates are officially invited to this congress. It is certain that the associations founded in the year 1905 almost all originated from either Socialist Revolutionary sindacalism, or were founded by the 'Mensheviki', that is, the supporters of the 'minority' of the divided socialist party (Plekhanov group), which is recognized as orthodox by the German Social Democrats. The Leninist 'majority' (Bolsheviki) look down on them with contempt.

Without exception the intellectually most outstanding groups of trade unions, for example the typographers, are the keenest and the most orthodox Social Democrats. The meeting of the Bureau of Trade Associations in Moscow on 4 June, although of decidedly Social Democratic persuasion, pleaded that the economic struggle should not be taken 'on to the streets' (*Russkiia Vedomosti*, 146/4). It was attended by delegates of the associations of print workers, bakers, boxmakers, metalworkers, marbleworkers, hatters, shoemakers, plumbers, technicians, bookbinders, chemists, tobacco workers, umbrella-makers, and messengers.

The May Day celebrations, held in Poland according to the Gregorian, and in Russia according to the Julian calendar (a very tangible distinction!), seem to have been observed rather more widely than in Germany; apparently the employers opposed the absence from work rather less than in Germany. At the moment they simply have no particular reason to wish to try to impress their rulers with their political 'zeal'.

The strikes which are now (June) breaking out with astonishing vigour seem to be at least *partly* politically inspired, and resemble those of autumn 1905.

The uniting of the entire *Social Democratic* Party of Russia, which emerged, at least formally, from the common congress in Stockholm in May, and had been planned for such a long time, has yet to prove its durability. As the foreign-based Social Democratic Russian press has closed down, and the native equivalent is only now being re-established, it is at the moment difficult to discover anything certain about events since December. According to reports so far available, the Stockholm Congress resolved as follows:

Pseudo-constitutionalism 195

1 Adoption by majority vote of the principle of 'municipalization' of land, with the additional clause that, if the peasants should demand distribution of the confiscated land among local peasant committees, they were to be supported in this. Further discussion on the present position was refused.
2 Against the violent protest of the 'Bolsheviki' and of almost all nationality groups, the boycott of the Duma elections was lifted.
3 By majority vote, the principle of party neutrality for the trade unions was accepted.
4 It was recognized that armed uprising was inevitable, but could only succeed with the participation of the bourgeoisie, and should be delayed until this was 'possible'.
5 The principle of autonomy for the nationalities was accepted.

The boycott of the Duma has particularly discredited the party. Its calculated attempts to disrupt the Democratic campaign meetings, with fiery speeches against the Duma and rowdy behaviour, were used by the government to justify its ban on assembly.

Certainly, the attitude of the socialists throughout the election period constituted a serious embarrassment and handicap for Democracy. The fact that the Duma elections did not have a reactionary outcome is no thanks at all to Social Democracy: in every way possible it simply played into the hands of the government.

More threatening at the start of the election movement was a certain sense that Bourgeois Democracy itself had lost its way.

On 5 January the Constitutional Democratic Party, usually known in the press by its initial letters KD, or 'Kadets', met for its second congress (till 11 January). To judge from the impression given by the negotiations, the mood was rather depressed, owing to fear of the effects of the Moscow uprising. In addition there was the impression of organizational uncertainty and the tendency to theoretical hair-splitting and speculation about the future.

It is astonishing that at such a serious moment there should be protracted debates on whether the Duma should in principle be a 'constituting' assembly; how this and the protest against the nature of the electoral law should be expressed; whether, in other words – if they did enter the Duma – they should refrain from all practical parliamentary work; or which subjects would merit discussion – the question of the so-called 'inner boycott' of the Duma.

Finally, though, participation in the work of reform, 'which could no longer be postponed', was resolved (by 91 votes out of 102). Moreover, party organization, which was then being very much neglected in the provinces, and election tactics, were discussed, a number of protest resolutions of a general character were passed, the party was renamed the Party of Popular Freedom ('Partiia narodnoi svobody') – although most people continued to refer to it as 'KD' or 'Kadets', as before – the reference to the minority vote against women's suffrage was deleted from the party programme, the decidedly nationalistic motions of Tartar, Kirgisian and Jewish representatives were rejected, and, most importantly, a resolution was passed which called for a strictly *parliamentary* regime.

All these resolutions, except those of a purely technical kind, indicated that the party was assuming that it would form at best only a small opposition group. Otherwise, the general political and social programme points were mostly retained in the same form.

There were protracted debates on the *agrarian programme*. No agreement was reached. Only on the concept of the 'just price' at which, according to the programme accepted in October, private land would be expropriated, was a resolution (No. V) passed, which declared that such a price should be calculated according to the yield which was 'normal' for the particular region, assuming expert economic management and without regard for the rent levels brought about by the shortage of land.

At the congress there were evidently two diametrically opposing views. Some delegates believed that forced expropriation of private land to meet the peasants' needs was undesirable; apart from allocation of the non-private land to the peasants, these delegates were merely in favour of regulation of leasing conditions and the introduction of progressive tax on land ownership, in order to depress the land prices to help meet the peasants' demand for land.

The opposing view – held by the majority – was in principle for 'nationalization' of the land by the formation of a land fund, to be created by the greatest possible degree of expropriation. From this fund the land was to be allocated to the peasants for utilization in exchange for a modest charge. Professor Luchitskii (Kiev), however, protested most vehemently against any idea of nationalization: the peasants of the south-west and south, who lived not in full communes but in a system of inherited farms (*podvornoe zemlevladenie*), would immediately turn their backs on the party if it were to resolve such a thing, and only the granting of full private land ownership could satisfy them.

Between these two extremes there were numerous views differing in individual points, and it became clear, in spite of a detailed address by A. A. Kaufmann, that the congress was obliged to leave all important questions in this area open for the time being, especially because no agreement on fixed *norms* could be reached, on the one hand on the scope of the intended expropriation, and on the other hand on the amount of land to be granted to the peasants. The disputed points were finally passed to a committee, which then presented the third congress with a prepared programme which agreed in all essential points with the bill which the party later introduced in the Duma.

It is perhaps appropriate at this point to discuss, at least in condensed form, this agrarian programme and the differences of opinion which emerged regarding it, in order to give some idea of the unbelievable difficulties which need to be overcome if anything whatever is to be 'achieved' in Russia in this most important question. First some general remarks:

In the first place it is undoubtedly true that for almost all regions of the Empire, except the extreme north and the new land areas, there exists the ('subjective') phenomenon of acute 'land hunger' amongst the peasants, which is at its strongest in, though is by no means limited to, a zone which comprises the purely or almost purely agrarian, *cereal*-growing, 'Black Earth' regions, and those areas bordering on them, from the west bank of the Volga through the southern central area as far as and beyond the Dnieper.

'Objectively', this pressing demand for land expresses itself most clearly in the fact that for two decades, in spite of almost continually *falling* cereal prices and (relatively!) stable farming technology, rents and prices of farm land have been constantly *rising*, sometimes exorbitantly: in these regions, land is sought not for the purpose of economic exploitation of 'investment capital' or as a means of acquisition, but simply . . . as a means of subsistence; the goal is not profit, but the satisfaction of the most immediate needs. Thus the price of land is limited *solely* by the amount of money (however acquired) at the disposal of those who wish to buy it. [. . .]

If one assumes the business and economic qualities of the peasant as an element which at best can only change gradually, then the increase of a peasant's land ownership, at whatever cost, seems to be an essential precondition of everything else, especially of the possibility of 'self-help'.

A good deal of such increase is taking place today by way of free commerce or that mediated by the Peasant Land Bank, but at prices which in general undoubtedly rule out the possibility of 'surplus yields' from land bought or leased, because (1) the yield from peasant farms already is 20 per cent below those of the estates from which they buy their land; the peasant is often better off working for the landlord than as leaseholder or buyer, even if one only considers the 'yield value' of the estate land, and especially because (2) the tremendous competition for land amongst the peasants needing leases or purchases drives up the prices without limit, to levels far above the capitalized yield value even of the estate land. Moreover, it is, of course, by no means the most needy who come into possession of the land they require in this frenzied race.

It is this situation that has given birth to the idea of establishing *compulsory* fixed prices, putting an end to land speculation, and systematically increasing the 'nadel' of those peasants who really need land to a level which at least relieves them from the constant pressure of hunger; in other words, the idea of expropriation.

Let us look briefly at the *problems* it entails. The question arises of what should be the norm for the size of the peasant nadel, which is to be achieved – as far as possible – by allocation of land. Proposals and demands such as the following vie with each other:

1 The demand that the land owned by the peasant should be of an appropriate size for him to make full use of his labour upon it. 'The land is God's, and it must be given to the man that will work on it – to each just enough for him to work.' The impossibility of attaining this aim in Russia is statistically completely beyond doubt. There just is not that much land available; nevertheless not only the Socialist Revolutionary Peasants' and Workers' Party has advocated this *trudovaia norma* ('work norm'), but occasionally well-known agrarian politicians have done so too.

2 The 'need principle' (*potrebitelnaia norma*): enough land is to be distributed to the peasant farm to allow it to meet its elementary needs (food, housing, clothing); it is clear that this norm could only be established with regard to all concrete circumstances, i.e. there would be local variation. The 'trudovaia norma' is based on the 'right to work', and the 'potrebitelnaia norma' on the 'right to a living'. The former assumes, like the 'right to work' itself, that the purpose of economic activity is acquisition; it is a revolutionary child of capitalism; the latter treats the purpose of economic activity as the satisfaction of one's 'needs', and its philosophical basis is the 'subsistence' standpoint. The principle of 'potrebitelnaia norma' may be formulated in two different ways:

i. that the criterion should be a quantity of land which is sufficient for his needs, if the peasant's technology has been raised as near as possible to the level of modern farms; or
ii. that the criterion should be the *present* technology of the peasant, and the average efficiency 'customary in that locality' (since one should not directly *favour* the lazy and the stupid).

3 Finally, since these norms, especially point ii, would require the most minutely detailed surveys and the appearance of arbitrariness would

be unavoidable, a 'historical' norm has been proposed, namely *either* (a) the maximum peasant land share of 1861 as variously reckoned in the different regions; *or* (b) today's *average* land share of the individual areas as *minimum* nadel. Against proposal (a) the argument was put forward that the tremendous upheavals in Russia's economy since 1861 would be bound to make the application of this norm today extremely arbitrary and quite uneven in its effects.

The draft produced by the agrarian commission of the Constitutional Democratic Party has accepted the *need* principle. [. . .]

Added to these material difficulties and uncertainties concerning the extent of the problem, which so far have only been partially dealt with in the negotiations, is the fact, important for the political fate of Democracy, that the majority of its supporters from zemstvo circles do not wish to go as far, even in the case of the most desperate need, as to expropriate the *entire* private landed property. The first result of doing this would be to get the whole body of small private landowners up in arms against them. Also to be borne in mind is the importance of the large farms for cultivation and the feared sudden rapid fall in agricultural production, at a moment when a huge amount of capital needs to be raised. This was why, under protest from the Socialist Revolutionaries, the official speakers at the Agrarian Congress in May 1905 advocated conservation of parts of the large landholdings.

[*Weber provides details of what, according to the Kadet draft, was not to be expropriated.*]

The question which divided *all* the reforming parties, as the Duma negotiations again showed, is whether land should be *leased* or *sold* (in limited quantities). The agrarian commission of the Duma was split by 30 votes to 26, among the latter (for sale of the land) being a member of the extreme left Labour Group (Trudovaia Gruppa) and several Kadets. The whole of the west, for quite understandable *national* reasons, was opposed to the state land fund. It feared that the Russians would be favoured by leasing and that the 'nationalization' of land would simply serve the interests of those striving for Russification. For the same reason the west was in favour of reserving the land for the *local* population.

The negotiations on the whole draft in the congress were detailed and at times passionate. *No* resolution in the matter was actually passed. There was a fear that no agreement with the *peasants* could be reached, and the principle was expressed – more for reasons of party opportunism than genuine principle – that their wishes should on *no* account be disregarded (Gurevich-Tula et al.).

Even the draft itself was a compromise between the supporters of 'nationalization' of the land and the more cautious social politicians: A. A. Kaufmann and the outstanding agronomist and reformer of peasant agriculture in the Volokolam district A. A. Subrilin had been members of the commission. Miliukov and Struve described it as the 'maximum that could be achieved by the path of legislation – i.e. peacefully', and saw in it, if it should be carried out, 'the greatest reform the world had ever seen', whilst the radicals called it a 'bureaucratic product'. Private landowners had not been elected to the commission – but it should not be forgotten that the party had to take account of their many supporters from this group. Finally the draft was handed over to the future parliamentary party for its use and possible modification, together with a resolution which established the transfer of land 'into the hands of working people' as 'guiding' principle of the party.

Drafts calling for *systematic* expropriation and division of private landed property will doubtless continue to multiply. But it must seriously be doubted whether ultimately any of them will ever be carried out by any Russian government in a manner which comes anywhere near the ideals of their authors.

Even the really moderate Constitutional Democratic draft is a proposal for a kind of auto-vivisection; it makes proposals, the execution of which presuppose a 'completely dispassionate approach'. But if one considers for a moment the terrible passions and especially the chaos of conflicting interests *within* the peasantry which any attempt at *systematic* and *general* land distribution would arouse, one can only conclude that such action would require a government which was *at the same time* inspired by strictly democratic ideals *and* was prepared to repress any opposition to its orders with iron authority and power.

The implementation of the reforms themselves as well as the periodic renewed leasing of such vast areas to a huge number of interested individuals can, as far as historical experience can judge, only be done by despotic governments in *stable* economic conditions. The millions of small state leaseholders would form a class of *coloni* [tenant farmers] on a scale that only ancient Egypt and the Roman Empire have known.

A bureaucratic regime lacks any possibility of pursuing those ideals, and in general of ruling ruthlessly against the nobility and the landowning class, whilst a democratic ministry would not have the necessary undemocratic 'iron' authority and the ruthlessness against the peasants. A forced expropriation on a large scale is therefore not very likely, whatever may happen in the future in Russia.

Voluntary purchase of land at relatively low prices is possible, as long as the peasants remain as restless as they are now: the cossack guards are expensive for the estate owners, and they are in an uncomfortable si-

Pseudo-constitutionalism 201

tuation, but the credit necessary for this [purchase] is scarcely affordable, especially for a really big operation running into thousands of millions, and the peasants will not buy. However, once the country is 'calm' again, given the constant demand from the state or the Land Bank, the price of land will shoot up even more sharply than it did here in the province of Posen: in the space of about 15 years (in spite of falling product prices) there has already been a five- and occasionally even ten-fold increase in *individual* regions.

Realization of the idea of *dopolnitelnyi nadel* [see Glossary] seems – unfortunately – very unlikely, not because the idea represents anything 'impossible' in itself (there is no question of that!) but because, as the controversial situation just outlined has shown, and the figures illustrate, an immense number of obstacles threaten to wreck any serious attempt to transform it into reality.

Added to these difficulties is the fact that the peasants are now politically 'aware', and powerful revolutionary parties, filled with the most glowing hopes, are appealing to their imagination.

Any real 'solution' of this unbelievably complicated question (such as that attempted, on a broad basis, by the Constitutional Democratic programme) is only achievable by means of objective and unbiased work. However, this is not possible when both social and purely political passions have reached their current level of intensity, and the leaders of the extreme left want to use the hopes of the peasants in the service of these passions. It is 'too late' for that, as for so much else, thanks to the policies of the last 20 years.

And with all due respect for the intellectual abilities of the peasants – and even antidemocratic Russian observers have gained an impression of them which has surprised them – it would be a fatal self-deception to attribute to the peasants *today* the ability to achieve agrarian reform *themselves*.

An upstart of genius like Napoleon or a citizen like Washington, if in possession of military power and borne along on the confidence of the nation, could perhaps produce a new Russia based on the small farmer out of thin air. Legitimate monarchies are probably as little able to do this as some very new parliamentary body, fighting wearily for its life and under attack from right and left.

If the agrarian reform were to be implemented even partially in the manner in which the party proposes, then – as I have previously shown[53] – a powerful increase in the spirit of 'natural law' resting on a 'communist' base, and long-lasting political, social and spiritual changes to the character of Russia would be the probable result. These would be truly 'unheard of' – but their exact nature seems impossible to predict. A great economic *collapse*, however, lasting some 10 or 20 years, until this 'new' petty bourgeois Russia is again saturated with capitalism, seems quite certain: *one must choose between 'material' and 'ethical' goals.*

An expropriation operation limited to the *leased* land which is already de facto in the possession of the peasants would be a very different matter, perhaps along the lines of the new leasing regulations introduced by the authorities for land leased from 1 January 1896 or, alternatively, in the form of redemption of the lease and transfer to the communes or (as now happens with the Peasant Bank) freely formed cooperatives of peasants, i.e. a combination of a 'regulatory legislation' and the work of the Peasant Bank.

Economically, this would fit much better into the structure of today's social order than, for instance, the Irish land legislation, but – as the great preponderance of individual and free cooperative land purchase over purchase by communes by means of the Peasant Bank shows – it would rest on 'economic selection', and would therefore be strictly contrary to the Socialist Revolutionary principles of ethics and natural law, which – in diluted form – also underlie the agrarian programme of the Kadets. They would therefore reject it and the mass of the peasants and their ideologists in the radical intelligentsia would reject it even more emphatically.

Even if the measures outlined were to be applied to all farm land which on 1 January 1906 was being worked with peasants' farming equipment only, whereby, for instance, the employment relationship was converted by law into one of 'employment lease', with officially fixed fees, which could continue to be redeemed – such a policy would be 'conservative' in character. Conversely, the Kadet idea of the systematic provision of the landless and land-poor *as such* with a minimum amount of land would be essentially Socialist Revolutionary (and indeed is intended to be).

Perhaps neither of these paths will be followed, and the Russian peasant will have to continue to carry his cross in torment and anger until a combination of modern agrarian capitalism and the modern small farm on inherited soil trying to gain a foothold in the market has finally emerged victorious in Russia too, and thus the last refuge of communism in Europe and of the peasant revolutionary natural law which arises from it is finally buried. The policies of those who today hold the physical power in their hands are certainly moving in this direction, in spite of considerable concessions to the ideas of the Narodniki.

However that may be, the attitude of the party to the most important practical question had not been finally and completely clarified even by the opening of the Duma, let alone at the start of the election. In the discussions it became clear that the degree of expropriation that the draft envisages met with the most decided resistance even from leaders of the party. It was furthermore evident that the party's reform proposal would never satisfy the strata of peasants whom the Socialist Revolutionaries had awakened to political awareness. On the other hand, at the start of the election movement, when the less thoroughly researched but similar draft was available, it inevitably appeared that the decided inclination of the majority of the organized party to take over the role of representative of the peasant class would cost them the support of the great mass of the larger and medium landowners.

And, lastly, not only the organization of the party, which *at the time* (in January) still seemed extremely inadequate outside the big cities, but especially the inner unpreparedness and uncertainty, and the tendency to discuss purely theoretical questions in the greatest detail while leaving everything open in the formulation of programme points of practical importance – as in the agrarian question – seemed undoubtedly to depress their chances greatly.

Added to this was the departure of some of the most respected members of the right wing, Prince Eugene Trubetskoi at their head, whose decision had been prompted by these very weaknesses, especially the pointless debate on the question of the 'constituent assembly' and the like. Maxim Kovalevskii too had joined a group which stood rather on the right, the 'Party of Democratic Reform'. Thus the difficulties seemed to be mounting.

Thanks to the dedicated work of its members up to the beginning of the elections, the party had brilliantly compensated for the deficiencies of its organization – but the inner discord was not really healed, and it had in the meantime come up against party organizations which had to be regarded as extremely dangerous opponents, in view of the strong bias of the franchise in favour of property ownership, and especially landed property. Let us take a brief look at them.

The most significant opponent of the Kadets, in terms of its intellectual and material powers, the party of the Union of 17 October, developed as a special group out of the differences of opinion on *national* questions revealed by the Congress of the Zemstvos and Cities, in September 1905.

It came into being immediately after the manifesto from which it takes its name, in Moscow, as a result of the demise of the old National Progress Party of D. N. Shipov, which had embraced the principle of a people's assembly, which was to emerge from the self-governing bodies – divested of their estate character – and whose purpose would be to *advise* on the laws and the budget. Shipov and A. J. Guchkov assumed the leadership.

At the November Congress of the Zemstvos and Cities, at which the Constitutional Democratic Party had the overwhelming majority – although a dozen members supported Guchkov – the clash of views was particularly evident on the occasion of the debate on the imposition of martial law in Poland, which Guchkov defended. The members of the Union, which had just been formed, also voted against the Constitutional Democrats on the question of the 'constituting function' of the Duma, the franchise (Guchkov was in favour of the 'two-stage' electoral system) and the autonomy of the border countries (especially Poland).

On 4 December the party was constituted under the leadership of Shipov, Guchkov, Stachovich, Count Heyden and the moderate members of the zemstvos.[54] The leading elements were overwhelmingly recruited from the circles of the liberal rural bourgeoisie, while some were from the wealthy urban classes (especially from Petersburg), from a section of the academic intelligentsia (Miliutin, Pilenko), plus liberal civil servants, clergy and officers. The Germans joined the Union both in Moscow and in Petersburg (Baron Meyendorf), and the Baltic Constitutional Party, under purely German leadership, but including a few members of the Latvian bourgeoisie, considered itself to be in solidarity with it.

Relations with Witte were at first excellent; Guchkov could without doubt have obtained a ministerial portfolio at any time; in April the Tsar requested him to accept the appointment as a member of the Imperial Council, a request which he refused. Towards the end of January, after Witte's ambiguous statements on the continued existence of the autocracy had become known, the relationship cooled: the united Moscow and Petersburg committees, under the chairmanship of Shipov, expressed the conviction that the Emperor *had* restricted his power voluntarily, that the basis for a 'constitution' was thus in place, and the Union had the task of building on this basis. Similar views were expressed in a lively meeting held in Petersburg on 29 January, which included fierce personal attacks on Witte.

The Union began to feel that it was a force to be reckoned with; according to its own information it had about 10,000 members in Moscow by the end of January; the 'Peasant Union based upon the Manifesto of 17 October', which had been formed as a counterweight to the radical 'Bund' on the one hand, and the 'black hundreds' on the other, refused to join the Monarchist Party or the Party of Legal Order, and instead forged links with the Union of 17 October. [. . .]

In the absence of a strong agrarian programme the Union was quite unable to rely on the peasant vote. Conversely, it was only to be expected that all 'class-conscious' private landowners, at least those with large land holdings, would support it, as did the entire 'class-conscious' bourgeoisie in the cities, except for those who belonged to the Trade and Industry Party, which was in any case closely allied to the Union. In view of the great indifference of the masses which was reported almost everywhere in January and February, prospects for the Union were excellent.

The Union of 17 October was essentially the party of the constitutional *zemstvo right*. Thus those economic groups which, thanks to the composition of the zemstvos, were not represented in them at all, did not join the Union. This applied particularly to the specifically modern classes representing owners of moveable property, classes which had been created by capitalism, and which in the 1880s and 1890s stood firmly on the side of the bureaucracy, since only the latter had supported its interests against those of the liberal landowners.

The *Trade and Industry Party* grew out of the 'Trade and Industry Association', whose spiritual leader was, and remained, the Chairman of the Moscow Stock Exchange Committee, G. A. Krestovnikov. This party was the actual and specific representative of the 'bourgeoisie' in the strictly economic sense of the word. Big industrialists and traders donated money in support of the quite vigorous agitation which it undertook, and did not scruple to use their position of authority to put gentle but firm pressure on their commercial employees, officials, and other white-collar workers dependent upon them, to join the association. The results showed that these members reluctantly supplied the party with their signatures and subscriptions at the elections, but did not vote for it.

The party saw itself as a class representative, and its members, who had studied and understood Marx just as much (or just as little) as their socialist opponents, had the honesty to state this openly in a Moscow meeting: every party *must* stand for 'class interests'; everything else was an illusion. It was quite successful in getting recruits, even among the petty bourgeoisie, although the attempt to found a special Artisans Party [*Handwerkerpartei*] ended in failure. Certain protectionist interests, which emerged in individual workers' associations and amongst home workers, worked in their favour in the lower social strata too.

A Pan-Russian congress of the party took place on 5 February 1906 and the days following. At that time, according to the report of the committee, the party comprised 60 sections and had at its disposal over 30 newspapers with a circulation of 3 million. In the debates it became clear that the party was essentially in agreement with the Union of 17 October, except that the constitutional question was handled with a considerably greater degree of caution, the guarantees of personal rights in the Manifesto of 17 October were stressed, universal and equal suffrage was seen as being for the moment a 'purely theoretical' question, and the *centralist* idea of unity was even more strongly emphasized. The party spoke out strongly against 'red tape', i.e. for the removal of bureaucratic control of capital, and regarded both the socialists and, on account of their decentralist (and of course also antiprotectionist) tendencies, the Constitutional Democrats, as their particular enemies.

Although the initial attempt (in March and July 1905) to unite the whole of big industry politically *and* economically proved unworkable, and as a result the representation of economic interests became divorced from the formation of political parties, nevertheless the bedrock of support for the political party of the bourgeoisie was formed by the powerful *employers' associations*, which have sprung up in the course of the past year. Thus, after initial resistance to centralist control, by the industry of Lodz on the one hand, and of Moscow industry on the other, a union of big industrialists from all over the Empire has come together in Petersburg whose concerns are twofold: firstly to ensure that the views of the employers on the reorganization of social legislation are jointly presented to the government in the negotiations which have already begun and will be continuing; secondly, to facilitate the importation of the most up-to-date methods in the struggle against the workers. A strike insurance association for employers has been constituted for the Moscow district and is due to spread throughout the country in the near future; the creation of 'welfare institutions' for the purpose of social domination has also begun here and there.

One can see that the country is jumping straight into the middle of the most modern form of economic struggle, without passing through any of the intermediate phases of Western development. In Moscow, the first major lockout, in retaliation against a strike of typographers, is about to take place.

Prior to the elections, big industry was powerfully armed; the question was only whether its power could be put into effect, given the nature of the electoral law.

The so-called Party of Legal Order (Partiia pravovogo poriadka) was not, unlike the Trade and Industry Party, divided by differences in the economic situation of the different strata which it represented, but by the accident of its origins in the Union of 17 October. It first emerged in public with a statement of principle, after the deliberations of the September Congress of the Zemstvos and Cities on the national question.

The statement declared that in essence it differed from other zemstvo members, even though it did not necessarily oppose the main concern of other groups of moderates, namely their radical agrarian programme, in that (1) it regarded even the smallest degree of experimentation with the idea of autonomy for the *krais* [regions] as extremely dangerous: the party itself inclined only to absolute equality for all nationalities with regard to civil rights and the civil service, concessions in the language of schooling, and complete implementation of religious tolerance; (2) it regarded absolute maintenance of a 'strong state power' as vital, but felt that the liberal programme placed this in jeopardy. [. . .]

One could not fail to notice the rather loose organization of the groups to the right of the Kadets, their inferior 'technique' of electoral agitation, and the lesser number of ruthlessly dedicated party workers who were both talented agitators *and* academically trained.

Much of the intellectual burden of the agitation for the Union of 17 October was carried by Dr Pilenko, that of the Progressive Economic Party by Prof. Oserov, whilst the distinguished politicians of the 'centre', like Shipov, held themselves back. The Trade and Industry Party and the Party of Legal Order believed they could rely on the social and economic strength of their members, while the right relied on their nationalist antisemitic demagogy. Nevertheless, the chances of these groups in the election campaign looked favourable compared with the endless frustrations suffered by the Democratic movement – which were so great that even just before the elections the Central Committee of the Kadets considered whether perhaps a boycott of the Duma might be more advisable for them.

What seemed to weigh more heavily against the Democrats and in favour of the centre parties and conservatives than all these frustrations caused by the administrative authorities was the volte-face in the mood of those circles who were especially favoured by the electoral law, namely the *private landowners.*

After the suppression of the Moscow uprising and after the experience of the peasant riots,[55] the reaction of the bureaucracy began to spread to 'society', that is to say, primarily the *zemstvos.* Obviously, the dominant role was played here by the peasant riots, with their serious threat to the economic basis of private land ownership, whose representatives were after all the best minds of zemstvo liberalism. The process is a telling example of the conditions necessary for successful ideological work within a landowning class and of the limits to the force of humanitarian ideals as compared with economic interests. As long as the economic basis of the landowners, who were dominant in the zemstvos, remained essentially undisturbed, they accepted the leadership of the political and social ideologists amongst them. However, when they were directly threatened with physical and economic destruction, the whole weight of latent conflicts of interest rushed upon them, and it was inevitable that, torn out of their daily existence and painfully reminded of the material basis of their own position, they modified their position not inconsiderably. [. . .]

When by the middle of January the flood-waters had receded, the changed mood of those affected became clear. The ideologists' scope for action had been considerably narrowed. Those circles of the nobility and big private landowners who hitherto had either submitted to the leadership of the progressive liberals or had simply abstained from political activity, began to swamp the January zemstvo meetings, and whereas, as a result of the reticence of the 'moderates', the minority led by Guchkov at the October Congress had been almost infinitesimal – only 15 to 20 persons – now material 'class interests' went on to the offensive all along the line.

[*Weber describes certain policy vacillations within the government, particularly the furore from landed interests that greeted the news that the Minister of Agriculture, Kutler, was considering partial expropriation of land in private ownership. Weber states:*]

As far as is known, the draft [of the Ministry of Agriculture] established norms for the size of three types of farms for the different areas of the Empire: small ones, which ran without paid labour; medium, in which the owner worked personally alongside waged workers; and large. That part of any landed property which exceeded the norm for the class in which it had been placed was to be expropriated. This, together with the state and appanage lands, was to form a 'land fund' out of which peasants with little or no land were to be supplied. However, the debate on the draft in the Council of Ministers, which was scheduled to begin on 7/20 January, never took place, because in the meantime the storm of protest from interest groups had begun: the Congress of the Nobility, which had hastily convened in Moscow (4/17 to 11/24 January) protested against any expropriation other than that for railways, and against the decree of an agrarian law before the Duma had assembled, and also rejected the institution of a special commission consisting of the nobility, the zemstvos and peasants to draw up an agrarian draft.

[*Of the alternative proposals mooted by landed interests, Weber adds:*]

The main aim of these guardians of national traditions was – as with us – the achievement of a boom in land prices. And in the main the interests of agrarian capitalism were victorious. The fate of the expropriation idea was soon decided in the ministry.

[*Kutler resigned from the government and joined the Kadet opposition.*]

In numerous statements, the most emphatic of which was on 18/31 January in a speech to the peasant deputation from the Kursk Province, which was then officially published throughout the Empire, the Tsar

reiterated his commitment to the *absolute inviolability of property*.
The class distinctions between nobility and peasantry now emerged most distinctly. The landowning nobility had suffered such a shock that it immediately set about making comprehensive preparations for a union of (if possible) the entire estate, in order to work most vigorously against the social and political democratization of the country. [. . .]

In highly characteristic manner, the huge change in attitude of the ruling classes with regard to the *obshchina* compared to the time of Alexander III was revealed. Once the darling of the Slavophile and reactionary romantics and regarded as a pillar of 'authority', the Congresses of the Nobility now saw it (as had the bureaucracy of Witte for years) as the source of the revolutionary mood of the masses. [. . .]

In any case 1 January 1907 was destined to become a turning-point in the fate of the obshchina, because, as decreed by the Manifesto of 3 November 1905, on that day the redemption payments were due to be discontinued. (Hitherto the existence of outstanding payments bound the peasant to the obshchina – since 1893 this applied even if the individual had paid off his own share.)

The question was whether in reality, and then under what conditions, the government would permit resignation from the obshchina on that date.

On 25 January/7 February a 'special commission' met to discuss this and on 19 March/1 April, as it had resolved to do, the Interior Ministry took the question before the Imperial Council. As in previous years, Count Witte expressed his conviction that there would be no peace until the special position of the peasants had been done away with. A. P. Nikolskii, the successor to Kutler, added that the sooner the obshchina disappeared the sooner would any plans for compulsory expropriation of land disappear, and a member of the Imperial Council consequently recommended giving the peasants the general right to demand distribution of the land *in one piece* on resignation from the commune: the obshchina would then soon cease to exist.

However, the Imperial Council absolutely refused to go so far without the agreement of the peasants themselves, and approved the Interior Minister's draft, according to which distribution of land could only be requested periodically, namely once every four years, and by a minimum of five peasants simultaneously. The size of land share should be determined by the current ownership situation; when no redistribution had taken place for 25 years it should be established by resolution of the commune.

Alongside this last idea, which contained a kind of parting gesture of respect for the old 'right to land', what was politically characteristic in this whole procedure was the eagerness to use the short time remaining before the opening of the Duma to make a final effort to promote the idea of peasant private ownership; the government's pretext was that it was merely 'interpreting' an act of autocracy, the November Manifesto. It was not only the left-wing press that protested, but even opportunist publications like *Novoe Vremia* disapproved, at least for the moment, of the bureaucratic attack on a 'national' institution. Sanction was therefore withheld, and the draft was added to the others to be submitted to the Duma.

Considerations similar to those responsible for the government's hostile attitude will no doubt, the more social antagonisms intensify, drive the private landowning classes to join the opponents of the obshchina. Opinions of their representatives in the well-known Witte committees 'on the needs of agriculture' were divided, partly out of mutually contradictory considerations of class interest (the need for workers for the estates), partly owing to opposing social and general political points of view. There seems to have been no sudden unanimity, but rather a gradual shift of the consensus of opinion toward opposition to the obshchina. For example, the provincial zemstvo of Kazan passed a strongly worded resolution this spring against the obshchina, though not without an equally determined protest from a dissenting minority.

As far as the peasants are concerned, their attitude to the obshchina remains divided; of those who would be substantially the *losers* by a redistribution – that is, in general, those with much land but with small families with few children – a certain proportion normally declare themselves against the obshchina when directly asked. Additionally, there is, of course, always a small stratum of peasants who have developed so far economically as to feel the obshchina to be a shackle. But the numerically overwhelming *majority* of peasants, in the regions where it exists, is undoubtedly favourably disposed to its basic principle: right to land according to need, and in favour also of its fundamental institutional function, the redistribution of land where there has been a shift in the 'correct' proportion between size of family and land share.

The once often heard view that after abolition of joint liability for tax, which was always a feature of the commune, there would be a tendency for the peasants to go their separate ways, has *not* been borne out so far, and the abolition of redemption payments has of course only made the right to redistribution of land ownership all the more attractive for the masses, who are either landless or own very little land. Certainly, wherever the peasants have publicly stated their view, they have come out for the preservation of the obshchina. Finally, it is well known that amongst leading 'bourgeois' Russian scholars, including those educated

Pseudo-constitutionalism 211

in the German tradition, the idea of legislation which would directly destroy the obshchina or indirectly encourage its decline is usually rejected vigorously even today.

In Germany, of course, even the technical nature of the obshchina, which admittedly, measured by the standards of agrarian capitalism, is an 'archaic' but by no means 'primitive' or crudely communist institution, is frequently insufficiently known. We should therefore make an effort to appreciate the motivation for the support it enjoys before we judge it, and must then be clear that, as so often, 'value stands against value'.

Any closer examination of the viewpoint of Russian scholars must be reserved for another occasion; suffice it to say here that the obshchina, when it feels the effects of capitalism, will probably be subject to such changes that, in the eyes of *non*-interested parties, both the favourable view of the obshchina taken by most observers in Russia and the prevailing unfavourable 'value' viewpoint here in Germany will undergo a shift.

Here it has simply been my intention to establish the characteristic change in the attitude of the *government*. Having pledged itself to end the domination of the village commune over the individual peasant, it showed, almost in the same breath, that it was nevertheless quite prepared to make use of this domination for its own ends. The government did this – as previously briefly mentioned[56] – by attempting to exploit one of the most odious of the powers of the mir in order to assist the police: the right of the mir, under certain circumstances, to get rid of troublesome members by means of banishment to Siberia. This power was employed against the revolutionaries by encouraging the peasant communes to pass resolutions *denouncing* to the state authorities people who were 'supporters or instigators of peasant riots', whereupon the minister, 'using his discretion' could order immediate banishment (in such cases the transport costs were assumed entirely by the state).

In a similar way, the abolition of joint liability for taxes (1904) was cancelled out by the introduction of joint responsibility for damage which had occurred during agrarian riots. Then, immediately before his resignation in April, the Interior Minister drafted a law which aimed to make the civil liability of the peasants for damage in the case of riots more 'effective' by making subject to seizure by bailiffs even those items of their equipment which had previously been exempt. However, this measure, dictated by anger, was met with scepticism by both the Justice Minister and Witte, and was rejected.

On the other hand, the government attempted to meet the class interests of the landowners, at least to the extent of creating, in contrast to the legislation which was moving in the direction of abolition of punishment for strikes, a special anti-strike law for *farm labourers*, on the Prussian model, formulated in such a way as to make it possible to include peasants labouring on estate land. The government took this so seriously that it published this law on the day before the opening of the Duma, 26 April, dating it 15 April, under the puzzling heading, which betrayed the haste with which it had been edited: 'Regarding the *draft* (!) of a ruling against the outbreak of strikes among farm labourers'. Any strike contrary to contract by agricultural workers and any incitement to such, even if it is unsuccessful, is here made a criminal offence, even if no violent means are employed.

Set against all this progress towards the preservation of the 'inviolability of private property', the only in any sense 'positive' step in the area of agrarian politics was the development of the *Peasant Bank*, after an earlier unsuccessful attempt by Kutler. (One can disregard financial assistance for transportation to Siberia and a number of discussions by the various departments of domain and forest administration concerning leasing of land to the peasants.)

[*Weber describes the powers of the Bank and the attitudes of various social strata, particularly the peasants themselves, towards it – see Glossary.*]

The question is only whether the peasants will use the favourable opportunity offered [by the Peasant Bank] or whether they will let it pass in the hope of better things from the Duma.

[*Weber describes a rightward shift in the attitudes of the zemstvos. He then gives an account of the composition of the proposed new Imperial Council, in which zemstvo members were prominent.*]

It might appear a priori that the most advisable path for the Government (and, indeed, one that was easy to tread) would have been for it to come to an agreement with the legally or actually privileged classes, and in particular, since the nobility would have provided too thin a base, with circles of 'moderate' zemstvo constitutionalism. However, it did not follow this course. We have seen that in the case of the zemstvos – the example of Moscow cited is the proof – fear of the revolution was *outweighed* at the decisive moment by suspicion of the government. Similarly, in the case of the government, the desire for a pillar of support against the revolution was outweighed by the old hatred of the zemstvos. The bureaucracy was simply not prepared to make really far-reaching sacrifices of its *arbitrary* administrative power – the absolute and primary necessity for any understanding with the propertied classes.

There was no change in the bureaucracy's extreme jealousy of the zemstvos, which was revealed at the time of the war in the almost unbelievable behaviour of the 'Red Cross' towards the organizations made available by the zemstvos to assist it. For instance, the purely charitable zemstvo organization created for the benefit of the districts suffering starvation was again subjected to petty harassment, surveillance, and obstruction, like all other charitable activity engaged in by zemstvo circles, right down to the provision of free meals: despite the crying need, these efforts were subject to blanket prohibition.

Instead of leaving repression of the 'Third Element' to the 'class interest' of the propertied strata, whose interest operated promptly enough when it came to the 'preservation of the state', the administration of the governors and governors-general insisted, as usual, on playing its part in a manner which by its abruptness was bound to wound the self-esteem of the zemstvos; it simply could not get used to the idea of giving up anything at all of its omnipotence, for whoever's benefit.

The reply from the other side was not long in coming. Even the moderate zemstvo members (like Shipov) had refused the portfolios offered by Witte at the end of October, as cooperation with Trepov or Durnovo was unthinkable for them.[57] In January Witte sent a circular to the zemstvos, inviting them to send suitable representatives to take part in his regular consultation on political questions. The zemstvos almost all refused and after a certain time Witte had no choice other than to let it be known that the intended consultations had proved to be 'unnecessary'. The two sides were unable to reach agreement.

The bureaucracy of Witte (which was *economically* liberal), had, by the way in which it had framed the electoral law and devised the system of representation in the Imperial Council, condemned its closest friends, the entrepreneurial bourgeoisie, to insignificance, treated its most steadfast ally in the ministry, Timiriasev, with contempt, and, finally, constantly aroused suspicions that it was resorting to 'zubatovshchina' [use of *agents provocateurs*]. It was therefore unable politically to utilize these circles.

Analysis of the Duma Elections

[*A section follows analysing the Duma election results in various parts of Russia. The salient points made by Weber relate to the quite unexpected degree of electoral success enjoyed by the Kadets. Parties to its right – like the Union of 17 October – fared, on the other hand, very badly. As he remarks,*] the victory of Democracy was regularly achieved by an alliance of the urban voters with a section of the landowners, and especially with the *peasants*, for whom the radical land programme and the fierce opposition to arbitrary administrative action was particularly attractive. Once the period of electoral agitation got under way, the reactionary and centre party 'peasants' alliances' brought forth by the winter dispersed like chaff in the wind.

[*Still, Weber cautions,*] the fact that vast numbers of Social Democrat voters cast their vote for the Democratic candidate has not only been directly testified to, but was also evidenced by the fact that these election results persuaded the Social Democrats to abandon the boycott and put up their own candidates at the subsequent elections: thereupon Democracy was beaten in Tiflis by the socialist list, which was able to return nine-tenths of all their electors. At the same time this shows that the Democratic election victory does not stand on a very secure base: a very high turnout by the extreme left would do so much damage to Democracy in a great number of big cities that – as with us – the balance would swing solely between socialists and bourgeois class parties, and ideological Democracy would be squeezed out.

[*And Weber concludes,*] Bourgeois Democracy is not as strong as it outwardly appears: if Social Democracy participates in the election in the cities, then there too the election result will shift, and so, equally, will the class interest of the private landowners be accentuated to the detriment of Democracy. To what extent the paths of the urban Social Democrats and the Socialist Revolutionary peasants will merge is likewise uncertain, just as it is uncertain what effect inevitable disillusionment will have on the peasants. And even a relatively minor change within the electoral bodies could remove Constitutional Democracy from its present position of power.

The election result is primarily the consequence of the arbitrary actions of the Durnovo regime, against which all voters capable of political judgement came together to protest under the banner of Democracy. Without firm legal guarantees, which this regime, by its very nature, *could* not give, an alliance with broader bourgeois strata was not possible, and only extreme political exhaustion could have caused the breakup of the mass of opponents, forced together as they were by a level of oppression which could scarcely be exceeded, and which silenced all 'class antagonism'. The centre parties in particular were quite right when they accused the government of having succeeded only in furthering the cause of Democracy by their conduct.

After the Elections

Although the election itself became fragmented into a series of separate contests with only the election of the deputies themselves taking place on certain fixed days for groups of provinces, by the last week of March it was already becoming clear what the result would be. The first consequences showed themselves in the life of the *parties*. Although they formally numbered only one-third of the deputies, the Kadets were the leading party by virtue of their tactical unity, and the consequence was that at their Third Congress – 24 to 26 April – not a word was said about the 'constituent' assembly, and there was no further talk of holding aloof from 'organic' legislative work.

The party's agrarian programme was completed, and here the old antagonism emerged again and led to a resolution which was phrased in very general terms, describing the draft as only a provisional 'sketch', and declaring that contact with the peasants should be maintained; furthermore a commission on the workers' question was appointed, and there was discussion of the ranking order in which the party should place the individual reform proposals on the agenda. Regarding tactics in general it was stated that the party would not flinch from confrontation with the government, but would ensure that if such a confrontation should occur then the government alone would bear the responsibility for it. Tactically, this was a significant 'shift to the right', but one which retained a sober [*sachlich*] radicalism.

Things were different on the opposition side. The Party of Legal Order made itself look ridiculous with a 'Congress' of 23 people (24 April). The Trade and Industry Party was dissolved altogether and the members devoted themselves to strictly economic interests. Even during the elections themselves the Union of 17 October had broken off the alliance with this party in many places (e.g. Kharkov), as the electorate was evidently not going to be persuaded to vote for 'capitalists'. Thus the 'bourgeoisie' formally relinquished any parliamentary representation.

The general mood of factory-owning circles on the one hand and of the government on the other emerged clearly when (immediately after the elections) the administration of Trade Minister Fedorov presented its *social-political programme* and invited the factory owners to consult with him on this.

The programme itself was the most comprehensive imaginable. But what was *essentially* new about it and what appealed most strongly to the factory owners was the freeing of industry from administrative control and supervision, allied to the legal establishment of certain rights for the workers and, at first sight, relatively far-reaching legal measures along the lines of West European, and especially German, labour legislation. Supported as it was by powerful interests and employers' associations, which it was in the process of creating, industry felt strong enough to face the struggle with the workers. It was prepared – although this was by no means unanimous – to accept the element of 'social policy' required of it, provided only that the employment contract was taken out of the control of factory inspectors and the intervention of the state in its management was restrained *by law*.

This was indeed promised by the 'constitutional' ministry, unlike the government of the previous winter. Tactically the step taken was absolutely right from the viewpoint of the bureaucracy: liberated from the state in the pursuit of its economic interests, the Russian 'bourgeoisie' would be inclined to become that much more of a reliable pillar of 'strong state power' – though not, of course, *within* the parliament.

The Union of 17 October at first also intended to dissolve itself after the elections in the capital cities: even *Novoe Vremia* advocated this. However, after further consideration, the central committee came out in favour only of reorganization and 'rejection of undesirable elements'. They broke off all relations with the parties of the right, and at a party conference in Petersburg the motion that the Tsar should embark on a revision of the 'Fundamental Laws' was passed unanimously, but the further motion, that the ministry should be formed from the majority, was rejected – although, it was stated, they were not opposed to it in principle. Nonetheless, the rejection of this motion resulted in Pilenko's resignation.

Certainly, the party revised its programme in a leftward direction, and unmistakably narrowed the gap between it and the Kadets – as Count Heyden's conduct in the Duma showed. Its completed nationalities programme came close to that of the Democrats, with the sole exception of the *political* autonomy of Poland. Their party programmes were almost identical on the questions of self-government and language. Even in the elections some sections of the Union had advocated possible expropriation of land – and now this was heard in the Duma from the leader himself, Count Heyden, who declared that even the principle of sanctity of property must yield to considerations of the 'good of the state' – although only as far as this was unavoidable; this, then, represented a sharp 'shift to the left'.

Only the monarchists, even after their miserable results, remained 'unmoved' and held a congress with precisely the same old speeches and resolutions. But even within their ranks no friend of 'bureaucracy' could be found.

On the eve of the opening of the Duma the centre parties within the 'Constitutional Monarchist League of Law' had listened to speeches by workers who threatened the outbreak of the 'revolution' if the 'Fundamental Laws', which downgraded the Duma to the level of 'a purely consultative assembly', were not revised.

Finally, the electoral success of radicalism had the expected effect on the extreme *left*: namely, the Social Democrats took part in the forthcoming Caucasus elections with significant success, having *rescinded* their boycott resolution (which had originally only been passed with the votes of 1,168 branch meetings to 928) and having now formed themselves again into a single party, as already mentioned.[58]

Whilst in the case of the Kadets the concern that the parliamentary party could fall victim to the dominance of *extra*parliamentary 'clubbism' immediately gave rise to consideration of how this could be avoided, Social Democracy sought to hold the parliamentary representation, which it had at first received against its will, and which was about to increase, on a strict leash and to bind it to the directives of the newly created central authority. Besides this, the Stockholm agreement had by no means brought to an end the dispute between Mensheviki (Plekhanov) and Bolsheviki (Lenin), the old dispute in the party, which continued throughout the whole election period.

The last named group, evidently to the delight of the government, which on this occasion was happy to tolerate the most extreme speeches, continued its tactics of antiparliamentary sindacalism[59] – which is admittedly an unduly flattering name for their idiotic behaviour – aiming it this time at the Duma. When Plekhanov called for support for the Duma with an 'Appeal to the Russian Workers', the Bolsheviki began to break up the meetings of the Mensheviki. In the light of this, one must await the further development of the official party situation, about which doubtless next year's congress will provide information.

The Socialist Revolutionaries had, albeit reluctantly, found considerable support for their party amongst the *peasants*, though the latter were of relatively moderate orientation. The government booked special accommodation, including full board, at an amazingly low price, for the peasant deputies, and sent them the rail tickets in plenty of time before the opening of the Duma, but its efforts were in vain. First the police searched the suitcase of a peasant deputy at the station for secret documents. Then one of the staff of the inn where they were staying let slip that he had been instructed to 'keep an eye on' the deputies to see what they got up to. Indignantly, the overwhelming majority of the peasants moved out (on 21 April) and from then on held private meetings under the chairmanship of the fiercely radical F. M. Onipko, in accordance with a request previously sent to them; these meetings were attended at first by about 80, and later by 122 and occasionally more deputies.

At once the practised old agitators of the radical Narodnichestvo – Aladin, Anikin, Bondarev, Nazarenko, Onipko, Shilkin etc. – began to dominate proceedings. Amongst the participants were also those supporters of the Kadets (there were quite a few of them) who were members of the peasant estate. In accord with their wishes, two members of the party executive were included in the consultations from time to time, and they also regularly attended the meetings of the Kadets as guests. However, they stopped short of actually joining the party. The peasants found the Constitutional Democratic programme 'not sufficiently oriented to the people', the *dvorianskii dukh* ('air of the nobility') was wafting through it; they assumed from the fact that some of the big private farms were to be maintained that the Kadets too were interested in 'high rents and low wages' – but the land was God's and each peasant must receive as much as he could 'cultivate with his own hands' (the 'trudovaia norma', already discussed).[60]

Fierce protests against the expulsion of workers from Petersburg, absolute condemnation of the death penalty – 'everyone can change for the better' – followed; the radical mood intensified and the resolution which soon followed, to join no other party, led to the formation of the 'trudovaia gruppa', which comprised at first 60–70, and finally 107 'peasants' (including workers and radical intelligentsia) whilst the Constitutional Democratic participants now returned to their party, and a section of the peasants, frightened off by the strident tone, stood aside and simply voted with the group. The 'trudovaia gruppa' (with 107 members) was internally less strong than it appeared. Its three components, Socialist Revolutionary intelligentsia, radical peasants, and socialist workers, could not possibly hold together permanently.

In June the Social Democrats declared that now, following the rescinding of the boycott of the Duma, their supporters were to form a special parliamentary group [*Fraktion*] – which they have now done.

The peasants were all more or less indifferent to any political problems which went beyond the land question and the removal of arbitrary police actions affecting them personally; they were very much opposed to equal rights for the Jews, at least with regard to 'rights to land', and women's suffrage, and their deep suspicion of the leaders who were from the 'intelligentsia' remained unabated: even when it was a question of something like the hire of a party meeting hall the provenance of the money paid in advance by these leaders from the 'intelligentsia' aroused their suspicion. It was only the peasants' 'shortage of land' and the tremendous pressure of administrative tyranny that held this group together. The influence of the street and of 'clubbism' upon them was, naturally, quite tangible, and some of their leaders reached considerable heights of oratory, whilst the success of several vain windbags (Aladin, Anikin) only too clearly showed the effect of the government's electoral policy in depressing the intellectual level of debates in the Duma.

All parties, in order to succeed in the elections, had been obliged to include so many peasants on their ticket that there was no place for many of their most talented leaders, especially since the government had brought charges against a significant section of these men with the aim of excluding them from candidature; others had been excluded from candidature by the requirement of selection 'from amongst the members themselves'.

Thus all the government's expectations with regard to the outcome of the elections and the attitude of the peasants were disappointed, and – this could already be seen by the end of March – it was faced with an overwhelming majority of absolutely antibureaucratic and socially and politically radical elements.

The first thing it did in this situation was rapidly to take up a 'war loan' against the 'enemy within' on conditions which the banks dictated. And the banks now held the whip hand. They had at first persistently called for the convening of the Duma, and now that this was about to take place, they too had the most pressing interest in getting the loan 'signed and sealed' before the Duma met, for it was clear that the Duma would never agree to the conditions under which the government, which had been delivered helpless into their hands, was inclined to conclude the deal. What was more, a collapse of the bureaucracy or its subjection to the Duma would inevitably hand all Russia's government stocks to an uncertain fate and completely ruin the deal. [. . .]

The financial situation of the government was such, however, that it had to subject itself either to the Duma or to the banks, and, preferring the latter, agreed to virtually any condition: in spite of a bank rate of around 9 per cent at the end of January, which was about to jump to 10 per cent at any moment, the cash reserves of the bank were falling, and the tax boycott by the peasants was making itself felt. Higher wages for railway and post office employees, improvements in army catering, grants to the cossacks, relocation of garrisons, increased police costs, the substantial 'provisions budget' to alleviate the famine, remission of redemption payments, and finally the direct losses of state property and taxation income – these caused massive shifts within the budget which either contributed to the previous year's deficit or had still to make themselves felt. It was no longer possible to do business with short-term treasury bills of exchange. Thus the government accepted conditions which were in almost grotesque contrast to the price of Russian stocks even at the worst period of the war with Japan (achieved by the clever tactics of the big financial institutions in handling the stock exchanges) and were amongst the harshest which Russia or any other hitherto 'reputable' great power has ever tolerated. [. . .]

At least the loan was 'home and dry' – and Count Witte was thus dispensable; indeed, since he had to share all the odium attaching to the Minister of the Interior, even the foreign banks were apprehensive at the idea of his coming into contact with this Duma. Any pretext would therefore serve – and the nature of the pretext used is hard to make out – to have him and his cabinet disappear ignominiously from the scene and to replace them with an assortment of dutiful conservative officials, who were also still relatively 'uncompromised' in their relations with 'society'. The new ministry 'modified' in a few places the draft of the Fundamental Laws (which had reached the press through an indiscretion), to make it more constitutional, but still obtained the Tsar's signature and thus caused an immediate angry protest not only from Democracy but also from the centre parties.

Otherwise, the bureaucratic machine proceeded in the same tempo after the elections as before it. The outlines of the draft for a comprehensive programme of social legislation was made known and showed among other things that the government was giving up any attempt to regulate capitalist development as hopeless; property would be deprived of the freedom it had enjoyed from intervention from *above* and would fall into the lap of 'capital' – with a few social and political restrictions. [. . .]

On the other hand we have seen how property, especially landed property, received increased protection against attacks from *below*. April 26 – the day of the opening of the Duma, thus legally the last day of the *ancien régime* – must have been a day of hard 'work' for the Tsar: not only the Law on Agricultural Labourers, but also various ukases regarding the Peasant Bank, financial decrees etc., which were published only 10 to 12 days after the opening, bear this day's date.

The day of the opening arrived, and amid the excessive pomp and solemnity of the courtly procession the Tsar mounted, 'unsteadily' (according to press reports), the steps of the throne and read out his totally vacuous 'greeting'; the generally expected 'speech from the throne' is said to have been postponed owing to 'irresponsible' influences, but the real reason was probably simply that no one could agree on what it should contain.

The most powerful – negative – effect achieved by the address arose from the fact that it contained no mention at all of the amnesty which was awaited in all the prisons in the land and in all those tens of thousands of villages in which banishments and arrests had been carried out. It would have been a symbol that an end was to be put to the practice of punishment without trial – and this after the government, whether it liked it or not, had just had to have a number of exiles returned from Siberia and Arkhangelsk because they had been elected to the Duma. A professor (Muromtsev), who had been dismissed from his post, was elected president, and a professor (Gredeskul) who had just been banished was elected vice-president of the Duma from his enforced domicile in Arkhangelsk.

At once, amid tempestuous outbursts, Petrunkevich, one of the veterans of the Liberation Movement and former president of the Union of Liberation when it was clandestinely constituted in the Black Forest in Germany, departing from official procedure, raised the question of the amnesty demand. And now the real drama began: neither side thought that it would end in anything other than 'powder and shot'. The official *Pravitelstvennyi Vestnik* had published the Emperor's speech of greeting. But it continued to ignore the existence of the Duma: it seemed in doubt, as the Petersburg press put it, whether it should regard it as an institution of the state or rather as a revolutionary club. The same could be said of the 'leaders' of the 'old' Russia. Before the meetings began, Muromtsev was, as the law required, received by the Tsar, and was said to have been 'favourably impressed'.

When, in the tumultuous amnesty debate, all the pent-up anger was vented – although some restraint was observed – and the answering address, which was hard-hitting in both form and content, had been agreed, Muromtsev had again to appear at court for the birthday of the Tsar. Placed with studied courtesy at a seat of honour, he was not spoken to by anyone who might have had anything of significance to say. The Tsar refused to accept the address personally and requested that it be sent to the court minister – undoubtedly a procedure which would forcibly strike the peasants, who with one accord desire their representatives to have 'direct communication' with the Tsar. Indeed, more generally, the crumbling of the romance surrounding the Tsar in the eyes of the mass of the peasants will probably be the most lasting legacy of all these events.

However, not only did the ministerial benches in the Duma remain physically unoccupied for 16 days, but the government, which since December had justified the postponement of the convening of the Duma by the need to be 'prepared' to come before it, had not presented a *single* substantial bill by the *end of May*. Until that time its entire activity consisted in formulating its reply to the address.

This address, which, after long deliberation, the Duma accepted unanimously – Count Heyden had declared that he and his supporters, since they were only in disagreement with the way the address was presented and did not wish to jeopardize the unanimity, would leave the chamber – contained the following programme points: the 'four-part' franchise formula, parliamentary control of the executive, with the aim of eliminating the arbitrary rule of civil servants, which put a barrier between the Tsar and the people, ministerial responsibility, a parliamentary regime, abolition of the Imperial Council, guarantee of personal rights, freedom of speech, of the press, of associations and of assembly, freedom to go on strike, the right of petition, equality of all before the law, abolition of the death penalty, expropriation of land for the purpose of provision of land for the peasants, labour legislation, free elementary schooling, taxation reform, reorganization of self-government 'on the basis of universal franchise', justice and the rule of law in the army, 'cultural autonomy' for the nationalities, amnesty for all religious, political and agrarian crimes.

In reply the following points were conceded: changes to the franchise (but not just yet, as the Duma was only just beginning its work), labour legislation, universal elementary education, fairer distribution of taxation (especially income tax and inheritance tax), reform of self-government with special consideration for the particular character of the borderlands, personal and freedom rights (though with 'effective' means to prevent 'abuse' of freedoms), legal responsibility of civil servants, abolition of internal passports, abolition of the special 'estate' status of the peasants and means for their provision with land through the Peasant Bank and, additionally, from state domains and by resettlement, but without expropriation. All other demands were more or less categorically rejected, especially the amnesty; all that was agreed was 'careful examination' of the circumstances of those internees who had not been charged.

It was only in order to read out this reply to the Duma's address that the Prime Minister, on the seventeenth day after the opening of the Duma, first spoke, and from that day on the proceedings of the Duma appeared in the columns of the evening supplement to the *Pravitelstvennyi Vestnik*, which replaced Witte's *Russkoe Gosudarstvo*. Verbatim reports were promised, and indeed began to appear, but, perhaps because the speeches of Aladin, Nazarenko and others seemed too 'wild', they soon diminished to the level of mere lists of speakers, with nothing about the content; the Duma itself, on the other hand, resolved to undertake mass distribution of their proceedings throughout the land and set aside a sum of money for the purpose. [. . .]

The ministerial benches remained unoccupied. Thus in its relations with the Duma the government at first followed the same formula as

Turkey when faced with inconvenient demands: ignore it and do nothing.[61] Since there was a danger that the Duma would become embroiled in endless talking and lose touch with the real interests of the masses [...] the Democrats rapidly introduced legislative proposals [*Direktiven*].

[*Weber gives an account of government attempts to frustrate legislation by means of a procedural device. He goes on to describe the differences of view between the Democrats and the 'trudovaia' (labour) group of the Socialist Revolutionaries.*]

The latter took no part in practical parliamentary work, which seemed to them pointless, and instead made use of the Duma as a centre of revolutionary propaganda. When 15 members of the group addressed the public with an appeal in which the behaviour of the government towards the Duma was criticized as obstruction, the government charged them with incitement, and the governors vied with one another in public 'refutations' of this assertion – and, in their zeal, did not hesitate sharply to criticize the Duma itself in the process.

The ever more impatient mood in the country had its effect on the mood in the Duma, and this in turn – since the deputies were beginning to travel about in their constituencies to hear the views of their electorate – had its effect on the country. In the meantime the most uncontrollable rumours were rife concerning the intrigues aimed at imposing a military dictatorship, the alleged infighting of cliques in Peterhof and the machinations of what was known in the press as the 'star chamber'.

The massacre of Jews in Belostok then showed the Duma at the height of its authority: the deputies which it sent to report immediately restored calm, though the relationship with the government became more strained.[62] The Duma countered reports from the commanding military (which were naturally quite one-sided) with the equally one-sided report of its delegates, who had no legal authority to cross-examine the *civil servants*. Interpellations [official questions] regarding illegal behaviour by civil servants mounted up into the hundreds, and were answered in stereotyped fashion. No sooner did the ministers and their civil servants attempt to go beyond strictly factual statements to make political comments than they were angrily interrupted by the left, and those of them 'with blood on their hands' (e.g. General Pavlov) were prevented from speaking. The 'two Russias'[63] stood beside one another with no contact; military revolts, political strikes and peasant uprisings began afresh.

A dual party-formation in the Duma now seemed a possibility: either the Kadets would form an alliance with the right wing of the trudovaia gruppa (the 'legal' wing), or they would ally themselves with the 'Party of Peaceful Renewal', which Count Heyden was organizing, and which was also attracting a section of the 'non-party' deputies.[64] As long as no firm constitutional guarantees had been given, the preference of the dominant party clearly had to be for the former option, if only because this was in keeping with its whole history; the moderates were anxious to maintain contact with the Kadets, but a premature pact with the moderates risked exposing the Kadets to the demagogy of the government, which clearly benefited from the attacks of the radical Social Democrats on the Duma and the Kadets.

The Kadets therefore, in the course of secretly conducted discussions, consistently refused to enter a ministry formed not from their membership *alone* but including men like Shipov, Count Heyden or Stakhovich.[65] Whether, even had they taken over the government, they would have been able to hold together is another question, which probably must be answered in the negative: Kotliarevskii and several others inclined to right-wing party groups, Shchepkin and others to left-wing groups. The release from the powerful pressure of police tyranny would also, under a liberal ministry, have led to an upsurge of wild excesses not only of radicals but also of class – and then of national – antagonisms. But the main factor was that the Tsar, who was solely concerned for his personal position and security, could not be persuaded to entrust himself to them.

There is no point in describing the *substance* of the proceedings of the Duma, as they led nowhere. When, after the government's obstructive tactics, they were finally able to begin, they were engaged in with an intensity equal to that in any parliament in the world. For the real work, of course, was done not in the plenary sessions, which is all the press reported, but in committee. A glance at the weekly gazette of the committee meetings shows how busy the deputies were behind the scenes.

All the drafts introduced by the Duma deputies were close to completion by the beginning of July. The agrarian draft, after far in excess of 100 members had spoken to it in plenary session for 14 days, and the 91-member committee with numerous subcommittees had worked on it for four weeks, had reached the point where the basic outlines, upon which a large majority was prepared to agree, were almost all established: they corresponded almost exactly to those of the Constitutional Democratic draft. What court circles objected to was not that the Duma promised to achieve *too little*, but rather that it promised to achieve *too much*, most of it highly inconvenient for the government.

The government attempted to manoeuvre it into a corner by introducing the draft of a 50 million rouble *loan* to alleviate the anticipated bad harvest. The Duma approved 15 million for the present, but determined that the amount was to be obtained out of *savings* and reserved further approval, since Kokovtsev's financial report (which, incidentally, was singularly lacking in lucidity) had failed to demonstrate the necessity for a loan. As the majority of the *Imperial Council*, led by the 'Centre' group, accepted this view (Samarin's motion for voting by name having been, typically, defeated), this affair represented a major defeat for the ministry. The situation became increasingly difficult: there remained only dissolution or subjection.

[*Weber describes how the government, basing itself on the principle of the absolute inviolability of property,*] attempted to play off the interests of the landowners and peasants against the Duma and at the same time if possible to sabotage the Duma itself. Simultaneously with the introduction of its own agrarian drafts the government (on 20 June) addressed the country directly with an official public announcement (*Pravitelstvennyi Vestnik*, no. 137). The demagogic character of this action is evident from the mere fact that – although, as we have seen, the Duma rejected most emphatically any expropriation of nadel land and of privately owned smallholdings – the government was here proposing that the 'consequence' of *any* expropriation of land must be the division of *all* land into equal portions, i.e. the taking away of all private and 'finally also' nadel land for the purpose of an 'insignificant' increase in peasant ownership of land (in truth, according to the government's own reckoning, an increase amounting, on average, to *over a third* of the land held by all peasant villages, including the most prosperous!)

The government of course knew full well that a procedure like this direct, official and public ministerial polemic (and, what is more, one so full of crass untruths) against the Duma could not and would not be taken lying down, especially as Gurko's quite unfounded arguments from the recent stormy Duma session were merely being rehashed. It was also well aware that these arguments would not make the slightest impression on the peasants. The only possible *political* purpose of this completely worthless pronouncement was to make difficulties for the Kadets in the Duma by whipping up the revolutionary passions of the left. That is to say, fearing that the continued existence of the Duma would lead to the crumbling of its own power position and of army discipline, it wanted to encourage a formal conflict before a gun was pointed at the head of the Tsar by a draft for agrarian reform being passed by the Duma. And indeed it succeeded in that aim.

The step taken by the government was undoubtedly irreconcilable with every custom of a well-ordered state. The same could of course also be said of the counter-move taken by the Duma when it resolved, against the votes of the moderates (Count Heyden, Stachovich), to *reply to* the government's communiqué. The 'statement' proposed by the agrarian commission for this purpose, which, though very restrained in form and content, was nevertheless also addressed to the public, set the fundamental resolutions of the agrarian commission, which were already available, against the ministerial statement of 13 May (reply to the Duma address), and remarked in regard to the government communiqué of 20 June (which repeated this statement) that a law could not be passed without the approval of the Duma, but that the Duma would not abandon its demand for compulsory expropriation. It then stressed that an agrarian law could only be passed after the most careful deliberation, and accordingly requested the public to 'wait calmly and peaceably' for the law to be passed.

In the sitting which lasted until 2 o'clock in the night of 6–7/19–20 July, Petrunkevich then introduced an amendment which had been formulated after long negotiations in the Constitutional Democratic Party – an amendment to which Count Heyden also agreed. It deleted any mention of the resolutions of the commission on the grounds that they were not yet officially known to the Duma and, severely censuring the ministry for 'undermining the peaceful solution of the agrarian question', referred instead to the Duma's answering address.

The expectation that the people would wait 'calmly and peaceably' had been expressed in the introduction to the statement. But the left (in the person of Shilkin) fiercely attacked the amendment as a 'dilution' and demanded instead that the public be called upon to mobilize in support of the Duma. This was rejected.

After acceptance of Petrunkevich's amendment the statement was accepted, with 124 votes from the Kadets (who, however, did not all vote for it), against 53 votes of the Social Democrats (who were opposed to the call for calm) and of the right (who were opposed to any 'statement') – and with the abstention of 101 'trudoviki'.

It is obvious that any direct 'appeal to the public' on the part of a parliamentary body goes against the custom and the spirit of constitutional governments, as Petrunkevich himself admitted. (The only analogy – although an inexact one – might be the 'public display' of the resolutions of the French chamber.) It also contrasted with the principle of the Kadets, to which they otherwise strictly adhered, to remain firmly within the existing 'order' *despite* all the government's illegal actions. However, the issuing of that 'statement' did not *in itself* constitute stepping outside this order. For, according to Petrunkevich's expressly declared intention, it was *not* to be communicated to 'the *people*' by means of the press, but to the *Minister* of the Interior for the purpose of printing it in the official *Pravitelstvennyi Vestnik*. The Duma was, in a sense, claiming the right of 'correction' in the press against the ministry's statement.

However, the fact that the ground of formal legality had not been departed from does not alter the fact that the resolution, from the point of view of the Kadets, was a political *error*, which, under the circumstances, was admittedly difficult to avoid. It was bound to mean a setback for the Duma if only because it had no means of enforcing publication 'in accordance with the regulations'. For even Petrunkevich himself could hardly have believed that *Pravitelstvennyi Vestnik* would publish it. The Duma therefore simply had the *choice* of either going along 'unconstitutional' paths, or leaving publication to the press as it thought fit. Of course, a resolution which branded the government communiqué as 'untruthful' – indeed, one could, in all honesty, have spoken of its 'frivolous demagogic mendacity' – would have achieved the same effect, since the press could be counted on to give it the widest circulation. [. . .]

Tactically the moment seemed right for dissolution (although no one was prepared for this), in view of the split in the Duma and the isolation of the Kadets, and the government seized its opportunity.

The dissolution of the Duma and the adjournment of the Imperial Council (with the exception of the two purely bureaucratic departments) was directly followed by the publication of an Imperial 'Manifesto', which must be described as an astonishing piece of work, even for Russia. It first maintains that the Duma, '*instead* of operating in the field of legislation', had departed from the area of its competence by concerning itself with an investigation of the actions of 'local authorities appointed by our orders' and 'with the imperfections of the "Fundamental Law", which may only be altered by our Imperial will'.

The latter assertion is a pure invention, as the Duma has made no attempt to arrogate to itself the initiative reserved for the Emperor. What is more, the right of interpellation in cases of illegalities by the authorities is its constitutional right. And as regards the creative work in the field of legislation (since what matters is not the speeches in the plenary sessions but the activity of the committees), no parliament in the world – let us repeat this – has done more work than the Russian one, only not in ways which were acceptable to the Tsar.

There follows the (untrue) description of the Duma statement of 7–8 July as an 'appeal to the people', a 'patently' illegal action. Then comes the assertion, of unparalleled irresponsibility, that the peasants had *thereby* – i.e. by an 'appeal' which had not even been published – been incited to revolt. Furthermore the promise is made that 'the Russian worker, without touching property not his own . . . should have a legal and just means to extend his land ownership', a task which should be carried out by the future Duma; the convening of the Duma was announced for 20 February/5 March 1907 – which meant that the *budget* for 1907 could not be passed in the legally required form.

It is hard to find adequate words to describe the *concluding* section, which commences with the grandiose and menacing sentence: 'We shall impose our Imperial will on the disobedient.' The opening section of the Manifesto remarks, with that insincere religious unction which has now become a repulsive ingredient of all monarchical statements, that the Emperor had 'firmly trusted in *divine grace*', but immediately adds that he had been 'disappointed in his expectations by a cruel trial'; and the conclusion states that he is now resolved to place his trust in *men*: '*We believe (!)* that *heroes of thought and deed will appear* and that, thanks to their self-sacrificing work, the glory of Russia will shine out.'

Yet even if such a confession of impotence could so rouse those 'heroes', who were supposedly somewhere in the background, that they came out of hiding and revealed themselves, there would be no place for them in the police system of this regime – unless individuals like the former minister Durnovo or General Trepov or Interior Minister Stolypin (who was promoted to Prime Minister at the same time as the publication of this pronouncement) were regarded by the writer of the Manifesto as such 'heroes'. In fact, the most one can say of them is that 'any fool can rule with a sabre'.

The Duma deputies – with the exception of the 'moderates' – protested to the Duma from Vyborg [in Finland] against the unconstitutional attempt to govern without a budget and against the statement that 'the Imperial will was to be enforced on everyone'. In this protest they called for the non-payment of taxes – a method already criticized above – and the non-provision of recruits. It remains to be seen whether this agitation will be successful. For the moment – since no preparations have been made – everything may remain calm, unless the leaders lose control of the masses, as happened late last autumn.

The fall in the rate at which the loans are offered is not very great: the banks can only do 'business' with the absolutist regime and now have to dispose of their stocks; the rate will therefore be 'artificially pegged'. Anyone who allows himself to be deceived by this or by a docile parliament which has been blackmailed by violation and deception is *beyond help*. For the moment it seems quite out of the question that this regime can find any way to achieve *lasting* 'calm' in the land – this much must have been clearly shown by this chronicle: the regime can only attempt to pull itself up by its own bootstraps. And, disregarding 'tactical' questions, the lasting effect of the government's behaviour can only be a further devaluation of the Tsar in the eyes of the peasantry, even if this effect may appear to be delayed in the immediate future by the expected manipulation of the election results.

At this point we must break off this chronicle. It has only been possible to give a very rough outline of the more intimate background of the recent events, especially the conflicting views at court – even in Russia itself these events are inadequately known. But my intention has not been to write some kind of 'history' of the last six months – my task, as far as the existing sources have allowed, has been to illustrate the general social and political situation into which police absolutism, the political legacy of Alexander III (which was not repudiated soon enough), and, most recently, the work of Witte's Interim Ministry, has led the country, and out of which it must now – and who can say how? – find its way. Prophecies, even for the next few months, seem to me quite impossible, and are not even attempted by the best informed politicians in Russia itself.

So much can be said: the almost inevitable tendency and necessity of modern dynastic regimes to work for *prestige* domestically, as well as abroad, to 'save face', led the government in Russia to fail to give what it had to give *in time*, and then when one concession after another was forced out of it, it tried and continues to try to restore its lost 'prestige' by remorseless police tyranny. This awareness that victims were being slaughtered for reasons of pure vanity was the reason why the coarse and uncivilized form in which the left in the Duma insulted the ministers and drove them from their seats failed to call forth a more severe repudiation from those parties who held fast to the 'parliamentary solution'. One can no longer imagine *what* concession by the government would now be needed for the Duma to agree with it on any programme, in view of the way its voters have been incited to a red frenzy by the government's actions. It is equally hard to imagine how any civilized government could emerge out of the quicksand this bureaucracy has created. There is no longer any doubt that the crass intensification of class antagonisms must inevitably make any attempt to rely on 'property' look *reactionary*.

At times like this, when Russia is going through terrible birth pangs, the Germans have the absurd habit of looking for somebody 'to blame' – and since 'of course' no blame can attach to the Monarch and his immediate servants and an extremely shabby kind of 'criticism' of parliamentarism is currently fashionable, in the eyes of the German philistine it must be the Duma that is at fault. It is said to be 'politically incapable' and to have achieved nothing 'positive', and the German reader is then reminded that the Russian nation is in any case not yet 'ready' for a constitutional regime. (This leads one to ask oneself: for what, then, are those people on and near the throne 'ready', who have brought the country to the state it is in?)

In six weeks the only material for 'positive' work presented to the Duma by the government has been one draft bill on university courses for women and another on an orangery and a laundry. At the same time the government has obstructed its own right of initiative (under a crazy constitutional regulation which it created itself) by demanding *postponement* of debate for a month. Under these circumstances, it is inconceivable that a newly created parliamentary body could really have achieved more than the Duma has achieved. Only crass arrogance, which condemns with no knowledge of the facts on the basis of sensational press reports, or blinkered, dyed-in-the-wool conservatism, could thus, ignoring the facts, use such trite and offensive language.

For nine months – this much should be clear from the foregoing chronicle – the existing regime has done nothing but try, with truly oriental cunning, to emasculate the 'rights' it has just granted. Not until the middle of June (Old Calendar) did the *first* real modest reform proposals come forward, *all* of them bearing the hallmarks of their origins in the thought world of zemstvo liberalism: the bill on Magistrates' Courts was sure of acceptance, and the agrarian drafts were sure of the most serious consideration. But the government did *not* take decisive action to guarantee protection against the absolute tyranny of the police (abolition of administrative arrest and banishment, making all civil servants, without exception, responsible before independent courts), and without this it could find no groups of the population to rely on for support. However, the dissolution of the Duma will only lead to a favourable result for it if – as seems likely – it is really determined to *rig* the elections.

It blames the activities of terrorists for the police's insane rule of tyranny. Yet the *statistics* demonstrate that the imposition of martial law, i.e. of a state of lawlessness, has caused these activities to *increase* and created sympathy for them. Just as a revolution from below is not possible without aid or toleration by the middle class, so also no containment of the violence is possible from above without such support either. The well-known saying could in this case be applied to the government: 'Que messieurs les assassins commencent!'[66] Instead, it evidently falls back on the expectation that 'the machine' – in this case the bureaucratic mechanism – 'never tires', whilst even the keenest enthusiasm eventually does so. But it is by no means certain that today's regime or its like will succeed (for more than brief spells) in sapping the indefatigable energy of Russian radicalism, especially once the cadres of the Social Democratic and Socialist Revolutionary organizations are in place – and certainly not before the total economic ruin of the country.

True, the Russian freedom struggle reveals few of the features of 'greatness', as usually understood, to arouse the emotions of the un-

Pseudo-constitutionalism 231

committed observer. This is because, firstly, with the exception of the agrarian programme (which is difficult to understand), the demands made are largely ones which have long since lost the appeal of *novelty* for us in the West: they *seem* to lack the originality which they would have had in Cromwell's and Mirabeau's time and, in as much as they are purely political in content, they actually *do* lack it. For *us* they (mostly!) seem trivial – as one's daily bread is trivial. Furthermore, there is a lack on both sides of really 'great leaders' on whom the emotional interest of observers could focus – for not even the most outstanding political journalist or social-political expert (and there is no lack of such) is a political 'leader', any more than the boldest 'practical' revolutionary is one.

All this easily gives the impression of a lack of originality: all the ideas which are discussed here by the participants are, not only in terms of content, but even the very words used, 'collective products'.[67] And the eye of the spectator, especially that of politically and economically 'sated' nations, is not accustomed, and, from afar, not able, through the veil of all these programmes and collective actions, where such masses are involved, to perceive the stirring spectacle of the individual fate, the uncompromising idealism, the relentless energy, the ups and downs of tempestuous hope and agonizing disappointment experienced by those in the thick of the fight.

To the outsider, all those individual fates, so dramatic in themselves, become interwoven, to form an impenetrable tangle. It is a continuous, unrelenting struggle, with wild deeds of murder and merciless acts of tyranny in such numbers that even these horrors finally become accepted as normal. Modern revolution is like modern warfare, which, robbed of the romantic aura of knightly contest of days gone by, *represents itself* as a mechanical process caught between the instrumentalized products of the intellectual labour of laboratories and workshops, on the one hand, and the icy power of money on the other, but at the same time actually *is* a terrible, unending test of *nerve* both for the leaders and for the hundreds of thousands of the led. Everything – at least in the eye of the beholder – is 'technique' and a question of nervous stamina.

In Russia, where the police authorities – as this description should have shown – exploited their position of power by the most subtle methods and the most cunning oriental wiles, the struggle with it had inevitably to consume so much strength in mere 'tactics', and place so much emphasis on 'technical party considerations', that scarcely any room was left for 'great leaders'. One cannot accomplish 'great' deeds against vermin. And on the opposing side great deeds are completely absent: the very last thing the numerous outstanding individuals in the Russian civil service, whose existence is obvious to even an outsider's cursory glance, can become, under the present system, is great 'statesmen' producing great reforms; dynastic ambitions will see to that – in Russia as with us. Even the great mass of intellectual effort (in individual cases often amazingly painstaking) that has evidently been expended on the state documents of this regime merely leads, as we can see, again and again to the service of the single and absolutely self-regarding goal of police self-preservation.

The terrible objective pointlessness of this goal, the complete impossibility of imagining any values embodied in this regime, be they 'moral' or 'cultural', does indeed lend to the activities of these rulers and to the 'professional work' of these servants of the state – especially the 'efficient' amongst them – something of that wraith-like quality which Leo Tolstoy's apoliticism conveys so eerily in his *Resurrection*.[68] The Russian Revolution has been compared to the French Revolution. Apart from numerous other differences it suffices to indicate the decisive object which, in contrast to that time, is *no longer* 'sacred' even to the 'bourgeois' representatives of the freedom movement and is *missing* from the catalogue of benefits which it is hoped liberation will bring, namely '*property*'. Today the Tsar proclaims its 'sanctity' – rather belatedly from the point of view of his own interests.

Whatever happens now, this is the end of every kind of Slavophile romantic notion, and indeed of 'old' Russia. In Russia, though, the imported ultramodern forces of big capitalism run up against a subterranean world of archaic peasant communism, and unleash, for their part, such radically socialist feelings among their work-force (which they then meet with equally uncompromising 'antifreedom' organizations of the most modern character) that one can scarcely imagine what kind of development is in store for Russia, even if – as is overwhelmingly probable – the 'sanctity of property' ultimately gains the ascendancy over the Socialist Revolutionary peasant ideology. All those intermediate stages are missing, which in the West placed the powerful *economic* interests of propertied strata in the service of the bourgeois freedom movement.

The tiny percentage of the population represented by the industrial proletariat can have little significance at the moment, while the ideals of the peasants lie, in spite of everything, in an unreal world.

Never has a freedom struggle been waged under such difficult conditions as the Russian struggle, never with such a degree of unconditional readiness for martyrdom; and with such an attitude, it seems to me, any German who has not lost all the idealism of his forefathers should feel deeply in sympathy.

The familiar German reactionary exponents of *realpolitik*, however, should ponder whether they are wise to awaken feelings in Russia against them like those Napoleon III awakened in us against him before 1870. One only needs to read the reactionary and semi-official Russian newspapers to see with what skill they exploit the foolish hostility to democracy of our 'state-preserving' journals as a means of diverting the hatred of the masses outwards – against us. Certainly, the pathetic rule of the Tsar, to which any war poses a fundamental threat, may make Russia appear to be a 'comfortable' neighbour. A truly constitutional Russia would be a stronger and, since it would be more sensitive to the instincts of the masses, a more restless neighbour. But, let us not deceive ourselves, this Russia is coming, one way or another – and even *realpolitik* dictates that it is better that we reach an amicable agreement now, while we are strong, on the chaotic mass of questions which lie between us, than to hand these problems down to succeeding generations and in the meantime set in motion against us all the ideal forces within the upwardly striving peoples of this Empire.

The two great neighbouring nations have little understanding of each other at the moment. On the one hand, I have met no Russian Democrat with that inner sympathy with German culture which can only come from real understanding. On the other hand, the pressures that come with increasing wealth, linked with the habit, which has now become automatic, of thinking in terms of *realpolitik*, makes it difficult for Germans to feel sympathetic towards the turbulent, excitable and nervous nature of Russian radicalism. But we, for our part, in spite of the need to remain clear-headed in a world of enemies, should not forget that we bequeathed to the world our most enduring legacy at a period when, as a nation, we ourselves were feeble and other-worldly, and that the future for 'sated' nations is bleak.

Notes

1 [M–D] On 17 Oct. 1905 Tsar Nicholas II issued the so-called October Manifesto, which promised 'civil liberty', an extension of the franchise and the right of the Imperial Duma (the parliament which was to be newly created) to play a part in legislation.
2 [M–D] From 7 to 17 Dec. 1905 there was an armed uprising in the streets of Moscow led chiefly by the Moscow Soviet (Workers' Council). It was defeated after a few days thanks to the loyalty of the military and the weakness of the rebel forces.
3 [M–D] There was a general strike from about 12 to 21 Oct. 1905; the Petersburg Soviet called a second general strike (for the 8-hour day) on 1 Nov.

1905, but this had to be called off after only a few days. The third general strike was declared on 6 Dec. 1905. The strike call was virtually ignored in St Petersburg and the provinces, but in Moscow it led to the armed uprising of 7 to 17 Dec. 1905.

4 [M–D] In autumn and winter 1905–6 there were serious peasant riots in the Black Earth provinces, in central Volga, in the Ukraine and in the Baltic region, which were only put down by means of massive military intervention. Cf. Maureen Perrie, 'The Russian peasant movement of 1905–1907: its social composition and revolutionary significance', *Past and Present*, 67 (Nov. 1972).

5 [M–D] Weber is referring to the so-called first political general strike, which began on 6 Oct. 1905 with a rising by the railway workers in Moscow and in the next few days spread to almost every branch of industry and a major part of the country. This strike was one of the reasons why Nicholas II, on the advice of Witte, issued the Manifesto of 17 Oct.

6 [Weber] Although it is often denied, it is now beyond doubt that the 'Black Hundreds' (their activities included threatening letters to liberal politicians, beating up of real or supposed socialists, and bloody massacres of Jews), who made their first appearance in 1905 at the time of the Tsar's February Manifesto, were organized *by the police* with the knowledge of the central authorities. It is, of course, quite possible that 'volunteers' joined them as well.

7 [M–D] The reason why they declined was that Witte refused to agree to have any *other* liberal ministers in his cabinet.

8 [M–D] 'All wheels shall rest, At the workers' behest.' Georg Herwegh: 'Bundeslied für den Allgemeinen Deutschen Arbeiterverein' (Anthem for the General German Workers' Association).

9 [M–D] On 3/16 Apr. 1906 a consortium of French, English, Austrian and Dutch banks issued a loan of 2,250 million francs. Cf. Dietrich Geyer, *Russian Imperialism: The Interaction of Domestic and Foreign Policy 1860–1914*, tr. Bruce Little (Leamington Spa, 1987).

10 [M–D] Reference to the 'Soiuz Russkikh Liudei' (League of Russian People), which was founded in Mar. 1905 under the leadership of Count P. Sheremetev. [Tr. Weber regularly refers to it as the 'League of Russian Men'.] The League of Russian People drew most of its members from the zemstvos and the associations of the nobility. It advocated the creation of an advisory body, elected from the traditional estates, known as the 'zemskii sobor', in order to re-establish the links between Tsar and people which had been broken by the bureaucracy. Cf. Hans Rogger, 'The formation of the Russian Right', *California Slavic Studies*, 3 (1964).

11 [M–D] From the period of the Severi at the end of the second century, when civil war was becoming increasingly common, the rulers gave more and more gifts of money to the Roman armies.

12 [M–D] The French elections to the National Assembly, held on 13 Feb. 1871, a short time after the signing of the cease-fire, brought a clear conservative and rural majority which pressed for an ending of the war.

Pseudo-constitutionalism 235

13 [Weber] In Brest-Litovsk the school administration refused to pay the salaries of the many schoolteachers who had been detained and held without charge for months to their *wives* [. . .]. Distribution of assistance to peasants who were suspected of taking part in the riots was prohibited by the Minister, Durnovo, by a special decree. Priests who had distributed bread to peasants out on strike were arrested (*Pravo*, p. 1258). In areas where there was starvation, there was a ban on all *free meal distribution* to the unemployed and the poor which was organized by persons in any way politically suspect, *not* only by party politicians, but also e.g. – 2 cases are known to me – by the sons of liberal university professors. At a time in which *Novoe Vremia* counted 30,000 unemployed in Petersburg, there were massive bans on free meals and 'people's kitchens' if their organizers were regarded as politically interested (see *Novoe Vremia*, 3 Feb., pp. 4ff).

14 [M–D] On 16 Jan. 1906 the Socialist Revolutionary Mariia Spiridonova shot Luzhinovskii, a senior civil servant, in Tambov. After her arrest and torture by the cossack officer Abramov the latter was shot in broad daylight on 1 Apr. 1906.

15 [M–D] The ukase of 17 Apr. 1905, known as the Edict of Toleration, proclaimed religious toleration and removed legal discrimination against non-Orthodox Christian confessions. The ukase of 12 Dec. 1904 had announced some vague measures in the direction of legal equality for the peasants, and the introduction of religious toleration, press freedom and other civil liberties.

16 [M–D] Rationalist Christian sect, founded mid-18th century. On Stundists, see above, BD n. 78.

17 [M–D] Sect believing that salvation lay in the 'baptism of fire' of circumcision.

18 [M–D] See above, n. 15.

19 [M–D] In Feb. 1899 a demonstration of students of Petersburg University calling for more rights for students was brutally smashed. Thereupon there was a nationwide student strike in protest against the poor social and material situation of the students and against the rigid university system. The strike was ultimately unsuccessful.

20 [M–D] By the university statute of 23 Aug. 1884 the power of the inspectors, who were directly answerable to the State Registrar, was considerably extended. Rector, Deans and Professors were appointed, or 'called', by the Minister, not by the university. The universities were deprived of the autonomy which they had enjoyed since the statute of 1863. The tasks and functions of the inspectors were supervision of order and good behaviour among the students and 'Guest Students' [not fully enrolled] within and, where possible, outside the universities. Until the law of 23 Aug. 1884 the inspectors were elected by the University Council for 3 years and were answerable to it. According to the university statute of 1884 the inspectors were directly subordinate to the State Registrar.

21 [Tr.] Privatdozent: Unsalaried lecturer, remunerated directly by students' fees.

22 [Tr.] Habilitation: Qualification for a professorship.

23 [Tr.] Dozent: University lecturer.
24 [M–D] In the German Reich the composition of the 'Core Senate' [*engere Senat*] was fixed by *Land* law. It consisted of the Rector (or the Pro-Rector), the Deans of the Faculties, and a certain number of Professors elected by the Great Senate. The Core Senate was the true executive committee of the university. The Great Senate consisted of all the active full [*ordentliche*] professors of a university. It elected the Rectors (or Pro-Rectors) and Senators of the Core Senate and made decisions on the establishment of new university institutions.
25 [Tr.] Extraordinarius: Professor without a department of his own.
26 [Weber] According to today's terminology there are (1) 'ordinary' [*ordentliche*] and 'extraordinary' professors, both on the establishment [*etatmäßige*] i.e. *university* teachers; (2) 'Privatdozenten', who may receive some payment from a special fund, but otherwise, as in Germany, have to rely on the students' fees (by law, an average of 1 rouble per hour is payable); (3) Lektors (for languages etc.), as in Germany; (4) Other personnel in science institutes (pro-sectors [M–D: term for an anatomy professor's assistant, who prepares the anatomical samples required in teaching], assistants etc.) [. . .]
27 [M–D] Until the issuing of the Imperial Law of Associations on 19 Apr. 1908 the Laws of Association in force in the German Reich were those of the *Länder*. On the strength of the Laws of Association in Bavaria, Saxony, Prussia, Baden, Alsace-Lorraine and some smaller *Länder* the police were authorized to send officers into assemblies and, if there was a 'disturbance', to disperse them.
28 [M–D] See above, p. 156.
29 [Tr.] Schöffengericht: court in which lay magistrates officiate alongside a professional judge.
30 [M–D] See above, p. 209.
31 [M–D] References to the official Russian Compendium of Laws, a systematic compilation of the laws of the Russian Empire (*Svod Zakonov Rossiiskoi Imperii*).
32 [M–D] A reference to Bismarck's invoking of the cabinet order of 8 Sept. 1852, which obliged the Prussian ministers to first notify the Minister President of 'Immediatvorträge' for his approval [reports normally presented directly to the Head of State]. This led to a serious conflict with Kaiser Wilhelm II, who accused the Chancellor, in his capacity as Prussian Minister President, of restricting the royal prerogative and preventing ministers from having free access to the monarch. This conflict contributed materially to the fall of the Chancellor.
33 [M–D] Reference to the introduction of the office of Prussian Minister President on the occasion of the inauguration of the ministry of Count Arnim-Boitzenburg on 19 Mar. 1848. The Minister President was now accorded the role of *primus inter pares*, whereas previously there had been a purely collegial system, though with some regional variations. It is not known what publication Weber is here referring to.

Pseudo-constitutionalism 237

34 [Weber] Witte created yet another indispensable method of bureaucratic government: a big, semi-official journal, the *Russkoe Gosudarstvo*, with capital of 600,000 roubles. The vile sycophancy of this journal recalled the worst periods of the press under Bismarck. [. . .]
35 [M–D] See above, p. 181.
36 [Weber] Addressing a 'petty bourgeois' audience, Witte made the doubly astonishing remark that the King of England was 'dependent on Jewish bankers'. Now, there is no need to take too literally the assertions of leading English journalists that a powerful increase in English Crown prerogatives is in the offing [. . .], but it is certain that so far this King, thanks to his sense of tact (not everywhere observable among today's monarchs) and his ability, without any leaning towards outward show, to preserve *modest* forms, has kept his dignity *just as* surely as, and has probably rendered more significant *practical* services to his country than, some potentates invested with stronger formal and legal prerogatives than he. (This is equally true of matters of form: cf. his conversation with John Burns.) [M–D: Possibly Weber is referring to the presentation of the new cabinet of Sir Henry Campbell-Bannerman to King Edward VII on 11 Dec. 1905. The labour leader John Burns, as the newly appointed President of the Local Government Board, was present.]
37 [M–D] Allusion to the conduct of the Prussian Finance Minister Johannes von Miquel in 1894 before the fall of Reich Chancellor Caprivi. During the debate on the 'Umsturzvorlage' (the bill to increase the penalties for subversion) Miquel was accused of intriguing against Caprivi, with the aim of making himself Reich Chancellor and Prussian Minister President.
38 [Weber] The big capitalists will of course *always* stand by the bureaucracy against the Duma, and be happy for it to have the most far-reaching *formal* rights. Here in Germany too, before the negotiations with the Verein für Sozialpolitik in autumn 1905, a number of representatives of the cartels begged in delightful fashion for 'the state' to enter a community of interest with them, to *educate* them (*sic!*) etc. – in the full knowledge that in this yearned-for embrace the cartels would play the role of Brunhilde and the 'state', should it permit itself too many liberties, would suffer the fate of King Gunther. [M–D: Reference to the *Nibelungenlied*. Brunhilde, wife of King Gunther, who was endowed with supernatural strength, tied up her husband and hung him from a hook in the bedroom to escape from his embraces.]
39 [M–D] See List of Parties and Associations.
40 [M–D] See above, pp. 205f.
41 [M–D] See above, pp. 156ff.
42 [M–D] In its new form after 24 Apr. 1906 half the members of the Imperial Council were appointed by the Tsar and half elected along estate lines.
43 [Tr.] Weber here makes reference to the device of 'Pairsschub', i.e. the simultaneous nomination of a fairly large number of sympathetic peers to a chamber in order to secure a majority either for the Crown or for the ruling party. Cf. Meyers Lexikon, 1930.

44 [M–D] On 6 Mar. 1862, in the Hagen motion, in order to render impossible the financing of the Army Bill, which the House had rejected, from other budget codes, the Prussian House of Deputies decided on 'specification (lit. 'specialization') of the budget'. In this point, and this alone, Bismarck complied with the wishes of the deputies, but soon afterwards withdrew the budget for 1863 entirely, on the grounds of irreconcilable differences.

45 [M–D] *Leges saturae* (*per saturam*) is the term for the grouping together of factually distinct issues in one and the same ballot; inadmissible since the Gracchi period. Theodor Mommsen, *Römisches Staatsrecht* (Leipzig, 1887), pp. 336f and 377.

46 [M–D] See BD: p. 147 n. 231 above.

47 [M–D] The Duma franchise was an indirect curial franchise based on a wealth and property census (see Glossary). The only curia to be unrestricted by a census was the peasants' curia. [. . .] In the provinces of European Russia there were 4 curiae: landowners, peasants, urban dwellers and workers (only in firms employing 50 or more). In each provincial district the curiae of the landowners and of the peasants elected the prescribed number of electors, though the small landowners had first to elect their delegates for the landowners' curia. In the peasants' curia up to district level voting was in two stages; every 10 households elected 1 delegate for the volost assembly, in which 2 electors were elected for the district electoral meeting. The urban voters and the workers elected their electors separately, the workers first electing delegates for each factory, who then had to elect the electors. All these electors assembled in the provincial electoral assembly, in which the number of deputies assigned to the province were elected to the Duma. Before this common election the peasant electors had the right to elect separately one deputy for the Duma from their own members. The peasant electors then united with the other electors of the other curiae, who elected the remainder of the deputies from their own members. Cf. H. D. Mehlinger and J. M. Thompson, *Count Witte and the Tsarist Government in the 1905 Revolution* (Bloomington, Ind., 1972).

48 [M–D] See above, pp. 152ff.

49 [M–D] See Glossary: 'tretii element'.

50 I have already reported on the Union of Unions in the supplement to vol. 22. [M–D: See above, pp. 70ff.] In Feb. it proposed that its members should debate a scheme for insurance against arrest and dismissal, and also to pass a resolution on the 'permissibility' of holding non-conspiratorial meetings. I do not know what came of these proposals.

51 [M–D] From 1881 to 1888 Robert von Puttkamer was the Prussian Interior Minister. This period saw the intensified application of the anti-socialist law, the construction of a comprehensive system of informers for the suppression of Social Democracy, the development of the political police and the appointment of politically conformist judges.

52 [M–D] The term is derived from the Italian 'sindacalismo'. In using this term Weber was taking over a distinction made by Robert Michels between

French syndicalism and Italian sindacalism. According to Michels sindacalism is similar to French syndicalism insofar as it is anti-parliamentary, but at the same time it supports the viewpoint that the workers' movement should participate in elections. Cf. Robert Michels, 'Proletariat und Bourgeoisie in der sozialistischen Bewegung in Italien', *Archiv für Sozialwissenschaft und Sozialpolitik*, 22 (1906), pp. 715f.

53 [M–D] Supplement to the *Archiv*, 22 (1). [M–D: = 'Bourgeois Democracy', pp. 92–3 above.]
54 [M–D] The Union of 17 October (Octobrists) had already been founded on 10 Nov. 1905. It first entered the public arena on 4 Dec. 1905 with a meeting in St Petersburg: *Russkiia Vedomosti*, 322 (6 Dec. 1905), p. 1. (See List of Parties and Associations.)
55 [M–D] See nn. 2 and 4 above.
56 [M–D] See above, pp. 170f.
57 [M–D] Cf. above, n. 7.
58 [M–D] See above, pp. 195f.
59 [M–D] See above, n. 52.
60 [M–D] See above, pp. 198f.
61 [M–D] Reference to the political strategy of the Ottoman empire, which usually merely prevaricated when repeatedly requested by the Great Powers to introduce reforms in the regions of European Turkey.
62 [M–D] From 1 to 3 June 1906 in Belostok (Polish: Białystok) there was a pogrom, in the course of which, according to official statistics, 82 Jews were murdered (unofficially, the number was put at several hundred). The commission of investigation set up by the Duma dispatched a three-man delegation to Belostok, whose task it was to investigate the actions of the authorities and of the military, and at the same time to give assistance.
63 [M–D] The expression 'the two Russias' was probably coined by Alexander Herzen, who, in the 1850s, spoke of an unbridgeable gulf between the autocratic government and the mass of the people. Others picked up the expression, in particular P. Miliukov, who used it in his *Ocherki po istorii russkoi kultury* (St Petersburg, 1902). Cf. Robert C. Tucker, 'The image of dual Russia', in Cyril E. Black (ed.), *The Transformation of Russian Society: Aspects of Social Change Since 1861* (Cambridge, Mass., 1967).
64 [M–D] The Party of Peaceful Renewal (Partiia mirnago obnovleniia) was founded in the course of the legislative period of the First Duma, and consisted of Octobrists, right-wing Constitutional Democrats and one deputy from the Trade and Industry Party. (See List of Parties and Associations.)
65 [M–D] The leader of the Constitutional Democrats, Pavel Miliukov, in secret talks on the possibility of his party joining the government, demanded that the cabinet be formed exclusively from the members of his party, and that this cabinet should be confirmed by parliament. Dmitrii Shipov, who negotiated with government representatives a short time later, refused to form a cabinet of this nature on the grounds that the Duma would not support it. Cf. Robert L. Tuck, 'Paul Miljukov and negotiations for a Duma Ministry',

American Slavic and East European Review, 10 (1951). The Constitutional Democrats denied all rumours of secret negotiations.

66 [M–D] 'Si l'on veut abolir la peine de mort, en ce cas que messieurs les assassins commencent,' Alphonse Karr (journalist) – *Nouveau Dictionnaire de citations françaises*, ed. Jeanne Matignon et al. (Paris, 1970).

67 [Weber] This is not to imply that such 'leaders' were lacking. The iron will of a man like Petrunkevich, for instance, would appear to be ideally suited to take over the role of Carnot. [M–D: Lazare Carnot was the founder of the French Revolutionary armies, and had the reputation of being a stern Republican and a man of inflexible principles.] And the intellectual potency of the brilliant names of which the Democratic Party can boast, in the areas of both scholarship and the political skills of local self-government, cannot be bettered in any foreign party. However, some of these were excluded from the work by the electoral law, and some were forced by malicious police harassment and the attitude of the government to act in a purely 'negative' way.

68 [M–D] Tolstoy, *Resurrection*. The Russian version, *Voskresene*, was published in instalments from 13 Mar. 1899 in the journal *Niva*, which was forced by censorship to cease publication on 4 Dec. 1899. The following year a revised version was published in St Petersburg. In Tolstoy's view, salvation of the world was only possible by complete restoration of humanity, love, work and equality – not through political action.

3
Russia's Transition to Pseudo-democracy

The undersigned claims no special expert knowledge of Russia beyond that which anyone else could acquire for himself. The author does, however, feel he may be capable of forming a sober judgement on what may be expected from the men who are now at the helm. Despite my very strong sympathies for the Russian Liberation Movement the following must be clearly stated: given the present composition of the Russian governing powers there can be *no question* of the majority of the politically prominent men in Russia having sincerely peaceful intentions, let alone being well-disposed towards the German people. (I say advisedly 'the German *people*', not 'the present German Government'). Not only were the peaceful declarations[1] of the Central Powers honest, having been made in spite of the highly provocative, indeed, warlike utterances of Professor Miliukov,[2] but it also remains politically absolutely right to make them again, in spite of and, indeed, because of this behaviour. For we must think of the future. Of course, other events, or great shifts of power, would have to occur for these declarations to have immediate success.

Any prophecy regarding the further course of the revolution is impossible even for the best-informed observer. Even those who are far better informed on the situation than I am had serious doubts as to whether the Tsar would be overthrown during the war, or even after the war. Stolypin's agrarian reform[3] had made the clever tactical move of splitting one of the core units of the Socialist Revolutionaries, the peasants of the regions of Old Russia, into two differently sized but inevitably profoundly hostile parts: on the one hand the new private owners who had emerged from village communism, that is, the economically strongest elements of the peasantry, whose new possessions tied them closely to the regime in power, and on the other hand the proletarianized masses of the peasantry, who had remained within village communism, and who regarded the granting of that private ownership as a blatant injustice, favouring the other group.

It did seem possible that another important representative of old Socialist Revolutionary ideas might take a different attitude from previously: the so-called Third Element. This group comprises the huge numbers of permanent but poorly paid employees of the great associations of self-government, the so-called zemstvos [see Glossary]. These include almost the entire 'intelligentsia' engaged in administration, that is, all personnel engaged in work for what we should call the 'national economy' (agronomic, veterinary and similar work) and also in secular elementary-school teaching; it also includes country doctors employed on a fixed salary (unlike the practice in our country). That is, it encompasses almost all those circles of the 'intelligentsia' who are concerned with the peasants in their daily life on a confidential basis. During the previous revolution they were in the sharpest contrast to the state administration, which served police purposes almost exclusively, and were the representatives of Socialist Revolutionary propaganda in the rural areas. Similarly, however, they were opposed to the honorary zemstvo members themselves, whose origins were in land ownership, particularly in the rural areas. (Certain changes in the practical directions of zemstvo work, as well as in the composition of this stratum, which were not unexpected following the measures taken by the Stolypin Government and of the zemstvos after the revolution, have made the present attitude of this element towards revolution more uncertain.)

As a result of the proletarianization of broad lower strata of the peasants, and as a result of the new system of private ownership, the landless industrial proletariat, which was not tied to the village by claims to land, had greatly increased. It had been one of the motivating forces in the previous revolution. But it was limited in numbers, and the course of events after the constitutional manifesto confirmed the experience, which has since been repeated everywhere, that revolutions today, if they are to have more than a short-term success, can be carried out *neither* by the middle classes and bourgeois intelligentsia alone, *nor* by the proletarian masses and the proletarian intelligentsia alone either.

Every general strike and putsch failed from the moment when the bourgeoisie and specifically that part of the bourgeoisie which is most important in Russia, namely the landowning zemstvo circles, had refused any further participation. Even when rebellious masses have leaders who

Pseudo-democracy 243

are as able and at least to some extent unselfish, as they undoubtedly are in Russia, there is *one* weapon they lack which will always be vital: *credit-worthiness*. This weapon is, however, possessed by the bourgeoisie. And on the basis of this credit-worthiness the bourgeoisie can obtain the funds which today are as necessary for the organization of a permanent administration, whether or not it calls itself 'revolutionary', as for any organization which exercises power. People need first and foremost to subsist, and in order to pay a host of employees, however idealistic, one needs money so as to obtain the numerous material means necessary to hold power.

The question was, therefore, how bourgeois circles would react to another revolution. It was, of course, clear that the few giant enterprises in heavy industry in Russia would adopt an absolutely reactionary stance. (However, they were so reactionary that their attitude was bound to provoke a mood of rebellion in the masses – as in our own country.) Neither did there seem to be any doubt about the attitude, since the revolution, of the majority of the bourgeois intelligentsia and the zemstvo circles, who were once the bearers of the reform movement. Their self-esteem, broken by the disappointment of their hopes of acquiring domestic power, took refuge all the more fervently in the romantic dream of exercising power abroad. This is quite understandable: the members of the higher Russian bureaucracy as well as of the officers' corps are recruited very largely out of these propertied strata – as they are elsewhere. Constantinople and the so-called liberation of the Slavs (meaning in reality their domination by the nationalist Greater Russian bureaucracy) now replaced the enthusiasm for 'human rights' and the 'constituent assembly'. This imperialist legend, and especially the Greater Russian claim to dominance within Russia itself, remained alive even in the bourgeois intelligentsia, and even during the heyday of the whole Liberation Movement. Before the slightest guarantee of the achievement of liberty, which was supposedly the only goal, as early as 1905 almost all the leading personalities of the Union of Liberation[4] (though *not* the unjustly maligned Mr Peter Struve) had turned their gaze towards Constantinople and the Western border.

They disputed the existence of a Ukrainian identity, and acknowledged Polish autonomy only with a view to creating external 'friends on the Western border' for a future expansion of Russia, and they proclaimed the 'liberation' of every imaginable nation as the task of Greater Russia, whilst at home everything remained to be done towards the achievement of 'liberation'. Meanwhile, the little group of ideologues belonging to the old Dragomanov school,[5] who were striving for the transformation of Russia into a genuinely equal federation of nationalities, were, even then, either deceivers who had themselves been deceived or completely without influence and in constant fear of arousing the Greater Russian chauvinism of their comrades. The question of the *autonomy of the nationalities* within Russia, as Professor *Johannes Haller* rightly emphasized in his recent work on the 'Russian Peril in the German House',[6] was used by Stolypin to arouse Greater Russian nationalism and thus became his most important instrument for defeating the democratic opposition.[7] The firm conviction of the supposed 'inevitable' decline of Austria-Hungary and the weakening of Turkey in the Balkan war inflated the hopes of this imperialistic intelligentsia to an extreme degree. In the Duma it became the main agitator for war preparations, and once the war had started, its motto was 'war to the end'. Since Grand Duke Nikolai's consultation with the leaders of the 'Kadets' in July 1914 (referred to by Prof. Haller),[8] these politicians switched quite suddenly to the camp of the warmongers. They hoped that the war would bring a strengthening of the financial position of the bourgeoisie. As representatives of the Kadet Party said at the outset of the war in private conversation, the politically liberal development of Russia would 'come of its own accord'. *How* this would ever happen if autocracy and bureaucracy had emerged with tremendous prestige from the war, by means of a victory over us, remained mysterious. It would only have been possible as the result of a crushing defeat such as these Russian imperialists did not expect at all. For all that, revolution appeared extremely improbable.

The fact that revolution has come after all is due, as well as to the success of our weapons, to the *purely personal conduct of the Tsar*. True, he used the defeat of 1915 to neutralize the present 'bourgeois king' in waiting: the Grand Duke Nikolai.[9] But he failed to make use of the partial success of 1916[10] to escape from the war with an honourable peace. This failure was determined by his hope for greater success and perhaps also by his profound personal hatred of the German Kaiser. After the defeat in Romania, the path was open to agreement with the thoroughly nationalistic, bourgeois, monarchical majority of a Duma elected by a blatantly class-based franchise. However, the Tsar was evidently prevented from taking this path and thus embracing parliamentarism by his fatal *vanity*. It remains an open question whether slightly pathological factors also had a part to play – a possibility suggested by his brand of 'religiosity', which seems to have deeply affronted the dignity of even his closest supporters.

His overriding and fundamental error lay in his fatal insistence on *wanting to rule on his own*. It was only possible for a monarch like the Tsar to even imagine that he could do this because, fortuitously, a quite unusually gifted statesman helped him to preserve the *appearance* of doing so. The Tsar would have been lost at the previous revolution, when his jealousy and vanity prompted him to dismiss Count Witte,[11] had it not been for the quite unexpected emergence of a personality of the stature of Stolypin, to whom he was willing to submit unconditionally. Without such support he was revealed as a complete dilettante, whose fickle and unpredictable interference would have rendered any purposeful politics impossible even had he been far more talented, and who was simply gambling with the very existence of the country and of his crown. Having ascended to the throne at an early age, he was unable to acquire technical mastery of modern administration. But this was not the decisive factor. Given the necessary restraint on the part of the monarch, efficient civil servants could take care of that. However – and people often forget this – even the most outstanding civil servant is not necessarily a good *politician*, and vice versa. And the Tsar was certainly not a good politician. The special qualities necessary for this difficult area of responsible activity – including the strict *objectivity*, the steady sense of *proportion*, the restrained *self-control*, and the capacity for *unobtrusive* action which it calls for – are not necessarily inherited along with the crown. And while it is hard for all monarchs to maintain these qualities, since their situation tends to stimulate romantic imagination, this particular monarch found it incomparably harder to do so. In monarchical states there is today a need for quite firm and strong powers of a different kind to make possible the *removal* of politically inept monarchs, in their own interest, where this is necessary.

The longer the war continued, the more the need to remove the monarch was borne in upon the Russian Imperialists themselves (absolutely undemocratic though they were), particularly their most able elements. And this would have been true whether or not England had been fomenting the revolution.[12] Circumstances being as they were, the (in part) highly socially conservative circles of the so-called 'Progressive Bloc'[13] in the Duma reached the same conclusion.

Great politics is always achieved by small groups of people. What is decisive for success is: (1) that their resolutions are not interfered with by the notions of a monarch so lacking in political talents; (2) that they have the *freely given* dedicated support of a sufficiently broad, powerful social stratum; (3) that they know how power struggles are carried out in situations where regulations, commands and military or bureaucratic obedience are *not*, in the nature of things, appropriate methods – and this is the case in great politics.

It is very strong and broadly based autonomous *parliamentary power alone*, consisting of men with the confidence of the voters, that can provide an apparatus capable, where necessary, in his own and the country's interest, of removing a monarch lacking all political talent, without at the same time overturning political institutions. The humanly understandable jealousy of trained civil servants, the flattery of plutocratic interested parties posing as 'monarchist', and the aesthetic snobbery of philistines and literati (those slavish followers of whatever the current fashion regards as 'refined') have for decades treated this simple truth with contempt.

Few people will be inspired by the aesthetic attractions of parliament. From the standpoint of pure administration it is nothing but wasted energy and a chance for speech-making by vain men to whom any efficient civil servant feels far superior in mastery of his subject; such men have to be offered the bait of little privileges and some concealed share of the patronage of office, the better to exclude them from real power and responsibility. These are precisely the qualities which do in fact characterize every *powerless* and therefore politically irresponsible parliament, which shuts its doors to the politically talented, with their morally justified ambition for power. This is 'pseudo-constitutionalism' and it inevitably harms the quality of political performance. Germany, for example, has the finest and most honest civil servants in the world. The German achievement in this war has shown what efficiency and military discipline are capable of. But the terrible failures of German politics have also shown what can *not* be achieved by these means.

The *untalented* ruler, and only he, is condemned to impotence by parliamentary power – and that is its greatest positive achievement by far – by a simply operating process of selection. By contrast, parliamentary power confers on the politically talented monarch that tremendous influence exercised by Edward VII, for example, a more dominant figure in recent times than any other monarch. The Tsar had to make the choice between the *real* possession of that power which his actual influence on the leadership of the state (which is always great) guarantees any monarch who displays political wisdom and self-control, and the vain romanticism and self-pity of the outward *appearance* of power; the striving for this appearance of power caused his ostentatious and blustering interventions to be ruinous for the calm and steady practice of politics, and imperilled his crown. Unlike Germany, in Russia any *publication* of speeches and telegrams of the monarch was a punishable offence ('Publication of a Court Report') if it had not been first checked by the appropriate official. However, since this official was a court official and had no parliamentary power as an independent basis for his position vis-à-vis the monarch, this was not enough to prevent politically injudicious remarks made by the Tsar from becoming known. Least of all was there any barrier to the clumsy unpredictability of his interventions in politics. For this reason even conservative circles within the Russian propertied classes, indeed especially they, became supporters of parliamentarism during the war. The Tsar, however, preferred romantic illusion, and, even at the eleventh hour, could not bring himself to share formal power even with the socially conservative forces of the bourgeois propertied classes, who are dominant in the present Duma.

However, the country, in its present situation, could not be held in check merely by means of the police, who, in their own power interests, were absolutely loyal to him, and the 'Black Gangs' [see Glossary], which had been specially recruited. They demonstrated their ability to arrange assassination attempts, general strikes, and pogroms to intimidate the bourgeoisie and inconvenient ministers, as events proved beyond doubt. They operated completely on their own authority and were in fact a considerable force. But, inevitably in a state characterized by police functions, almost the whole material administration lay in the hands of precisely those zemstvo circles which the Tsar so profoundly hated. Most important of all, if these representatives of 'society' were deliberately pushed to one side, forbidden to organize or even driven to engage in obstruction, the economic provision of the country and of the capital cities was sure to be brought to a complete standstill. This evidently occurred and, added to the failure of the Russian railway system resulting from the demands of the Romanian campaign, led directly to the outbreak of the revolt.

Without the opposition of the *bourgeois* intelligentsia to the old regime, any mass revolt, no matter how successful, would have quickly run into the sand and have been drowned in blood, as happened in the winter of 1905–6 and as would happen to a putsch by that bunch of windbags in our 'Liebknecht Group'[14] if one imagines them increased in size twentyfold. But not only all trained workers' leaders but also the leading strata of the bourgeois intelligentsia joined in, as a result of the behaviour of the Tsar. The majority of even the active reserve officers (as most officers now were) would not in the long term have been prepared to send their battalions in against members of those families from which most of them came themselves. Moreover, the most able amongst them took the view that the elimination of the unpredictable personal interference of this monarch was a *practical* necessity, once the consequences of his dilettantism had become clear. The fact that this 'elimination' took a quite different course from that which the majority of them had wished, namely that it led to the fall of the dynasty and *not* to a bourgeois monarchy in the person of a Grand Duke or to a military dictatorship, forced the leaders of the movement in the capitals to look to the *proletariat*, whose power was indispensable in the struggle against the Tsar.

The famine occurred simply because the Russian railways were unavailable for civil purposes on account of the demands made on them by the extension of the front due to the Romanian campaign. And it now became clear that the leaders of the proletarian strata of the 'intelligentsia', of lower officialdom (both state and non-state) and of workers in railways, post, and telegraph were so firmly in their people's hands that they were obliged to accept Kerensky's taking of power and the complete sweeping away of the dynasty. It is, however, very unlikely that an open or disguised military dictatorship can be permanently kept at bay, *if the war continues*. The propertied strata would of course need to be given some consideration. However, the majority of professional officers, and certainly the bourgeois strata of today's class-based Duma and the provisional government, fear genuine democracy. Above all the *money-providers*, both domestic and in the allied countries, fear it. This is partly because they wish the war to continue, but partly also because they fear for the security of the money they have advanced. Their influence is the most significant. In the previous revolution one could follow step by step how the government of Count Witte did whatever the foreign banks and stock exchanges regarded as being advantageous for the *creditworthiness* of the regime, whether this meant making concessions or applying repression. The bourgeois leaders of the present regime, if they wish to have credit, have no choice other than to behave likewise. In 1906 it was receipt of a foreign loan[15] that placed the Tsar in a position to dismiss Witte, to impose pseudo-constitutionalism[16] and above all to re-establish the police and the Black Gangs, and then first to treat the Duma as though it did not exist and then to proceed to the coup d'état.[17] If the right personalities can be found, then they will receive the money to tame the country this time too, under whatever *apparently* democratic forms. The task is, in itself, not insoluble, the question is only whether the personalities can be found. No foreign observer can know the answer to this question. At any rate, everyone will say to themselves that a regime financially supported by people like Morozov and the other leaders of arch-reactionary big capitalism cannot possibly be a 'democracy'.[18] Messrs Miliukov and Guchkov are casting glances towards the banks, both domestic and foreign, and now also towards America, in order to obtain money from there[19] – not primarily for the conduct of the war, but in order to ensure that they are firmly in the saddle *against the radicals*.

In this connection what is now decisively important and characteristic is the position of the government vis-à-vis the *peasants*, who in the previous revolution were a kind of weather-vane of the current power situation in the field of domestic politics.

Objectively, it is the *peasants* in particular who have a real interest in

Pseudo-democracy 249

peace, and they represent the overwhelming majority of the Russian people. In terms of their own ideals, their real interests cannot be satisfied without (1) the expropriation in entirety of non-peasant land, and (2) *cancellation of Russia's foreign debts*.

The latter is particularly important. If the peasants have to shoulder the interest on foreign debts, then the process described so graphically by Russian economists would have to begin all over again: this severely undernourished stratum would have to hand over the grain for export to pay the interest, and would have to be highly taxed in order to force them to sell. This is how it was before. The difficulties presented by the *first* point, which will presumably be insuperable this time too, lie not so much in the thing itself as in the conflicts of interest which inevitably arise between the individuals when it comes to carrying it out, in particular between the local and regional groups amongst the peasants themselves. If in one district expropriation produces 6 hectares for the peasants and in the neighbouring district it produces 15, the peasants from the first district naturally demand an equal amount in the distribution, whilst those from the other district would like to have all the land in their district for themselves. These conflicts existed in the early stages of the previous revolution.

Additionally, there is the problem that they do not wish to pay anything for the land, and thus get into hopeless conflict with the bourgeois landowners. These difficulties could only be resolved by means of a Socialist Revolutionary *dictatorship* lasting for years (whereby 'Socialist Revolutionary' should not be taken to imply rule by some firebrand but simply that of a politician who is prepared to disregard the 'sanctity' of private land ownership, which in Russia is still quite a new idea). I do not know whether Russia has such men. However, they could only gain permanent power if *peace* were concluded. *For only then would the peasants even be at home and available.* At the moment it is only women and children and the old who are at home, whilst the peasants are at the mercy of 'discipline', which means in this case the violence of the dominant property-owning strata and their military officers and civil servants. The discipline may be relaxed and the army's offensive capability weakened, but the continuation of the war does at least *this* service for the propertied classes.

These strata are, of course, *sworn enemies of any peasant movement*, for they are allied to the landowning interests which dominate the zemstvos. Thus, *in order to keep the peasants away from their homes*, they are absolutely in favour of prolonging the war *for its own sake*, even if the prospects are completely hopeless. Only in this way can firstly the mass of the *peasants* be held in the trenches *under the control of the generals*, secondly the new power of the propertied classes be strengthened before the conclusion of peace, and thirdly *the financial support of the banks* at home and abroad be gained, in order to organize the new political power and keep the peasant movement under control.

The situation is similar to ours in so far as our conservatives also would like to go through the motions of a reform of the Prussian franchise *behind the backs of the army, while it is away.* Reactionaries like Guchkov and similar personalities would *never* have joined the present government without guarantees that any true peasant movement would be put down. It was only for this purpose that they came into the government. That much is obvious. On the other hand, the arch-reactionary leaders of heavy industry and the presidents of the chambers of commerce and the banks would *never* have subscribed to the 'freedom bond'[20] nor would the financial backers in the allied states have given credit to the new regime without the same guarantees, as they would otherwise risk losing the money they had lent. That too is obvious. True, money cannot achieve everything. But *without* money you can, in the long run, do nothing. With the aid of the thousands of millions provided by the 'freedom bond' it should, as far as one can tell, be possible (1) to keep the mass of the peasants in the trenches and thus without power; (2) to frustrate any attempt by the true democrats within Russia to seize power.

This power of money may be restrained and its significance as an offensive force in war crippled, but short of the complete liquidation of the war it can never be completely broken. *So far* the only fact to emerge that is symptomatic of the power situation of the two hostile parties is that a section of domestic capitalism *refuses* to subscribe to the 'freedom bond', thus apparently having no confidence that the bourgeois plutocratic government will last. Quite an important indication.

The Democrats have not yet shown that they too pose a serious threat to the power of finance. Concessions have, of course, been made to them by permitting a certain degree of freedom of movement, especially in the practically important field of agitation, and also by the promise of a 'Republic' as well as by *vague promises* for the future, as vague as those the Tsar had given. For the time being they still have control over a section of public transport and communication, especially the inland telegraph and railways. But *they* do not receive credit from the banks, and as long as the war continues, their power to establish a permanently functioning government apparatus is strictly limited. Even the many civil servants loyal to them chiefly want to be *paid*, and for this one needs bank credit. However, the banks will only give credit to those who (1) continue the war for the time being; and (2) whatever happens, keep the peasants in subjection, as their ideals

Pseudo-democracy 251

are incompatible with the interests of the Russian state creditors.

The government has never promised the 'constituent assembly'.[21] If (1) genuinely free elections were to take place and (2) the peasants could be given proper information on the situation, such an assembly would undoubtedly result in a tremendous majority of peasant representatives, who would be in favour of (1) expropriation of land, (2) cancellation of the state debt, and (3) peace. Thus the ruling propertied strata and the leading officers, like the powerful financial interests at home and abroad, have an interest in (1) falsifying the information getting to the peasants, falsifying the elections; and (2) if this is not possible, postponing the constituent assembly. Most of all they have an interest in ensuring *at any price* that those serving in the *army*, namely the mass of the most powerful peasants, do not participate in the elections to the constituent assembly.

However, many representatives of the social-democratic Russian industrial workers cannot work up any enthusiasm for any of the three points of the peasant programme, based on the 'natural order'. To the Marxist Social Democrats, especially Plekhanov, the real hopes of the peasants appear just as utopian and 'backward' as they did in 1905. Plekhanov and similar ethical thinkers, as Marxist evolutionists, are sworn enemies of all 'petty bourgeois, peasant ideals of equality and sharing', and material factors play a part too. The workers demand the highest prices [for their goods] and cheap bread, whilst the peasants hold back the grain and would, if they could, oppose confiscation with violence. Workers' earnings in war-related enterprises are very good. Any successes for the real aspirations of the peasants could slow down the pace of capitalist industrial development for years. And just as everywhere else in the world (as for example in Sicilian cities) where socialist workers have achieved government, they have shown themselves to be committed promoters of capitalist development, which does, after all, provide them with work. Most of all, though, they would have to share power with a movement of quite a different kind, forming a huge majority, a movement of whose profound 'immaturity' they are as much convinced as any German literary man. This does not, of course, stand in the way of a quite sincere *emotional* feeling of solidarity with the peasants. Neither does it prevent those socialists who have no interest in the war industry, and are not committed to evolutionist thinking, from working for peace. Finally, it does not prevent them from advocating 'in principle' the sole competence of the constituent assembly, as their programme requires. It does, however, influence the actual *practical* attitude of those socialist politicians in the government, despite their principles.

By obstructing the administration the socialist workers' leaders may be able to extract political concessions from a *bourgeois* government – but they *cannot* do this from a 'constituent assembly' of *peasants*. Neither can they organize any steady administration of the country as long as the war continues. Here the decisive point is the lack of *credit-worthiness*, which remains a crucial factor *as long as the war continues*. However, they will not risk determined opposition to such continuation. For they cannot do without the alliance with the bourgeois strata, who alone are *credit-worthy*. Without the continuation of the war, this credit would not be available. Thus, as long as the situation remains as it is, the Social Democrats and Socialist Revolutionaries can only play 'second fiddle' and are happily tolerated in that role, because they provide the illusion of a 'revolutionary' character for the government. However, for the time being, it is not they who can resolve the decisive question of war and peace, but the propertied bourgeois strata, the officers – and *the banks. So far, there has been no 'revolution' but merely 'the removal' of an incompetent monarch.*

At least half of the real power is in the hands of purely monarchist circles, who are only going along with the present 'republican' sham because, to their regret, the monarch has not stayed within the necessary restraints to his power. It is a matter of practical indifference whether (and these circles would certainly *not* welcome it) the 'republic' will ultimately establish itself for a longer period (or even permanently) as a result of the follies and shortcomings of the dynasty. Everything depends on whether the truly 'democratic' elements, peasants, tradesmen, and industrial workers *outside* the arms industry, gain real power. That is not out of the question, but is not the case at the moment. However, when once the bourgeois participants in the government, Guchkov, Miliukov etc., have the *money* from America or from the banks in their hands, *then* the time will be ripe for an attempt to get rid of the socialist hangers-on entirely with the aid of the officers and the Guards. If the socialist ideologists were then *really* to proceed to 'revolutionary' action, they would find powerful financial interests and the ruling bourgeois circles solidly against them. Even the most radical politicians who want to rule *with* these powers have no choice other than to accept the miserable role that people like Kerensky and Chkheidze are forced to play.[22]

Those, quite simply, are the facts of the situation. Those who doubt them – and there are sure to be such simple souls in neutral countries and perhaps in our country too – should put them to the test by considering the following points, the force of which, if they are honest, they must acknowledge:

1 The mass of the peasants are at the front. The radicals, who claim to be against 'militarism', ought now to press for the right of these people

Pseudo-democracy 253

to *express* their opinion in secret ballot and election (the secrecy of which would need to be carefully supervised). The *reactionaries* and *only they* have, as we have said, a clear interest in (a) *keeping the peasants at the front* and (b) *preventing front-line soldiers from participating in voting.* As long as there are only old men, children and women in the villages, the peasants are powerless. It is all too easy for those who have stayed at home to call loudly for the continuation of the war. They earn money from it and use the opportunity to gain the custom of the armed forces. That much is as clear as day. So if the radicals agree to the army being kept away from the elections they do *not* want peace – because they are 'not allowed to'. The test is conclusive, if the news has not actually been falsified: the deputies of the new government, including the reactionary Guchkov on the one hand and the revolutionary Kerensky on the other, have been to see the (arch-reactionary) General Brusilov.[23] What happened? *They gave in to him.* According to the latest news, some form of participation by the army does seem to have been achieved after all. But there are further tests.

2 There has been a public, absolutely unambiguous statement by the Central Powers[24] and, what is more, a telegram from the German Social Democratic Party[25] to the (supposedly) 'radical' Petersburg leaders. The simple test is: whether thereupon the present government, whose most powerful man in internal affairs is Kerensky, or whether at least the rival government, whose most powerful man is Chkheidze, attempts to enforce peace negotiations between the Central Powers and the alliance of Entente Powers or not. We shall learn the answer in the near future.

3 There are still further tests: it is impossible to undertake peace negotiations by means of public proclamation of conditions to which the opponent must agree *before* the beginning of negotiations as to an 'ultimatum'. No opponent would accept that. Yet that is what Professor Miliukov has done by means of his manifesto on *Poland*[26] and his declaration on *Serbia*[27] – without contradiction from the 'radical' Kerensky. The manifesto on Poland does not state *what territory* Prof. Miliukov understands by the term. As he well knows, there is no one in the whole of Germany willing to negotiate about those territories belonging to the German Reich in which German inhabitants are inseparably intermingled with Poles. The point is rather that the autonomy of Poland *guaranteed* by Russia in 1815,[28] which was abruptly snatched away by the Tsar, should be restored with new guarantees. The main question is: what should be the *eastern* border of this territory? The German point of view would be that the *view of the Poles* should be decisive. The Poles have now withdrawn from the Duma, as it no longer represents them.[29] Prof. Miliukov, to whom the

Duma has given power, will thus evidently have no more to do with them.

In addition there is the internal Russian nationalities question. The Ukrainian, Dragomanov, had, at one time, drawn up a genuinely democratic programme for this: a completely free federation with a federal parliament and control only over the formal *legality* of the acts of the autonomous local parliaments [*Landtage*] and assemblies of the individual nations.[30] The present government could not avoid the setting up of a nationalities programme which promises *equality*.[31] But it contains *nothing* about *autonomy*, i.e. the replacement of *Greater Russian officialdom* and the officers' corps by civil servants freely determined by the individual nationalities, nothing about *Landtage* [provincial parliaments] or about rights such as those enjoyed by Czechs, Croats and Slovenes in Austria.

This is where democracy has its strict limits, as long as the present bourgeois government remains in power in Russia. Its Imperialist members, especially those in the Duma, want to *dominate* the other foreign nations by means of a bureaucracy and an officers' corps drawn from their own ranks, that is, from the propertied *Greater Russian* strata. It has always been like this in Russia, no matter who the rulers were. The previous revolution was also defeated by the arousal of Greater Russian chauvinism. Even the socialists will at first have to conform in this respect – for fear of this possibility. Neither any of the foreign nations within Russia nor Mr Guchkov himself, and least of all Messrs Kerensky and Chkheidze, believe that 'national' promises made by Mr Guchkov and the other members of the Duma (which emerged from class elections) are any more likely to be kept than those of the Tsar. They must nevertheless take them at face value.

I repeat – the politicians currently holding power, of whatever persuasion, need money from the *banks*. Only a tiny proportion of this money is used in the struggle against the Central Powers. The great mass of it is used to consolidate the domination of the country by capitalist interests and those representing the Russian propertied intelligentsia. One element of this consolidation is the creation of an army which will be as reliable for the bourgeois regime as the Tsar's Black Gangs were for him. It is designed to be used *primarily* against *internal* enemies. This is happening now – with the financial advances from the banks and the big industrialists. What is also necessary to achieve this is the *arrest* of all those people whom the peasants are capable of influencing in their favour. These are the same means that the Tsar's regime employed. These arrests have already begun. They are carried out on the pretext that these radicals are secret 'German agents'.[32] At the same time the elections to

Pseudo-democracy 255

the constituent assembly (if they should take place at all during the war) are being unfairly influenced by the spread of untrue allegations that Germany 'supported the old regime'. A word about that.

In 1905 I was repeatedly asked in all seriousness by academically educated Russians who had lived in Germany for a long time (1) whether Germany would intervene in the case of expropriation of privately owned Russian land; (2) if so, whether the Social Democrats would be able to prevent this. A negative answer to *both* these questions, which for those familiar with the situation in Germany are equally absurd, met with total disbelief. Undoubtedly the attitude of the conservative Prussian police has done its bit towards the rise of this belief. I do not wish to enumerate again their undignified and politically pointless services. I believe that is now all in the past. However, the direct cause of the ridiculous notion was the arch-reactionary military governor of Warsaw, Skalon, in 1905, who knew very well what he was doing.[33] None of those in power in Petersburg *today* believe this nonsense. And yet they use it every bit as much as Skalon did. And it seems that the representatives of Russian socialism have the choice of either joining in this pathetic game *or* giving up a share of power. Equally they have to *go along with* the ignoring of the message of peace issued by the Central Powers, and have to tolerate the issuing of war manifestos and interviews which have the warlike aim of 'destruction of Prussian militarism' or 'the overthrow of the Hohenzollern' or the dismemberment of Turkish or Austrian or German territories.[34] *Otherwise there will be no money* for the preservation of their own dominance in the country.

This crystal-clear situation of Russian pseudo-democracy and in particular of the socialist leaders in Russia places the German *Social Democratic Party* and its leaders in a position of great responsibility.

The situation is now as follows: alongside material factors the attitude of Russian socialist leaders rests on a fundamental assumption: with an army of negroes, ghurkas and all the barbarian rabble in the world standing at our borders, half crazed with rage, lust for vengeance, and the craving to devastate our country, they assume that German Social Democracy will still be a party to the fraudulence of the present Russian Duma plutocracy and, morally speaking, stab the army which is protecting our country from savage nations in the back. It rests also on a *tremendous underestimate* of German military power and of our resolve if need be to take upon ourselves any privation in order to enforce a lasting peace if the Russian rulers once more succeed, as it appears they may, in frustrating the peace negotiations. It is absolutely necessary for the German workers to *know* that at the moment there can be no question of any genuine 'democracy' in Russia, and why this is so. We could make an honourable peace at any time with a *genuinely* democratic Russia. We could probably *not* do so with the present one; for those in power need the war to maintain that power.

It is undoubtedly an unpleasant thought that after almost three years of war our troops must still remain far from their homeland, simply because the plutocratic half of the present government in Russia is obliged to secure its power in its own country by keeping the peasants in the trenches and making use of bank credit, and because the socialists, thanks to their lack of credit-worthiness, are too weak and are therefore compelled to howl with the wolves. Unless there is another coup or there is some shift in the power situation it will be several months before broad areas of the *bourgeois* elements in Russia, who have an interest in achieving the ordered conditions for which an honourable peace is a necessary precondition, are able, in one way or another, to assert themselves.

This moment will come with absolute certainty. But until it does we must be prepared to fight on implacably; we have no choice. It is in the natural order of things that, as long as there is any real hope that the peaceful tendency will emerge dominant, the Russians should be allowed to sort things out among themselves. When those groups with an interest in war gain the upper hand there is no longer any justification for this.

There is nothing we can 'learn' from this *present pseudo*-democracy other than the fact that one should not allow the fraudulence of the present *Duma franchise* to *jeopardize the moral credit of a crown*. Unfortunately it still seems timely, even today, to emphasize this.

Notes

1 [M–H] In a speech in the Reichstag on 29 Mar. 1917 Bethmann-Hollweg declared that Germany would not interfere in the internal affairs of Russia and would not ask Russia to accept a dishonourable peace.
2 [M–H] In an interview with the newspaper *Rech* on 5 Apr./23 Mar. 1917 Miliukov expressed himself very forcefully on Russian war aims and the preparedness of the Russian people for war (*Rech*, 70 (23 Mar. 1917), p. 2, reprinted in *The Russian Provisional Government 1917: Documents*, selected and edited by Robert P. Browder and Alexander F. Kerensky, vol. 2 (Stanford, Calif., 1961), p. 1044. Likewise, the circular telegram from Miliukov to the diplomatic representatives of Russia abroad of 17/4 Mar. (Browder and Kerensky, *Documents*, vol. 2, pp. 1042–3), in which he stated that foreign policy would continue as before, became known in Germany on the same day.

Pseudo-democracy 257

3 [M–H] Reference to the agrarian reform of the Russian Minister President Stolypin of 1906, whose main object was removal of peasants from the obshchina without their consent and thus the transformation of collectively owned land to individual property.
4 [M–H] See List of Parties and Associations.
5 [M–H] Dragomanov was one of those in the vanguard of the struggle for the restructuring of the tsarist state in the direction of the granting of far-reaching autonomy to the nationalities.
6 [Weber] The work is an attack on the book by and also on the activities of Prof. *Hötzsch* for the *Kreuzzeitung*. [M–H: Reference to Otto Hötzsch, *Rußland. Eine Einführung auf Grund seiner Geschichte von 1904–1912* (Berlin, 1913), and additionally to his reviews of the foreign policy of the week which appeared regularly in the *Neue Preußische Zeitung* (*Kreuzzeitung*) from Nov. 1914.] It is indeed astonishing that a man who has frequently been to Russia, and whose book makes considerable claims for itself, should demonstrate such a complete ignorance of decisive political party groupings as in fact is the case in this book, which is shallow in every respect, and cannot be taken seriously as a source of political information. My own chronicles of the revolution of 1905–6 ('Zur Lage der bürgerlich Demokratie in Rußland' and 'Rußlands Übergang zum Scheinkonstitutionalismus' (Tübingen, Mohr, 1906) [M–H: Published as supplements to the *Archiv für Sozialwissenschaft und Sozialpolitik*. See BD and PC, this volume]), which were written contemporaneously with the events they describe, can *only* be given consideration if one bears in mind (1) that we know a great deal more in Germany today than we could glean from incomplete reports at that time, and (2) that since then the Stolypin reform has been undertaken. It was not possible to recognize the significance of Stolypin at that time. To the completely uninformed person who is willing to make the effort of reading them (as e.g. Herr Hötzsch was not), these modest chronicles may perhaps offer a certain degree of orientation on the *party tendencies* in Russia (which have since partially shifted) and the degree of support they enjoyed.
7 [M–H] Cf. Johannes Haller, *Die Russische Gefahr im deutschen Hause* (Stuttgart, 1917).
8 [M–H] Cf. ibid., p. 80 n. 1.
9 [M–H] After their defeat by the German and Austrian troops between May and Oct. 1915 the Russian armies had to quit Poland, the Baltic region and a large part of Galicia. In Sept. Tsar Nicholas II took over supreme command of the army from his uncle, Grand Duke Nikolai Nikolaevich. The Grand Duke enjoyed a certain popularity with the public. Possibly Weber's characterization of him as 'bourgeois king' derives from this.
10 [M–H] In May 1916 the Russian army achieved a partially successful offensive on the south-eastern front under General Brusilov.
11 [M–H] On 14 Apr. 1906, immediately before the convening of the new Duma, which had just been elected.

12 [M–H] German government circles, especially the leader of the Russia department of the Foreign Office, Count Pourtalès, took the view that the revolution had been fomented by the British. Cf. Wolfgang Steglich, *Die Friedenspolitik der Mittelmächte 1917–18* (Wiesbaden, 1964), p. 59.
13 [M–H] The overwhelming majority of the Duma deputies, with the exception of the extreme right and the left, and a section of the conservative Imperial Council, merged in the summer of 1915 to form the 'Progressive Bloc', which called for 'a government of trust' as well as for social and political reforms.
14 [M–H] Reference to the 'International Group' or 'Spartacus Group', which brought together opposition Social Democrats surrounding Karl Liebknecht and Rosa Luxemburg from 1 Jan. 1916.
15 [M–H] In the spring of 1906 an Anglo-French consortium granted Russia a new loan, which eased the financial problems of the Empire.
16 [M–H] The 'Pseudo-constitution' is a reference to the constitution imposed by the Tsar on 23 Apr. 1906.
17 [M–H] On 3 June 1907 the Russian Minister President Stolypin dissolved the Second Duma and, in contravention of the existing constitution, imposed a new electoral law for the Duma.
18 [M–H] The Morozovs were a well-known family of textile industrialists. Weber's source here is an article in the *Frankfurter Zeitung*, no. 99, 11 Apr. 1917, (evening edn): 'Freedom bond – Issuing the Freedom Bond'.
19 [M–H] Shortly after it came to power, the Provisional Government attempted to secure American, Japanese and even English credit. From 3 May 1917 the Provisional Government received American credit. Cf. Browder and Kerensky, *Documents*, vol. 2, pp. 500–3.
20 [M–H] 'Freedom Bond' was the name of the state bond issued by the Russian revolutionary government on 9 Apr./27 Mar. 1917 (issue price 85%, interest 5%, to run for 49 years).
21 [M–H] Nevertheless, on 20/7 Mar. 1917 the government published the following vaguely worded statement: 'As soon as possible the government will convene the constituent assembly on the basis of universal, equal, direct and secret franchise, and guarantees the glorious defenders of the fatherland participation in these elections.' *Vestnik Vremennago Pravitelstva*, 2 (7 Mar. 1917), p. 1.
22 [M–H] The Trudovik A. F. Kerensky, the only socialist minister in the first Provisional Government, was at the same time deputy chairman of the Petersburg Workers' and Soldiers' Council. N. S. Chkheidze, a Menshevist, was the chairman. Kerensky in particular played the part of mediator between the soviet and the Provisional Government.
23 [M–H] No such meeting is known to have taken place. Weber may be referring to the agitation tour undertaken by Duma deputies to the front line, which took place after 8 Mar./23 Feb.

Pseudo-democracy   259

24 [M-H] Cf. p. 256 n.1.
25 [M-H] The telegram from the German Social Democrats, signed by Friedrich Ebert, was sent on 31 Mar. 1917 via Copenhagen to the Duma in Petersburg. In it the German Social Democrats congratulated the Russian Social Democrats 'on their successes on the path to political liberty. They earnestly desire that the political progress of the Russian people may contribute to securing that peace for the world for which German social democrats have fought ever since the outbreak of war.' Quoted in Heinrich Schulthess (ed.), *Europäischer Geschichtskalender* (Nördlingen, 1917), part 1, pp. 389f.
26 [M-H] On 29 Mar. 1917 the Provisional Government had issued a proclamation to the Poles relating to the territorial autonomy of Polish regions: 'the Provisional Government regards the creation of an independent Polish State, formed from all those regions, the majority of whose population consists of Poles, as a pledge of a lasting peace in the new Europe of the future.' Ibid., part 2, p. 673.
27 [M-H] In a reply to the recognition of the new Russian Government by Japan, Belgium, Portugal, Serbia and Romania, Miliukov expressed himself in favour of restoring freedom to Belgium, Romania and Serbia. (Report in *Frankfurter Zeitung*, no. 96, 7 Apr. 1917, morning edn.)
28 [M-H] Reference to the ruling of the Vienna Congress of 1815, that Russia should grant a representative constitution and national institutions to the parts of the Grand Duchy of Warsaw which it would receive. Thereupon this part of the territory was granted autonomous status as 'Kingdom of Poland'. After the Polish uprising of 1830, however, it was abolished.
29 [M-H] Cf. *Frankfurter Zeitung*, no. 93, 4 Apr. 1917, evening edn: 'The Poles in Russia'.
30 [M-H] Dragomanov's programme, entitled 'Free Union, draft of Ukrainian political and social programme', for the Ukrainian Liberation Movement, contained amongst other things the draft of a new constitution for Russia. The principal aspect of this was the granting of greater rights to Ukrainians and the other non-Russian nationalities within the Russian Empire.
31 [M-H] In its decree of 2 Apr./20 Mar. the Provisional Government lifted all restrictions on the rights of the individual based on his religion or nationality. Browder and Kerensky, *Documents*, vol. 1, pp. 211ff. In declarations to the Poles and Finns, dated 29/16 Mar. and 21/8 Mar., it guaranteed free self-determination for the Poles and the re-establishment of the autonomy of Finland.
32 [M-H] Cf. *Frankfurter Zeitung*, no. 89, 31 Mar. 1917, 2nd morning edn: 'The Russian Revolution – Workers' Rally for Peace'. According to this report, soldiers returning from the front who agitated for peace were arrested as German spies.
33 [M-H] It has not been possible to trace this incident.

34 [M–H] In a speech to the Workers and Soldiers Council (29/16 Mar. 1917) the chairman, Chkheidze, declared: 'The motto of the revolution is "Down with Wilhelm"!' (Browder and Kerensky, *Documents*, vol. 2, p. 1077). In *Rech* (23 Mar. 1917), Miliukov stated that the liquidation of European Turkey and the reorganization of Austria-Hungary with the aim of liberating oppressed nationalities, and the separation of Armenia from Turkey, remained Russian war aims.

4

The Russian Revolution and the Peace

The fall of that government which desired war against us more intensely than any other could of course signify a fundamental change in our whole position towards Russia. It is clear that we could live in enduring peace and friendship with a Russia in which there was a real likelihood of the lasting existence of a *non*-imperialist, that is, a federalist democracy, and that we would break off the war with such a country *and give up our demand for any further guarantees*. It is also clear that such a Russia would permit us to develop our own internal conditions without the continual presence of that terrible threat which proximity to this country has meant for us for three decades, so that supervised arms control treaties with Russia would acquire the practical significance they have hitherto always had for the pacifists. The question is whether a democratic and federalist Russia has indeed truly come about, or is likely to come about, and will continue to exist. My very great appreciation for the Russian Liberation Movement cannot prevent me from expressing doubts about this, *so long as the situation remains as it is*.

The Russian government is evidently playing a double game. Some of its members make statements aimed at those Russian radicals who are inclined towards an honourable peace,[1] whilst others make statements designed to satisfy the Entente and the imperialist bourgeoisie.[2] A diplomatic seesaw operates between the two. Collectively, the government, whose most powerful man in domestic politics is (or at least was) *Kerensky*, declared that it wanted no annexations or indemnities and as 'guarantees' wanted only treaties of disarmament and arbitration.[3] However, the Foreign Minister, Professor *Miliukov*, carries on his secret correspondence, describes himself as 'indispensable' for maintaining relations with the Entente, and identifies himself with its imperialist aims.[4] These statements have been denied, but he remains in office, with the approval of the others, and periodically he repeats his imperialist utterances, despite all denials. He may no longer do this publicly, but he undoubtedly will continue to link himself with the Entente by means of correspondence.

The composition of the bodies holding power decides the chances of a non-imperialist policy. There exists an official 'Provisional Government'. Alongside this there is a de facto secondary government in the 'Council of Workers and Soldiers', which sees its function as keeping a check on other bodies. The official government is formally legitimized by the *Duma*. The Duma's majority is extremely imperialist. Its President *Rodzianko*, a *monarchist*, still describes 'inseparability' from the Entente and the 'victory' of Russia as conditions of peace,[5] which is tantamount to an indefinite postponement of any consideration of peace. Mr *Guchkov* has a seat in the provisional government; he is an efficient administration official, who is a member of the liberal-conservative Union of 17 October, and is allied to large landowning interests and the bourgeoisie. He *has no intention* of aiming for democracy and federalism. For the Union of 17 October was founded to fight *against* both of these things,[6] in contrast to the Kadets, who were at least officially democratic and to a certain degree federalist too. The latter make up the greater part of the official government. They are imperialist and supporters of a 'bourgeois monarchy', which would leave power with the bourgeoisie, because the monarchy would not be completely legitimate. In July 1914, after its principal journal, *Rech*, whose policy had hitherto been opposed to war, had held discussions with the Grand Duke Nikolai, the Kadets began to support the war.[7] Professor Miliukov, their most prominent member, a highly respected scholar, is held in thrall by the romantic appeal of the imperialist idea, and has been one of the principal propagandists for this idea in Russia and abroad during the war. As a consequence of its relations with England, this party will surely do nothing against English wishes. A bourgeois monarchy is not possible at the moment, it is true, but at a suitable time it could rapidly be set up. The war aims of Professor Miliukov are absolutely *identical* with those of the Tsar. This government will never bring about a real federalism, that is, autonomy for the non-Russian peoples, with their own provincial parliaments, their own, non-Russian, officer corps and civil servants elected from amongst their own people. Even the Kadets are much too closely tied to the selfish interests of would-be Greater Russian office-holders and to the pan-Slavic myth.

How do things stand with the *radical* members of the government, like

Kerensky, and with the unofficial government, whose most powerful member is Chkheidze? The Ukrainian autonomists place great hopes in Kerensky.⁸ These hopes are doomed to disappointment as long as a government like the present one remains at the helm. Even if he really wanted to, Kerensky would not be able to execute seriously federalist demands. It can be seen that although he can make a public disavowal, he *cannot* truly abandon the imperialist demands of his Kadet colleagues, that he cannot even prevent inflammatory speeches like those of Rodzianko, and that he can do nothing to stop the imperialist Duma from being treated as the decisive court of appeal. His power, though quite considerable in itself, is not as great as that of the bourgeois strata, with their connections with the British Envoy. For reasons soon to be stated, however, no fundamental change in the composition of the government is likely. All the Kadet members have declared themselves to be in solidarity with Miliukov.

True, there can be no doubting the subjective honesty and integrity of Chkheidze and of other members of the secondary government. But they are 'intellectuals', and so far experience has always shown that whatever party a Russian intellectual professes, as soon as he has a share of *power* in the state he not only becomes, as all radical parties of every country do, 'national', he becomes, in one way or another, national*ist* and imperialist. This may take different forms, but remains essentially true.

There is *only one* reliable *test* of a genuinely democratic and non-imperialist attitude. Does the politician in question restrict himself to cleaning up in his own backyard, i.e. to creating a democracy within his own country *or not*? If he does not, he is an imperialist, whether or not he intends to be one or believes himself to be one. Having scarcely come to power, Chkheidze has called upon German workers to 'depose the Hohenzollern' – otherwise there would be war to the death. Such interference in our internal affairs by foreigners is imperialism. For whether Russian imperialism takes a despotic, a liberal or a socialist form is neither here nor there. Anyone who wishes to *intervene by force* in the affairs of *other* nations from *outside* the sphere of interest of his own nationality is an 'imperialist'. This is what is being proposed here. For Chkheidze and his party everything still remains to be done in Russia. If they still act in the manner of all Russian intellectuals; if instead of setting their own house in order, they concern themselves with the 'liberation' of *other* nations (an aim of the tsarist regime too), then *war* is the only possible answer to them, just as it was against the tsarist regime, and the creation of military *guarantees* in the East is the only possible war aim. However little the German people may wish to be ruled by the plutocracy of the Prussian Three Class Parliament, it wishes far less to be ruled by imperialist literati from abroad. Refusal to interfere in the affairs of other nations is the *only test* of whether a Russian politician is an honest democrat.

In view of the above, we must also ask ourselves what guarantees there are that the Russian government, even if it were a democracy now, would continue to be one *in the future*, and what guarantees there are that statements made by the present rulers will be binding on a future regime. And for that there is *only one test*: whether the Russian government forces its allies to begin *peace* negotiations on the basis of its own programme immediately, under the threat of otherwise doing this itself, independently of them. If Democracy does not have the strength to do this, it does not have the strength to play a part in ruling Russia.[9] It would then be certain that sooner or later the imperialist bourgeoisie would gain the upper hand. If there is any fear of this, *then* we must of course continue the fight, and, though this would be to our great regret, eventually demand guarantees of our own security. Our *interest* in peace is, at the moment, objectively viewed, no greater than it was at the outset. The problems with food supplies to be expected in the coming months could *not* be solved by a peace settlement. The world-wide crop failure and the tremendous rise in prices abroad would prevent import of foodstuffs to Germany. However, once our crops have been harvested, our interest in peace becomes less than that of the enemy. For it is only as long as the war continues that we shall be in possession of the *Romanian corn-growing land* and can dispose of these crops as we choose. Everyone in Germany knows this, or could do so. It would therefore be extremely unwise of the Russian Democrats to assume – as it almost seems that they do – an increasing interest in peace in Germany. I suspect, however, that the reason for their behaviour lies elsewhere entirely. I repeat, it does not lie, as some maintain, in the fear that, should they leave the Entente, there would be a Japanese attack on Russian possessions in Asia. At least, Russian Democracy would be very foolish to allow itself to be intimidated by this, and I cannot imagine that it does not know this itself. By acting in such a way, the Japanese government would draw the revenge of Russia on its head in any future instance of conflict, and would not be safe from the American threat from the rear. Japan knows this. The reason lies, essentially, in Russia's *domestic* political situation.

The socially reactionary elements of the Duma and of the provisional government, amongst which the large landowners figure prominently, must first secure *their own power position* within the country. To do this they need, first, to hold down the peasants who are demanding free distribution of private large landholdings, and secondly, they need *money*. The Democratic peasants can be held down by keeping them in

The Russian Revolution and the Peace 265

the trenches under the discipline of the generals. Money can only be obtained if Russia's own banks and big industrialists, or the Entente powers, provide it. Neither their own, nor foreign financial powers, will provide money except on condition that the radical and revolutionary peasants are suppressed, and the war continues. All government loans are primarily directed against the enemy within, who threatens its position of power, and not against the external enemy, who it knows will not attack it without provocation. This has been clearly shown by the information that has come to light on the most recent negotiations.[10] The Duma government continues the war *in order to stay in power*. The continuation of the war and that alone will enable the Russian plutocracy to falsify the elections to the constituent assembly to its advantage, should these elections really become unavoidable. The radical members do not have the strength, and more particularly they do not have the money and the credit-worthiness, to maintain themselves in power, should they form a government themselves. *For this reason* they tolerate the duplicity of the others and even go along with imperialist demonstrations. By doing this, they will, in the long run, dig their own graves.

All this places the *German* government in a difficult position when making public declarations on its war aims. At the moment these appear to lead *nowhere*. It is to be hoped, however, that it will do what is honest and *therefore* politically right, namely that it will declare that, on the basis of the most recent statement of the *entire government*, Germany *is prepared for an immediate peace with Russia*.[11]

Notes

1 [M–H] On 9 Apr./27 Mar. the Provisional Government published a statement in which, on the insistence of the Workers' and Soldiers' Council, the phrase 'no appropriation of alien territories by force' was inserted. See Reinhard Wittram, *Studien zum Selbstverständnis des 1. und 2. Kabinetts der russischen Provisorischen Regierung (März bis Juli 1917)* (Göttingen, 1971), p. 37 n. 43.
2 [M–H] Allusion to a press interview by the Russian Foreign Minister Miliukov, 8 Apr./27 Mar. Under the heading 'Miliukov on War Aims' the *Frankfurter Zeitung*, no. 98, 10 Apr. 1917, 1st morning edn, reproduced this interview.
3 [M–H] Under the heading 'Kerensky's War Aims', the *Frankfurter Zeitung*, no. 79, 21 Mar. 1917, evening edn, reported: 'In international politics Mr Kerensky seemed to be a lively supporter of the *internationalization of Constantinople*, of an *independent Poland* and of an *autonomous Armenia* under Russian protection.' In a statement of 5 May/22 Apr. the Provisional

Government announced that: 'By the terms "*sanctions and guarantees*" for a lasting peace, it understood *disarmament, international* courts, etc.' *Frankfurter Zeitung*, no. 125, 7 May 1917, morning edn.

4 [M–H] Presumably Weber is here referring to a speech given by Miliukov on 4 May/21 Apr., published in the *Frankfurter Zeitung*, no. 124, 6 May 1917, 1st morning edn, in which, amongst other things, he said: 'Citizens! When I heard that demonstrators had this morning displayed banners reading "Down with Miliukov!" I did not fear for Miliukov, but for Russia. What will the envoys of our allies say? This very day they will dispatch telegrams to their governments with the message that Russia has betrayed its allies and has removed itself from the list of allies. The Provisional Government cannot adopt this standpoint. *Russia will never agree to a separate peace.*'

5 [M–H] The *Frankfurter Zeitung*, no. 125, 7 May 1917, evening edn, published the following declaration by Rodzianko, to which Weber is presumably referring: 'Russia *cannot and must not abandon the war. Russia must be absolutely victorious.* Russia cannot break with her allies.'

6 [M–H] See List of Parties and Associations.

7 [M–H] Weber is referring to Haller, *Russische Gefahr* [see above, PD n. 7], p. 80 n. 1.

8 [M–H] The Ukrainian Central Rada, formed on 4 Mar. 1917 by bourgeois and socialist nationalists, advocated autonomy for the Ukraine. Kerensky had backed this demand in the Duma. The Rada thanked him in a telegram of 6 Mar. and at the same time expressed the hope that Kerensky would now make every effort to ensure that the political demand for autonomy was achieved. See Browder and Kerensky, *Documents*, vol. 1, p. 370 [see above, PD n. 2].

9 [M–D] In 'A' (the original text published in the *Berliner Tageblatt*) there follows the editorial note: 'We are unable to agree with this conclusion. The Editors.'

10 [M–H] Reference to negotiations on the so-called 'Freedom Bond' and American credit. See Browder and Kerensky, *Documents*, vol. 1, p. 161, vol. 2, pp. 487ff and 500ff. In its issue 109 of 21 Apr. 1917, 2nd morning edn, the *Frankfurter Zeitung* reported on the commencement of subscriptions to the Russian 'Freedom Bond'.

11 [M–H] Presumably a reference to the Provisional Government's statement of 4 May/21 Apr. and that of the Petersburg Workers and Soldiers Council of 5 May/22 Apr., in which abandonment of the aim of conquest of foreign territories and the willingness to conclude peace on the basis of the self-determination of nations was reaffirmed. Cf. Wolfgang Steglich, *Die Friedenspolitik der Mittelmächte 1917/18* [The Peace Policy of the Central Powers], vol. 1 (Wiesbaden, 1964), pp. 90f.

Political Parties and Associations in Russia, 1905-1906

Compiled by Dittmar Dahlmann

Bund (General Jewish Workers League in Lithuania, Poland and Russia)
Founded 25-7 November 1897 in Vilna. Aimed to achieve a federal, socialist republic; organized as a mass party, but as an autonomous body it was a member of the RSDRP (q.v.).

Constitutional Democratic Party (Official title: Party of Popular Freedom; commonly known as Kadets)
Founded 12-18 October 1905. Second party conference 5-11 January 1906; advocated a new order for Russia on the Western constitutional model; strongest party in the First Duma, with 179 deputies.

Labour Group (Trudovaia Gruppa or Trudoviki)
Founded late April 1906. Coalition of those radical peasant deputies, Social Democrats and Socialist Revolutionaries who did not observe their parties' election boycott; chiefly represented the interests of the peasants; in the First Duma it had at first 96, and later 107 deputies; first party conference 3-7 October 1906.

League of Russian People (or Men) (Soiuz Russkikh Liudei)
Founded spring 1905. Extreme right-wing, antisemitic organization, which, in autumn 1905, called for the formation of militia units to oppose the revolution.

League of Zemstvo Constitutionalists
Founded 17-20 November 1905 in Moscow. Right-wing organization of the landowning nobility. The association, which made an unsuccessful attempt to gain the allegiance of landowners from outside the nobility, had faded into insignificance by May 1906.

Party of Legal Order
Founded 15 October 1905 in St Petersburg. Emerged from the St Petersburg City Duma; conservative party situated on the extreme right fringe of the bourgeois parties; dissolved in 1907.

Party of Peaceful Renewal
Founded July 1906. In the Duma, the left wing of the Union of 17 October and the right wing of the Constitutional Democratic Party merged to form the 'Fraktion' (Parliamentary Party) of Peaceful Renewal; constituted as a party on 11 August 1906; represented by 29 deputies in the First Duma.

Peasant League (Krestianskii Soiuz)
Came into being in the spring or early summer of 1905 as an illegal organization linked with the Socialist Revolutionary Party (q.v.); in late July/early August and in November 1905 the Peasant League held two congresses in Moscow; actively involved in the peasant riots of autumn 1905 to spring 1906; in the course of 1906 it ceased to have any political significance.

Russian Social Democratic Workers Party (RSDRP)
Founded 1-3 March 1898. At the party conference in London in 1903 the party split into Mensheviks and Bolsheviks; it was reunified at the Stockholm party conference in April 1906; the final split came in 1912; at first it boycotted the Duma elections, but at the party conference of 1906 the boycott was abandoned; in the First Duma, in June 1906, a Social Democratic 'Fraktion' (Parliamentary Party) of 16 deputies was constituted.

Socialist Revolutionary Party
Founded winter 1901-2. Socialist party in the tradition of the Narodniki; first party conference late 1905/early 1906. Boycotted the elections to the First Duma.

Trade and Industry Party
Founded 12 November 1905 in Moscow. Right-wing party representing the industrial bourgeoisie and led by G. A. Krestovnikov; for the Duma elections of March 1906 it formed an alliance with the Union of 17 October; represented by one deputy in the First Duma.

Union of 17 October (Octobrists)
Founded 10 and 14 November 1905 in Moscow and St Petersburg; first party conference 8–12 February 1906; based on Manifesto of 17 October; conservative party which comprised the right wing of the zemstvo movement and the industrial bourgeoisie; represented in the First Duma by, at first, more than 20, later by 13 deputies.

Union of Liberation (Soiuz Osvobozhdeniia)
Founded unofficially 2–5 January 1904. Left liberal organization, operating to some degree in exile; formed the left wing of the bourgeois opposition movement.

Union of the Russian People (Soiuz Russkogo Naroda)
Founded November 1905. In 1905–6 the Union absorbed the great majority of the rightist groups and became the strongest group on the political right; antisemitic; organized the 'Black Hundreds' (combat units); the Union was disbanded in 1907.

Union of Unions (Soiuz Soiuzov)
Founded 8–9 May 1905. Organization of trade or professional unions, especially of the radical intelligentsia. The individual unions had a large measure of autonomy; partly socialist, partly radical-liberal; after the strike of October 1905 the Union lost its importance.

References

Note: Dates in square brackets in the Introduction denote original year of publication.

Anderson, Perry 1974: *Lineages of the Absolutist State*. London: New Left Books.
Antoni, Carlo 1962: *From History to Sociology: The Transition in German Historical Thinking*, tr. Hayden V. White. London: Merlin Press.
Ascher, Abraham 1992: *The Revolution of 1905: Authority Restored*. California: Stanford University Press.
—— 1988: *The Revolution of 1905: Russia in Disarray*. California: Stanford University Press.
Ash, Timothy Garton 1990: Eastern Europe: the year of truth. *New York Review of Books*, 15 Feb., 17–22.
Ashworth, Clive, and Dandeker, Christopher 1987: Warfare, social theory and West European development. *Sociological Review*, 35 (1), 1–18.
Baehr, Peter 1989: Weber and Weimar. The 'Reich-President' proposals. *Politics*, 9 (1), 20–5.
—— 1988: Max Weber as a critic of Bismarck. *European Journal of Sociology*, 29 (1), 149–64.
Baehr, Peter, and O'Brien, Mike 1994: Founders, classics and the concept of a canon. *Current Sociology*, 41 (1), 1–151.
Beetham, David 1989: Max Weber and the liberal political tradition. *European Journal of Sociology*, 30 (2), 311–23.
—— 1985: *Max Weber and the Theory of Modern Politics*. Cambridge: Polity Press.
Bellamy, Richard 1992: *Liberalism and Modern Society*. Pennsylvania: Penn State University Press.
Breuer, Stefan 1992: Soviet communism and Weberian sociology, tr. John Blazek. *Journal of Historical Sociology*, 5 (3), 267–90.

References

Collins, Randall 1986: *Weberian Sociological Theory*. Cambridge: Cambridge University Press.
—— 1981: Long-term social change and the territorial power of states. In idem, *Sociology since Midcentury: Essays in Theory Cumulation*. New York: Academic Press.
—— 1978: Some principles of long-term social change: the territorial power of states. In Louis Kriesberg (ed.), *Research in Social Movements, Conflicts, and Change*, vol. 1. Greenwich, Conn.: JAI Press.
Doctorow, Gilbert S. 1975: The government program of 17 October 1905. *Russian Review*, 34, 123–36
Fleischhauer, Ingeborg 1979: The agrarian program of the Russian Constitutional Democrats. *Cahiers du monde Russe et Soviétique*, 20, 173–99.
Gellner, Ernest 1992–3: The price of velvet: on Thomas Masaryk and Vaclav Havel. *Telos*, 94, 183–92.
Giddens, Anthony 1972: *Politics and Sociology in the Thought of Max Weber*. London: Macmillan.
Greenberg, Martin 1993: A defense of translation. *New Criterion*, 2 (9), 24–32.
Harcave, Sidney 1964: *First Blood: The Russian Revolution of 1905*. New York: Macmillan.
Hennis, Wilhelm 1988: *Max Weber: Essays in Reconstruction*, tr. Keith Tribe. London: Allen and Unwin.
Hinkle, Gisela J. 1986: The Americanization of Max Weber. *Central Perspectives in Social Theory*, 7, 87–104.
Hintze, Otto 1975: Military organization and the organization of the state. In idem, *The Historical Essays of Otto Hintze*, ed. with an Introduction by Felix Gilbert; tr. Felix Gilbert and Robert M. Berdahl. New York: Oxford University Press, 180–215.
Hirst, Paul 1991: The state, civil society and the collapse of Soviet communism. *Economy and Society*, 20 (2), 217–42.
Hobsbawm, E. J. 1973: *The Age of Revolution*. London: Cardinal.
Hutton, Will 1994: Markets threaten democracy's fabric. *Manchester Guardian Weekly*, 16 Jan., 21.
Jones, Robert A. 1983: The New History of Sociology. *Annual Review of Sociology*, 9, 447–69.
Kennedy, Paul 1988: *The Rise and Fall of the Great Powers*. London: Unwin Hyman.
Kimball, Alan, and Ulmen, Gary 1991: Weber on Russia. *Telos*, 88, 187–204.
Koselleck, Reinhart 1985: *Begriffsgeschichte* and Social History. In idem, *Futures Past: On the Semantics of Historical Time*, tr. Keith Tribe. Cambridge, Mass.: MIT Press, 73–91.
Lapidus, Gail W., and Zaslavsky, Victor, with Goldman, Philip (eds) 1992: *From Union to Commonwealth: Nationalism and Separatism in the Soviet Republics*. Cambridge: Cambridge University Press.
Lenin, Vladimir I. 1967: Lecture on the 1905 Revolution. In idem, *Selected Works*, vol. 1. Moscow: Progress Publishers, 778–802.

—— 1964: Can 'Jacobinism' frighten the working class? In idem, *Collected Works*, vol. 25. Moscow: Progress Publishers, 120–1.
Mann, Michael 1986: *The Sources of Social Power*, vol. 1: *A History of Power from the Beginning to AD 1760*. Cambridge: Cambridge University Press.
Merleau-Ponty, Maurice 1973: *Adventures of the Dialectic*, tr. Joseph Bien. London: Heinemann.
Michnik, Adam 1990: My vote against Walesa. *New York Review of Books*, 20 Dec., 47–50.
Mommsen, Wolfgang J. 1984: *Max Weber and German Politics, 1890–1920*, tr. Michael S. Steinberg. Chicago: University of Chicago Press.
—— 1974: *The Age of Bureaucracy: Perspectives on the Political Sociology of Max Weber*. Oxford: Basil Blackwell.
Mommsen, Wolfgang J., and Dahlmann, Dittmar 1989a: Einleitung (= Introduction). In Max Weber 1989: 1–54.
—— 1989b: Editorischer Bericht (= Editorial Report for Bourgeois Democracy in Russia). In Max Weber 1989: 71–80.
—— 1989c: Editorischer Bericht (= Editorial Report for Russia's Transition to Pseudo-constitutionalism). In Max Weber 1989: 281–92.
Murvar, Vatro 1984: Max Weber and the two nonrevolutionary events in Russia 1917: scientific achievements or prophetic failures? In Ronald M. Glassman and Vatro Murvar (eds), *Max Weber's Political Sociology: A Pessimistic Vision of a Rationalized World*. London: Greenwood Press, 237–72.
Oakes, Guy 1982: Methodological ambivalence: the case of Max Weber. *Social Research*, 49 (3), 589–615.
Parkin, Frank 1982: *Max Weber*. Chichester: Ellis-Horwood; London: Tavistock.
Perrie, Maureen 1972: The Russian peasant movement of 1905–1907: its social composition and revolutionary significance. *Past and Present*, 57, 123–55.
Pipes, Richard 1954–5: Max Weber and Russia. *World Politics*, 7, 371–401.
Rigby, Thomas Henry 1980: A conceptual approach to authority, power and policy in the Soviet Union. In T. H. Rigby, Archie Brown and Peter Reddaway (eds), *Authority, Power and Policy in the USSR*. New York: St Martin's Press, 9–31.
Röhl, John C. G., and Sombart, Nicolaus (eds) 1982: *Kaiser Wilhelm II. New Interpretations*. Cambridge: Cambridge University Press.
Roth, Guenther 1992: Interpreting and translating Max Weber. *International Sociology*, 7 (4), 449–59.
Runciman, Walter G. (ed.) 1978: *Max Weber: Selections in Translation*, tr. Eric Matthews. Cambridge: Cambridge University Press.
Scaff, Lawrence A. 1989: *Fleeing the Iron Cage: Culture, Politics, and Modernity in the Thought of Max Weber*. Berkeley and Los Angeles: University of California Press.
—— 1984: From political economy to political sociology: Max Weber's early writings. In Ronald M. Glassman and Vatro Murvar, *Max Weber's Political Sociology: A Pessimistic Vision of a Rationalized World*. London: Greenwood Press, 83–107.

References 273

Scaff, Lawrence A., and Arnold, Thomas Clay. 1985: Class and the theory of history: Marx on France and Weber on Russia. In Robert J. Antonio and Ronald M. Glassman (eds), *A Weber–Marx Dialogue*. Kansas: University Press of Kansas, 190–214.
Schluchter, Wolfgang 1979: Value-neutrality and the ethic of responsibility, tr. Guenther Roth. In Guenther Roth and Wolfgang Schluchter, *Max Weber's View of History: Ethics and Methods*. Berkeley and Los Angeles: University of California Press, 65–116.
Skocpol, Theda 1979: *States and Social Revolutions: A Comparative Analysis of France, Russia, and China*. Cambridge: Cambridge University Press.
Suny, Ronald 1992: State, civil society, and ethnic cultural consolidation in the USSR – roots of the national question. In Lapidus et al. 1992, 22–44.
Szamuely, Tibor 1974. *The Russian Tradition*, ed. with an Introduction by Robert Conquest. London: Secker and Warburg.
Tribe, Keith 1989: Prussian Agriculture – German Politics: Max Weber 1892–7. In Keith Tribe (ed.), *Reading Weber*. London: Routledge, 85–130.
Warren, Mark 1988: Max Weber's liberalism for a Nietzschean world. *American Political Science Review*, 82 (1), 31–50.
Weber, Marianne 1988, 2nd edn [1st English edn 1975]: *Max Weber: A Biography*, tr. Harry Zohn, with a new introduction by Guenther Roth. New Jersey: Transaction.
Weber, Max 1989: *Zur Russischen Revolution von 1905. Schriften und Reden 1905–1912*. In *Max Weber Gesamtausgabe*, I/10, ed. Wolfgang J. Mommsen in collaboration with Dittmar Dahlmann. Tübingen: J. C. B. Mohr [Paul Siebeck].
—— 1986: The Reich President, tr. Gordon C. Wells. *Social Research*, 52 (1), 128–32.
—— 1984a: *Zur Politik im Weltkrieg. Schriften und Reden 1914–1918*. In *Max Weber Gesamtausgabe*, I/15, ed. Wolfgang J. Mommsen in collaboration with Gangolf Hübinger. Tübingen: J. C. B. Mohr [Paul Siebeck].
—— 1984b: Deutschland unter den europäischen Weltmächten. In Max Weber 1984a: 161–94.
—— 1978a, 2nd edn [1st English language edn 1968]: *Economy and Society*, ed. Guenther Roth and Claus Wittich. Berkeley: University of California Press.
—— 1978b, 2nd edn [1st English language edn 1968]: Parliament and government in a reconstructed Germany, tr. Guenther Roth. In *Economy and Society*, ed. Guenther Roth and Claus Wittich. Berkeley: University of California Press, 1381–469.
—— 1977: *Critique of Stammler*, tr., with an introductory essay, Guy Oakes. New York: Free Press.
—— 1976: *The Agrarian Sociology of Ancient Civilizations*, tr. R. I. Frank. London: Verso.
—— 1971: Socialism. In J. E. T. Eldridge (ed.), *Max Weber: The Interpretation of Social Reality*. London: Thomas Nelson, 191–219.

—— 1949a: 'Objectivity' in social science and social policy. In Edward A. Shils and Henry A. Finch (eds and trs), *The Methodology of the Social Sciences*. New York: Free Press, 49–112.

—— 1949b: The meaning of 'ethical neutrality' in sociology and economics. In Edward A. Shils and Henry A. Finch (eds and trs), *The Methodology of the Social Sciences*. New York: Free Press, 1–47.

—— 1948a: Capitalism and rural society in Germany, tr. C. W. Seidenadel. In H. H. Gerth and C. W. Mills (eds and trs), *From Max Weber*. London: Routledge, 363–85.

—— 1948b: Politics as a vocation. In H. H. Gerth and C. W. Mills (eds and trs), *From Max Weber*. London: Routledge, 77–128.

—— 1947: *The Theory of Social and Economic Organization*, ed., with an introduction, Talcott Parsons; tr. A. M. Henderson and Talcott Parsons. New York: Free Press.

—— 1930: *The Protestant Ethic and the Spirit of Capitalism*, tr. Talcott Parsons. London: Unwin University Books.

Wolin, Sheldon S. 1981: Max Weber: legitimation, method, and the politics of theory. *Political Theory*, 9 (3), 401–24.

Zaslavsky, Victor. 1992: Nationalism and democratic transition in postcommunist societies. *Daedalus* (Special number on The Exit from Communism), 121 (2), 97–121.

Glossary

Compiled by Dittmar Dahlmann

arkhierei. Church dignitary; bishop, archbishop, metropolitan.

arteli. (See kustar.)

ataman. Elected leader of the Don Cossacks, later appointed by the Imperial Russian government.

Black Gangs. (See Chernye sotni.)

Bulygin Duma. This was intended, by manifesto and statute of 6 August 1905, as an Imperial Duma with solely advisory functions, and was to be formed on the basis of an indirect curial electoral system, which was based on a census (q.v.) measured by taxation level. Named after the Interior Minister A. G. Bulygin, who led the commission which worked out the statutes of the Duma.

bunt. Uprising, revolt.

Byt po semu. Let it be so! formula of confirmation or authorization.

Caesaropapism. The combination of State and Church rule, in which the secular ruler is granted the supreme leadership of the Church, including internal Church affairs, also on the basis of his divine consecration. From the 18th century the concept was applied especially to the late Roman and Byzantine ecclesiastical system, in which the spiritual and secular Empires were unified. It was and is applied also to the Russian situation, especially since the abolition of the Patriarchate by Peter I (1721) and the institution of the Holy Synod as state body for the control of the Church.

census (Russian: *tsenz*). Qualification for the franchise by wealth or property.

Chernye sotni. Black hundreds. Term for the right-wing radical fighting units which were active from spring 1905 and had the covert approval of the government. Used both pejoratively and by the members themselves. Frequently also used for the whole political right.

chernyi peredel (literally: black redistribution). Distribution of the land to working people of the whole country. Term for the group founded by G. Plekhanov within the party 'zemlia i volia' (1878–81), which rejected terrorist actions (see also Narodnichestvo).

Chin. Rank. In the 18th and 19th centuries the rank of a soldier or of a government official according to the 'Tabel o rangakh' of Peter the Great in 1722, who classified the military, court officials and civil servants into 14 categories of rank.

Chinovnik. Possessor of 'chin' (see above). Official; also, pejorative, bureaucrat.

deiateli. Men in public life; those active in society.

desiatina. Desiatin: Russian area measure = 1.09 hectares.

dopolnenie. Supplement (see next entry).

dopolnitelnyi nadel. Share of land which needed to be added to the peasants' land to enable them to subsist.

Duma. Originally: idea or thought; then: advice; finally: a group or assembly of advisers. Gorodskaia duma: City Duma; from 1870 (altered 1892) the City Duma was elected by a census franchise. The City Duma elected the mayor. Its tasks were principally restricted to economic, medical and educational problems. From 1906 also the term for the Russian parliament: Gosudarstvennaia Duma (Imperial or State Duma). (See also Bulygin Duma, Soiuznaia Duma.)

dvornik. Caretaker, porter.

edinovertsi. Those members of the Old Believers who accepted priests; between 1788 and 1800 they concluded agreements with the Orthodox Church in which the right was granted to them to hold services according to the old rites and use the books printed before the Nikon reform of 1654–5. (See also Raskol, Old Believers.)

Eparchie. Diocese.

glasnyi. Member of the local self-governing body. Member of the city council elected by the qualified city assembly (by the statutes on local self-government of 1879 and 1892). Zemskii glasnyi: member of the zemstvo assembly elected according to the zemstvo statutes of 1864 and 1890.

Glossary 277

Holy Synod (Sviateishii Sinod). From 1721 the supreme administrative organ of the Russian Orthodox Church.

iavochnyi poriadok (literally: without previous permission). The meaning is that the founding of unions or associations no longer required previous permission from the authorities; they merely had to hand in their statutes subsequently for approval by the authorities. This also applied to newspapers and periodicals.

Kadets. Constitutional Democratic Party (see List of Parties and Associations).

krai. Region, border area.

kramola. Conspiracy, uprising or revolt.

Krestianskii pozemelnyi bank. Peasant Bank or Peasant Land Bank. Mortgage bank founded by the state on the basis of the law of 18 May 1882; its aim was to enable peasants to acquire land – individually or in groups, by granting favourable credit. The loans, up to 75 per cent of the value of the land, ran for a period of 24½ or 34½ years; the interest rate was 2.75 per cent.

kulak (literally: 'fist'). Peasant owning large farm, also rural profiteer.

kustar. Peasant who engages in home industry. The kustar industry was of great importance in Russia, especially in the textile, metal and wood industries. Frequently the kustari joined together to form arteli, voluntary cooperative organizations, which had an elected elder at their head.

Marshal of the Nobility. By the laws of 1775 and 1785 the nobility of each province formed the Society of the Nobility (*dvorianskoe obshchestvo*), which elected the provincial Marshal. There was also a Marshal of the Nobility at district (uezd) level. The Marshals of the Nobility were responsible for important functions in the administration of the provinces and districts, and from the time of the institution of the zemstvo in 1864 were *ex officio* members of the zemstvo assemblies.

mir. Peasant commune, which administered its own affairs. Unlike the term obshchina (q.v.), refers to the people, rather than the institution.

nadel. Share of commune land which has been given to a peasant family for their use.

narodnaia rada. Popular council.

narodnaia volia (The People's Will). Organization founded in the 1870s by a section of the Narodniki, which aimed to bring about a revolution in Russia by means of terror. The most prominent victim of this movement was Tsar Alexander II, in 1881.

Narodnichestvo. Movement within the Russian intelligentsia from the 1870s (Populism). Political education was to be carried out by means of propaganda amongst the people (*narod*), in order to bring about a change in conditions. The theories of the Narodnichestvo were based on the view that the germ of a social organization of society already existed in the form of the Russian mir, but also on modified Marxist ideas and on the ideas of Mill, Comte and Spencer. It was the view of the Narodniki that the formation of Western capitalism in Russia could be avoided because the mir already contained within it socialist forms of organization. At the end of the 1860s the activities of the Narodniki led to a mass 'going to the people' (*idti v narod*); this was eventually ended by a wave of arrests. From within the movement a clandestine organization 'zemlia i volia' was founded, which aimed to change society by actions of terrorism and conspiracy rather than peaceful propaganda. In 1879 'zemlia i volia' split into 'chernyi peredel' and 'narodnaia volia', a moderate and a radical wing.

Oberprokuror Sviateishego Sinoda. Chief Procurator of the Holy Synod. From 1722 government representative in the Holy Synod who at first had only to supervise the activity of this body of the Church leadership as state official, but after a short time became the minister in charge of Church administration. The office existed until 1917.

oblast. In Imperial Russia a territorial unit of administration corresponding to a province.

obrezki. Land which the peasants lost as a result of the Emancipation in 1861. After the 1861 reform the obrezki were taken away from the peasants' allotment of land in numerous provinces in instances where their allotment per head exceeded the size laid down for that region, or if the landowner was left with less than one-third of the good cultivable land for his use.

obrok. Before the Peasants' Emancipation of 1861, interest to be paid by the peasants to the landowner or the state in kind or in money.

obshchina. Peasant commune. The obshchina supervised the dividing of the communal land and of the pasture land and was, until 1903, collectively responsible for payment of taxes. It was also responsible for the maintenance of order in the village.

obshchinoe obshchestvo. Official title of the village commune as self-governing organization of the peasants.

Old Believers (Raskol). Raskol is the official term for the split in the Orthodox Church in the second half of the 17th century, in which the so-called Old Believers (*raskolniki* or *staroobriadtsy*), who maintained the old rites, split from the official Church. The Old Believers split later into one group which retained a sacerdotal

Glossary 279

order (*popovshchina*), and one group which rejected any form of sacerdotal order (*bezpopovshchina*). The latter split up into numerous sects.

Peasant (Land) Bank. (See Krestianskii pozemelnyi bank.)

peredel. Redistribution of the land.

potrebitelnaia norma. Norm of consumption, i.e. the basic unit of ownership necessary to secure the existence of a peasant family.

prigovor. Legal judgement. Also the decision of a village assembly: *prigovor selskogo skhoda*.

prisutstvie. In the official terminology of Imperial Russia, a permanent government institution which administered or supervised certain matters.

prodovolstvennaia norma. Subsistence norm.

Raskol. (See Old Believers.)

Raskolnik. Official term for the Old Believers up to the Edict of Toleration of 17 April 1905.

redemption payments. The regular payments that peasants were required to make in return for land received at the time of the Emancipation of the Peasants in 1861.

samoderzhavnyi. (See next entry.)

samoderzhets. One of the titles of the Russian monarch: autocrat.

selskoe obshchestvo. Official designation since 1861 of village commune.

Senat (Full name: Pravitelstvuiushchii Senat). Governing senate. Created in 1711 as the supreme Imperial Office for domestic administration and justice. After the judicial reform of 1864 the senate was mainly a court of cassation (appeal). It conducted the supervision of local administration and the courts, published the laws and was responsible for their interpretation. From 1898 it consisted of six departments.

skhod. Village assembly.

skreplenie. Counter-signature, certification, accreditation (by signature).

sobor. Council, assembly, also in the sense of church council.

Soiuznaia Duma. Federal assembly; intended as supreme representative organ in Dragomanov's 1884 constitutional draft.

Staroobriadchestvo. The Old Believer Movement.

Staroobriadchik. Old Believer; since the Edict of Toleration of 17 April 1905 the term 'Raskolnik' has been replaced by 'Staroobriadchik'.

Starost. Selskii starosta. The village head elected by the village commune after the Peasants' Emancipation of 1861.

Third Element. (See tretii element.)

tretii element. Literally: Third Element. Term for the zemstvo officials: doctors, statisticians etc., in the early 20th century, who belonged neither to the administration nor to the representatives of the estates in the zemstvo, and were regarded as particularly radical.

trudovaia norma. Work norm, i.e. the size of landownership which a peasant could work with the members of his family.

uezd. District, fairly small administrative unit within a province.

ukase (Russian: *ukaz*). Decree, order. An Imperial order having the force of law.

ulozhenie. Statutes; Code of Law.

uprava. Administrative body (see zemstvo).

usucapion. In Roman Law, acquisition of property by prior possession.

volost. After the Emancipation of the Peasants in 1861 several villages or hamlets were united into a volost, with a population of between 300 and 2,000 males.

volostnoi skhod. The volost assembly comprised both peasant representatives and officials elected by the peasants.

zakon. Law, statute.

zemlia i volia. (See Narodnichestvo.)

Zemskii Nachalnik. Land captain. Since the reform (on 12 June 1890) of the zemstvo statute of 1864, a government-appointed official – usually from the local nobility – who had control over the decisions of the obshchina. He possessed both legal and administrative functions.

Glossary

Zemskii Sobor. Imperial or provincial assembly. The term was coined by the Slavophile Konstantin Aksakov in 1850 and adopted by S. M. Solovev as an academic term.

zemstvo. Official designation: *zemskoe uchrezhdenie*. Organ of self-government in rural Russia created by statute of 1 January 1864 in 34 provinces of European Russia. The zemstvo was responsible for the building and repair of roads, development of local trade and industry, public education and medical provision for the population, veterinary provision, and assessment of taxation on local property. The district and provincial zemstvos held regular meetings to elect an executive body (for a period of 3 years) known as the *uprava* (board). The district and provincial Marshals of the Nobility were *ex officio* members of these boards. The chairmen of the upravas had to be approved by the Governor or Interior Minister. The deputies to the district zemstvo assembly were elected by the following groups of voters: (1) private owners of a certain minimum amount of land; (2) the village commune; and (3) urban owners according to a fixed census. In 1890, in the reign of Alexander III, the franchise was changed and a greater share of seats accorded to the noble landowners. From that time, too, all members of the upravas had to be approved by the Governor.

zubatovshchina. Term for the attempt undertaken at the end of the 19th and beginning of the 20th centuries by S. V. Zubatov, head of the Moscow department of Okhrana (secret police), with the approval of the government, to establish workers' organizations, chiefly in order to combat the influence of revolutionary propaganda. In 1903 the government put an end to this enterprise, which had met with strong resistance from the employers.

Index

Numbers in **bold** denote glossary entries. Numbers in *italics* indicate major section devoted to the subject.

Academic Congress, 166–8
Academic League, 165, 166
Agrarian Congress, 199–200
Agrarian Manifesto, 141(n195), 149, 209, 210
agrarian reform, 7, *75–101*; difficulties in implementation of, 7, 197, 199, 200–1; government and, 91, 92, 101, 141–2(n195), 208–10, 211–12, 225–6; Imperial Duma draft, 224–5, 226; land ownership, 86–8, 89–90, 91–2, 95–7, 101, 197–9, 202; and landowners, 97, 207–8, 209, 210, 211–12; measures needed for, 201–2; and the obshchina, 76–8, 83–4, 87–9, 92, 209; party programmes for *see* individual parties; Peasant League Congress, 94–7; peasants' demands for, 7, 93–4, 138(n176), 251; and Stolypin 13, 241, 257(n3)
Alexander II, 138(n169), 277
Alexander III, 80, 161, 163, 229
amnesty, 220–1, 222
army, 153, 253; mollification of by government, 8, 154–5; and Moscow uprising, 151
Austria-Hungary, 57, 123(n60), 244

banishment, 170, 171, 172, 211, 221
banks: and First World War, 250, 256; relationship with government, 15, 219, 220, 228, 248, 252, 254, 265

Beetham, David, 17
Black Gangs, 247, 248, 254, **275**
'black hundreds' (*Chernye sotni*), 104, 149, 204, 234(n6), **276**
Bolsheviks, 6, 13, 194, 217
bourgeoisie, 14, 45, 72, 73; creditworthiness of, 13, 242–3; and government, 18, 216; members, 5; 'petty', 7, 74; and Trade and Industry Party, 205, 206
budget, state, 182–3, 219
Bulgaria, 52, 121(nn45–6)
Bulygin Duma, 3–4, 43, 50, 71, **275**
Bulygin Electoral Law, 169, 184–6
Bund (Jewish League), 191, 204, **267**
Bureau of Trade Associations, 193–4
bureaucracy, 176–9, 180, 184, 220, 243

Caesaropapism, 63, 64, 124–5(n77), 128(n84), **275**
capitalism, 79, 86, 107–8; disadvantages of, 27, 49, 66, 81, 109, 110
censorship, 159–60
census, 48–51, 74, 185, 238(n47), **275**
Chernye sotni see 'black hundreds'
chernyi peredel (black redistribution) 79, 135(n147), **276**
Chkheidze, N. S., 13, 15, 252, 253, 258(n22), 263
Christian Fighting Brotherhood, 18, 126(n84)

Index 283

Church: and Christianity, 126-8(n84); priests, 64, 98, 125-6(n83), 141(nn188-9); and the State, 63-5; see also Caesaropapism; Orthodox Church
civil service, 93, 105, 176, 245, 251
Collins, Randall, 25, 37-8(n24)
Committee of Ministers, 175, 177
Congress of the Nobility, 208-9
Constitutional Democratic Party (Kadets), 2, 5, 6, 43; and agrarian reform, 19, 90-1, 100, 196-7, 199, 200, 202-3, 215; and Duma, 217, 223-4, 225, 226-7, 239-40(n65); and Duma elections, 8, 11, 146(n228), 207, 213, 215; formation, 45-6; party programme, 49, 53, 54, 63, 121-2(n48), 204; peasants' view of, 98, 218; in Provisional Government, 13, 262, 263; Second Congress, 195-6
Constitutional Draft see Union of Liberation
cossacks, 8, 154-5, 200
Council of Ministers, 183; reorganization of, 175-6, 177-8; and the Tsar, 10-11, 178
Council of Workers' Deputies (SRD), 69-70, 73, 74, 133(n115); formation, 69; and strike movement, 148-50

Dragomanov, M. P.: on self government, 48, 60, 243, 254, 257(n5)
Duma, 244, 254, 264, **276**; City 114(n3); dissolution of Second, 258(n17); and effect of universal franchise, 51-2; and Provisional Government, 14, 262; see also Bulygin Duma; Imperial Duma
Durnovo, I. N., 107, 144(n220), 149, 180, 187, 214; and repression policy, 8, 143(n211), 146(n228), 153, 154, 172
dvornik 74, 134-5(n137), **276**

Economy and Society (Weber), 20, 22, 25, 26, 33(n9)
Edict of Toleration, 65, 160, 162, 235(n15)
education see schools; universities

elections (First Imperial Duma), 11, 145-6(n228), *191-213*, 215; analysis of results, 213-14; background of parties, 195-202, 203-7; boycott of, 191, 195; campaigning, 187-8; and electoral law, 184-6; and government, 188, 219; Kadet success in, 8, 11, 213, 215; and peasantry, 98-100, 185, 189-91, 214, 218-19, 238(n47); registration, 188-9
electoral process, 99; and Bulygin Duma, 50-1; Bulygin Electoral Law, 169, 184-6; census franchise, 9, 49-50, 238(n47); extension of franchise, 9; and universal franchise, 48, 49, 51-2, 121(n39)
emergency laws, 170-1
executions, 157

factory owners, 215-16
First World War, 12, 244; and bank credit, 250, 256; and control of peasantry, 14-15, 248-9, 252-3, 256, 265; Germany and, 2, 12, 246, 255-6, 263; Provisional Government and, 14-15, 253, 256, 261-3, 265, 266(n11)
franchise see electoral process
Fundamental Laws (1906), 9, 174, 184, 216, 217, 220

Gapon, Father George, 73, 126(n84), 134(n128)
George, Henry, 79, 135(n148)
Germany, 170, 236(n27), 237(n38); and agriculture, 19, 97; Army Bill, 106, 143(n213); comparisons with Russia, 17-20; and First World War, 2, 12, 246, 255-6, 263; and liberalism, 19-20, 107, 129(n85); and the Poles, 62, 124(n72), 253; rule of Wilhelm II, 121(n47), 177, 236(n32); universities, 236(n24); view of Russia, 232-3
government (1905-6), 181; and agrarian policy, 91, 92, 101, 141-2(n195), 208-9, 211-12, 225-6; mollification of army, 8; and October Manifesto, 8; relationship with banks, 15, 219, 220, 228, 248; relationship with Duma, 9, 221,

government (*Cont.*)
  222–3, 224–7, 229–30; repression policy, 8, 146(n228), 153–4, 155–7, 229, 230; and students, 164–6; and zemstvos, 42, 47–8, 72, 106–7, 212–13; *see also* Council of Ministers
Guchkov, A. J., 203, 204, 208, 250, 254, 262

Herzen, A., 67, 131(n105), 239(n63)
Heyden, Count, 115(n6), 216, 222, 224, 226

Imperial Council, 178, 209, 227, 237(n42); composition, 175, 146(n229), 181; and Duma, 9, 158, 181, 225; Shipov proposal for, 179
Imperial Duma, 8, 20, 72, 106, 175; agrarian draft, 224–5, 226; conflicting ideas within, 225–6; constitutional rights of, *181–4*; dissolution of, 11, 227, 230; elections to *see* elections; and Imperial Council, 9, 158, 181, 225; and Imperial Manifesto, 227–8; and October Manifesto, 4, 9, 51, 158; opening address, 173, 220–2; and peasantry, 50, 120(n36), 217–18, 222; programme, 222; relationship with government, 9, 219, 221, 222–3, 224–7, 229–30
Imperial Manifesto, 227–8
industry, 13, 14, 206; *see also* Trade and Industry Party
intelligentsia, 14, 20, 70–1, 82, 93; disunity within, 71, 107, 108; and Duma elections, 185, 190; and zemstvos, 71, 89; *see also* Third Element
Interior, Ministry of, 105, 149, 153 *see also* Durnovo, I. N.
Iskra, 66, 130(n96, 98)

Jacobinism, 33(n7), 89
Jewish League (Bund), 191, 204, **267**
Jews, 142(n203), 151, 223, 239(n62)

Kadets *see* Constitutional Democratic Party
Kautsky, K., 140(n184), 160
Kerensky, A. F. 13, 15, 248, 253,
  258(n22), 261, 263
Khrustalev-Nosar, G. S., 70, 133(n118), 150
Kovalevskii, Maxim, 72, 203
Kulaks 19, 50, 82, 88, 97, **277**
kustar 79, 85, **277**

Labour Group *see* Trudovaia Gruppa
land captains (*Zemskie Nachalniki*), 93, 98, 138(n173), 191, **280**
landowners, 50, 82, 88, 97; and agrarian reform, 97, 207–8, 209, 210, 211–12; Moscow Congress of, 137(n162); and peasantry, 50, 82, 210, 249
language, 57, 59, 60–2, 162–3
Lavrov, P., 67, 86, 131(n106)
laws, 174–5, 176
League of Russian People, 234(n10), **267**
League of Zemstvo Constitutionalists 41, 45, **268**
Lenin, V. I., 4, 5, 24, 33(n7); and RSDRP, 66, 67, 68, 130(n96)
liberalism, Russian, 101–2, 108, 143–4(n214); failure of, 23, 106; obstacles to, 5, 6–7, 17–18; vocation, 108; and zemstvos, 6
literature, 160

Manifesto of 17 October *see* October Manifesto
Martov, L., 66, 130(n96)
Marxism, 27, 108, 131(n103); Weber and 16, 17, 21, 23–4
meetings: banning of during Duma elections, 188; and Law of Assembly, 169–70
Mensheviks *see* Plekhanov, G. V.
Mikhailovskii, N. K., 82, 85, 86, 115(n6)
Miliukov, P., 64, 72, 253–4; and Constitutional Democratic Party, 46, 200, 239(n65); and First World War, 241, 256(n2), 261–2, 263; and Provisional Government, 13, 14, 241
Ministry of the Interior, 105, 149, 153 *see also* Durnovo, I. N.
mir 35(14)n, **277**; *see also* obshchina
monarchists, 216–17, 252
Moscow: armed uprising (1905), 102,

103, 142(n197), 148, 151–2, 233(n2); lockout, 193, 206; worker movement in, 193

Nachalo, 68, 132–3(nn109–10, 114)
nadels, 90, 137(n159), **277**
narodnaia volia (The People's Will), 79, 135(n147), **277**
Narodnichestvo (Populism), 67, 79, 93, 115(n6), 202, 218, **278**; and agrarian reform 80, 82–4, 85–6
nationalities problem, 6, *54–63*, 124(n71), 254, 259(n30); disunity over, 54–8, 59, 60; *see also* Poland; Ukraine
newspapers: censorship of, 159–60
Nicholas II, Tsar, 3, 149; and constitutional draft, 53; and Duma, 20, 220–1; failings, 14, 233, 244–5, 246–7; and October Manifesto, 4, 152; and peasantry, 7, 50, 80, 208–9, 221; relationship with Council of Ministers, 10–11, 178; removal of, 13, 26, 241, 245–6, 247, 252; and Witte, 152, 245, 248
Nikolaevich, Grand Duke Nikolai, 244, 257(n9)
Novaia Zhizn, 68, 132(n109)

Objectivity in Social Science and Social Policy (Weber), 16
obshchina, 18, 209, 211, **278**; and census franchise, 49; functions, 35–6(n14); influence of, 76–7; opposition to, 209–10; party programmes and, 76–8, 82, 83–5, 87–9, 138(n171); peasants' attitude to, 19, 92, 210
October Manifesto, 4, 102, 104, 151, 152, 154, 181; failings, 9–10, 122(n52), 173; promises, 116(n12), *158–73*, 233(nl), academic freedom, 163–4, extension of franchise, 51, 185, freedom of assembly, 169–70, freedom of conscience, 160–2, freedom of speech, 159–60, inviolability of person, 170–2, and languages, 162–3, and creation of a good impression abroad, 8, 153, 158
Old Believers (Raskol), 65, 146(n228), 161, 162, **278–9**
Orthodox Church, 128(n84); and October Manifesto, 160–2; and Patriarch, 63–4; resistance to liberalism, 6, 18, 65; *see also* Old Believers
Osvobozhdenie, 42, 115(n8)

Party of Democratic Reform, 203
Party of Legal Order, 11, 46, 74, 215, **268**; policies, 59, 104, 123(n63), 206–7
Party of Peaceful Renewal, 224, 239(n64), **268**
passport system, 77–8, 135(n144), 171, 173
Patriarch, chair of, 63–4
Peasant Land Bank, 101, 141(n195), 197, 201, 202, 212, 222, **277**
Peasant League, 70, 72, 139(nn178–9), 187, 191, **268**; Congress (1905), 94–7, 150
peasantry, 101, 218–19, 232; anti-bureaucracy, 98–9; and census franchise, 49–51; control of during First World War, 14–15, 248–9, 252–3, 256, 265; demands of, 7, 93–4, 138(n176), 251; and Duma, 50, 120(n36), 217–18, 222; and Duma elections, 98–100, 185, 189-91, 214, 218–19, 238(n47); and land ownership, 86–8, 89–90, 91–2, 95–7, 197–9, 202, 249; and obschchina, 18, 35–6(n14), 76–7, 92, 209, 210–11; riots, 149–50, 207, 211, 234(n4); rise of resistance amongst, 95, *see also* Peasant League; split of under Stolypin's reform, 13, 241–2; suppression of, 191, 211–12, 264–5; and Tsar, 7, 50, 80, 208–9, 221; *see also* agrarian reform
People's Will, The (*narodnaia volia*), 79, 135(n147), **277**
periodicals: censorship of, 159–60
Peshekhonov, A. V., 84, 86, 87–8, 89
Petersburg Soviet *see* Council of Workers' Deputies
Petrograd Soviet, 13, 14, 15, 262, 263
Petrunkevich, Ivan I, 41, 114(n6), 221, 226, 240(n67)

Plehve, V. K., 73, 93, 102, 103, 119(n29); and zemstvos, 41, 44, 48, 115(n7)

Plekhanov, G. V., 66, 68, 132(n114), 251; dispute with Lenin, 66, 130(n96), 217; and Mensheviks, 67, 68, 131(n102), 194

Poland, 72, 259(n26); and autonomy, 54–6, 57, 58–9, 60–1, 104, 122(n55), 253, 259(n26); imposition of martial law, 149, 150, 204; language, 163

police, 74, 111, 171; mollification of by government, 8, 154; tyranny of, 47, 190–1, 229, 230, 231, 247

Populism *see* Narodnichestvo

priests, 64, 98, 125–6(n83), 148(nn188–9)

Prime Minister: enhancement of power, 10, 177, 178

Protestant Ethic and the Spirit of Capitalism (Weber), 16, 17, 36(n20)

Provisional Government, 13; finance obtainment, 248, 254, 258(n19); and First World War, 14–15, 253, 256, 261–3, 265, 266(n11); nationalities question, 254, 259(n26, 31)

PSR *see* Socialist Revolutionary Party

Raskol *see* Old Believers

Red Terror, 105, 153, 180, 187

redemption payments, 75, 101, 209, **279**

RSDRP (Russian Social Democratic Workers' Party), 66, 72, 150, 250, 255, **268**; and agrarian reform, 67, 80, 89, 138(n171); and Duma elections, 11, 41, 191, 195, 211, 217; and Federal Council, 68, 131–2 (n107); formation of Fraktion, 218; split, 66–9, 130(n96), 217; and Stockholm Congress, 194–5

Russia, 18, 110–11; Collins on, 25, 37–8(n24); comparisons with Germany, 17–20; as 'debtor state', 8–9, 151; obstacles to liberalism in, 17–18; parallels between 1905 and present, 25–6; prospects, 27–8

Russian Social Democratic Workers' Party *see* RSDRP

schools, 57, 62–3, 120(n30), 163

Second Element 5, 33(n9), 45, 118(n23)

Shipov, D. N., 44, 49, 149, 179, 203, 204, 207, 239(n65)

Slavophiles, 43, 60, 79, 103, 105, 175, 179, 180

Social Democracy, 21, 69, 110

Social Democratic Party *see* RSDRP

Social Democrats *see* RSDRP

Socialist Revolutionaries, 13, 69; and agrarian reform, 78–9, 82–7, 88–9, 90, 91, 94–7, 202, 203; and Duma, 191, 217, 223; extreme, 73, 93, 102; and Provisional Government, 72, 252

Socialist Revolutionary Party (PSR), 80, 135–6(n150), **268**; and agrarian reform, 80, 81–2, 83–4, 94; programme of, 136(n151)

Solovev, V. S., 52, 60, 121(n42)

SRD *see* Council of Workers' Deputies

Stockholm Congress, 194–5

Stolypin, P. A., 228, 244, 258(n17); and agrarian reform, 13, 241–2, 257(n3)

strikes: anti-strike law for farm labourers, 212; general (1905), 4, 104, 148, 233–4(n3); June (1906), 194; October (1905), 148–9, 150, 234(n5); student: (1899), 163, 235(n19), (1905), 165

Struve, Peter, 46, 65; and agrarian reform, 75, 76, 92, 100, 200; and nationalities question, 55, 62; and newspapers, 42, 115(nn8,10)

students, 163–4; emergence of associations of, 164–5, 166, 168; strikes: (1899), 163, 235(n19), (1905), 165

Stundists, 63, 65, 125(n78), 161–2

Supreme Decree (1906), 172

Syn Otechestva, 86, 116(n12)

Third Element (tretii element), 118(n21), 213, **280**; composition, 5, 242; and peasantry, 98, 190; split with Second Element, 33(n9), 118(n23); views, 5, 71; and zemstvos, 45, 71, 242

Tolstoy, Leo, 70, 141(n194), 166; *Resurrection*, 232, 240(n68)

Trade and Industry Party, 11, 145–6(n228), 180, 207, **269**; dissolution, 215; policies, 205–6

tretii element *see* Third Element
Tribe, Keith, 33-4(n10)
Trubetskoi, Prince E., 149, 203
Trudovaia Gruppa (Labour Group), 218, 223, 224, **267**
tsarism, 14, 144(n220), 184; and Council of Ministers, 175-6, 177-8; Weber's view of, 14, 20, 36(n16); *see also* Nicholas II

ukase, 174-5, **280**; of 21 October 175-7, 177, 179
Ukraine, 48, 123(n68), 159; and autonomy, 61-2, 254, 263, 266(n8); and peasantry, 76, 94
Union of Liberation, 66, 67, 69, 71, 243, **269**; and agrarian programme, 76, 77-8; Constitutional draft, 4, 6, 32(n1), 41, *45-54*: and decentralization, 48, 57-8; dissolution of, 46; founding, 41, 114(nn4-5); and nationalities problem, 48, 54-6, 61, 122(nn53-4); and *Osvobozhdenie*, 42, 115-16(8n); on relations between church and state, 63; and schools, 62-3; and Supreme Tribunal, 53-4; and Tsar, 53; and universal franchise, 48-50, 51, 52
Union of the Russian People, **269**
Union of 17 October, 74, 207, 216, **269**; and Duma elections, 213, 215; formation, 203, 204, 239(n54); support, 204-5
Union of Unions, 46, 67, 118(n22), 165, 191, 238(n50), **269**; and the intelligentsia, 45, 70-1, 72; policies, 72, 73
United States, 58, 99, 110, 123(n62), 141(n193)
universities, *163-9*, 235(n20); and Academic Congress, 166-8; appointment procedure, 163-4, 167-8, 235(n20); student unrest, 164-5, 166
uprava, 42, 43-4, **280**

village commune *see* obshchina

Weber, Marianne, 2
Weber, Max, 12; characteristics of

writing, 21-2, 26; *Economy and Society*, 20, 22, 25, 26, 33(n9); and Germany in First World War, 12; phases in work of, 16, 33-4(n10); political ideas, 2, 20-1, 23-4, relevance of, 25-8, 39(n26); reputation, 22; sources for writing, 12, 32(n1); style, 1-2; translations of work, 24-5; (1905-6 essays) 2, *3-15*, objective, 23, portrayal of individual in, 23, reaction to, 24; (1917 essays), 2, *12-15*
White Terror, 156, 234-5(n13)
Witte, Count Sergei, 8, 204; and Durnovo, 154, 180; and finance, 102-3; and October Manifesto, 4; policies, 71, 98, 105, 174, 213; and position of Prime Minister, 178, 179-80; replacement of, 220; and the Tsar, 152, 245, 248; and zemstvos, 43, 72, 106-7, 144(n215), 145(n221)
women: emancipation 139-40(n181), 196; Leagues 187
workers, 216, 251-2; revitalization of movements of, 192-4; *see also* RSDRP; strikes

Young Populists, 83-6, 89

Zemskie Nachalniki see land captains
Zemstvo Congresses, 42-3, 117-18(nn15-16), 203; and agrarian reform, 75; composition of, 44-5; and constitutional draft, 46, 119(n25); development of, 42-3; and nationalities question, 56-7, 59, 60-2, 204; resolutions, 72, 117(n14)
zemstvos, 3, 22, *41-5*, 54, 89, 205, 243, **281**; achievements, 5-6, 47-8, 54; agrarian reform, 75; effect of universal franchise on, 51; landowners within, 207, 242; and liberalism, 6, 54; organization of, 42; suppression of, 42, 47-8, 212-13; and Third Element, 45, 71, 242; and Union of Liberation, 6, 41-2, 46; and *uprava*, 42, 43-4; and Witte, 43, 72, 106-7, 144(n215), 145(n221)
Zhivago, Sergei I., 4, 53, 54, 122(n53)
zubatovshchina, 134(n130), 180, 213, **281**

www.ingramcontent.com/pod-product-compliance
Ingram Content Group UK Ltd.
Pitfield, Milton Keynes, MK11 3LW, UK
UKHW021558230326
469232UK00007B/232